Global Fashion Business

Global Fashion Business

International Retailing, Marketing, and Merchandising

Byoungho Ellie Jin

BLOOMSBURY VISUAL ARTS
LONDON · NEW YORK · OXFORD · NEW DELHI · SYDNEY

BLOOMSBURY VISUAL ARTS
Bloomsbury Publishing Plc
50 Bedford Square, London, WC1B 3DP, UK
1385 Broadway, New York, NY 10018, USA
29 Earlsfort Terrace, Dublin 2, Ireland

BLOOMSBURY, BLOOMSBURY VISUAL ARTS and the Diana logo
are trademarks of Bloomsbury Publishing Plc

First published in Great Britain 2024

Copyright © Byoungho Ellie Jin, 2024

Byoungho Ellie Jin has asserted her right under the Copyright,
Designs and Patents Act, 1988, to be identified as Author of this work.

For legal purposes the Acknowledgments on p. xvi constitute
an extension of this copyright page.

Cover design by Holly Capper
Cover images © andersphoto and WinWin/Adobe Stock

All rights reserved. No part of this publication may be reproduced or transmitted in
any form or by any means, electronic or mechanical, including photocopying, recording, or
any information storage or retrieval system, without prior permission in writing from the publishers.

Bloomsbury Publishing Plc does not have any control over, or responsibility for, any third-party
websites referred to or in this book. All internet addresses given in this book were correct at the
time of going to press. The author and publisher regret any inconvenience caused if addresses
have changed or sites have ceased to exist, but can accept no responsibility for any such changes.

A catalogue record for this book is available from the British Library.

Library of Congress Cataloging-in-Publication Data
Names: Jin, Byoungho Ellie, author.
Title: Global fashion business : international retailing, marketing and
merchandising / Byoungho Ellie Jin.
Description: 1 Edition. | London ; New York : Bloomsbury Visual Arts, 2024. |
Includes bibliographical references and index.
Identifiers: LCCN 2023035319 | ISBN 9781350180185 (paperback) | ISBN 9781350180192 (pdf) |
ISBN 9781350180208 (epub)
Subjects: LCSH: Clothing trade. | Fashion merchandising. | International trade.
Classification: LCC HD9940.A2 .J56 2024 | DDC 381/.45687–dc23/eng/20231023
LC record available at https://lccn.loc.gov/2023035319

ISBN: PB: 978-1-3501-8018-5
ePDF: 978-1-3501-8019-2
eBook: 978-1-3501-8020-8

Typeset by Integra Software Services Pvt. Ltd.
Printed and bound in India

To find out more about our authors and books visit www.bloomsbury.com
and sign up for our newsletters.

Online resources to accompany this book are available at bloomsbury.pub/
global-fashion-business. If you experience any problems, please contact
Bloomsbury at: onlineresources@bloomsbury.com

To the Lord, to whom I give all glory
To Andrew and Lauren, love of my life.
BEJ

Contents

List of Figures xii
List of Tables xiii
Preface xiv
Acknowledgments xvi

Part One
An Overview 1

1 The Nature of the Global Fashion Business 3
Characteristics of the Fashion Business 4
The Status of Fashion Brand Internationalization 5
Fashion Brand Internationalization: Motivators, Enablers, and Benefits 7
   Motivators of Fashion Brand Internationalization 7
   Enablers of Fashion Brand Internationalization 8
   Benefits of Fashion Brand Internationalization 8
Trends That Affect the Scope and Speed of Fashion Brand Internationalization 8
   Everything Is Online 9
   Dominance of Social Media 9
   Increasing Popularity of M-commerce, Especially in Developing Countries 10
   Increasing Popularity of E-payment System 10
   D2C Startups Becoming Mainstream 11
   Emergence of Livestreaming Commerce 12
   Acquisition of Global Fashion Brands by Companies in Asia 13

Case Study 1.1. Beaucre's Timely Entry into China in 1999 15
Case Study 1.2. Anta's Ascent to World's Ninth Largest Sportswear Company 17
Summary 19
Class Activities 20
Key Terms 20
Appendix 1. Top 250 Global Retailers 2023 21
Appendix 2. Global Fashion Industry: Size, Growth, and Potential by Region 21
Appendix 3. Apparel and Footwear Market Sizes by Region: 2016–26 22

2 Global Fashion Marketing Strategy 23
Global Fashion Marketing Defined 24
Global Marketing Strategy 26
   Decision to Enter a Foreign Country 26
   Marketing Mix Development: Standardization and Adaptation 29
   Coordination of Marketing Activities 32
Inherent Challenges Associated with Global Fashion Marketing 33
   Four Risks Coming from Different Environments 33
   Self-reference Criterion 34
   Coordinating Marketing Activities across Countries 35
Case Study 2.1. Macy's Exit from China 36
Summary 38
Class Activities 38
Key Terms 38

Part Two
Global Environments Affecting the Fashion Business 41

3 Economic Environment of Global Markets: Why and How It Matters 43

Economic Development Level: Classification and General Characteristics 44
- Country Classification and Characteristics 44
- Apparel Industry Development Patterns 46

Characteristics and Challenges of Retail Markets by a Country's Economic Development Level 48
- Retailing in Least Developed Markets: Characteristics and Challenges 48
- Retailing in Emerging Markets: Characteristics and Challenges 49
- Retailing in Mature Markets: Characteristics and Challenges 52

Implications of Economic Environment on Global Fashion Marketing 52
- Do Not Assume the Current Economic Status Will Remain the Same 52
- Do Not Underestimate Market Opportunities in Less Developed Countries 53
- Find a Balance between Mature and Fast-growing Markets 53
- Do Not Just Rely on Economic Environment When Making Business Decisions 54

Case Study 3.1. An Overview of China: It Will Be a Mistake to View China As One Country 55

Case Study 3.2. Strong Prospects of India's Apparel Market 56

Summary 58

Class Activities 59

Key Terms 59

4 Cultural Environment and Its Impact on the Global Fashion Business 61

Defining Culture and Cultural Elements 62
- Some Cultural Elements Related to the Apparel and Retail Industry 62

Hall's Cultural Dimensions and Implications for the Fashion Business 64
- High- vs. Low-context Culture 64
- Monochronic vs. Polychronic Time Culture 65

Hofstede's Cultural Dimensions and Implications for the Fashion Business 66
- Individualism vs. Collectivism 66
- Strong vs. Weak Uncertainty Avoidance 67
- High vs. Low Power Distance 68
- Masculinity vs. Femininity 69
- Long- vs. Short-term Orientation 70

Other Cultural Frameworks 72
- Trust Building: Task-based vs. Relationship-based Cultures 72
- Information-oriented vs. Relationship-oriented Cultures 72

Implications of Cultural Environment on Global Fashion Marketing 73
- Know Your Enemies and Yourself to Win 73
- Do Not Assume All Are the Same Within a Culture 74
- Does a Country's Economic Development Change the Culture? Culture Does Change but Slowly 75

Case Study 4.1. Two Boycott Cases: Muslims against Danish Brands and Chinese against Dolce & Gabbana 75

Case Study 4.2. Why Are Secondhand Markets Not Thriving in China? 77

Summary 79

Class Activities 79

Key Terms 80

Appendix 1. Dolce & Gabbana's Advertisement Accused of Racism in China 82

Appendix 2. Dolce & Gabbana's Apology 82

5 Legal and Regulatory Environment: Playing by the Rules 83

Government Regulations in the Retail Sector 84
- Gradual Retail Market Liberalization 84
- Other Government Regulations on Retail Operations 85

Intellectual Property Issues in the Global Fashion Industry 87
- Protection of Intellectual Property: Why It Matters 87
- Definition and Types of Intellectual Property 88
- Infringement of Intellectual Property 88
- Ownership of Intellectual Property Rights: Prior Use vs. Registration 90

Red Tape, Bribery, and Corruption: Implications for Global Fashion Companies 91
- US Foreign Corrupt Practices Act (FCPA) of 1977 91
- China's Anti-corruption Campaign and Its Impact on the Luxury Market 92
- South Korea's Improper Solicitation and Graft Act 92

Case Study 5.1. Ralph Lauren's Bribery in Argentina 92
Summary 94
Class Activities 94
Key Terms 95
Appendix 1. Corruption Perceptions Index 95

Part Three
Assessing Global Market Opportunities 97

6 Internationalization Theories 99

Internationalization Process Model 99
Ownership-Location-Internalization (OLI) Model 102
Transaction Cost Analysis (TCA) Framework 104
Network Model 105
Case Study 6.1. Why Target's First Internationalization Failed 106
Summary 108
Class Activities 109
Key Terms 110

7 Where to Enter: New Market Selection Decision 111

International Market Selection Approaches: Systematic vs. Non-systematic 112
- Systematic Approach 112
- Non-systematic Approach 113

Host Country Factors That Affect Fashion Firms' Market Entry Decision 116
- Consumer Demand for Branded Apparel Goods 116
- Consumer Acceptance of Global Brands 117

Firm Factors That Affect Market Entry Decision 117
- Firm Size 118
- Brand Image and Home Country Image 118
- International Experience 118

Case Study 7.1. Havaianas's Flip Flops: From a Commodity to a Premium Product 119
Summary 121
Class Activities 122
Key Terms 122

8 How to Enter: Entry Mode Decision 123

Market Entry Choices 124
- Exporting 125
- Contractual Entry: Licensing and Franchising Agreements 127
- Investment Entry: Joint Venture, Concession, Flagship Store, Acquisition, and Wholly Owned Subsidiary 130

Factors Related to Entry Mode Decisions 135
Implications for Fashion Companies 136

Case Study 8.1. Two Sides of Licensing: The Case of Burberry in Japan 139
Summary 140
Class Activities 141
Key Terms 141

Part Four
Developing Global Marketing Strategies 143

9 Brand Management for Global Markets 145
Types and Benefits of Global Brands 146
   Global vs. Local Brands 146
   Types of Global Brands 146
Strategic Global Brand Management Process 147
   Global Brand Naming 147
   Global STP Strategy 149
   Global Marketing Mix Strategy Options 150
Consumer Culture Positioning Strategy 150
Country of Origin and Country Image for Global Fashion Brand Management 152
   Country of Origin (COO) 152
   Country Image: How It Is Different from Country of Origin 152
   Foreign Branding 153
Case Study 9.1. Tommy Hilfiger's Different Positioning across Countries 154
Summary 155
Class Activities 156
Key Terms 157

10 Product Development for Global Markets 159
The Importance of Offering Products and Services Suitable for Global Markets 159
   Modification Addressing Culture 160
   Modification Addressing Season 161
   Modification Addressing Religion 161
   Modification Addressing Economic Development Level 161
Developing Culturally Appropriate Products 162
   Use of National Flag in Product Design: Not Suitable for Some Countries 162
   Slogans on a Hooded Sweatshirt Perceived as Racism: Interpretation May Differ by Countries 162
   Graphics Could Resemble Important Symbols: Be Aware 163
Product Localization Approaches for Global Markets 163
   Localizing Size 163
   Localizing Clothing Terms 164
   Localizing Colors 165
   Developing Limited Editions 167
   Developing a Product Line for Certain Markets 168
   Developing a New Brand for Certain Markets 168
Case Study 10.1. How Gentle Monster Achieved Its Wild Success 169
Summary 170
Class Activities 171
Key Terms 172
Further reading 172

11 Pricing for Global Markets 173
Taxes and Tariffs on Imported Goods 174
Price Escalation and How to Minimize Its Effect 176
   Price Escalation: Definition and Contributing Elements 176
   Approaches to Lessening Price Escalation 178
Approaches to Pricing for Global Markets 179
Factors That Affect the Pricing Decision 179

Costs and Company Goals That Affect Pricing Decision 179

Market Factors That Affect Pricing 180

Parallel Importing and Its Implications for Global Fashion Companies 184

Case Study 11.1. Cross-border Shopping and Luxury Fashion 185

Case Study 11.2. Chanel Handbag Pricing 187

Summary 188

Class Activities 189

Key Terms 189

12 Retail and Distribution for Global Markets 191

International Distribution Channel Decision 192

International Distribution Channel Decisions Aligning with Brands' Strategy 192

Why Channel Localization Is Needed 193

International Distribution Channel Selection 193

Establishing Distribution Channels: Indirect Involvement 194

Establishing Distribution Channels: Direct Involvement 196

Factors Influencing a Firm's Choice of Distribution Channel 197

Digital Distribution: Opportunities and Challenges in the Global Marketplace 198

Selling through Online Marketplaces 198

Digital Distribution via Fashion Brand's Own Brand Website 200

Setting Up a Brand Store on an Online Marketplace 201

Challenges in Developing Countries: Payment and Logistics Challenges 205

Case Study 12.1. WeChat and Mobile Shopping in China 206

Summary 208

Class Activities 209

Key Terms 209

13 Communications and Advertising to Global Consumers 211

Global Advertising: Standardization vs. Adaptation 212

Cultural Implications of International Advertising 216

Differing Goals of Marketing Communications: Individualistic vs. Collectivistic Cultures 216

Effective Website Design: High- vs. Low-context Cultures 217

Effective Advertising Appeals: Masculine vs. Feminine Cultures 218

Regulations and Challenges Related to Advertising across Countries 218

Comparative Advertising Is Ineffective or Banned in Some Countries 218

Communication Challenges in Arab Countries 218

Regulating Advertising Hours and Content 219

Regulating Unhealthy and Provocative Images in Advertising 219

Regulating False Claims 220

Specifying Disclosure Requirements for Social Media Influencers 220

Regulating Digital Modifications 220

Case Study 13.1. Gymshark's Impressive Rise: Social Media and Brand Community Strategies 221

Summary 223

Class Activities 224

Key Terms 224

Further Reading: Burberry Ad in China 224

Appendix 1. Shiseido Advertisement on Instagram 225

Appendix 2. Puma's Run the Streets Campaign: US vs. Korea 225

Appendix 3. Patagonia Houdini Jacket Ad: Individualistic vs. Collectivistic Culture 225

Appendix 4. Estée Lauder's Advertisements: Masculine vs. Feminine Culture 226

Appendix 5. Clarks' Advertisements: Saudi Arabia vs. Kuwait 226

Appendix 6. Yves Saint Laurent's Banned Ad in the UK 226

Appendix 7. Miu Miu's Banned Advertisement in the UK 226

Appendix 8. Lancôme's Banned Advertisement in the UK 226

References 227

Index 247

Figures

1.1 Top 10 highest m-commerce growth rates by country 11
2.1 Ansoff's product and market growth matrix 26
2.2 SWOT analysis example 29
2.3 Global marketing mix strategy options and degree of adaptation 31
2.4 Pros and cons of standardization and adaptation 32
3.1 Unorganized retailing in India 50
3.2 Coexistence of modern retail and wet markets in Shanghai, China 51
3.3 Coexistence of modern retail and tailors in Mumbai, India 51
4.1 A shutter is down during prayer time, Tashkent, Uzbekistan 63
5.1 Three examples of associative counterfeit goods 89
5.2 New Barlun logo and store in China 90
6.1 Internationalization process model: an incremental approach 100
6.2 U model vs. born global's expansion pattern 102
8.1 Risk, resource commitment, and control and involvement level by entry mode 124
8.2 Licensing agreement 127
8.3 A Pierre Cardin lingerie corner in a Vietnamese department store 128
8.4 Direct franchise agreement 130
8.5 Master franchise agreement 131
8.6 Joint venture between Muji and Reliance Brands in India 132
8.7 Factors related to international market entry mode decisions 136
8.8 Resource commitment increase within a country: Tiffany & Co. and Ralph Lauren in Japan 137
8.9 Fashion brands' resource commitment increase after 2012 lifting of Indian government regulations 138
9.1 Global strategic brand management process 147
9.2 Global STP strategy 150
9.3 Country image: its concepts and dimensions 153
10.1 Sizes and care labels in multiple languages 166
11.1 Drivers of global brand profitability 180
12.1 International distribution channels in the fashion industry 194
12.2 A building with many showrooms (left) and a showroom inside (right) 196

Tables

1.1 Selected apparel companies in top 250 global retailers 6
1.2 Selected e-payment systems worldwide 12
1.3 Acquisition of global fashion brands by companies in Asia 14
3.1 Country classification and characteristics by the World Bank 45
3.2 Korean apparel industry development by Toyne et al. (1984)'s six stages 47
3.3 Comparison of characteristics of retail market environments 53
3.4 Comparison of selected economies in some indices 54
4.1 Summary of Hall's cultural dimensions 65
4.2 Individualistic vs. collectivistic cultures 67
4.3 Implications of high vs. low power distance in business settings 69
4.4 Summary of Hofstede's five cultural dimensions 70
4.5 Information-oriented vs. relationship-oriented cultures 73
5.1 Summary of retail market liberalization in South Korea, China, and India 85
7.1 Two markets compared 113
7.2 Comparison of systematic and non-systematic approaches 114
8.1 Brief description of each entry mode and fashion industry examples 125
8.2 Fashion trade shows and their specialty areas 126
8.3 Advantages and disadvantages of the franchise system 131
10.1 Women's apparel size conversion chart 165
10.2 Different clothing terms in selected English-speaking countries 167
11.1 Taxes on imported goods by country 175
11.2 An example of escalation of costs through exporting 177
12.1 Major luxury distributors in selected countries 195
12.2 Major online marketplaces in selected countries 199
12.3 Comparison of three digital distribution options for global brands 202

Preface

The fashion business is truly global. In production, no single apparel item is entirely produced within one country. Materials needed for apparel production such as fabric, trims, buttons, and zippers often come from different countries. In retailing, fashion companies ranking in the top 250 global retailers operate in 30 different countries on average and the highest percentage of their revenues are generated from foreign operation (38.5 percent), compared to other sectors. Take Inditex, the parent company of Zara, as an example. It operates in 215 countries, and 86 percent of its revenue is from global operations. In the fashion business world, "global" is not an option: it is a necessity. So, many fashion programs across countries require their students to take global fashion business, marketing, or branding courses; yet only a limited number of textbooks devoted to the global fashion business have been available. The existing global marketing or business textbooks insufficiently use fashion brands as examples. This encouraged me to commit my time to develop and update my lecture notes from multiple sources and share them by writing this book.

I have direct research experience in many parts of the world, which is reflected in the text. For the past 23 years of my career as a professor of fashion marketing in the US, I have been researching retail and consumer behaviors across the globe. Through funded projects, I have been fortunate to visit many parts of the world researching retail and fashion consumers, visiting apparel factories, and interviewing business professionals and retail and factory owners. The countries I have visited so far include Korea, Japan, China, India, Vietnam, Bangladesh, Indonesia, Malaysia, and Uzbekistan in Asia. In Europe and North America, I have experience in the UK, France, Germany, Spain, Portugal, Croatia, Monaco, Sweden, the Netherlands, Denmark, and Canada, in addition to a three-month stay in Italy for my research leave in 2016. Moreover, as a native of South Korea born in the 1960s, I have observed the entire spectrum of apparel business development from original equipment manufacturing to selling in the global marketplace. These experiences have enabled me to understand the varying needs of countries that are culturally and economically different. Insights from my observations and first-hand experiences, together with 140 published academic papers showcasing my research findings, are incorporated into this book.

Global Fashion Business took almost six years from the initial conversation with Bloomsbury in 2018 during the International Textile and Apparel Association conference to final production. During those six years, the way global fashion does business changed dramatically. The world experienced the unprecedented Covid-19 pandemic, leading technologies, such as artificial intelligence, virtual reality, augmented reality, and blockchain, are being utilized for fashion businesses, and new emerging business models are putting pressure on incumbent fashion brands. The paradigm is shifting; no fashion company will survive solely with a traditional, store-based model. The use of social media marketing and influencers is pervasive, while traditional mass media is less popular. The scope of internationalization is also quickly broadening. The rise of m-commerce, e-payment systems such as PayPal and Alipay, and platform business enables many small fashion retailers to expand into the global market with fewer hurdles. Take the example of a small clothing store in Asia; it can sell to US consumers via Amazon.com without establishing any stores or websites. Accordingly, selling to global consumers is not as difficult as before, which means more competition for existing fashion brands.

Given this shift, this book attempts to reflect the recent changes while explaining the core concepts. It is intended to be a comprehensive global fashion business book for readers across countries, so several aspects were kept in mind for this purpose. Major concepts are explained with actual examples as far as possible. Fashion brand examples, big or small, new or established, from many different countries are incorporated. Perspectives and insights are also provided for fashion brands from emerging countries that aspire to be global with their own brands.

Global Fashion Business consists of 13 chapters in four parts: Part 1, An Overview, comprises Chapters 1 and 2; Part 2, Global Environments Affecting the Fashion Business, comprises Chapters 3–5; Part 3, Assessing Global Market Opportunities, comprises Chapters 6–8; and Part 4, Developing Global Marketing Strategies, comprises Chapters 9–13. Several pedagogical features (case studies, summary, class activities, key terms, and QR codes for further readings) are found at the end of each chapter; they are designed to be relevant to students from any country. Case studies help readers understand major concepts in each chapter with real-world examples, and discussion questions added to enrich their critical and strategic thinking. Full references are also included.

This book will be most beneficial for junior or senior level undergraduate students in fashion marketing programs and graduate students without much fashion business background. Industry professionals will equally benefit from this book, in that it deals with many real-world examples that could be applied to many different settings. A book may not be the ideal medium to capture the speed of the global fashion business; however, there should be a comprehensive understanding that gives a big picture. This first edition will serve this purpose, but I promise to update it in the future with more insights reflecting global fashion industry trends and feedback from peers and students.

Acknowledgments

I would like to express my sincere gratitude to many brilliant individuals, mostly my doctoral, master's, and undergraduate students, who were willing to assist with finding materials and case studies. They are Reagan Dunnam, Meredith Gaskill, Da Eun Chloe Shin, Gwia Kim, Heekyeong Jo, Hyesim Seo, Md Sadaqul Bari, Jiwoon Kim, and Yoo-Won Min. A special thanks to the anonymous reviewers who gave me practical tips and support and to Georgia Kennedy and Rosie Best at Bloomsbury, who guided this book project from proposal stage to final hard copies. My profound gratitude is extended to the late Dr. Brenda Sternquist, professor at Michigan State University, who ignited my passion for international retailing. An honorable mention is reserved for the students in my Global Brand Management class who, with a gleam in their eyes, pose insightful and critical questions. You have been my source of inspiration and I have written this book for you all.

An Overview

PART 1

Part 1 aims to lay the foundation to help understand the subsequent three parts emphasizing unique aspects of the global fashion business. Chapter 1 illustrates the global nature of the fashion business and the reasons for and benefits of fashion brand internationalization. In particular, Chapter 1 details the factors related to the scope and speed of fashion brand internationalization to help readers understand the subsequent chapters with these changing environments in mind. Chapter 2 provides an overview of global fashion marketing concepts and strategies. Major concepts pertaining to global fashion marketing (standardization and adaptation) and the inherent challenges associated with the global fashion business and marketing are outlined.

CHAPTER 1
The Nature of the Global Fashion Business

Learning Objectives

After studying this chapter, you will be able to:

- Explain the characteristics of the fashion business.
- Describe the current status of fashion brand internationalization.
- Articulate the reasons for and benefits of fashion brand internationalization.
- Discuss the trends that affect the scope and speed of fashion brand internationalization.

The apparel industry is one of the oldest and largest export industries in the world. Clothes are a basic human need. Since ancient times, humankind traded clothes, as evidenced by the Silk Road. The apparel industry is the second largest consumer goods industry globally, after packaged food (Euromonitor International, 2018). Another definite fact is that the apparel industry is truly global. Almost every country is involved in either producing, importing or exporting fibers, yarns, fabrics, clothes and accessories, and so on. Thanks to global sourcing, a large portion of apparel production is performed in low-wage countries, while apparel product development, marketing, and retailing are the focus of many advanced economies. This is not true for other industries such as the automotive industry; not every country is involved in the product development, production, and marketing of automobiles.

Another aspect highlighting the global nature of the apparel industry is that very few apparel items are entirely produced within one country. In the apparel industry, it is common that a US apparel company, for example, develops the designs and product specifications (collectively referred to as the "tech pack") and a partner factory in Hong Kong sources fabrics and trims from a number of different countries, such as zippers from Japan, fabrics from China, and buttons from South Korea, and arranges the garment assembly in Vietnam. Thus, multiple countries are involved in the production of any apparel item. Moreover, many fashion companies enter international markets to sell their goods. Gap Inc., for example, sells its products to consumers worldwide, with 2,799 company-operated stores and 591 franchise stores across 44 countries (Gap Inc., 2022). While Gap is an American company, its production and marketing activities are carried out in locations well beyond the domestic market. Being international in the fashion industry is no longer an option but a common business practice to stay competitive.

This chapter lays the foundation for subsequent chapters, by highlighting the characteristics of the fashion business, the status of fashion brand internationalization, and the reasons for and benefits of internationalization. It ends with a discussion on how the emerging trends in fashion brand internationalization are broadening the scope and accelerating the speed of internationalization.

Characteristics of the Fashion Business

An analysis of the global fashion business should start with an understanding of fashion products and business characteristics, which are quite different from other industries. The characteristics of the fashion business are as follows (Jin, 2004, 2006):

1. *Shorter product life cycle*: The most important aspect of the fashion business is that the fashion product has a short product life cycle due to fashion and seasonal changes. Because of that, apparel companies need to sell their products within a season. Otherwise, they cannot sell unsold inventory in the next season, which creates a huge problem. This is why there are heavy markdowns, such as 60–70 percent off after a season. This contrasts with other industries such as the consumer electronics industry, where the markdown rate is small: it is rare to see 60–70 percent markdown for computers after a season. In fact, the companies may not even need to mark down unless a model is discontinued. This is because the product life cycle is long, compared to fashion goods.

2. *High number of stock-keeping units (SKUs)*: The second characteristic is the high number of stock-keeping units (SKUs). An apparel company typically develops 15,000 SKUs in one collection. Consider automobiles. How many designs does a car company offer in a year? It is just one or two designs per model. Even if we count different colors or different add-ons, it is not even close to 15,000 SKUs (Jin, 2004).

3. *A wide variety of products from basic to fashion items*: Moreover, a wide variety of products from basic to fashion items are offered in a season. Depending on the product characteristics, some items, such as socks, can be treated as a commodity that allows for standardized volume production. Other items, such as blouses, lend themselves better to small batches, instead of volume production. Thus, the economies of scale cannot be applied to every apparel item.

4. *Demand uncertainty*: Unlike other consumer goods, it is difficult to predict when and what items and sizes consumers will purchase. It is extremely hard to produce accurate amounts to the size level. Therefore, we need the highest level of management technologies to estimate consumer demand, control inventory, and respond quickly to ever-changing consumer demand.

5. *Low barrier to entry*: Another aspect of the fashion business is the low entry barrier, because compared to other businesses, you can set up a fashion business with little capital and few skills or technologies. A couple of sewing machines may be all you need. You can start even without a sewing

machine because you can arrange production in other countries. With the low entry barrier, many developing countries start their economic development with apparel production by utilizing their abundant cheap labor.

6. *Easily copyable trade secrets*: One downside of the fashion business is that trade secrets, such as product design, assortment, price, store layout, window display, and even store format, are exposed to competitors, meaning that your competitors can easily copy them if they so wish. Therefore, intangible assets such as brand image are more critical in the fashion business.

7. *Subjective product evaluation and greater symbolic benefits*: The last but probably most important aspect of the fashion business is that the evaluation of fashion goods is quite subjective. Consumers can judge the quality of other consumer goods such as electronic goods and automobiles relatively easily, since there are specific evaluation criteria, such as CPU or RAM for computers and fuel consumption for automobiles. In contrast, for fashion products, there are no universally agreed objective measures to say "good design" or "good quality" as these essentially depend on personal tastes. Thus, brand name often primarily drives the evaluation of fashion products.

Kumar and Steenkamp (2013) viewed electronics and cars as product-driven products, packaged goods in the middle, and clothes, alcohol, and cosmetics as brand-driven products. This implies that the quality of cosmetics is the hardest to judge, followed by clothes; product quality of clothes and cosmetics is solely dependent on brand image. Thus, symbolic meanings created by brand image, rather than functions, play a bigger role in evaluating fashion products. This can be one of the reasons why consumers are willing to pay a high price for luxury handbags even though the functional value of the handbag itself is not much different from that of less expensive alternatives.

These characteristics show that the fashion industry is substantially different from other consumer sectors. This may create additional sets of challenges and opportunities in the internationalization process; thus, these characteristics should be considered when analyzing fashion brands' internationalization activities.

The Status of Fashion Brand Internationalization

An industry is global to the extent that a company's industry position in one country is interdependent with its industry position in other countries. Among many globalization barometers that show how an industry is global, industries select indicators that fit their analysis purpose. For fashion brand internationalization, two indicators generally explain how a fashion brand is global: retail revenue percentage from international operations and the number of countries entered. Levi's is one of the global apparel brands that represents the US like Coca-Cola. You will see Levi's jeans in almost every country you visit. They sell in 110 countries, and 55 percent of their revenue comes from international operations (Levi Strauss & Co., 2022). From this, we can say Levi's is a global brand.

Like Levi's, most global fashion brands operate in many international markets, generating a significant proportion of their revenues outside their home countries. A large number of global brands earn more than half of their revenue from international markets. For example, revenues from international operations are 96 percent for H&M, 94 percent for LVMH, 86 percent for Inditex, which is Zara's mother company, and 59 percent for Nike (H&M Group, 2022; Inditex, 2022; LVMH, 2022; Nike, 2022). Table 1.1 shows selected apparel companies that made the top 250 global retailers listed in Deloitte's report published in 2023 (see Appendix 1 for the report). All those apparel brands operate in many countries. As Table 1.1 shows, Inditex sells in 215 different countries, and Kering Group has a presence in 95 different countries. Most of these apparel companies' compound annual growth rates (CAGR) for the past five years (2016–21) are impressive. JD Sports's CAGR is the highest (30.2 percent), followed by Nike (16.7 percent) and Kering (15.4 percent).

Table 1.1 Selected apparel companies in top 250 global retailers

RETAIL REVENUE RANKING	COMPANY NAME	COUNTRY OF ORIGIN	RETAIL REVENUE IN 2021 (MILLIONS OF US$)	NUMBER OF COUNTRIES OF OPERATION	2016–21 RETAIL REVENUE CAGR
20	LVMH	France	56,305	80	14.4%
23	The TJX Companies	US	48,550	9	7.9%
35	Inditex	Spain	32,567	215	3.5%
52	H&M	Sweden	23,343	75	0.7%
57	Fast Retailing	Japan	19,884	24	3.6%
59	Nike	US	19,657	74	16.7%
61	Ross Stores	US	18,916	1	8.0%
69	Kering	France	16,898	95	15.4%
71	Gap	US	16,670	40	1.4%
107	JD Sports	UK	11,391	32	30.2%
120	Hermès	France	9,663	46	14.4%
121	Adidas	Germany	9,662	60	10.3%
129	Foot Locker	US	8,958	28	2.9%
159	Primark	UK	7,650	14	−1.2%
173	Victoria's Secret	US	6,785	74	−2.7%

Note: Revenue includes wholesale and retail sales.
Source: Global powers of retailing 2023

According to the 2020 report, 38 apparel companies on the list, on average, have a retail presence in about 30 countries, and 38.5 percent of their revenue comes from foreign operations. This level of globalization is the greatest among all sectors. In comparison, on average, the top 250 global retailers have a retail presence in 10.8 countries and 22.8 percent of their revenue comes from foreign operations (Kalish and Eng, 2020). The apparel sector is also the *fastest growing* and *most profitable*, with the highest net profit margin and highest return on assets among all sectors.

In summary, among all consumer sectors, the apparel sector operates in the highest number of foreign countries, generates the highest revenue from foreign operations, is the fastest growing, and is the most profitable. From these facts, we can say the apparel industry is truly global.

Fashion Brand Internationalization: Motivators, Enablers, and Benefits

Motivators of Fashion Brand Internationalization

Why do apparel brands operate in other countries? What makes them go global? Seeking growth opportunities is the most important reason for fashion brands entering other countries. Intense competition in the saturated domestic market makes it difficult for fashion firms to keep growing. Gap's entry into China in 2010 is a good example. Gap could not find growth opportunities in the US because there are so many Gap stores (that is, the market is saturated).

Another factor that deters a retail firm's growth is restrictive legislation. Some governments do not allow large retailers to establish multiple stores within certain areas to protect small businesses and employees. This type of restrictive legislation can be found in many European countries and Japan. Japanese department stores chose to enter Hong Kong in the 1980s to avoid the restrictive legislation in its domestic market.

A third reason for entering other countries is to access products or services that can be sourced cost-efficiently or do not exist in home markets. A fashion brand can source pashmina scarves from India or Nepal because pashmina, the finest cashmere, can be found only in these countries.

Another reason for internationalization is to exploit first-mover advantage. When a fashion brand enters an emerging market for the first time (for example, the first women's brand in the country), the brand can enjoy first-mover advantage because competition in the country is often low or nonexistent. By entering a country early before competitors, firms can build brand recognition and positive brand image easily. This is because consumers tend to remember the first brand in a category. Think of Kleenex and how we often use the brand name to refer to facial tissues. However, there are drawbacks for first movers. Since the market is not yet developed, companies need to do preliminary jobs such as training channel members and educating customers about new products or services. For this reason, some firms decide to enter later after observing the first mover's performance. These followers usually take a me-too approach, so the operation might be easier than the first mover's, but they may need more time to establish brand recognition and loyalty. For example, South Korean (henceforth Korean) company Beaucre entered China in 1999 with its brand On & On much earlier than global brands entered. Because of this early timing, the firm enjoyed first-mover advantages, but also faced some difficulties. Case Study 1.1 discusses Beaucre's entry into China.

Enablers of Fashion Brand Internationalization

So what makes fashion retailers' active internationalization possible? One of the reasons may be that fashion brands require a small-scale retail space, compared to other sectors such as food and home improvements, entailing little financial investment and low management setup costs. Therefore, economies of replication can be maximized in the international market. Economies of replication means that by having the same store across countries, firms can save on their setup costs while keeping brand image consistent.

Benefits of Fashion Brand Internationalization

Fashion brand internationalization brings numerous benefits to companies. We can think about three aspects of benefits: production and operation, production development and marketing, and building brand name.

1. *Production and operation*: fashion brands can achieve economies of scale in sourcing, production, marketing, and R&D so they can reduce cost. By multiplying stores across countries, firms can increase their market size, so they can earn higher margins and profits.

2. *Product development and marketing*: fashion brands can pool resources such as human capital (creative designers, directors) and leverage best practices. If a firm operates only in one country, their talent pool may be limited. By operating globally, firms can leverage the best resources they can access. Firms can borrow innovative product and promotion ideas from other countries. For example, Christian Dior learned of the popularity of cushion foundation while operating in the Korean market and developed it for its own product line. Dior's website explains: "originating in Korea, cushions have now won over the whole of Asia. This portable technique enhances and protects the skin wherever you are" (Campbell, 2016).

3. *Building brand image*: by entering multiple countries, fashion companies can build a global brand image more rapidly than when selling just in one country. In addition, if a brand can make a name for itself in economically advanced countries like the US, the UK, and France, it can easily build brand reputation in other markets. For this reason, many brands from emerging countries or a country with a weak fashion image strategically enter economically advanced economies. This aspect will be discussed more in Chapter 7, which delves into market selection decisions.

Trends That Affect the Scope and Speed of Fashion Brand Internationalization

Fashion brand internationalization has been mostly limited to large companies in economically advanced economies. Now, with changes occurring around the industry, the speed and scope of fashion brand internationalization becomes faster and broader. Here, the internationalization speed indicates how soon a company enters a foreign market after its establishment. It is often operationalized as how many years it took to enter an international country after its inception. The internationalization scope denotes the geographic dispersion of international businesses (George et al., 2005), and it is thus operationalized as the total number of foreign markets a firm has entered. Some trends that affect the speed and scope of fashion brand internationalization are discussed below.

Everything Is Online

You will all agree that everything is now online. When e-commerce (electronic commerce) was first introduced, online was just one of many distribution channels that supplemented offline stores. It now serves as a major distribution channel offering diverse business models and platforms, such as resale (e.g. The RealReal), rental (e.g. Rent the Runway), and curated services (e.g. Stitch Fix). Social media has also become an important promotion tool. With the Covid-19 pandemic, sample garment development, fashion show, and showroom functions are increasingly accomplished virtually. The dominance of online operations has prompted luxury brands, which have been reluctant to offer goods online for a long time, to rely on online sales. Many different online luxury platforms such as Yoox, Net-a-Porter, and Farfetch have become popular (Sherman, 2020). The norm of fashion business was opening brick-and-mortar stores and adding an online shop later. Now, many small businesses and startups begin with an online store and then expand offline later.

Statistics support the size and the growth of online sales. The channel size of internet retailing (e-tailing) is the largest, followed by specialty retailers, department stores, home shopping, and so on. In terms of growth, internet sales recorded a CAGR of 18.1 percent between 2014 and 2019. In contrast, the CAGR of specialty retailers was −0.8 percent and that of department stores was −3.1 percent over the same period (Euromonitor International, 2020). Having a store presence in foreign countries, especially establishing a flagship store in a major fashion capital like Paris, London, and New York, requires hefty resources. Thanks to the growing popularity of e-commerce, apparel companies, big or small, old or young, can establish a presence in foreign countries via their own websites or third-party online platforms, which can expedite the internationalization speed and scope.

Dominance of Social Media

No one can doubt the dominance of social media. The use of traditional mass media such as TV commercials and fashion magazines is becoming unpopular. An increasing number of global fashion brands use social media and influencers in their promotion and marketing. One report projects that, by 2023, digital ad spending will be 60.5 percent of total media ad spending, meaning that digital will be dominant (Enberg, 2019a).

A growing number of fashion brands sell their product on social media sites. The most notable example is Instagram, where brands make shoppable posts in which the viewers can click and make a payment without ever leaving the app. Postings on social media serve as a reservoir of rich information on consumer trends. With the help of big data and artificial intelligence (AI) analytics, apparel firms can explore, in real time, consumer trends and their likes and dislikes. This implies that fashion brands can use social media for every aspect of the fashion business: product development, selling, marketing, and communicating with global consumers. The cost of social media marketing, compared to that of magazine or TV advertising, is much lower. Thus, the financial burden stemming from advertising and building a brand name in the global marketplace is reduced, enabling more apparel companies to partake in internationalization.

Increasing Popularity of M-commerce, Especially in Developing Countries

The next trend is the increasing popularity of m-commerce (mobile commerce). Compared to e-commerce, the global sales volume of m-commerce is still small, but its growth for the past five years (2014–19) was 43.7 percent while that of e-commerce was 18.1 percent. In particular, developing countries show the highest m-commerce growth rates. Figure 1.1 represents m-commerce growth during the periods 2018–19 and 2022–23. In 2018–19, Uzbekistan shows a remarkable growth rate, 119.5 percent, followed by Azerbaijan (110 percent), Romania (105.2 percent), Algeria (85.1 percent), Pakistan (74.9 percent), Thailand (71.2 percent), Argentina (70.5 percent), Malaysia (70 percent), Peru (69.9 percent), and Egypt (67.4 percent).

Many developing countries leapfrogged landline phones and moved directly to mobile phones. Smartphone use is especially common among younger and more educated groups (Silver et al., 2019). In many developing countries, online shopping often means mobile shopping, indicating that instead of computers, consumers in these countries use their mobile phones to shop. Limited access to the internet was a major hurdle for e-commerce development in developing countries. Thanks to the widespread use of mobile phones, apparel firms now have more flexibility in marketing their goods to consumers in developing countries via m-commerce.

Increasing Popularity of E-payment System

It is a mistake to assume that a credit card is a popular payment method across the globe. In developing countries, credit cards are not widely available or accepted. So you may wonder how consumers in developing countries pay. Another important trend, together with m-commerce growth, is the increasing popularity of e-payment systems in developing countries. With e-payment systems, consumers can pay without a credit card. This function is critical, especially in emerging countries where credit card usage is not popular. PayPal, started in 1998, is an initial form of e-payment. Now you can pay via PayPal in 200 countries. Alipay is the Chinese version of PayPal, which is extremely popular in China and can be used in 40 countries via the Alipay app. M-Pesa is a popular form of payment in Kenya. As Table 1.2 shows, there are many e-payment systems that allow consumers to pay with an app on

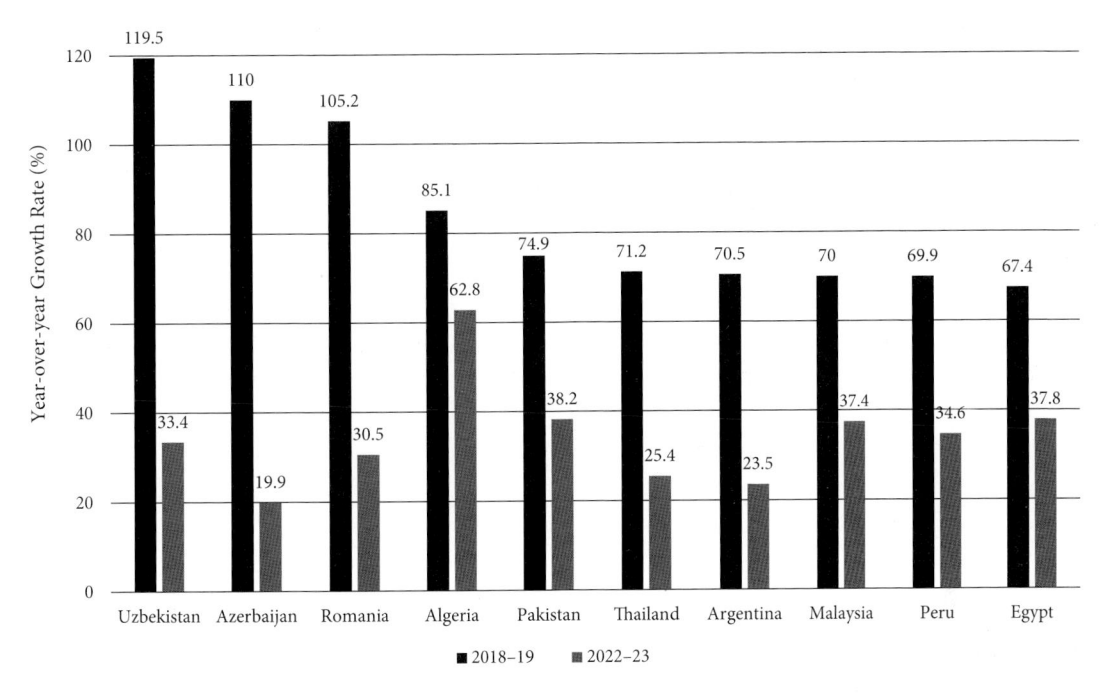

Figure 1.1 Top 10 highest m-commerce growth rates by country.
Source: Developed by the author based on Euromonitor International (2020)

their cell phone or website. E-payments will help speed the growth of m-commerce worldwide because they reduce friction by allowing consumers to browse and pay on the same device. The growth of m-commerce and e-payment systems will enable firms to enter many different countries, broadening the scope of internationalization.

D2C Startups Becoming Mainstream

Small startup companies have been emerging since the 2010s. They are mostly online D2C (direct-to-consumer) brands that sell directly to consumers without intermediaries like department stores. This group of apparel firms is growing rapidly and becoming mainstream. An example is Bonobos, a menswear brand founded in the US in 2007. It was acquired by Walmart in 2017. Startups offer innovative business models with unique competitive advantages that traditional retailers do not have, such as resale, customization, rental, and curated services. There are a huge number of examples: ThredUP in resale, Indochino and Knot Standard for customization, Rent the Runway for rental, and Stitch Fix for curated service. These startups are emerging globally, not just in the US. For example, Son of a Tailor in Denmark offers men's custom-made zero-waste pullovers utilizing 3D knitting technology.

Table 1.2 Selected e-payment systems worldwide

PAYMENT PLATFORM	YEAR LAUNCHED	COUNTRY	OVERSEAS MARKET REACH
PayPal	1998	US	200 countries
Alipay	2004	China	40 countries
M-Pesa	2007	Kenya	Democratic Republic of Congo, Egypt, Ghana, Lesotho, Mozambique, Tanzania
GoPay	2007	Indonesia	Philippines, Singapore, Vietnam, Thailand
Paytm	2010	India	Canada
WeChat Pay	2013	China	25 countries
MobilePay	2013	Denmark	Finland
KakaoPay	2014	South Korea	Japan
Apple Pay	2014	US	51 countries and regions

Like Uber and Airbnb, these startups often provide a platform. The RealReal is such an example. The RealReal sells pre-owned luxury items online on a consignment basis. It does not own the items but takes a commission for each item sold. The implication of these D2C startups for fashion brand internationalization includes that, with unique value propositions and competitive advantages, fashion companies can easily go global via online and mobile applications, as long as they can ship to other countries. Many D2C startups in the luxury sector are global, such as GOAT (est. 2015), Moda Operandi (est. 2010), and Gilt Groupe (est. 2007), meaning that consumers in many different countries can order online and receive their goods via international shipping. This aspect will be detailed in Chapter 12.

Emergence of Livestreaming Commerce

The next trend is the emergence of livestreaming commerce, which is similar to TV home shopping but through a livestreaming app. Influencers hired by brands showcase products to consumers in real time, and viewers can ask questions and order while watching the livestream, just like home shopping (Amed and Berg, 2020). China pioneered this trend. In 2015, Mogu Inc., a fashion-centric social commerce company, offered a livestreaming feature. Livestreaming became so popular that many leading Chinese e-commerce companies started their own livestream units (Yokoi, 2020).

In 2018, Taobao Live in China, Alibaba's dedicated live streaming shopping app, sold over 600,000 different products and generated 100 billion yuan ($14.93 billion). American actress Kim Kardashian West sold 150,000 units of her perfumes during a livestreaming session on Alibaba's Tmall on a single day in 2019 (Vogue Business, 2020; Yokoi, 2020). Another noteworthy Chinese livestreaming company is ShopShops. This company aims to sell US-based brands to Chinese shoppers. It has partnered with over 150 brands and retailers, ranging from luxury designers to multi-brand stores and independent retailers including T.J. Maxx, Everlane, and Theory. ShopShops' hosts manage the livestreaming events, acting as stylists, fitting models, and translators for the viewers. ShopShops takes about 25 percent commission (Lieber, 2019).

While livestreaming gained in popularity in China, especially during the Covid-19 pandemic when consumers were unable to shop offline, the trend is not yet global. However, recently, Amazon launched Amazon Live where brands can livestream on amazon.com and its mobile app. Tommy Hilfiger hosted a livestream show in China and sold 1,300 hoodies in just two minutes (WARC, 2020). Walmart held the first shoppable livestream fashion event in 2020 and celebrated its one year of livestreaming shows on Twitter in 2021 (White, 2021). As with social media, livestreaming commerce has the potential to become a distribution channel, especially among young consumers. This trend will therefore help apparel firms mitigate some of the challenges associated with entering other countries. Global brands should be aware of this emerging opportunity.

Acquisition of Global Fashion Brands by Companies in Asia

Acquisition is the purchase of one business or company by another company or business entity to grow larger. It usually refers to a large firm's purchase of a smaller firm, or firms in developed countries acquiring competitors or less strong firms. Examples include VF's acquisition of Supreme in 2020 (O'Connor and Fernandez, 2020), Coach's acquisition of Kate Spade in 2017 (Duguid, 2017), and Michael Kors acquisition of Versace in 2018 (Ell, 2018).

Over the past decade, however, many companies or brands in the US and Europe have been taken over by companies in Asia. Table 1.3 lists such cases. Why are Asian fashion companies buying global brands? Acquisition is not just about buying a brand name. It comes with the brand's unique capabilities such as global reputation, store locations, networks, marketing, management and innovation skills, distribution networks, and even customers. Acquisition is regarded as the fastest way of establishing a global presence because it takes less time than establishing a global brand from the ground up.

After active participation in the apparel production for the world's market, many Asian companies now focus on internationalization with their own brands. Japan's Uniqlo and Hong Kong's Giordano are examples. China now is the world's biggest apparel and footwear market, and the US is the second largest (see Appendix 2). Asia and the Pacific region account for the biggest apparel and footwear market (38 percent), followed by North America (23 percent), Western Europe (20 percent), the Middle East and Africa (7 percent), Latin America (6 percent), Eastern Europe (5 percent), and Australia (1 percent) (see Appendix 3). The acquisition of global fashion brands will help a leading Chinese company like Anta achieve its dominance in the domestic market and potentially build a global presence (see Case Study 1.2).

The implication of this trend is the increasing participation of Asian companies in global fashion business. That is, fashion brand internationalization is not confined to large fashion companies in the US and Europe. While the acquiring companies may not be involved in the day-to-day business operations, this trend will help Asian apparel companies access the

Table 1.3 Acquisition of global fashion brands by companies in Asia

ACQUIRED BRAND (COUNTRY)	ACQUIRER	COUNTRY OF ACQUIRER	YEAR OF ACQUISITION	AMOUNT ($)
Sergio Tacchini (US)	F&F	South Korea	2022	63 million
Amer Sports (Finland)	Anta Sports	China	2019	5.2 billion
Jason Wu (US)	Green Harbor	China	2019	n.a.
De Fursac (France)	Shandong Ruyi	China	2019	47.1 million
Lanvin (France)	Fosun International	China	2018	n.a.
Aquascutum (UK)	Shandong Ruyi	China	2017	117 million
Maje, Sandro, Claudie Pierlot (France)	Shandong Ruyi	China	2016	1.5 billion
Balmain (France)	Qatar	Qatar	2016	563 million
Sonia Rykiel (France)	Fung Brands	Hong Kong	2012	n.a.
Valentino (Italy)	Qatar	Qatar	2012	858 million
Harrods (UK)	Qatar	Qatar	2010	1.5 billion
Escada (Germany)	Mittal	India	2009	n.a.
Fila (Italy)	Fila Korea	South Korea	2007	450 million
MCM (Germany)	Sungjoo Group	South Korea	2005	n.a.
Pringle (UK)	Fang & Sons	Hong Kong	2000	8.8 million

learning and know-how that acquired brands have accumulated, which can potentially facilitate the speed and scope of internationalization. Learning (that is, foreign market knowledge) is a critical component of internationalization. This aspect will be further discussed in Chapter 6, which delves into internationalization theories.

What are the implications of these trends for apparel companies? All the above trends have accelerated the speed and broadened the scope of fashion brand internationalization. In the past, companies could not globalize at the outset. It took some time and resources because internationalization mainly relied on store openings in major cities. For example, it took Zara 13 years to enter the first international market, Portugal. In contrast, Farfetch, a UK luxury e-tailer, sold internationally within three years after its establishment in 2007.

The explosive growth of the internet and the associated digital, information and communication technologies have transformed the global marketplace into a borderless world (Schu et al., 2016). Now with the technologies via e-commerce (e.g. amazon.com), m-commerce, and livestreaming commerce, it became easy to sell goods overseas, accelerating the speed of internationalization in the global marketplace. Without much financial investment, social media can also serve as an effective venue for identifying market needs in real time, developing positioning and segmentation strategies, and ultimately developing marketing mix strategies for foreign markets. In addition, many hindrances in developing countries (such as low internet usage, credit card penetration, and so on) have become less critical with many different e-payment systems and a widespread use of mobile phones. This means substantially lower barriers to entry for companies.

In summary, fashion brand internationalization or selling fashion goods in overseas markets has become less challenging with advanced technologies and increasingly diverse business models and distribution channels. Therefore, more small and young companies can go global with fewer resources than before (see Case Study 13.1 on the UK's Gymshark). This means that there will be more exciting globalization opportunities, regardless of firm size, history, or experience. This also suggests that more entrepreneurial opportunities will emerge in the global marketplace, requiring a more globally competent workforce who can analyze and seize market opportunities.

CASE STUDY 1.1

Beaucre's Timely Entry into China in 1999

Established in 1991, Beaucre Merchandising Co. Ltd. (Beaucre) is an apparel company based in Seoul, South Korea. In its early years, Beaucre served the domestic market but soon expanded internationally. Beaucre's international expansion began in 1999 when the company entered China with its first brand On & On, which offers premium business attire for women in their twenties. Over the years, the company received awards from Chinese department stores for its outstanding sales.

In the early phase of the entry, however, Beaucre faced challenges. Because the Chinese government did not allow foreign companies to enter China without local partners, Beaucre partnered with a Chinese fashion firm. To Beaucre's dismay, the partnership lasted only three months because the partner company copied On & On's designs and sold them under its own brand name (Jin and Chung, 2016). After the dissolution of the first partnership, Beaucre worked with a Korean businesswoman who was active in the textile business in Hong Kong. With the help of the new partner's networks, Beaucre was able to open a store at one of the luxury department stores in Shenzhen, making huge sales on the first day of opening. However, Beaucre and the new partner had a diverging view on the brand's growth strategy. The partner sought to make profits through an aggressive expansion that sacrificed the prestige image, which resulted in a loss of popularity among consumers. As a result, the second partnership also ended bitterly after a nine-month legal battle with the closure of the majority of stores in China. In the end, enabled by the relaxation of trade regulations, Beaucre established a wholly owned sales subsidiary in 2004 in Shanghai, the first Korean apparel company to be established in China with 100 percent investment (Jin and Chung, 2016).

While it was important for On & On to deliver premium customer service to establish its premium brand image, the local sales associates had little understanding of customer service. The idea of serving customer needs by delivering professional, high-quality assistance had not yet taken root in the Chinese market. Beaucre overcame this difficulty with an innovative approach to staff training. The company invited selected Chinese sales associates to Korea, took them to a variety of low-end and high-end establishments, including hair salons, hotels, and restaurants, and had them experience the different levels of customer service by the price level. This approach proved successful because the staff's first-hand experiences of superior customer service translated into their own delivery of excellent customer service, which helped solidify On & On's premium brand image in China (Jin and Chung, 2016).

When Beaucre first entered China in 1999, the Chinese apparel market was just emerging with a limited number of apparel brands. At that time, there was one Chinese national brand (Li Ning), only a handful of global brands such as Nike, several luxury brands, such as Burberry, and a few international casual wear brands, such as Giordano and E-land (Jin and Chung, 2016) (see below figure). There were even fewer brands offering business attire for young women, despite a growing demand. Thus Beaucre was able to capitalize on first-mover advantage by filling the void. Upon launch, On & On soon gained traction from working women wanting more choices, which translated into great sales.

Another first-mover advantage On & On enjoyed was influencer marketing at virtually zero cost. Anchorwomen on major news channels in Beijing voluntarily contacted the brand to ask if they could borrow On & On's clothes to wear on their shows. This was made possible because the concepts of paid marketing and sponsorships were relatively underdeveloped at that time. At today's prices, it would

Three phases of international brands' entry into the Chinese apparel market

1 [Late 1970s to early 1980s]
- International brands
  - Nike, Adidas, Lacoste, Montagut, and Foxerc
- Global luxury brand entry was restricted by the Chinese government
  - Pierre Cardin was the first global luxury brand to enter China

In 1989, the first Chinese national brand was created: Li Ning (a sportswear brand)

2 [Mid 1990s]
- Luxury brands in first-tier cities
  - Ermenegildo Zegna, Louis Vuitton, Dunhill, Burberry, and Hugo Boss
- Casual wear brands
  - Giordano and E-land

3 [Late 1990s to 2000s]
- More luxury brands in first-tier cities and expansion into second-tier cities
  - Gucci, Christian Dior, Hermès, Armani, Givenchy, and Chanel
- More casual wear brands
  - Esprit, Mango, Zara, H&M, Uniqlo, Muji, GUESS, and Gap

In 1999, Beaucre entered with On & On, which offers premium business attire for young career women in their twenties have cost the brand millions of dollars. These sponsorships provided publicity for On & On and led to a number of contacts from fashion magazines (Jin and Chung, 2016). In addition, as one of the first Korean fashion companies to enter China, Beaucre was able to benefit from the enthusiasm for the "Korean Wave" (also called Hallyu or K-pop) prevalent in most Asian countries. For instance, BoA, one of the most popular South Korean singers (dubbed the "Queen of K-pop"), was featured as a model in commercials for W., Beaucre's second brand to be launched in China. The result of these promotion efforts was an explosion in brand awareness of W. among Chinese consumers (Jin and Chung, 2016).

Discussion Questions

1. What enabled On & On to enjoy first-mover advantage in China?
2. What were the first-mover advantages On & On enjoyed in China?
3. What challenges did On & On face during the initial entry and how did the company overcome them?

Reference

Jin, B. and Chung, J.E. (2016). Beaucre Merchandising Co. Ltd: A successfully internationalizing Korean apparel company. In B. Jin and E. Cedrola (eds.) *Fashion brand internationalization: opportunities and challenges*, pp. 115–37. Basingstoke: Palgrave Macmillan.

CASE STUDY 1.2

Anta's Ascent to World's Ninth Largest Sportswear Company

Established in 1991 by Ding Shizhong and headquartered in Jinjiang, Fujian province, China, Anta Sports Products Limited (from now on Anta) is a Chinese sportswear company. Anta is one of the "Fujian Tigers," a term referring to dozens of sportswear companies that emerged in mountainous areas of Fujian province where Nike and Adidas shoes were stitched. Anta grew out of a small workshop run by the founder's father. The low-cost manufacturer for global brands is now the world's ninth-biggest sportswear company and ranked third in China in apparel, footwear, and sportswear after Nike and Adidas (Euromonitor International, 2018, 2019a, 2019b).

At the heart of Anta's impressive performance is the company's "Single-focus, Multi-brand, and Omni-channel" strategy (Anta Sports, 2019). This means that the company has been growing by building a house of brands that touches all levels of consumer segments while focusing on the sportswear category and creating synergy among its distribution channels as well as its brands. Anta currently has nine brands, and Anta's portfolio spans both high-end and mass markets, as well as fashion-oriented and performance-oriented products (see below figure). By successfully reaching a broad range of consumer segments, the company was able to grab a significant market share.

Anta has been building its multi-brand portfolio primarily through partnerships and acquisitions since 2009. In 2009, Anta entered into a joint venture with a Korean sportswear brand Fila to operate it in mainland China, Hong Kong, and Macau (J. Kim, personal communication, September 29, 2019). In 2016, Anta formed a joint venture with a Japanese brand, Descente, and Itochu for the rights to distribute Descente in China. In the same year, Anta acquired Sprandi, a Russian brand that offers leisure footwear products. In early 2017, Anta formed a joint venture with Kolon Sport, a Korean outdoor brand, to operate it in mainland China, Hong Kong, Macau, and Taiwan. In late 2017, Anta acquired Kingkow, a children's clothing brand based in Hong Kong (Anta Sports, 2019).

Anta is now aiming to rival Nike and Adidas with a takeover of Finland's Amer Sports. Amer Sports will be operated independently with a separate board of directors (Amer Sports, 2019; Baigorri et al., 2018). Amer Sports owns internationally recognized brands including Salomon, Arc'teryx, and Wilson. The acquisition would enable Anta to diversify into a number of different categories, including ball sports (Wilson, DeMarini, Louisville Slugger), winter sports (Atomic, Armada), cycling (ENVE Composites), and sports accessories and equipment (Suunto, Precor) (Ryan, 2018).

Discussion Questions

1. What are the implications of Anta's case for global apparel companies? What did you learn from this case?
2. Do you think China's role in the apparel and footwear industry has changed? Is China transitioning from a manufacturing hub to a brand powerhouse? What makes you think so?

References

Amer Sports (2019, April 1). Final results of the subsequent offer period of Mascot Bidco Oy's voluntary recommended cash tender offer for all the shares in Amer Sports. www.amersports.com/2019/04/final-results-of-the-subsequent-offer-period-of-mascot-bidco-oys-voluntary-recommended-cash-tender-offer-for-all-the-shares-in-amer-sports

Anta's brand positioning matrix

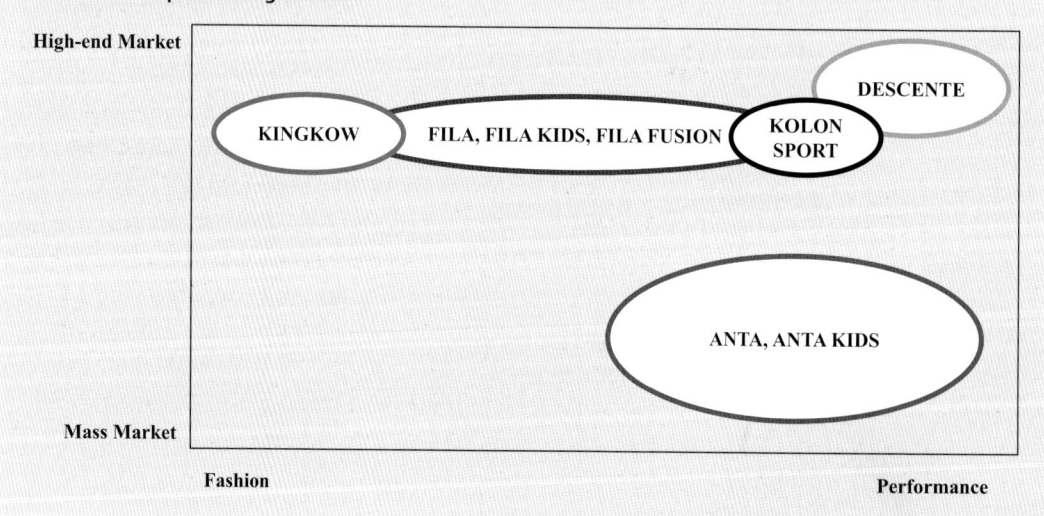

Anta Sports (2019, August 26). Anta delivers record-breaking performance with outstanding growth. www.prnewswire.com/news-releases/anta-delivers-a-record-breaking-performance-with-outstanding-growth-300906706.html

Baigorri, M., Zhong, C. and Chan, C. (2018, December 6). Anta-led consortium nears deal to acquire Amer Sports. Bloomberg. www.bloomberg.com/news/articles/2018-12-06/anta-led-consortium-is-said-to-near-deal-to-acquire-amer-sports

Euromonitor International (2018, November). World market for sportswear. www.euromonitor.com

Euromonitor International (2019a). *Anta (China) Co Ltd in apparel and footwear (China): Local company profile*. www.euromonitor.com

Euromonitor International (2019b). *Sportswear in China - data graphics: Country reports*. www.euromonitor.com

Ryan, T.J. (2018, September 12). What would Anta's merger mean for Amer Sports? SGB Media. https://sgbonline.com/what-would-antas-merger-with-amer-sports-mean

Summary

- The apparel industry is the second largest consumer goods industry globally, after packaged food.
- The apparel industry is the *fastest growing* and *most profitable* industry with the highest net profit margin and highest return on assets.
- The apparel industry is truly global. Virtually all countries are involved, whether it be producing, importing, or exporting fibers, yarns, fabrics, clothes, or accessories. The apparel supply chains span continents.
- The characteristics of fashion products and businesses are: shorter product life cycle, high number of stock-keeping units, a wide variety of products from basic to fashion items, demand uncertainty, low entry barrier, easily copyable trade secrets, subjective product evaluation, and greater symbolic benefits.
- The motivators of fashion brand internationalization are: intense competition in the domestic market, restrictive regulations in the domestic market, access to products, services, and business methods that do not exist in home markets or can be sourced cost-efficiently from foreign markets, and first-mover advantages.
- The benefits of fashion brand internationalization include: economies of scale in sourcing, production, marketing, and R&D, ability to pool various resources such as creative designers and directors, leverage best practices, and ability to build a global brand image more rapidly.
- The trends that affect the scope and speed of fashion brand internationalization are: everything is online, dominance of social media, increasing popularity of m-commerce, D2C startups are becoming mainstream, emergence of livestreaming commerce, and acquisition of global brands by companies in Asia.
- The aforementioned trends are accelerating the speed and broadening the scope of fashion brand internationalization by further lowering barriers to entry. Selling fashion goods in overseas markets has become ever more viable, thanks to the digital, information, and communication technologies that fuel diverse business opportunities from m-commerce to livestreaming commerce.

Class Activities

1. Discuss how the apparel industry is different from other industries in terms of production.
2. Discuss how the apparel products are different from other products in terms of selling them to consumers.
3. Form a pair with your classmate. One person argues why a fashion brand is easy to enter global marketplaces and the other person counters the argument by discussing the challenges of doing fashion business globally.
4. Other than the factors listed in the chapter, discuss what other trends facilitate fashion brand internationalization.

Key Terms

- **Tech pack:** The blueprint of a product, detailing all the components and steps needed to turn a design into a finished product, including materials, gradings, and trims.
- **Stock-keeping unit (SKU):** An SKU is a unique string of letters and numbers assigned to each product by a retailer for the purpose of inventory management. It identifies product characteristics, such as style, color, and size.
- **Economies of scale:** The cost advantage a company enjoys by increasing the production volume. The reduction in the average cost of production can enable companies to offer products at competitive prices.
- **Economies of replication:** The cost advantage a company enjoys by replicating its business operations across markets. For example, a company can set up stores in the same format in all markets it enters, so saving setup costs while keeping their brand image consistent.
- **First-mover advantages:** The competitive advantages a company gains as a result of being first to market in a new product category. One of the advantages is establishing strong brand recognition and customer loyalty before latecomers to the market.
- **Internationalization speed:** How soon a company enters a foreign market after its establishment, often operationalized as how many years it took a firm to enter an international country after its inception.
- **Internationalization scope:** The geographic dispersion of international businesses, operationalized as the total number of foreign markets a firm entered.

Appendix 1. Top 250 Global Retailers 2023

Source: *Global powers of retailing 2023*. Deloitte.
www2.deloitte.com/global/en/pages/consumer-business/articles/global-powers-of-retailing.html

Appendix 2. Global Fashion Industry: Size, Growth, and Potential by Region

In 2021, China overtook the US to become the biggest apparel and footwear market. By 2026, the size of the Chinese apparel and footwear industry will remain the largest.

Top 10 biggest apparel and footwear markets by country

	China	USA	India	Germany	UK	Japan	France	Italy	Canada	Russia
2016	$3,26,717	$3,42,625	$50,792	$74,812	$68,615	$79,941	$43,817	$43,525	$31,133	$40,219
2021	$4,27,154	$3,64,137	$53,149	$69,957	$70,734	$65,765	$40,097	$37,505	$32,961	$38,929
2026	$5,20,846	$4,57,901	$94,298	$90,701	$85,938	$80,713	$45,006	$44,191	$42,665	$42,435

Source: Developed by author with Euromonitor International market sizes data, 2022

Chapter 1 The Nature of the Global Fashion Business

Appendix 3. Apparel and Footwear Market Sizes by Region: 2016–26

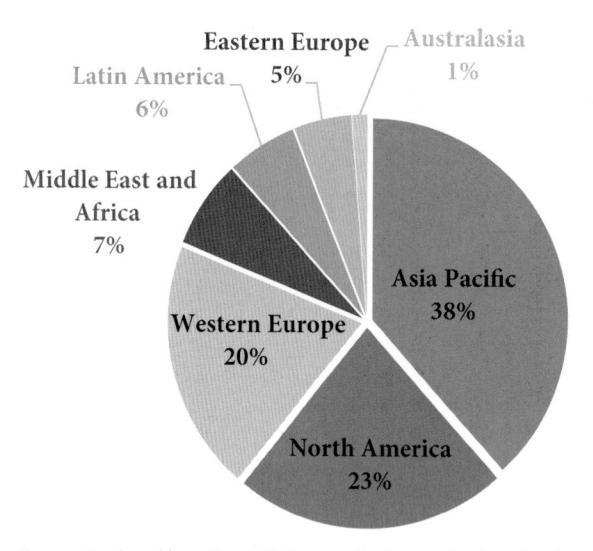

- Asia Pacific 38%
- North America 23%
- Western Europe 20%
- Middle East and Africa 7%
- Latin America 6%
- Eastern Europe 5%
- Australasia 1%

Source: Developed by author with Euromonitor International market sizes data, 2022

CHAPTER 2
Global Fashion Marketing Strategy

Learning Objectives

After studying this chapter, you will be able to:

- Define global fashion marketing and describe its difference from domestic fashion marketing.
- Define competitive advantage, describe its evolving nature, and explain why competitive advantage in domestic markets may not necessarily serve as a competitive advantage in global markets.
- Illustrate the factors that help fashion companies' decision to go global and the use of analysis tools such as SWOT.
- Discern the differences between standardization and adaptation approaches and the pros and cons of each approach.
- Discuss the inherent challenges associated with the global fashion business and marketing.

This chapter discusses the basics of global fashion marketing strategy. Global fashion marketing begins when firms decide to enter other countries. There are various factors influencing firms' global entry decisions. One of them is for continuous growth. In other words, global market entry is part of the firm's growth strategy. The basic concepts of fashion marketing apply to global fashion marketing. With the scope being broader (more than one country), compared to domestic marketing, firms need to pay attention to foreign environments. This is because varying market conditions may require firms to adjust their marketing elements accordingly. In global fashion marketing, therefore, the degree to which firms adapt their marketing elements and contents to foreign environments becomes a critical part of decision-making. Having defined global fashion marketing and outlined the difference from domestic marketing, this chapter illustrates the three steps of establishing a global marketing strategy. Major concepts related to a global marketing strategy such as standardization and adaptation will be explained. This understanding will lay the foundation for the subsequent chapters. The last part of this chapter is a discussion on the challenges inherent to global fashion business and marketing.

Global Fashion Marketing Defined

Before we define global fashion marketing, it is important to revisit the concept of marketing. As defined by the American Marketing Association in 2017, marketing is "the activity, set of institutions, and processes for creating, communicating, delivering and exchanging offerings that have value for customers, clients, partners and society at large" (AMA, n.d.). The essence of marketing is exchange; an organization offers competitive values that satisfy consumers' wants and needs, and in return consumers pay for its offerings. To fulfill marketing activities, companies utilize tools, typically known as the 4Ps of marketing—product, price, place of distribution, and promotion (communication)—also referred to as the "marketing mix." Marketing is more than selling goods. It starts with product development that addresses consumer needs and wants (product and price), followed by communicating what a company has to offer (promotion), and delivering the products to consumers (place of distribution). Later, in addition to the 4Ps, three additional Ps, people, physical evidence, and process, were introduced to explain unique activities in service industries (Booms and Bitner, 1981, 1982) (see Box 2.1).

BOX 2.1
The 7Ps of Service Marketing

The service marketing mix, commonly referred to as the 7Ps, encompasses the traditional 4Ps of marketing (product, price, place of distribution, and promotion) with the addition of 3Ps (people, physical evidence, and process). The 3Ps are introduced to explain the unique characteristics of services, that is, intangibility, heterogeneity, inseparability, and perishability. Haircuts are a good example of a service, involving no physical product (intangible), no identical haircut across people (heterogeneity), no way to separate a haircut from the service provider (inseparability), and cannot be made in advance and stored (perishability). Such characteristics make service quality control a challenge. The "people" who directly or indirectly provide the service to customers are critical. The "process" explains certain procedures and the protocols by which service activities are delivered. Lastly, "physical evidence" refers to the environment in which a service is provided.

Fashion retail is a major service sector wherein fashion goods are presented in a retail store or online (physical evidence) by sales associates (people), who follow certain procedures and protocols (process). The 7Ps may be more applicable to a growing number of fashion brands that have expanded into hospitality industries, such as hotels, restaurants, and cafés. In particular, several luxury brands have ventured into establishing their own landmark hotels in prestigious cities. Examples include Bulgari Hotel in Milan and Bali, the Palazzo Versace in the Australian Gold Coast and Dubai, and the Armani Hotel in Milan and Dubai. More recent examples include Muji Hotel in Ginza, Beijing, and Shenzhen. Fashion brands offering restaurant services include Armani (in Milan) and Polo Ralph Lauren (in Chicago). Similarly, French retailer L'Occitane en Provence operates L'Occitane Café in Taipei, while French apparel and accessories retailer Agnes B has established Agnes B Cafés in Hong Kong and Taipei (Jin and Cedrola, 2017). The Italian brand Harmont & Blaine has also opened a café in Porto Rotondo, Italy (Colurcio and Melia, 2017).

With the rise of online sales, the service aspects of offline retail stores have gained greater significance, as brick-and-mortar stores are no longer just destinations for purchasing physical goods. Increasingly, retailers are adding non-traditional services to their businesses. The upscale US department store Nordstrom now offers convenient services, such as alterations, gift wrapping, online order pick up, and easy returns and exchanges in New York and Los Angeles under the name of "Nordstrom Local." Thus, the additional 3Ps (people, process, and physical evidence) are significant factors in operating fashion retail stores across the globe.

References

Colurcio, M. and Melia, M. (2017). Harmont & Blaine: A successful dachshund to build the values and brand identity. In B. Jin and E. Cedrola (eds.) *Fashion branding and communication: Core strategies of European luxury and premium brands*, pp. 41–72. New York: Palgrave Macmillan.

Jin, B. and Cedrola, E. (2017). Brands as core assets: Trends and challenges of branding in fashion business. In B. Jin and E. Cedrola (eds.) *Fashion branding and communication: Core strategies of European luxury and premium brands*, pp. 1–39. New York: Palgrave Macmillan.

This concept of marketing also applies to global fashion marketing. A major difference between global marketing and domestic marketing is the scope of activities. While domestic marketing focuses on a single country, global marketing deals with the multiple countries that fashion firms enter. Each country has unique economic, cultural, legal, and political environments. Such variations in market environments are uncontrollable factors that companies encounter in international markets, making global marketing much more complicated than domestic marketing. Therefore, global marketing requires a comprehensive understanding of the differing environments. Part 2 (Chapters 3, 4, and 5) details the diverse economic, cultural, and legal environments across the globe.

A fashion firm's entry into the global market can be viewed as the firm's growth strategy. According to Ansoff's matrix, a firm can choose from four growth strategies that differ on product and market coverage: market penetration, product development, market development, and diversification strategy. Figure 2.1 shows this four-option matrix. Market penetration strategy is getting the existing customers to buy more of existing products, whereas product development strategy is developing new products and launching them in existing markets. Market development strategy is bringing existing products into new markets, and diversification strategy is developing new products for new markets. Doing business in other countries is a typical market development

	Existing products	New products
Existing markets	Market penetration strategy	Product development strategy
New markets	**Market development strategy**	Diversification strategy

Figure 2.1 Ansoff's product and market growth matrix.

strategy. By selling their existing products and services in new global markets, apparel firms can increase their market size. That is, if a fashion company enters three foreign countries, the market size is potentially three times larger than just operating in a domestic market. Therefore, global fashion marketing is actively pursued by companies from a small, saturated domestic market where growth opportunity is limited. Many economically advanced European countries are more active in entering other countries than the US. This is most likely because their domestic market size is small compared to the US. American companies are relatively slow in expanding to other countries partly because of their large domestic market size. Firms also consider entering other countries when the domestic market is saturated. The US and economically advanced European countries find growth opportunities in the global marketplace because of limited growth in their home countries. Taken together, global fashion marketing is defined as business activities designed to plan, price, promote, and direct the flow of a fashion company's goods and services to consumers or users in more than one market for a profit. As this definition shows, the major difference between single country marketing and global marketing is the number of countries involved.

Global Marketing Strategy

Global fashion marketing involves more than one country. Accordingly, there are additional strategic decisions a firm should make, even though the concept of marketing and the marketing mix are also applicable to global marketing strategy. In this section, three steps of global marketing strategy are explained.

Decision to Enter a Foreign Country

While single country marketing begins with segmentation, targeting, and positioning, global marketing begins with a decision to enter a foreign country. Not every company chooses to enter overseas markets. What factors drive this decision? People may assume that large companies internationalize more than small companies because of their ample financial resources. However, empirical studies confirm that the degree of internationalization is not related to firm size (Picot-Coupey et al., 2014). As we learned in Chapter 1, many hindrances of going global have been eased, thanks to digital, information, and communications technologies. Thus, some small companies choose to internationalize at their inception, and these companies are often referred to as "born globals." This born global concept will be discussed further in Chapter 6.

Instead of the size of the firm, it is the managerial mindset or founder's entrepreneurial orientation, defined as "processes, practices, and decision-making activities that lead to new entry" (Lumpkin and Dess, 1996, p. 136), that is related to a firm's decision to participate in global markets. The literature confirmed that entrepreneurial orientation is one of the most influential determinants of international scope and profitability (Jin et al., 2018).

In addition, if a firm has a competitive advantage in its home country, it is more likely to internationalize (for more on competitive advantage, see Box 2.2). That is, when a firm has a unique competitive advantage, the firm can decide to enter other countries with more confidence. An original retail concept or a unique and distinctive product can be the source of competitive advantage for global retailers (Hutchinson et al., 2009). For example, a strong brand identity is a major competitive advantage for many luxury brands, which assists them in expanding into global markets.

Take the Body Shop, the UK's retail chain, for example. Its unique retail store format selling skincare, body, and bath products was well accepted. However, the novelty of any unique retail concept eventually wears off. As products and brands have a finite life cycle, a unique retail concept can be novel and exciting when first introduced and gain popularity but eventually become less desirable over time. We use the term "product life cycle" (PLC) to depict how the sales of a product category, brand, or retail concept evolve over time. The PLC follows five stages: introduction, growth, maturity, saturation, and decline, typically shown in a bell-shaped curve. Its implication in the global marketplace is that the same unique retail concept can be in a different stage of PLC across markets. That is, although the Body Shop's store concept is not so new to consumers in the UK and the US, it can be novel in other countries and therefore can serve as a competitive advantage.

Here, it is important to note that what is considered a competitive advantage is contingent on the rivals in a given market. For example, if a sportswear company operates in the US, its competitors are other sportswear companies in the US. This implies that a competitive advantage in one country is not necessarily a competitive advantage in other countries and vice versa. The American shoe brand Toms' philanthropic idea may not be a competitive advantage in emerging markets where firms compete mostly on value for money. Likewise, a feature that is not a competitive advantage in the US can be a competitive advantage in other countries. Levi's is not perceived as a premium brand in the US, but in many other countries, Levi's is perceived as a leading American jeans brand, and this perception serves as a competitive advantage. In Japan, it is positioned as "the original," the "real" American jeans, with a high-end price; Levi's 501 jeans are roughly $95 in Japan, and about $40 in the US. Therefore, it is critical for a firm to analyze their competitive advantage in the country they enter, because the competitive advantage they enjoy in their domestic market may not necessarily translate into the countries they enter.

A SWOT analysis can serve as a useful tool in identifying whether a brand can enjoy a competitive advantage in a given country. A SWOT analysis is a commonly used strategic planning technique. It is versatile because it can be applied to a product, brand, or company.

BOX 2.2
Competitive Advantage

Competitive advantage is an attribute that allows a firm to outperform its competitors. When a company succeeds in creating more value for customers than its competitors, the company is said to enjoy a competitive advantage. Therefore, it is the leverage a firm can utilize over its competitors. The source that brings competitive advantages to a firm changes. Traditionally, cheap price, creative design, and agility can serve as important competitive advantages. Those features may not be enough because now there are so many fashion firms that can offer those advantages. Historically, JCPenney offered decent quality apparel and home goods at affordable prices. Today, many more competitors offer compelling products. JCPenney has been losing its customers to Target, Old Navy, H&M, off-price giants like T.J. Maxx, and e-commerce giant Amazon.com. In the end, it filed for bankruptcy in May 2020 (Maheshwari and Corkery, 2020).

Newly emerging competitive advantages include corporate social responsibility (CSR), supply chain transparency, and curated service. Toms, an American shoe company, is known for its CSR activity (e.g., buy-one-give-one: "you buy a pair of shoes, we give a pair to a person in need"). Everlane positions its brand well with its supply chain transparency strategy, and Stitch Fix's curated service is its competitive advantage that no other brands can offer.

Companies cannot prevent other firms from pursuing the same competitive advantage; thus, firm-specific competitive advantage is often unsustainable. Therefore, firms should continuously monitor whether their competitive advantage is strong enough to convince consumers in the market. In contrast, a country-specific competitive advantage such as country image can last a long time. Italian fashion brands are known for their premium quality and design. As illustrated in Chapter 1, consumers rely on country and brand image to evaluate apparel products. Therefore, brand name origin (such as Italian brand), rather than product country of origin (COO), serves an important competitive advantage in the fashion industry. Global consumers may buy Levi's jeans because of the American image embedded in the products. Whether the jeans are produced in Bangladesh or Indonesia, which is the products' COO, does not matter as much today because of the prevalence of global sourcing.

Reference

Maheshwari, S. and Corkery, M. (2020, May 15). J.C. Penney, 118-year-old department store, files for bankruptcy. *The New York Times*. www.nytimes.com/2020/05/15/business/jc-penney-bankruptcy-coronavirus.html?-auth=login-google

It has four aspects to analyze: two internal (strength and weakness) and two external to the organization (opportunity and threat). Strength and opportunity analyze the positive sides, whereas weakness and threat assess the negative aspects. A typical SWOT analysis looks like

	Positive side	Negative side
Internal to a firm	**Strengths** • Unique design • High quality • Strong digital marketing capability • Strong brand community	**Weaknesses** • Limited product range • Brand image being diluted • Unaffordable price • Heavy dependence on global sourcing
External to a firm	**Opportunities** • Rise of m-commerce • Growing popularity and accessibility of social media	**Threats** • Increasing labor cost • Knockoff merchandise • Changes in target consumers' shopping habits • Growing number of competitors

Figure 2.2 SWOT analysis example.

Figure 2.2. With this tool, Toms, for example, can analyze whether the brand has competitive advantages in Italy. If the analysis supports having competitive advantages in Italy, compared to the other shoe brands in the country, the brand can consider entering the market. However, additional market analyses should be conducted before finalizing the entry decision. Entry market decisions (where to enter) will be discussed in further detail in Chapter 7.

Marketing Mix Development: Standardization and Adaptation

Standardization and Adaptation Defined

Once a fashion firm decides to enter a foreign country, it needs to develop marketing plans with the marketing 4Ps. It would be ideal to sell exactly the same product at the same price with the same marketing campaigns in other countries because doing so makes the planning and execution very simple. However, each country has its own unique economic, cultural, and legal environments, all of which affect consumer needs and wants. Therefore, keeping the marketing 4Ps the same across countries may not work in practice; the firm must modify to a certain degree even though it takes time and resources. Not adapting to local conditions is often cited as a reason for a withdrawal from a market, as seen in Gap's exit from the UK market in 2021 (Faull, 2021; Timmins, 2021).

The former approach, marketing worldwide with the same marketing mix, is called "standardization." The latter, modifying the marketing 4Ps in response to local needs or conditions, is called "adaptation" or "localization." The term "customization" is also used. Initially, the two terms had slightly different meanings. Localization indicates mandatory modifications needed to make the product suitable for foreign environmental conditions, such as changing the voltage of electronic goods and using the metric system in Europe and Asia. In contrast, adaptation or customization is defined as discretionary modifications made to better cater to foreign consumer preferences. The difference between the two is that localization is mandatory and adaptation/customization is discretionary (Johansson, 2009). The term "adaptation" is more commonly used in global fashion marketing than customization because the latter is also pursued to address domestic consumer needs. Adaptation and localization are often used interchangeably in research and business, so this book treats the two terms as the same.

Related to the standardization vs. adaptation decision, a longstanding debate is the distinction between global and multinational retailers. Simply put, the global retailer is one that uses a standardized retail format utilizing similar products, branding, and marketing communications, whereas the multinational retailer is one that uses a decentralized management structure that allows for adapting the store format and marketing mix to suit the local culture and consumers (Salmon and Tordjman, 1989; Sternquist, 1997). Yet the distinction between global and multinational becomes blurred because even global retailers that rely on the standardized approach should modify to a certain degree in order to cater to local conditions. Therefore, the terms will be interchangeably used in this book.

Standardization and Adaptation: The Degree Is the Key

While standardization and adaptation/localization terms are used in literature and industry, numerous choices exist on a continuum between complete global standardization and complete local adaptation. Therefore, the global marketing strategy is not a matter of deciding between either global standardization or local adaptation; this dichotomous approach is not viable. The global marketing strategy involves deciding *the degree to which* a firm uses the standardized or localized approach in a host country with respect to the marketing 4Ps. In other words, a firm can modify all 4Ps in a foreign market, but in other markets, it can change only one aspect of the marketing 4Ps. For example, a firm can modify marketing campaigns and distribution channels but keep the products and price the same.

Fashion firms need to make strategic decisions at two levels: first, *which* marketing elements need to be changed or modified among the four marketing mix elements, and second, *how* the marketing elements can be localized (product positioning, product design modification, appropriate media, content of advertisement, and so on). In other words, fashion firms need to decide the localization level as to *what elements* among the marketing 4Ps as well as *how much* within an individual marketing mix will be localized. This decision should be based on the host country environments and the firms' long- and short-term strategic directions. In general, more adaptation is needed in a country where significant differences exist in consumer needs and wants. Competition intensity in a host country also necessitates that fashion brands differentiate their products. To summarize, the greater differences in local consumer wants and needs and the greater the competition in a host country, the greater adaptation is needed. A standardization strategy works well in countries that are economically, politically, and culturally similar to the home market (Szymanski et al., 1993). A standardization strategy can be also effective for fashion brands targeting young consumers such as ASOS, because their buying patterns are pretty much the same (Green, 2018).

Global marketing mix strategy can vary from offering the exact same element in all markets (standardization) to localizing all elements (adaptation). Degrees of localization are as follows (Steenkamp, 2017):

- *Same elements in all markets*: This is true to the definition of standardization, offering exactly the same marketing 4Ps (uniformity), unless there are some legal requirements and differing institutional capabilities. For example, fashion firms modify the alcohol percentage in perfume for Middle Eastern countries where alcohol consumption is banned.
- *Modest variations of a few elements*: This involves changing a few elements among the marketing 4Ps. This can be a slight modification in distribution.
- *Localization of more elements*: This involves modifying more marketing 4Ps.
- *Localization of all elements*: Localization occurs in every marketing 4P element. While a firm localizes all marketing elements, it refers to its global brand in each marketing plan. This level of localization may be risky for high-end fashion brands where brand image is their primary competitive advantage. This is because too much variation in products, price, commercials, and distribution channels may eventually jeopardize its brand image consistency across countries.

Figure 2.3 illustrates the differing degrees of localization on a continuum with examples. Gucci's New Year Capsule collection added piglets (zodiac of 2019, Year of the Pig) to its handbag, watch, and shoe designs to accommodate Chinese consumers' gift-giving culture for Chinese New Year. For European countries, the brand made no modifications to either products or commercials. This is an example of modest variations of a few elements. However, Dolce & Gabbana and Nike developed products for a new category, such as a hijab for Muslim consumers. In this case, a new product is developed for certain markets, so more localization is involved. Note that even within a single marketing 4P, for instance product adaptation, a firm has a wide spectrum of options, from just slightly modifying sizes to developing an entirely different product for the market (see Chapter 10, product development).

Standardized marketing strategy (Uniformity) ← **Standardization** — **Adaptation** → **Localized marketing strategy (Diversity)**

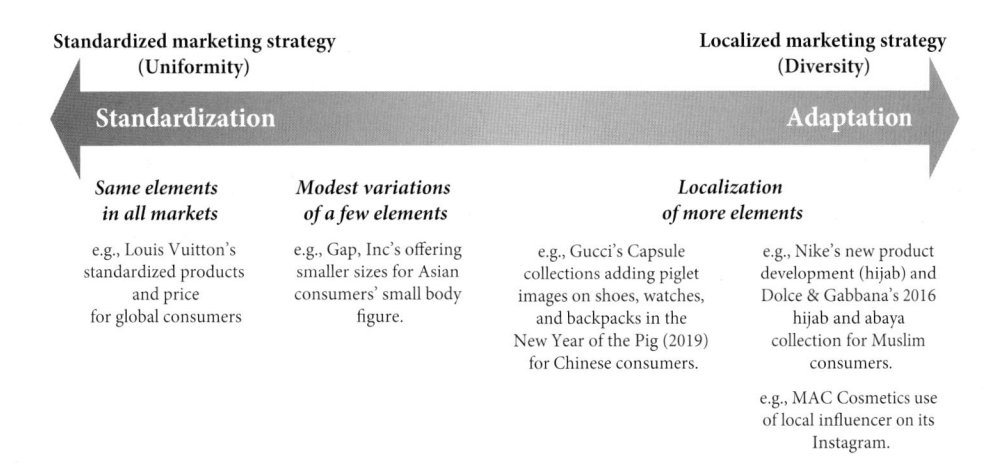

Same elements in all markets	Modest variations of a few elements	Localization of more elements	
e.g., Louis Vuitton's standardized products and price for global consumers	e.g., Gap, Inc's offering smaller sizes for Asian consumers' small body figure.	e.g., Gucci's Capsule collections adding piglet images on shoes, watches, and backpacks in the New Year of the Pig (2019) for Chinese consumers.	e.g., Nike's new product development (hijab) and Dolce & Gabbana's 2016 hijab and abaya collection for Muslim consumers. e.g., MAC Cosmetics use of local influencer on its Instagram.

Figure 2.3 Global marketing mix strategy options and degree of adaptation.

Figure 2.3 also shows that localization can occur in each of the 4Ps of marketing. In communication, for example, fashion companies can hire local influencers on social media and local celebrities in ad campaigns. In countries where popular social media platforms such as YouTube and Instagram are banned (such as China), local social media should be utilized, which is another example of localization (localizing communication channel).

Standardization and Adaptation: Pros and Cons

A product adaptation or localization strategy is chosen based on the assumption that it will increase the sales volume in foreign marketplaces by satisfying the needs and wants of local consumers. However, it is important to understand that adaptation of any element of the marketing program entails time and resources. Firms need to conduct market research to identify local needs and conditions and modify marketing elements accordingly. Adaptation requires time and resources and can therefore delay the product launch and add greater organizational complexity. Thus, it is critical to weigh the pros and cons of adaptation against the expected returns. The standardization and adaptation strategy entails a tradeoff between pros and cons. Figure 2.4 compares the pros and cons of standardization and adaptation decisions.

The decision should be about how much global standardization and local adaptation can be mixed strategically rather than choosing one over the other. A strategy that strikes the optimal balance between the two is referred to as "glocalization." The concept is well expressed in a motto "Think globally but act locally." One example of glocalization is marketing the same products with the same design and brand but localizing distribution and marketing communications. In doing so, fashion companies must consider the tradeoffs between standardization and adaptation.

Coordination of Marketing Activities

The last aspect of the global marketing strategy is coordinating the marketing activities across countries. If a fashion brand has to change all its product offerings, prices, distribution, and

	Standardization	Adaptation
Pros	• Minimal costs as firms apply the same marketing elements across countries • Easy to maintain brand image consistency across countries	• Can appeal to local consumers by accommodating local needs and conditions • Possible higher sales
Cons	• Uniform offering across countries may not appeal to certain local markets • Possible lower sales by not addressing local needs	• Difficult or time and resource consuming to identify local needs and conditions • More time and resources to develop or modify marketing elements • Greater organizational complexity

Figure 2.4 Pros and cons of standardization and adaptation.

commercials in each country the brand enters, it will be extremely complex to execute and, at the same time, hard to keep a consistent brand image. Therefore, a fashion brand needs to coordinate its marketing mix as much as possible so that it can offer consistent products and services across markets. "Global integration" is the degree of coordination of marketing mix activities across countries (Steenkamp, 2017). Global integration is critical for the effective management of brands across the globe, which allows fashion brands to optimize their resources and maximize the benefits of global branding. More explanations on global coordination are given later in this chapter. For effective coordination, fashion companies often group markets into a couple of regions where consumer characteristics and market environments are similar, such as Asian countries, South American countries, and so on. However, even within the region, subtle differences always exist; a nuanced understanding is necessary.

Inherent Challenges Associated with Global Fashion Marketing

Digital technologies have accelerated the speed of fashion brand internationalization more than ever, lessening the challenges of doing global fashion business. Thanks to digital technologies, just by selling online, a few startup brands, such as the UK's fitness apparel brand Gymshark, made a global success within a short period of time. Many well-established brands, however, failed in the global marketplace: American mass retailer Target exited Canada in 2015 with a $5.4 billion loss after less than two years of operation (Austen, 2015), while UK fashion retailer ASOS exited China after three years of online operation (Chambers, 2016). Topshop, another UK fashion retailer, exited both the US (Parisi, 2019) and China in 2019 after four years of operation (*Jing Daily*, 2020). Forever 21 exited Japan in 2019 by closing all 14 stores after 10 years of operation (Restar, 2019). These examples show that even brands with a great reputation in their domestic market do not always succeed in foreign markets. What makes global fashion marketing so difficult? What are the fundamental challenges of global fashion marketing? These challenges can be summarized in three factors discussed below.

Four Risks Coming from Different Environments

Entering foreign markets means operating in different environments, which inevitably engenders risks. The literature mentions four types of risk that companies face: cross-cultural risk, country risk, commercial risk, and currency risk (financial risk). These risks are inherent to global business because firms face different environments in any country they enter. If not handled properly, it can result in serious consequences such as damage to brand reputation, sales loss, and exit from the market.

1. *Cross-cultural risk*: This is ubiquitous as cultural differences can come from a variety of sources, from more obvious ones such as language and greeting etiquette to more subtle ones such as social norms and values. These differing values affect all aspects of global business: consumer behaviors, retail operation, communication, negotiation, management styles, and so on. For example, in high-context cultures, messages are implicit and indirect and legal documents are shorter than those in low-context

cultures. There are numerous products that failed because brands lacked an understanding of the subtle cultural nuances in host markets. Detailed cases will be handled in Chapter 10. In addition, some advertising messages may need to be modified because effective persuasion appeals are different from culture to culture. In Chapter 4, major concepts and frameworks related to culture are introduced.

2. *Country risk*: This comes from different economic, legal, and political environments. Some countries impose restrictions on foreign investments, so fashion firms should work with local partners. The extent of bribery, corruption, and red tape varies by countries. Generally speaking, the less economically developed countries are, the greater the bribery, corruption, and red tape levels. Fashion firms should be cognizant of how businesses are conducted in host countries. Chapter 3 deals with the risks stemming from economic environments.

3. *Commercial risk*: This can also occur because of differing business and retail environments. For example, in many Asian and European department stores, the consignment system is popular, whereas in the US, direct buying is common. Fashion firms need to be cognizant of the difference in order to manage their business in a proper manner.

4. *Currency risk*: This is an inherent challenge that fashion companies encounter in host countries. This is due to fluctuations in exchange rates, foreign taxation, and so on. Many South American countries are not easy markets to do business in because of high taxes on imported goods and high inflation rates.

Fashion companies should understand the implications of these risks on their businesses before entering. Adapting to environmental differences from one market to another is seen as the key to successful global marketing. It is vital for global marketers to be able to anticipate the uncontrollable foreign environments that have a great influence on the marketing mix.

Self-reference Criterion

People tend to see things from their own perspectives. The same pattern is observed in doing business globally. Fashion brands are inclined to see foreign markets as they would see domestic markets and thus often fail to see the differences. This tendency is called the "self-reference criterion" (SRC), defined as an unconscious reference to one's own cultural values, experiences, and knowledge as a basis for decisions (Lee, 1966). It occurs because people assume that what is suitable for domestic markets will also be suitable for foreign markets. Because of this tendency, fashion firms often do not test whether the product or service will work in a host country or not. US department store Macy's exited China in 2018 after three years of market presence (Parmar, 2018). Chinese consumers were not aware of how popular Macy's is in the US; they did not have reasons for shopping there. Moreover, products were not modified to Chinese tastes. Macy's may have assumed that they could attract Chinese consumers just as they could in the US and might have not tested the market thoroughly before making a huge investment (for more on Macy's, see Case Study 2.1).

This SRC can be observed at the negotiation table. A monochronic culture (such as the

US) values punctuality and discusses items in sequence within a given time frame. A polychronic culture (such as Brazil) considers promptness less important and multiple items can be discussed simultaneously. Applying the SRC, Americans may view Brazilians as unorganized and inefficient, while Brazilians view Americans as pushy and inflexible. Thus, it is important to understand cultural differences in order to have an effective, efficient meeting. Monochronic versus polychronic culture will be illustrated more in Chapter 4. The SRC is one of the primary challenges in global marketing, particularly for fashion firms entering foreign markets for the first time. A related concept is ethnocentrism, which is the attitude that one's own group, ethnicity, or nationality is superior to others' (Shimp and Sharma, 1987). However, the two are different, in that ethnocentrism refers to viewing one's culture as superior, while the SRC is applying one's own perspectives to making decisions. Firms with little global experience may have an ethnocentric view and put less effort into seeing differences among countries. In order to avoid any mistakes from applying the SRC and an ethnocentric view, fashion firms need to recruit a globally competent workforce and train them to be sensitive to cultural differences.

Coordinating Marketing Activities across Countries

Fashion firms may operate their brand stores in multiple foreign markets, which necessitates coordination and integration. As mentioned in Chapter 1, fashion goods are brand-driven, so brand is a critical asset for fashion companies. While companies choose to localize some of their marketing elements in certain markets, they need to coordinate them in order to keep a consistent brand image. Take Chanel as an example. If Chanel stores feel the same in every location you visit, whether in New York, London, Beijing, or São Paulo, we can say that Chanel is well coordinated across the globe. However, in practice, coordination is not that simple.

Imagine a scenario where a brand operates 5,000 stores across the globe via a licensing agreement. In a licensing agreement (more in Chapter 8), a brand allows its licensees to develop products and put the brand's name and logo on the products. Coordination can get tricky when multiple licensees across countries develop their own products for their own markets. Then products may look fairly different from country to country. Licensees can view their counterparts in other countries as competitors and do not share information with each other.

The pitfall of licensing agreements can hurt not only the brand identity but also the bottom line, as seen in the case of Burberry, a British luxury fashion house (Ahrendts, 2013). By 2006, Burberry had 23 licensees worldwide, each exercising full control over the product lines in their respective market. At the whim of the licensees in each market, the product offerings were inconsistent, ranging from kilts to dog leashes. The price was also very different among licensees. For example, the price of outerwear in the US was half of that in the UK. The trench coat price in Italy and Germany was even cheaper than the one in the US. Moreover, Burberry has a few regional websites. To create a consistent brand identity grounded in its heritage, Burberry terminated the licensing agreements, appointed one global design director to oversee every design that consumers are offered, and consolidated the regional websites into one platform. Fortunately, Burberry's coordination effort paid off, with its revenues doubling over the next five years.

Similarly, when US jeans brand Lee entered China in 1995 in a joint venture with a Chinese partner (WWD, 1994), it allowed the Chinese partner to develop products for local consumers. If Lee makes the same agreement in many different countries, the resultant variations in offerings across markets may confuse global consumers. Therefore, fashion firms need to ensure that the planning and execution of their marketing activities in different parts of the world are interdependent. Global integration is even more important for luxury and prestige brands because it targets a relatively uniform segment across the globe. With rapid information flows and market transparency thanks to digital technologies, brand consistency across countries becomes ever more important. Consumers can quickly compare differences in price, quality, and advertising messages with just a few clicks. This attests to the importance of global integration of brand strategies in building and maintaining brand trust.

CASE STUDY 2.1
Macy's Exit from China

In August 2015, Macy's formed a joint venture with Fung Retailing, an affiliate of the Hong Kong conglomerate Fung Group, to open an online store on Alibaba Group's Tmall Global platform, a leading e-marketplace that connects overseas brands and retailers to consumers in China (Parry, 2015). Tmall Global covers 16,400 brands from 68 countries and has 30 million active users. Tmall Global is a relatively low-commitment testbed for many foreign brands seeking to reach Chinese consumers and build brand awareness in China, not only because of its massive active user base but also because it does not require brands to have physical operations in China.

The joint venture, called Macy's China Limited, was Macy's foray into new avenues of growth, as Macy's had struggled to increase its sales in the US. With a 65 percent stake in the venture, Macy's invested more than $25 million (Parry, 2015). Even before Macy's opened its online store on Tmall Global, Chinese consumers were already able to shop on its official website, www.macys.com, but the merchandise offered was limited. Through the joint venture, Macy's sought to increase its presence in China by making itself more accessible and better able to understand Chinese consumers. Under the joint venture, Macy's launched an online store in late 2015 on Tmall Global, becoming the first US department store chain to open an online store on the platform. The joint venture partner Fung Retailing was responsible for merchandising an assortment of items tailored to Chinese customers and fulfilling orders through local logistics channels, including LF Logistics, an affiliate of Fung Retailing (Parry, 2015). Macy's chose Fung Retailing because the company had deep experience and expertise with retailing in Asia, particularly in China, as evidenced by its 3,000 stores spread across Asia, with at least 1,000 in China.

However, in late 2018, three years after the launch, Macy's shut down its online store on Tmall Global and went back to its previous method of serving Chinese consumers via its flagship site, www.macys.com (Bhattacharyya, 2018). So, now, Macy's ships directly to Chinese consumers from its US website (Parmar, 2018). According to Macy's annual report, the costs associated with the wind-down of Macy's China Limited amounted to $19 million.

Analysts attributed Macy's eventual exit to Chinese consumers' lack of awareness of the Macy's brand and Macy's inability to tailor its offerings to local preferences, which are fast-changing and varied. For example, while cosmetics and handbags sold well at most Chinese retailers, Macy's focused on clothes. More importantly, the company failed to localize its clothing options, which were deemed too old-fashioned and pricey for Chinese consumers (Weiduo, 2018). It is important to note that the company did make an attempt to adapt. There were merchandising teams in both Hong Kong and Shanghai that offered products to best satisfy local tastes. The problem might be with the method the company used to achieve localization. Macy's tried to localize by curating its merchandise assortment rather than developing products tailored to local preferences. However, since Macy's reputation is not as pronounced in China as in the US, Macy's curation might not have convinced Chinese consumers. Sticking to the US business model of curating brands and products proved ineffective in a marketplace like Tmall Global, because what Macy's offered was already available in Chinese marketplaces or through local distributors (Bhattacharyya, 2018). It turned out that if you have the wrong products to start with, true adaptation is difficult to achieve with curation alone, however sophisticated it may be.

Discussion Questions
1. What could Macy's have done differently to ensure it gained a competitive edge in the Chinese market?
2. What was Macy's biggest mistake that led to its failure in China?

References

Bhattacharyya, S. (2018, December 7). "An uphill battle": Why Macy's is pulling out of China. Digiday. https://digiday.com/retail/macys-pulling-out-china

Parmar, H. (2018, December 6). Macy's ends Tmall store in second China strategy shift of 2018. Bloomberg. www.bloomberg.com/news/articles/2018-12-06/macy-s-ends-tmall-store-in-second-china-strategy-shift-of-2018

Parry, T. (2015, August 12). *Macy's Testing Ecommerce in China, Signs Exclusive Deal with Alibaba*. Multichannel Merchant. https://multichannelmerchant.com/news/macys-testing-ecommerce-in-china-signs-exclusive-deal-with-alibaba

Weiduo, S. (2018, December 5). Retreat by Macy's from Chinese market shows localization woes. *Global Times*. www.globaltimes.cn/content/1130545.shtml

Summary

- A major difference between global and domestic marketing is the scope of activities.
- Each country has unique economic, cultural, legal, and political environments. Such variations in market environments are not under the company's control, making global marketing much more complicated than domestic marketing.
- Global marketing strategy starts with a decision to enter a foreign country. Having a unique competitive advantage allows the firm to enter other countries with more confidence. A SWOT analysis can be a useful tool in identifying whether a brand has a competitive advantage in a given country.
- Once a company decides to enter a foreign market, it needs to decide whether to standardize the 4Ps across markets (standardization strategy) or modify them to cater to local consumer preferences (localization/adaptation strategy).
- Numerous strategy options exist on a continuum between complete global standardization and complete local adaptation, and therefore the company needs to decide the degree to which the 4Ps are standardized or localized.
- Making modifications to the 4Ps can increase the operational complexity and make it challenging to keep a consistent brand image.
- To keep a consistent brand image, fashion firms should ensure that the planning and execution of their marketing activities in different parts of the world are interdependent.
- Inherent challenges in global fashion marketing include: the four risks stemming from different environments (cross-cultural risk, country risk, commercial risk, and currency risk), the tendency to believe that products and practices that succeeded in the home market will be successful in other markets, and coordinating marketing activities across the countries.

Class Activities

1. Choose a global brand such as Nike or Coach that is not from your home country. Compare the brand's website in its country of brand origin (the US in the case of Nike) with the one in your country. Discuss how the brand localized its product offering in your country. Also discuss whether its localization efforts were adequate and appropriate. If not, discuss what you would suggest to the company, considering the tradeoffs between the pros and cons of localization.

2. Find a fashion brand originating from your country that failed in a foreign market. Research the causes of the failure and discuss which of the three inherent challenges illustrated in this chapter can explain the failure.

Key Terms

- **Marketing mix (4Ps):** Also known as the 4Ps, refers to four core elements of marketing decisions: product, price, promotion, and place.
- **Ansoff's product/market growth matrix:** Developed by Igor Ansoff, a Russian American scholar in strategic management, Ansoff's matrix is used to identify the optimal portfolio of growth strategy in terms of product and market creation. It outlines four alternative directions for growth, which vary in risk: market penetration, market development, product development, and diversification.

- **Competitive advantage:** An attribute that allows a firm to outperform its competitors, which can lead to a higher market share and profits, compared to competitors.
- **Product life cycle (PLC):** The pattern of sales for a product, from the time it is first launched in the market until it becomes obsolete. The cycle follows a bell-shaped curve in five stages: introduction, growth, maturity, saturation, and decline.
- **SWOT analysis:** A SWOT (strengths, weaknesses, opportunities, and threats) analysis is a framework used to evaluate a company's competitive position for developing strategic plans.
- **Standardization:** A global marketing strategy where a company offers the same marketing 4P elements in all markets.
- **Adaptation:** A global marketing strategy where a company modifies the marketing 4Ps in response to local market needs or conditions.
- **Glocalization:** A combination of the words "globalization" and "localization," it refers to a global marketing strategy that achieves the optimal balance of standardization and adaptation.
- **Self-reference criterion (SRC):** An unconscious reference to one's own cultural values, experiences, and knowledge as a basis for decisions.
- **Ethnocentrism:** The attitude that one's own group, ethnicity, or nationality is superior to others.
- **Global coordination:** The alignment of the 4Ps across markets so that they are not disconnected from the company's overarching branding strategy.
- **Global integration:** The degree to which marketing mix activities are coordinated across countries.

Global Environments Affecting the Fashion Business

PART 2

The major difference between domestic business and global business is the environments where businesses are performed. Therefore, in marketing fashion goods globally, it is essential to understand how global markets differ from domestic markets. In addition, when significant events like war unfold in host countries, fashion companies must swiftly adapt to changing circumstances. For instance, when the war erupted between Russia and Ukraine in February 2022, fashion brands such as LVMH, ASOS, and Nike suspended their retail operations in Russia. Mango, on the other hand, halted online sales and deliveries to Russia (Paris, 2022). Such suspensions and withdrawals entail a loss of turnover and profit but are imperative to protect the brand image.

Furthermore, Brexit, the UK's withdrawal from the European Union (EU) on January 31, 2020, has significantly impacted fashion retailers. The privileges enjoyed by the UK as an EU member, such as the free movement of goods without paying duties and people without visas to other EU countries, are no longer available. Likewise, EU countries cannot freely move goods to the UK without incurring duties. This has varied implications for the UK and EU countries, including higher costs for the import of goods into the UK and moving fulfillment centers outside the UK to avoid new taxes and tariffs. To counter such issues, Gymshark, the UK sportswear brand, opened a warehouse in Belgium to provide uninterrupted delivery for EU consumers. Brexit also has several implications for consumers and retail sales. With the elimination of tax refunds for goods purchased by tourists in the UK, tourism sales, especially by luxury brands, will be diverted to other EU countries (Retail Insight Network, 2022). As seen in the above examples, fashion retailers must focus on environmental differences and changes, as they impact several aspects of the global fashion business.

In Part 2, the three types of global environments that fashion companies should be aware of will be examined: economic (Chapter 3), cultural (Chapter 4), and legal and regulatory environments (Chapter 5).

CHAPTER 3

Economic Environment of Global Markets: Why and How It Matters

Learning Objectives

After studying this chapter, you will be able to:

- Classify countries by their economic development level and explain the general characteristics of each classification group.
- Describe the development patterns of the apparel industry.
- Compare and contrast the challenges and opportunities in retail markets with different economic development levels.
- Explain the implications of differing economic environments on global fashion marketing.

Imagine you open a store in an African country where the economic development level is significantly lower than that of your country. The same strategies used in the domestic market would not be applicable. The products and brands you will carry, pricing of the products, store format, payment method, and promoting your products and brands should be different. This is because those aspects vary hugely by the country's economic environment. The economic level of a country is likely the single most important environmental element that fashion companies should look into before embarking on global business. Countries are often classified by their economic development level because each category's shared characteristics can provide a preliminary understanding of the countries. This chapter will begin by introducing the classification and characteristics of countries by their economic development level. Such differing characteristics pose different sets of challenges. These challenges will then be illustrated. The purpose of this chapter lies in helping fashion companies become aware of the implications of differing economic environments. Therefore, the last part of this chapter will address the implications of differing economic environments on global fashion marketing.

Economic Development Level: Classification and General Characteristics

Country Classification and Characteristics

Multiple indicators are used to assess a country's relative economic advancement. The most common metrics include gross domestic product (GDP) and gross national income (GNI). GDP is a widely used metric defined as the total monetary or market value of all the finished goods and services produced within the physical borders of a country in a given year. It is calculated considering the expenditure and investment of individuals, companies and government, and net exports. GDP does not, however, include monetary or market values beyond a country's border. GNI captures this aspect and adds income from foreign sources to GDP. GNI, therefore, is the total income earned by a country from its residents and businesses in a given year regardless of whether they are located in the country or abroad. It is considered accurate given the active movement of people and commerce across the globe. GNI per capita is the average income of a country's citizen before tax, calculated by dividing GNI by its population. Based on the GNI per capita, the World Bank classifies countries into four levels: high, upper-middle, lower-middle, and low-income countries. Table 3.1 summarizes the classification and characteristics of each category.

As shown in Table 3.1, the higher the GNI per capita, the richer the country. However, countries belonging to each category are not absolute, as the World Bank reevaluates the classification annually. GDP or GNI are largely correlated with other measures of economic wellbeing, such as life expectancy, infant mortality rates, and literacy rates, all of which improve as a country's GDP or GNI grows. Another tendency is decreased reliance on agriculture and increased focus on the service sector as countries' economies advance. Urbanization also increases with the economy. Other terms related to high-income countries include G7 (US, Japan, Germany, France, UK, Canada, and Italy), G20, and the OECD (Organisation for Economic Co-operation and Development). Thirty high-income nations belong to the OECD, often described as an "economic think tank" and a "rich man's club."

Other than this classification, classification based on economic growth or the size of the capital market, such as developed countries (or markets) versus developing countries (or markets), is also commonly used. Developing countries can be further grouped as newly industrialized economies (NIEs) or newly industrialized countries, emerging markets, or least developed countries in decreasing order of economic growth. NIE describes a country whose level of economic development ranks somewhere between the developing and developed classifications. Countries belonging to NIEs change. In the 1970s and 1980s, four Asian Tigers, Hong Kong, South Korea, Singapore, and Taiwan, were NIEs. In fact, the term NIEs appeared first to refer to these fast-growing Asian economies. These countries have now moved to developed countries. NIEs in the late 2000s include South Africa, Mexico, Brazil, China, India, Malaysia, the Philippines, Thailand, and Turkey. Common attributes of NIEs include a transition from agriculture to manufacturing, the presence of large national corporations, strong foreign

Table 3.1 Country classification and characteristics by the World Bank

COUNTRY GROUPS (GNI PER CAPITA)*	COUNTRY EXAMPLES	CHARACTERISTICS
Low-income countries ($1,035 or less)	Concentrated in Africa south of the Sahara	• Also called "least developed countries" • Limited industrialization • High percentage of the population engaged in agriculture and subsistence farming • High birth rates, short life expectancy • Low literacy rates • Heavy reliance on foreign aid • Political instability and unrest • Infrastructure is not well developed
Lower-middle-income countries ($1,036 to $4,045)	India, Sri Lanka, Uzbekistan	• Rapidly expanding consumer markets • Cheap motivated labor • Focus on labor-intensive industries like footwear, textiles, and toys
Upper-middle-income countries ($4,046 to $12,535)	Brazil, Russia, China, South Africa, Malaysia, Mexico, Venezuela	• Rapidly industrializing, less agricultural employment • Increasing urbanization • Rising wages • High literacy rates and advanced education • Lower wage costs than advanced countries
High-income countries ($12,536 or more)	US, Sweden, Japan, South Korea	• Also called "developed countries," "advanced economies," "industrialized countries" • Sustained economic growth through disciplined innovation • Service sector is more than 50 percent of GNI • Households have high ownership levels of basic products • Importance of information processing and exchange • Dominance of knowledge over capital, intellectual over machine technology, scientists and professionals over engineers and semiskilled workers

Note: * as of May 20, 2021.

direct investment, and rapid growth in urban centers resulting from migration from rural areas into larger and more populated city centers.

"Emerging markets" refer to countries and regions experiencing substantial and rapid economic growth and industrialization that are likely to emerge in the future as mature markets (Gielens and Dekimpe, 2007). Consumers in these markets are informed about and exposed to goods and services from mature markets, while still conforming to certain traditional habits, attitudes, and structures. Many acronyms are used to denote emerging markets. One of the notable ones is BRIC (Brazil, Russia, India, and China) coined by Goldman Sachs in 2001. Adding South Africa to it, BRICS is also commonly referred to as "emerging countries."

Four BRIC countries account for more than a quarter of the world's land area and more than 42 percent of the world's population. All four countries have a huge land size, with Russia having the world's largest land area, China the fourth, Brazil fifth, and India seventh. The population of China is 4.25 times that of the US, while the land size is about the same. Given the population, once those countries reach a certain economic level, the purchasing power for fashion goods will be great. According to one report, approximately half of mid-market apparel sales (55 percent) will come from emerging markets in 2025, up from 25 percent in 2004 (Keller et al., 2014).

The characteristics of NIEs and emerging markets are similar, in that NIEs are a subset of emerging countries. However, NIEs are close to becoming advanced economies while not fully reaching developed country status yet. The least developed countries show the same characteristics as the low-income countries described in Table 3.1.

Apparel Industry Development Patterns

The apparel industry in a country often develops as the country's economy advances. The apparel industry within a country evolves, following a certain pattern. Toyne et al. (1984) explained the pattern with six stages: embryonic, early export of apparel, more advanced production of fabric and apparel, golden age, full maturity, and significant decline. Each stage presents distinctive characteristics, as shown in Table 3.2. Apparel industry development in a country is often in parallel with its economic development. For example, the apparel industry in Korea was in an embryonic stage in the 1950s, right after the Korean War (1950–3). It underwent the early export of apparel stage in the 1960s, more advanced production of fabric and apparel stage in the 1970s, golden age in the 1980s, and full maturity in the 1990s (Jin et al., 2013). The country is now in a significant decline stage like many other advanced economies, which is characterized by an increase in global sourcing and decline in the number of factories.

The evolvement pattern described by Toyne et al. (1984) is, however, mainly from the apparel production perspective, lacking branding and retail perspective. The apparel brand concept emerges when a country reaches a certain economic level because it requires the understanding of consumer demands, financial capital, marketing concepts, and so on. In the case of South Korea and India, the branding concept does not emerge until the golden age (Jin et al., 2013). The export of branded apparel goods is observed to occur in the significant decline stage in many advanced economies (Jin et al., 2013).

Another model that explains the apparel industry development pattern is the flying geese model (Akamatsu, 1962). It explains that, first, a country imports certain goods, followed by production and export. Applying this model to the apparel industry, it is typical that in developing countries branded apparel goods are imported from advanced economies first, which motivates the developing countries to develop their own brands. After that, countries evolve to engage in the production of branded goods largely by utilizing their abundant labor. Finally, they progress to export their own branded goods overseas. The flying geese model can be further extended to explain the evolution pattern of industries in the same

Table 3.2 Korean apparel industry development by Toyne et al (1984)'s six stages

STAGES	CHARACTERISTICS	KOREA
Embryonic	• Produce simple fabrics and garments made from natural fibers for domestic consumption and import fibers, fabrics, and apparel	• 1950s
Early export of apparel	• Export of low-end mature varieties, native apparel, or apparel requiring elaborate handwork	• 1960s
More advanced production of fabric and apparel	• Domestic production of fabric increases sharply in terms of quantity, quality, and sophistication and export of fabric begins • Apparel exports are rapidly expanded and upgraded • Textile complexes become large, more diversified, more concentrated, and more internationally active • Movement to this stage is typically spurred by investment, contracting, or the provision of marketing or managerial assistance by large manufacturers and retailers in more developed countries as well as local government policies of import substitution and export development	• 1970s • The export of apparel and textiles increased by 13 times during the 1970s, accounting for about 40 percent of Korean total exports in 1971 (Kang and Jin, 2007)
Golden age	• Consolidation and diversification in product mix continue; huge trade surpluses result • Textile complexes spread internationally via foreign investment and contractual arrangement	• 1980s • Trade surplus increased • Textile companies established factories in Central America to export to the US market
Full maturity	• Employment in the complexes decline especially in the apparel sector; however, total outputs may be increasing • Industrial concentration continues and production and process sophistication reach high levels • The complexes move toward more capital-intensive production	• 1990s • Employment in the apparel sector was decreased due to declining of apparel export • Development of value-added textile products was emphasized
Significant decline	• Employment and the number of firms decline substantially • Offshore production increases significantly • Significant trade deficit appears in many sectors, especially in apparel and fabric	• Since 2000s • A significant increase in offshore production. • Significant fall in the number of firms and employees (Jin and Moon, 2006)

Source: Revised based on Jin et al. (2013)

country. For example, industry development in a country starts with textiles, followed sequentially by chemicals, iron and steel, automobiles, and electronic industries: Japan and South Korea followed this sectoral development pattern. The model also proposes that apparel production in a developing country moves to the next developing countries (Kwan, 2002). Just as geese fly in an inverted V shape, next tier countries emulate the leading geese country. Japan started its industrialization with apparel production in the 1950s, serving as a leading goose. After Japan, next tier geese (Taiwan, Hong Kong, and South Korea) followed the lead goose in the 1960s and 1970s. Then the third tier (China and India) followed the pattern in the 1980s. At present, Southeast Asian countries (Vietnam, Bangladesh, Pakistan, and Myanmar) are following the pattern. Bangladesh ranks second in the export of apparel goods after China, with apparel goods accounting for 84 percent of exports in the country (Bari and Jin, 2021).

The typical evolution pattern of apparel production in developing countries begins with OEM (original equipment manufacturing) and progresses into ODM (original design manufacturing) and then OBM (original brand manufacturing). In OEM production, manufacturers produce following a client's design and brand name. In ODM, it still produces under a client's brand name, but an in-house design team works with the client, suggesting and providing designs. In OBM, a company produces with its own design and brand name and distributes via its own distribution channels. Most advanced economies do OBM but outsource their production to developing countries (Scott, 2006).

Characteristics and Challenges of Retail Markets by a Country's Economic Development Level

As with the apparel industry, retail markets in a country progress as the country's economy moves forward. The level of retail market development roughly parallels the stages of economic development in the country. The more developed an economy, the more sophisticated and specialized the commercial entities become to perform retailing and marketing functions. Therefore, the challenges in the apparel retail markets differ by the country's economic development level. In this section, we will learn how retail markets in a country evolve. Then, the characteristics and challenges will be discussed by the country's retail market development level.

Retailing in Least Developed Markets: Characteristics and Challenges

Least developed markets are characterized by low per capita income, not being fully industrialized, and lacking a sophisticated legal or financial system. The characteristics of these markets' traditional retail systems are as follows (Reinartz et al., 2011; Samiee, 1993; Singh, 2019; Sternquist and Goldsmith, 2018; Varshney, 2021):

- Vendors move from village to village with a bag of assorted merchandise. In least developed markets, it is common to see vendors on the street approaching you to sell goods.

- Fragmented markets made up of small and independent stores.
- High percentage of unorganized retailing. In unorganized retailing, stores are not registered for sales tax. Typical unorganized retailers include owner staffed general stores, handcarts, and pavement vendors or street vendors.
- Permanent stores carry very scrambled merchandise—unrelated groupings of goods and broken assortments—and limited product variety.
- Shopkeepers in this system know their customers and call them by their name. Shopping is not just purchasing products. It includes socializing and information-gathering activities.
- Flexible prices, bargaining, and price haggling are common.
- Informal credit is common. Customers can buy without paying upfront. Because the shopkeepers know their customers, they can lend goods first and collect their money later when customers have money.

Figure 3.1 shows some aspects of the traditional retail system—street vendors with scrambled merchandise.

Retail challenges in the least developed markets are mainly related to infrastructure. These countries lack the infrastructure that supports distribution and modern retailing transactions, such as a postal system, road conditions, a credit card processing system, and modern banking. In lieu of credit card payment, cash on delivery is very common. This means that consumers pay a deliverer in cash when the items they ordered are delivered to their home. Imagine the deliverer needing to make multiple attempts to collect the payment if consumers are not at home. This adds to the costs of doing business in least developed countries. Because of the lack of a modern banking system, mobile phones are often used to transfer money. M-Pesa, a mobile phone-based money transfer service, is commonly used to pay online orders in many African countries (Reinartz et al., 2011; Sharma et al., 2018).

Retailing in Emerging Markets: Characteristics and Challenges

Thanks to their rapid economic growth, several distinctive characteristics appear in emerging markets—the rise of a middle class, increasing disposable incomes and urbanization, and a high share of a young population—all of which contribute to growing consumer demands (Reinartz et al., 2011). In emerging markets, the share of the population younger than 25 years is often more than 40 percent. In Brazil, it is 38.2 percent; India, 44.8 percent; Nigeria, 62.2 percent; and Egypt, 52 percent. This contrasts with many developed countries where a large share of the older population dominates. In the US, the proportion of people over 55 years was nearly 30 percent in 2021 (US Census Bureau, 2022). In contrast, in Nigeria, Africa's most populous country, only 7.3 percent of the population is older than 55 (Katabe and Helsen, 2020). A young population not only offers abundant labor for apparel production but serves as a stable consumer segment, offering tremendous opportunities to fashion companies.

Catering to the demand, global fashion retailers are eager to enter the markets. With the introduction of global fashion brands, consumers become conscious of brand name, and thus brand logo often serves as a status

Figure 3.1 Unorganized retailing in India.
Source: Courtesy of B. Ellie Jin.

symbol. Materialism is beginning to grow, and materialistic consumers tend to prefer goods that signal status (Cleveland et al., 2009). Therefore, consumer preferences toward global brands over domestic ones are prevalent (Batra et al., 2000). This contrasts with many advanced economies where consumers prefer domestic brands (Balabanis et al., 2001).

In terms of retailing, self-service and modern retail formats, such as shopping malls, department stores, and mass discount stores, are introduced but coexist with the traditional retail system (Reinartz et al., 2011). The markets are heterogeneous across products and services as well as geographic areas (that is, urban vs. rural). For example, infrastructure is being rapidly developed but centered in metro areas, while infrastructure in rural areas, such as paved roads, logistics, broadband internet, credit card usage, and so on, is still underdeveloped (Sheth, 2011). Modern retail formats are also growing quickly, especially in large cities, but coexist with traditional wet markets (Figure 3.2). Many modern shopping malls are popping up, but tailors and mom and pop stores still operate in the same city (Figure 3.3).

The next distinctive characteristic in emerging markets is huge diversity within a country. Regional differences are particularly immense in countries with a large land area, such as China and India (Cho et al., 2010; Jin and Son, 2013). These two countries are often described as a collection of countries with differing economic development levels, similar to the European Union. Cultural and ethnic diversity are also significant within these countries. China has 56 distinctive ethnic groups, the largest of which are the Han Chinese (92 percent) (see Case Study 3.1). In the case of India, each state has its own languages and alphabets, so two Indians coming from different states communicate in English, rather than in their mother tongue (see Case Study 3.2). With massive economic, cultural, and ethnic diversity within a country, consumers' tastes and acceptance of global fashion brands and products vary significantly.

Figure 3.2 Coexistence of modern retail and wet markets in Shanghai, China.
Source: Courtesy of B. Ellie Jin.

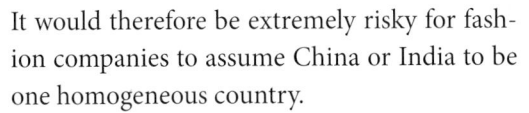

Figure 3.3 Coexistence of modern retail and tailors in Mumbai, India.
Source: Courtesy of B. Ellie Jin.

It would therefore be extremely risky for fashion companies to assume China or India to be one homogeneous country.

These distinctive characteristics of emerging markets present both opportunities and challenges. Growing consumer demand is a definite opportunity, but many challenges lie ahead of unfolding businesses there. One major challenge may come from unbranded products, which represent more than 60 percent of consumption (Sheth, 2011). Brand logos start to carry importance, but many products are still locally made without a brand concept. These products are reasonably priced and good enough for local consumers. Consumers gradually desire branded goods that convey good quality and status. Therefore, global fashion brands need to develop markets to convince consumers of the benefits of global brands that unbranded local products cannot provide. Another common challenge associated with underdeveloped countries is infrastructure. Hard infrastructure (such as load, internet, and IT systems) is itself an obstacle to overcome, but soft infrastructure (such as intellectual property, transparent transactions) might be more challenging as it takes more time. This issue will be discussed more in Chapter 5. Probably the most difficult challenge comes from market heterogeneity. Emerging markets are in the process of becoming advanced economies, so the markets are fairly heterogeneous across products and services. In urban areas, products and service levels can be similar to those in advanced economies. Yet the poorest area of an emerging country may show certain characteristics of underdeveloped countries. Urban consumers may be sophisticated through education and travel, while rural consumers can be illiterate and may not have access to the internet. There is a wide range of opportunities between the rich and the poor and between the urban and rural consumers. Therefore, fine-tuned strategies are needed to address the varying degrees of consumer needs.

Retailing in Mature Markets: Characteristics and Challenges

In mature markets, the infrastructure for the physical distribution of products and customer spending power are largely in place. The challenges of mature markets are not about infrastructure but about how to win over consumers as retail markets are quite competitive. Note that retailing in mature markets is a buyer's market. Consumers in these mature markets are pampered with strong domestic and global companies who compete intensely. Consumers are savvy and confident about their ability to make informed purchase decisions. For example, they know that a high price does not necessarily mean high quality. This implies that apparel companies need to be competitive enough to attract consumers by offering innovative goods, services, and experiences. Therefore, retailers in mature markets need to focus on how they can fulfill the higher order needs of consumers, such as experience, customization, corporate social responsibility, sustainability, and fair trade. The competitive advantage such as value for money may no longer provide opportunities in this market. Examples of brands with an innovative retail model in the US include Everlane for supply chain transparency, Stitch Fix for online personal styling service, and Rent the Runway for online rental service. Table 3.3 compares the characteristics of the retail market environment by the economic development level.

Implications of Economic Environment on Global Fashion Marketing

We have learned that the development of the apparel and retail market corresponds to the economic development in a country. Varying economic environments mean varying opportunities, which require differing marketing strategies. This section highlights some points related to the economic environment that global fashion companies should be cognizant of.

Do Not Assume the Current Economic Status Will Remain the Same

A country's economic environment keeps changing, especially in emerging markets where many economic indices are upgrading at a fast rate. With economic development, consumers in emerging markets are becoming increasingly sophisticated and digitally savvy. Thus, it is important to understand the dynamics of the changes and develop marketing strategies accordingly. To grasp the changes,

Table 3.3 Comparison of characteristics of retail market environments

	LEAST DEVELOPED (SELLER'S MARKET)	EMERGING (TRANSITION TO BUYER'S MARKET)	MATURE (BUYER'S MARKET)
Discount	Rare	Small	Common
Competition	Weak	Getting stronger	Fierce
Consumer markets	Embryonic	Strong	Saturated
Marketing and branding concept	Rare	Becoming important	Everywhere
Distribution	Weak	Complex	Streamlined
Major challenges	Overcoming lack of infrastructure	Understanding market heterogeneity	Winning consumer satisfaction

local market knowledge should be updated frequently, and decisions should not be made with outdated information. For daily operations, therefore, it is critical to hire local talent and find a good local partner who knows the local culture and language and can provide insights into the local markets and consumers.

Do Not Underestimate Market Opportunities in Less Developed Countries

There are many mistaken assumptions about less developed countries:

- Consumers in less developed countries have no money to afford fashion goods.
- Consumers in less developed countries are so concerned with fulfilling basic needs that they do not spend money on non-essential goods.
- The goods sold in developing countries are so inexpensive that there is no room for new market entrants to make a profit.
- People in less developed countries cannot use advanced technology.

The above assumptions are all false. There is a huge disparity between the rich and the poor in emerging markets and less developed markets (Reinartz et al., 2011). Consequently, even in poor countries, there are wealthy consumers who can afford luxury brands. As shown in Table 3.3, emerging and less developed countries are far less competitive; it can be more attractive than entering advanced economies. Technology spreads rapidly, so consumers in less developed countries adopt information technologies such as the internet, mobile phone, and social media just like consumers in advanced economies. As Chapter 1 showed, mobile shopping via mobile apps is growing even faster in some less developed economies than advanced ones.

Find a Balance between Mature and Fast-growing Markets

While emerging economies can offer huge market opportunities, it is risky as there are more challenges to solve. In contrast, advanced economies will be easier and lower risk places to do business, although their growth rate would be relatively slow and the retail market is competitive. With their stable consumer demand, North America and Europe will remain significant markets for many fashion companies for decades to come. Global fashion companies may need to choose the right balance between mature, lower risk advanced economies and faster moving but generally higher risk emerging markets. There is no single correct answer, and a good balance depends on each company's strategic directions. For instance, a risk-taking company may want to enter emerging markets more aggressively than advanced economies.

Do Not Just Rely on Economic Environment When Making Business Decisions

While a country's economic environment provides a fundamental understanding of the country, global fashion companies should not solely rely on it to inform decisions related to market entry and daily operations. For example, although the UK and the US are both advanced economies, the average home size in the UK is half of that of the US. This implies that closet size is smaller in the UK, so smaller quantities of clothes might be consumed compared to the US. Due to the small land size, walk-in closets, common in the US, are quite inappropriate in Hong Kong. This could imply that consumers in Hong Kong may prefer less quantity but more quality. Consider body mass index (BMI). Except in China, the average consumer in all countries listed in Table 3.4 is overweight (BMI above 25). This indicates that to gauge popular clothes size in a country, fashion companies should refer to BMI. This collectively suggests that beyond the economic environment, other environments and indices should be carefully examined. In Chapters 4 and 5, cultural and legal environments will be discussed, respectively.

Table 3.4 Comparison of selected economies in some indices

COUNTRY	GDP PER CAPITA[1]	POPULATION DENSITY (PEOPLE/KM)[2]	AVERAGE HOUSEHOLD SIZE (NUMBER OF PERSONS)[3]	AVERAGE HOME SIZE (SQ FT)[4]	AVERAGE BODY MASS INDEX (BMI)[5]
US	$76k	37	2.6	2,518	29
UK	$49k	279	2.4	1,100	27
China	$14k	151	2.6	500	24
Russia	$12k	9	2.3	600	26
Mexico	$10k	66	3.3	400	28
Brazil	$8k	26	3.2	1,288	27

Notes: 1. IMF (2022). 2. Ritchie (2019). 3. Euromonitor (2021). 4. Various sources. 5. BMI: Underweight = <18.5, Normal weight = 18.5–24.9, Overweight = 25–29.9, Obese = 30 or greater. Euromonitor (2021).

CASE STUDY 3.1

An Overview of China: It Will Be a Mistake to View China As One Country

China is the world's fourth largest country by area and the world's most populous country, with one-fourth of the world's population. Home to one of the world's oldest civilizations, China has about 3,500 years of written history. Starting with the Xia Dynasty (*ca.* 2070–1600 BCE), ancient China was ruled by a number of different dynasties. After the fall of the last dynasty (Qing) in 1912, a weak central government followed. In 1949, under Chairman Mao Zedong, China became a communist country.

Throughout history, the Chinese economy has undergone a process of prosperity, decline, and rise. Ancient China led the world's civilizations with four great inventions (gunpowder, papermaking, printing, and the compass). In the tenth century, China was better off than European countries. Up until 1820, China commanded a higher GDP than Western countries. With their pride, the Chinese had an ethnocentric ideology called "Sinocentrism" that regards China to be central or unique relative to other countries. The Chinese Sinocentric view is well reflected in the country name China, which literally means "central country."

However, the share of Chinese GDP in the world decreased continuously from 32.4 percent in 1820 to 13.2 percent (1890), 9.1 percent (1919), and 5.2 percent (1952) (Schlevogt, 2000). Between 1949 and 1978, the state took control of businesses on behalf of the people, so there was no private ownership. Its economy slowed down for decades under totalitarian socialism. The country became, by and large, an agricultural country, with a majority of its population living in abject poverty in the countryside (Biliang, 2018; Morisson, 2019). In 1978, two years after the death of communist leader Mao Zedong, the Chinese Communist Party began reforming its economy by introducing more flexible market policies such as private ownership. China's economy continues to be a socialist market where state-owned enterprises and public ownership coexist with private ownership.

Now, China is the world's second largest economy, with its GDP becoming commensurate with that of the upper half of OECD nations. China is the largest export economy in the world, and the world's leading exporter of goods ranging from labor-intensive ones such as textiles to mid-skilled ones such as smartphones. The export-led economy is evolving to one driven by domestic consumption, as Chinese people have more discretionary income to spend. China is also an increasingly important import country, in particular for other Asian countries (Colotla et al., 2018; World Bank, 2018).

However, China's 22 provinces, five autonomous regions, and four municipalities did not equally benefit from the economic boom. If each province's GDP is compared to that of other countries, there is a wide variability. Ningxia's GDP is equivalent to that of Ethiopia, while Jiangsu's is equivalent to Switzerland's GDP (*The Economist*, 2011). In fact, income disparity among regions is the highest in the world (*The Economist*, 2017a).

China is truly a diverse country with about 56 distinct ethnic groups, the largest of which are the Han Chinese (92 percent) (*The Economist*,

2017b). Its climate also varies widely, ranging from extremely dry in the northwest to tropical in the southeast. China has the greatest difference in temperature between its northern and southern regions in the world (Twitchett et al., 2019). Because there is so much variability across regions, China's cities are categorized in tiers based on factors such as GDP, population, and politics. There are 5 Tier 1 cities, which include Beijing and Shanghai, 30 Tier 2 cities, 138 Tier 3 cities, and 480 Tier 4 cities (*South China Moring Post*, n.d.).

Discussion Questions

1. What are the implications of China's vast income disparity for global fashion companies?
2. Do you think global fashion companies need to establish different marketing strategies by tiers? Why and how?

References

Biliang, H. (2018, January). China's economic transformation. https://doc-research.org/2018/01/chinas-economic-transformation

Colotla, I., Zhou, Y., Du, V., Wong, J., Walters, J. et al. (2018, December). China's next leap in manufacturing. www.bcg.com/en-us/publications/2018/china-next-leap-in-manufacturing.aspx

Morrison, W.M. (2019, June). China's economic rise: History, trends, challenges, and implications for the United States. https://fas.org/sgp/crs/row/RL33534.pdf

Schlevogt, K-A. (2000). The branding revolution in China. *The China Business Review*, May–June, 52–7.

South China Morning Post (n.d.). Urban legend: China's tiered city system explained. http://multimedia.scmp.com/2016/cities

The Economist (2011, February 24). Comparing Chinese provinces with countries: All the parities in China. www.economist.com/asia/2011/02/24/all-the-parities-in-china

The Economist (2017a, February 16). The great divide: A new paper finds China more unequal than France but less so than America. www.economist.com/finance-and-economics/2017/02/16/a-new-paper-finds-china-more-unequal-than-france-but-less-so-than-america

The Economist (2017b, July 15). Identity politics: Why China's Communists recognise just 56 ethnic groups. www.economist.com/china/2017/07/15/why-chinas-communists-recognise-just-56-ethnic-groups

Twitchett, D.C., Chan, H., Chen, C.-S., McKnight, B.E., Elman, B. et al. (2019, September 10). China. www.britannica.com/place/China

World Bank (2019, April). The World Bank in China. www.worldbank.org/en/country/china/overview

CASE STUDY 3.2

Strong Prospects of India's Apparel Market

The world's seventh largest country by area and the world's second most populous country, India has a long history. About 8,000 years ago, the Indus Valley Civilization, one of the early civilizations, arose from what is now northwest India. Between the 1100s and 1500s, Muslim conquests took place with a series of empires and kingdoms, such as the Maurya Empire and Chola Empire, ruling the Indian subcontinent. Between the 1500s and 1700, the Mughal Empire ruled most of northern India. India was subject to British influence from 1600 and was under the direct rule of the British Empire for about 89 years until the country gained independence in 1947 (Gannon, 2004).

Within about 70 years, India has become an important market for international brands thanks to its growing middle class and tech-savvy consumers (World Bank, 2019). The Indian middle class is expected to grow around 19 percent a year, outpacing China, Mexico, and Brazil. In 2008, there were only 5 million smartphone users and only 45 million with access to the internet in a country of 1.2 billion people. Within 10 years, the number of smartphone users has increased to 460 million and is expected to rise by 84 percent to 859 million by 2022 (Amed et al., 2018; *The Economic Times*, 2019). Furthermore, relaxed foreign direct investment regulations (such as allowing 100 percent foreign-owned single brand retail operations) have improved the ease of doing business in India (Kearney, 2017). As a result, India is becoming not only an increasingly important sourcing hub but also one of the most attractive consumer markets. It is estimated that India's apparel and footwear market will become the third largest globally by 2023 (Euromonitor International, 2019). The income of the population with discretionary income to spend on clothing is expected to triple between 2018 and 2025 (Amed et al., 2018).

However, India presents challenges. The apparel industry is largely unorganized, with modern retail comprising just 35 percent of sales in 2016. Its share is expected to grow to 45 percent by 2025, but it would still be relatively low. There are about 15 million small retail outlets called "kirana" shops, which nonetheless form the backbone of the market (Kumar, 2009). As a secular federal republic with 29 states and seven union territories, India is diverse in geography, climate, language, and cultures. Each state and union territory has one or more official languages; there are 23 officially recognized languages, along with hundreds of regional dialects spoken in different parts of the country. Learned individuals usually speak three languages: the mother tongue of the state where they are born, Hindi (the official language), and English (a medium for higher education). The climate ranges from tropical in the south to temperate and alpine in the north, where elevated regions receive snowfall in winter. Consumer preferences also widely vary from a price-sensitive tendency to conspicuous consumption (Kumar, 2009). An additional challenge comes from India's poor infrastructure, which continues to lag behind that of many other Asian countries (Amed et al., 2018). About 40 percent of India's population will be living in urban areas by 2025, which will account for more than 60 percent of consumption (Singhi et al., 2017). Therefore, brands are likely to focus on major urban areas with better infrastructure and consumers with rising spending power.

Discussion Questions

1. What advice would you give to brands seeking to enter India?

2. With the diversity in language, culture, and climate across the states, what suggestions can you give to apparel companies entering India?

References

Amed, I., Balchandani, A., Beltrami, M., Berg, A., Hedrich, S. et al. (2018, November). The state of fashion 2019: A year of awakening. www.mckinsey.com/~/media/McKinsey/Industries/Retail/Our%20Insights/The%20State%20of%20Fashion%202019%20A%20year%20of%20awakening/The-State-of-Fashion-2019-final.ashx

Batra, R., Ramaswamy, V., Alden, D.L., Steenkamp, J-B. and Ramachander, S. (2000). Effects of brand local/nonlocal origin on consumer attitudes in developing countries. *Journal of Consumer Psychology*, 9(2): 83–95.

Euromonitor International (2019). Market sizes: Apparel in all countries. www.euromonitor.com

Gannon, H.J. (2004). *Understanding global cultures* (3rd ed.). Thousand Oaks, CA: Sage Publications.

Kearney (2017). The 2017 global retail development index: The age of focus. data_file-the-1499331665.pdf (etb2bimg.com)

Kumar, S.R. (2009, October 20). Addressing diversity: The marketing challenge in India. *The Wall Street Journal*. www.wsj.com/articles/SB125601922922896025

Singhi, A., Jain, N. and Sanghi, K. (2017, March 20). The new Indian: The many facets of a changing consumer. www.bcg.com/publications/2017/marketing-sales-globalization-new-indian-changing-consumer.aspx

The Economic Times (2019, May 10). Smartphone users expected to rise 84% to 859m by 2022: Assocham-PwC study. https://economictimes.indiatimes.com/tech/hardware/smartphone-users-expected-to-rise-84-to-859m-by-2022-assocham-pwc-study/articleshow/69260487.cms?from=mdr

World Bank (2019, April). The World Bank in India. www.worldbank.org/en/country/india/overview

Summary

- Countries are often classified by their economic development level because each classification group's shared characteristics can provide a preliminary understanding of the countries.
- Multiple indicators are used to assess a country's relative economic advancement, the most common metrics being gross domestic product (GDP) and gross national income (GNI).
- Another commonly used classification is based on economic growth or the size of the capital market, such as developed countries (or markets) versus developing countries (or markets).
- Developing countries can be further grouped as newly industrialized economies (NIEs) or newly industrialized countries, emerging markets, or least developed countries in decreasing order of economic growth.
- Apparel industry development in a country is often in parallel with its economic development and follows certain patterns.

- Retail market development also parallels the stages of economic development in a country.
- Challenges in the apparel retail markets differ by the country's economic development level.
- Retailing challenges in least developed markets are mainly related to the infrastructure that supports distribution and modern retailing transactions, such as a postal system, road conditions, a credit card processing system, and modern banking.
- As income inequality is higher in the emerging markets, consumer needs and demands are heterogeneous across regions.
- Challenges in mature markets are not about infrastructure but about how to win over consumers as the retail markets are quite competitive.
- Varying economic environments means varying opportunities that require differing marketing strategies.
- Global fashion companies should not: assume a country's current economic status will remain the same, underestimate the market opportunities in less developed countries, fail to find a balance between mature or fast-growing markets when making entry decisions, and make business decisions solely based on a country's economic environment.

Class Activities

1. Choose a global fashion brand and research what countries the company has entered. Classify the countries by their economic development level and describe the company's market portfolio. Which classification group is represented the most and the least? What does the market portfolio say about the brand's expansion strategy?

2. Discuss the projected development pattern of the fashion industry in Vietnam, Bangladesh, Pakistan, and Myanmar, based on the flying geese model and the apparel development stages of Toyne et al. (1984).

Key Terms

- **GDP per capita:** The sum of marketed goods and services produced within the national boundary, averaged across everyone who lives within this territory.
- **GNI per capita:** The sum of a country's gross domestic product (GDP) plus net income (positive or negative) from abroad, averaged across everyone living in the country and abroad.
- **BRIC:** An acronym coined in 2001 to denote four major emerging economies: Brazil, Russia, India, and China.
- **BRICS:** BRIC plus South Africa, which was added in 2010.
- **Newly industrialized economies (NIEs):** A country whose level of economic development ranks somewhere between the developing and developed classifications.
- **Emerging market:** A country experiencing substantial and rapid economic growth and industrialization; likely to emerge in the future as a mature market.
- **Flying geese model:** An industrial development pattern where developing countries (follower geese) follow a sequential pattern of development led by a lead goose (i.e., advanced country). The pattern is characterized by a tran-

sition from import, domestic production, to export, as well as from simple to more sophisticated products.

- **Apparel development stages (Toyne et al., 1984):** A development pattern of the apparel industry characterized by six stages: embryonic, early export of apparel, more advanced production of fabric and apparel, golden age, full maturity, and significant decline.
- **OEM (original equipment manufacturing):** A factory manufactures products based on a client company's designs and specifications. The products will have the client company's label.
- **ODM (original design manufacturing):** A factory makes products based on its own designs and specifications for a client company. The products will have the client company's label.
- **OBM (original brand manufacturing):** A company makes products with its own design and brand name and distributes via its own distribution channels.
- **Seller's market:** Seller's market exists when customers want to buy more products than sellers can provide. The demand is greater than the supply, so the seller has more power than the buyer.
- **Buyer's market:** Buyer's market exists when sellers provide more products than consumers want to buy. The supply is greater than the demand, so the buyer has more power than the seller.
- **Unorganized retailing:** Stores are not registered with the government. Typical unorganized retailers include owner staffed general stores, handcarts, and pavement vendors or street vendors.
- **Cash on delivery:** A common method of payment in many developing countries in which consumers pay cash to the deliverer when their ordered items are delivered to their home.

CHAPTER 4
Cultural Environment and Its Impact on the Global Fashion Business

Learning Objectives

After studying this chapter, you will be able to:

- Define culture and the cultural elements that can affect the global fashion business.
- Identify and explain Hall's cultural dimensions and their implications for the global fashion business.
- Identify and articulate Hofstede's cultural dimensions and their implications for the global fashion business.
- Identify and understand other synthesized cultural frameworks.
- Explain the implications of cultural environments on global fashion marketing.

Along with the economic environment in Chapter 3, the cultural environment is another aspect that requires a thorough understanding in order to do business in dynamic global marketplaces. Self-reference criterion, a human tendency to see others through their own lenses, is one of the major challenges global fashion marketers encounter. To overcome this, it is imperative to comprehend global consumers from their cultural perspectives. A lack of cultural sensitivity often leads to boycotts, which can be detrimental to a brand image (see Case Study 4.1). Culture is a learned behavior passed on from generation to generation; it is difficult for outsiders to grasp. This chapter begins with the definition of culture and major cultural elements that can affect global fashion marketing strategies. Subsequently, major cultural dimensions and frameworks will be discussed relating to fashion products and marketing. Having read this chapter, you should have a better understanding of how global consumers think and behave according to the different cultures they belong to and how cultural differences are prevalent in every aspect of doing global business, particularly in negotiation, product development, and communication.

Defining Culture and Cultural Elements

Many definitions of culture exist but probably the most cited one is that of Geert Hofstede, the well-known Dutch social psychologist. He defined culture as "the collective programming of the mind that distinguishes the members of one group or category of people from others" (Hofstede, 1991, p. 5). Here, a category can be a nation, an ethnic group, a gender group, an organization, or a family. Each category can have its own culture, such as family culture or company culture. The collective programming of the mind is learned and passed on from generation to generation, so culture is a learned behavior. Individuals learn culture from social institutions (family, school, religion, media, government, and so on), through socialization (how one is raised), and acculturation (adjusting to a new culture) processes. We also learn and adapt to a culture through role modeling, or imitation of our peers. Culture affects every part of our lives; how we clothe ourselves, how we consume products, how we negotiate and do business, and so on.

Culture has many elements, which can largely be grouped into two categories: physical or material culture and nonphysical or nonmaterial culture. Physical culture is at the surface level and is easily observable, while nonphysical culture is underneath, unseen to the observer. Physical culture includes the society's tangible objects, such as clothing, tools, decorative art, and so on. In contrast, nonphysical culture is intangible, such as the values, beliefs, symbols, religion, norms, and language that define a society. These attitudes, values, and beliefs have a strong influence on decision-making, relationships, conflict, and other dimensions of global business. The influence of culture is pervasive in the global fashion and retail industry and thus will be discussed throughout this book. Some cultural elements relevant to the industries are discussed below.

Some Cultural Elements Related to the Apparel and Retail Industry

Religion

Religious influence in retailing is important, especially in countries where religious norms and rituals are firmly adhered to. As Case Study 4.1 shows, the misuse of a religious icon or symbol can trigger a serious boycott (Sari et al., 2017), yet fashion companies have often failed to understand the pervasive power of religion among Muslim consumers. In Muslim countries, daily prayer time is observed during normal business hours; sales associates go to a prayer room to abide by daily prayer times and the shutter of a store in a shopping mall is pulled down during prayer time (Figure 4.1). Having a separate prayer room, one for women and the other for men, within a shopping mall is also common. Some prayer rooms have an area where people can wash their hands, feet, and face before praying. In Saudi Arabia (a Muslim country), public interaction between men and women is strictly prohibited, so separate entrances, queuing, and eating zones for men and the rest of the family exist. Shops employing both men and women are required to erect separation walls to ensure that the two sexes remain separated while working together (Jin et al., 2018). However, the degree of gender separation varies among Muslim countries and thus fashion marketers need to check the extent of this when entering Muslim countries.

Figure 4.1 A shutter is down during prayer time, Tashkent, Uzbekistan.
Source: Courtesy of B. Ellie Jin.

Color and Number Symbols

Countries associate different meanings for certain colors and numbers. In China, red is considered an auspicious color symbolizing happiness and luck, so it is frequently used in fashion design and gift-wrapping. It is a tradition to give a cash gift in a red envelope on New Year's Day in China. Wearing a green hat refers to cheating in an old saying, so H&M did not include this color in its offering in China (Juliusson, 2015). The number eight means fortune/wealth in China, because the pronunciation of "eight" is similar to that of luck. The number four in East Asian countries (Korea, Japan, and China) is not popular because the pronunciation of number four and death are similar. You will often find "F", instead of the number 4, in elevators in those countries. Similarly, the number 13 is seen as an unlucky number, so the 13th floor is often skipped in many Western countries. This means that global fashion companies need to be mindful in using those ominous numbers in brand names, logos, and communications.

The same animal may symbolize different meanings in different cultures. For example, in many Asian countries, the pig symbolizes fertility and abundance, whereas it means laziness and greed in ancient Christian symbolism. In Muslim countries, the pig is seen as being impure, unhealthy, and uncertain, so pork is considered haram (that is, it is forbidden, so is not consumed) by Islamic law, which is based on the Holy Quran. Thus, wearing shirts decorated with pigs and pig-themed decorations are considered offensive in Muslim countries (BBC News, 2019a), while the same symbols may not convey these bad meanings in Asian countries.

Color symbols associated with death and funeral symbols are different by culture. Black is the color of mourning in Western countries but it is white in most Asian countries. H&M's global collection with a white daisy print was not launched in China since white flowers are associated with death (Juliusson, 2015). Colors, numbers, and animals may convey different meanings across cultures; therefore, fashion companies need to refrain from the use of any cultural elements that may create negative meanings in particular countries; their offerings need to be tailored to accommodate cultural differences.

Gift-giving Culture

Gifts are exchanged in every culture, but gift-giving is more frequent and widespread in Asian countries. In many Western countries, gift-giving is mainly found among family members for birthdays, Christmas, or other special events. In many Asian countries, gift-giving is expanded to people in business settings to express gratitude as well as to wish for long-term relationships. Gifts are also given over many occasions: Lunar New Year, Thanksgiving, home visits, special banquets, business trip, the signing of a contract, launch of a company, and so on. This gift-giving culture in business settings can be a new market opportunity, as fashion items are often exchanged as gifts. However, a gift with a high price tag, such as luxury watches and handbags, can be a form of bribery, so it has become a target of regulation. Recently, Korean and Chinese governments specified maximum values for gifts to prevent the use of gifts as bribes (Hancocks and Kwon, 2016; Moshinky, 2015; Ranasinghe, 2014).

Along with the above cultural elements, superstitions in a culture may also influence how clothes are consumed. A person's spirit is believed to reside in their clothes, so burning clothes that were worn by the deceased is common in China and Korea. This cultural superstition may impact the country's second-hand clothing market (see Case Study 4.2). In the next section, several cultural frameworks will be discussed together with their implications for the global fashion business.

Hall's Cultural Dimensions and Implications for the Fashion Business

American anthropologist Edward Hall (1914–2009) introduced two concepts to understand culture: high- vs. low-context culture, and monochronic vs. polychronic time culture.

High- vs. Low-context Culture

How people communicate with one another varies greatly from culture to culture. Hall views communication as important in culture. In his book *Beyond culture* (1976), Hall explained the communication differences across cultures by how explicitly messages are exchanged and how important context is in communication. He put high-context culture on one end and low-context culture on the other end of a continuum. In a low-context culture, messages are explicitly communicated in words, and thus context or situation is not so important in communication. Accordingly, nonverbal communications such as gestures, body language, voice tones are not much utilized. Low-context cultures include the US, Scandinavian countries, Germany, Australia, and New Zealand. In these low-context countries, words carry most information, not context.

On the other hand, in high-context cultures, meaning is based on context or situation, not necessarily on words, and messages are implicit, so nonverbal messages are important. Most Asian countries (Japan, Korea, Indonesia, Saudi Arabia) are high-context cultures, followed by Southern European (Italy, Spain, and Greece) and Latin American countries

(Chile and Mexico) (Meyer, 2014). In these countries, learning to interpret contexts or situations correctly is a key part of socialization.

This high- vs. low-context typology applies to business settings. In high-context cultures where information resides in context, agreements are based on trust and thus legal paperwork is less emphasized and often short. Establishing social trust should come first and negotiations are slow and ritualistic. The opposite is true in low-context cultures. Agreements should be specified in a legal contract, so legal paperwork is often long, explicit, and specific. Therefore, the role of lawyers is important, and they are present in many business meetings. In low-context cultures, negotiations proceed as quickly and as efficiently as possible.

Monochronic vs. Polychronic Time Culture

In his book *The dance of life: The other dimensions of time,* Hall (1983) further categorized cultures by their members' attitudes to time. On a continuum, Hall put monochronic time (M-time) on one end and polychronic time (P-time) on the other end. Monochronic time cultures view time as linear, focus on doing one thing (mono) at a time, and are concerned with promptness. Most low-context cultures (North America, Switzerland, Germany, and Scandinavia) have M-time perception.

Conversely, polychronic time cultures have a loose and flexible time perception, where several things (poly) are handled at once and interruptions are accepted. P-time cultures focus on people and relationships over scheduled work. Polychronic time cultures value promptness differently depending on the relationship or situation. For example, instead of serving people who come first, a customer in a hurry can be served first because they view people or relationships as more important. Most high-context cultures (Asia, Arab countries, Latin America, Spain, and Italy) belong to the P-time culture.

This differing time perception is well observed during negotiations. In Asia (mostly P-time cultures), all issues are discussed at once in no apparent order and concessions are made on all issues at the end of the discussion. In contrast, M-time cultures discuss one issue at a time with the final agreement being the sum or the sequence of smaller agreements. The monochronic sequential approach and polychronic holistic approach tend not to mix well. Therefore, fashion companies need to be aware of different time perceptions at the negotiation table. Table 4.1 summarizes Hall's two cultural dimensions.

Table 4.1 Summary of Hall's cultural dimensions

HIGH-CONTEXT CULTURE (JAPAN, KOREA, INDONESIA, MIDDLE EASTERN COUNTRIES)	LOW-CONTEXT CULTURE (THE US, SCANDINAVIAN COUNTRIES, GERMANY, AUSTRALIA)
The message is mainly context-bound Unclear communication Redundant style Oral communication is important One word often has different meanings	The message is mainly context-free Clear communication Concise style Written communication is important One word often has a precise meaning

Table 4.1 Summary of Hall's cultural dimensions. *continued*

POLYCHRONIC TIME	MONOCHRONIC TIME
Circular conception of time	Linear conception of time
Do many things at once	Do one thing at a time
Committed to relationships	Committed to the regulations
Change plans often and easily	Adhere to plans religiously
Tendency to build lifetime relationships	Accustomed to short-term relationships
Start and end meetings at flexible times	Prefer prompt beginning and ending
High flow of information	Prefer to talk in sequence
Synthetic and inductive thinking	Analytical and deductive thinking

Hofstede's Cultural Dimensions and Implications for the Fashion Business

Geert Hofstede (1928–2020) classified the world's culture into four dimensions based on empirical research in 20 languages with 116,000 IBM employees working in 72 countries between 1967 and 1973. The four dimensions are: individualism vs. collectivism, strong vs. weak uncertainty avoidance, high vs. low power distance, and masculinity vs. femininity. Later, a fifth dimension, long-term vs. short-term orientation, was added. Hofstede's dimensions are not without criticism but have been widely applied to international management. Details of each dimension are discussed below.

Individualism vs. Collectivism

Most low-context cultures (the US, the UK, Australia) belong to individualistic cultures, while most high-context cultures (Japan, Indonesia, Middle Eastern countries, Italy) represent collectivistic cultures.

In individualistic cultures, identity is in the person ("I" consciousness) and people look after themselves and their immediate family only. In collectivistic cultures, identity resides in the social groups to which one belongs ("We" consciousness) (Hofstede, 1980). A person is often referred to by their relationship with another person, rather than their first name. Let's say a lady has a daughter whose name is Lauren; she is called Lauren's mom, her husband is called Lauren's dad, and her brother, Lauren's uncle. Also, her aunt is known by the city where she lives, such as Chicago aunt, rather than her aunt's first name. Like this, a person's identity is based on a relationship, rather than the self.

In collectivist cultures, people are expected to be loyal to groups (nation, community, family, workplace, the church they attend, and so on) and these groups look after them in exchange for loyalty. Therefore, a person's status often comes from a big or strong group, such as employment with a large company or being born into a rich and well-known family.

In collectivistic cultures, there is a clear distinction between in-group and out-group and giving favor to in-group members is accepted and expected. This is called "in-group favoritism." This contrasts with universalism, applying the same rules to everybody regardless of group membership, in individualistic cultures. A person belongs to a group in collectivistic cultures, while one is outside a group in individualistic cultures. In addition, the distance between in-group and out-group is wide in collectivistic cultures but close in individualistic cultures (Nisbett, 2003).

The individualistic vs. collectivistic cultures further present very opposite values, motivation drives, and behaviors. As shown in Table 4.2, in individualistic cultures, consumers value individuality and independence, while collectivistic consumers consider relationships and connectedness important. Accordingly, in purchasing apparel, a greater preference is placed on differentiation and uniqueness in individualistic cultures but on conformity (a need to blend in) in collectivistic cultures. In individualistic cultures, personalization services such as engraving one's name or initials on towels, backpacks, and so on is often desired. Collectivistic cultures' group loyalty is extended to brands; brand loyalty is greater in collectivistic cultures (Thompson et al., 2014). Also, since group interaction is more active, information-sharing among groups is greater and thus the word-of-mouth effect is more prevalent in collectivistic cultures than in individualistic cultures (Lam et al., 2009; Shavitt and Barnes, 2020; Shneor et al., 2021). Group conformity, such as buying the same brand your peers purchase, is also greater in collectivistic cultures. However, in Confucian-based collectivistic countries (China, Korea, and Japan), face-saving was found to be more significant than group conformity in leading consumers to greater purchase intentions toward foreign brand jeans (Jin and Kang, 2010, 2011) and desire for unique consumer products (Jin and Son, 2014). Defined as a person's place in their social network, face-saving is the most important measure of one's social worth in those countries (Hu and Grove, 1999).

Strong vs. Weak Uncertainty Avoidance

Uncertainty avoidance is the "extent to which people feel threatened by uncertainty and ambiguity and try to avoid them" (De Mooij and Hofstede, 2002, p. 64). Cultures with a strong uncertainty avoidance have a lack of tolerance for ambiguity and thus maintain rigid codes of belief and behavior. People in these cultures are likely to feel uncomfort-

Table 4.2 Individualistic vs. collectivistic cultures

INDIVIDUALIST (THE US, THE UK, AUSTRALIA, SCANDINAVIAN COUNTRIES)	COLLECTIVIST (SOUTH KOREA, INDONESIA, ITALY, MIDDLE EASTERN COUNTRIES)
Self is defined by internal attributes, personal traits	Self is defined by important others, family, friends
"I" consciousness	"We" consciousness
Emphasis on separateness, individuality	Emphasis on connectedness, relationships
Focus on differentiation, relatively greater need to be unique	Focus on similarity, relatively greater need to blend in (conformity)
One's behavior is reflective of personal preferences and needs	One's behavior is influenced by preferences and needs of close others

able in uncertain and ambiguous situations and deviant persons and ideas are viewed as dangerous. Countries belonging to this culture include Germany, Italy, Greece, Mexico, Japan, and Korea. People in this culture are risk-avoiders, so purity and freshness in food and solid furniture that lasts a long time are preferred (De Mooij and Hofstede, 2002).

On the other hand, societies with a weak uncertainty avoidance maintain a more relaxed attitude in which practice counts more than principles, and thus people are likely to thrive in more uncertain and ambiguous situations, and deviation is not considered threatening. The US, Denmark, and Sweden have cultures that represent weak uncertainty avoidance. People in this culture are risk-takers and thus entrepreneurial and innovative ideas are encouraged and rewarded. In consumption, processed food and products that do not last very long (uncertain) are more acceptable. H&M and IKEA, clothes and furniture not intended to be strong and last long, are from Sweden, a culture with a weak uncertainty avoidance.

High vs. Low Power Distance

Power distance is the willingness to accept status and power differences among its members. In short, it refers to the degree of how well a society tolerates inequality. In high power distance cultures (hierarchical cultures), people accept inequality and steep hierarchical order in which everybody has a place with no further justification. A good example of high power distance culture is India where the caste system was in place for a long time (BBC News, 2019b). In India, older siblings can call the younger siblings by their first name, but younger siblings are expected to call older siblings by kinship terms such as older brother or older sister in their languages (Goldstein and Tamura, 1975). The same is observed in other high power distance cultures, such as China, Korea, and Japan. On the other hand, in low power distance cultures (egalitarian cultures), people are likely to expect equal power distribution and demand justification for power inequalities. Most Nordic countries, such as Denmark, Norway, Sweden, and the US belong to a low power distance culture.

The notion of high vs. low power distance is useful in understanding everyday social interactions, which largely extend to business settings. In high power distance cultures, those in power are expected to look and act powerful and thus people should show respect to the powerful people. In these cultures, people are often respectfully addressed by title and surname such as chairman Yang and manager Cao, rather than by their first name. Serving them first and going to the front without waiting in line is accepted. In business contexts, organizational structures are multilayered and fixed, the distance between a boss and a subordinate is high, and the best boss is a strong director who leads from the front (Table 4.3). In business banquets in China (high power distance culture), those of a higher position sit closer to the seat of honor and the guests of the lowest position sit furthest from the seat of honor.

Meanwhile, in low power distance cultures, everyone waits in the same line to be served and no special attention is expected or given to the powerful people. Since powerful people try not to look powerful, business attire tends to be more casual than in high power distance cultures. First names are commonly used in offices and bosses have less power than those in high power distance cultures. Organizational structures do not reflect the hierarchy as much and are thus flatter and the distance between

Table 4.3 Implications of high vs. low power distance in business settings

LOW POWER DISTANCE = EGALITARIAN CULTURES	HIGH POWER DISTANCE = HIERARCHICAL CULTURES
The ideal distance between a boss and a subordinate is small	The ideal distance between a boss and a subordinate is wide
The best boss is a facilitator among equals	The best boss is a strong director who leads from the front
Organizational structures are flat	Organizational structures are multilayered and fixed
It is okay to disagree with the boss openly even in front of others	An effort is made to defer to the boss's opinion, especially in public
If meeting with a client or supplier, there is less focus on matching hierarchical levels	If you send your boss, they will send their boss. If your boss cancels, their boss also may not come
With clients or partners, you will be seated and spoken to in no specific order	With clients or partners, you may be seated and spoken to in order of position

Source: Modified by the author based on Meyer (2014).

a boss and a subordinate is not so wide. The person who facilitates well, rather than dictates and leads, among equals is considered to be the best boss (Myer, 2014) (Table 4.3).

Masculinity vs. Femininity

This cultural dimension concerns how a society values stereotypical masculine or feminine traits. If a society emphasizes masculine-related values such as success, achievement, assertiveness, advancement, or title, the society belongs to a masculine culture. Feminine culture, in contrast, places more value on feminine traits such as humanistic goals (caring for others, friendly working climate, cooperation, and so on). This dimension is not about how much a society is male-like or female-like; instead, it refers to how much a society values typical masculine or feminine values. One phrase that contrasts the two cultures may be "big and fast is beautiful" in masculine cultures versus "small and slow is beautiful" in feminine cultures (Hosftede, 1980). The display of wealth via status goods such as luxury watches can be observed in masculine cultures, as those symbols represent success and achievement (De Mooij and Hofstede, 2002). At the same time, a greater degree of luxury consumption can be observed in high power distance cultures since it helps them show their power (Hofstede, 1980).

Another major difference that helps understand the two contrasting cultures is sex role differentiation, which is substantially different in masculine cultures. In feminine cultures, less sex role differentiation is observed; it is not frowned upon that a wife works as a business executive while the husband stays home taking care of the children. Japan and the US are classified as masculine cultures, while most Nordic countries (such as Sweden) and some Asian countries (such as Thailand) belong to feminine cultures. Japan is considered a very masculine culture and even gendered language is used. Some Japanese words and grammatical constructions are used only by females, not males, and vice versa.

The masculine and feminine cultural values are reflected well in business. In masculine cultures, people live to work because success and achievement are valued goals of the society. As a result, offline stores that are open for 24 hours are common. On the other hand, one of the feminine culture's dominant values is quality of life, so they work to live, not live to work (Hofstede, 1980). Consequently, a 24-hour shopping concept is not popular and retail stores are open for only a few hours on Sundays. Norway (a feminine culture) does not permit stores to open on Sundays and during holidays and most stores are closed before 6pm.

Long- vs. Short-term Orientation

This cultural dimension is the extent to which a society exhibits a pragmatic and future-oriented perspective. When a society values the future and is willing to delay short-term success and instant gratification in order to prepare for the future, the society's culture is said to have a long-term orientation. Therefore, future-looking values such as persistence, perseverance, saving for rainy days, and being able to adapt are essential in this culture. In contrast, a culture with a short-term orientation focuses on the present or past and considers them more important than the future. This culture cares about immediate gratification and current needs rather than long-term fulfillment. Initially called "Confucian dynamism," this long-term vs. short-term dimension was identified by Michael Bond in 1991 based on research with Chinese employees and managers, and later Hofstede added this dimension to his framework. China and Brazil represent cultures with a long-term orientation, while the US and the UK are classified as having cultures with a short-term orientation.

Some consequences resulting from this dimension are rather unclear, but some characteristics are the acceptance that business results may take time to achieve (long-term orientation) vs. results and achievements that are set within a time frame (short-term orientation). The other distinctive characteristic concerns employees' wish for a long relationship with the company (long-term orientation) vs. employees changing employers frequently (short-term orientation).

Table 4.4 presents the summary of Hofstede's five cultural dimensions. For more details, refer to Hofstede's (2001) book, which provides scores for each dimension across all countries studied, and thus multiple countries can easily be compared across the dimensions. Also refer to Hofstede (1980) to see 40 countries positioned on maps according to Hofstede's cultural dimensions.

Table 4.4 Summary of Hofstede's five cultural dimensions

INDIVIDUALISM	COLLECTIVISM
• "I" consciousness • Identity is in the person • Universalism • Most low context cultures • e.g., the US, the UK, Australia	• "We" consciousness • Identity is based on the social groups to which one belongs • In group favoritism • Most high context cultures • e.g., Japan, Indonesia, Venezuela

WEAK UNCERTAINTY AVOIDANCE	STRONG UNCERTAINTY AVOIDANCE
• Risk-takers • Deviation is not considered threatening (tolerable) • Entrepreneurial and innovative ideas are encouraged • Processed food and products that do not last long (uncertain) are accepted • e.g., the US, Denmark and Sweden	• Risk-avoiders • Deviant persons and ideas are dangerous (intolerable) • Purity and freshness in food and solid furniture that lasts a long time are preferred • e.g., Germany, Italy, Greece, Mexico, Japan, and South Korea
LOW POWER DISTANCE	**HIGH POWER DISTANCE**
• Expect equal power distribution and demand justification for power inequalities • Powerful people try to look less powerful and look younger • Purchases avoid the illusion of wealth and power • Everyone waits in the same line to be served • e.g., most Nordic countries	• Accept inequality and hierarchical order in which everybody has a place with no further justification • Those in power are expected to look and act powerful. Status is important to show power • Display of wealth and conspicuous consumption • The powerful go to the front of the line • e.g., India, Japan, Malaysia, Mexico, and Guatemala
FEMININITY	**MASCULINITY**
• Caring for others and quality of life are dominant values • Friendly working climate, cooperation, and nurturance are important • Less sex role differentiation • Small and slow is beautiful • Interdependence is ideal • Work to live • e.g., most Nordic countries and some Asian countries, such as Thailand	• Achievement and success are dominant values • Performance, advancement, title, and assertiveness are important • Substantial sex role differentiation • Big and fast is beautiful • Independence is ideal • Live to work • e.g., Japan, the US
SHORT TERM ORIENTATION	**LONG TERM ORIENTATION**
• Focus on present or past • Care about immediate gratification and current needs rather than long term fulfilment • Results and achievements are set and expected to be reached within time frame • Employees potentially change employer frequently • e.g., the US, the UK	• Focus on future and is willing to delay short term • success and instant gratification in order to prepare for the future • Perseverance (persistence), thrift (saving), and adapting to changing circumstances • Acceptance that business results may take time to achieve • Employees want a long relationship with a company • e.g., China, Brazil

Other Cultural Frameworks

The cultural dimensions discussed above are classic tools with which countries can be analyzed and interpreted. Recently, some simpler frameworks have been suggested, and two are now discussed.

Trust Building: Task-based vs. Relationship-based Cultures

In doing business, building trust with trading partners is important, but how to build trust differs by country. Meyer (2014) suggests two contrasting methods for building trust: through tasks (task-based) vs. through relationships (relationship-based). In relationship-based cultures, trust is built through knowing each other over the long term. Business is personal, so it is like: "I've seen who you are at a deep level. I've shared personal time with you. I know others well who trust you, so I trust you." Most collectivistic countries belong to this category. In these countries, the notion "I do not trust you until I find you trustworthy" applies, so to build trust, spending time together over meals, evening drinks, and golf outings, for example, is common. Trust is built on deep emotional connectedness, so that once the relationship is built, it is not broken easily.

On the other hand, in task-based cultures, trust is built through business-related activities. So business is business: "You consistently do good work, you are reliable, I enjoy working with you, so I trust you." Most individualistic countries represent task-based cultures. In these countries, trust can be instantly built, so "I trust you until I find you untrustworthy" applies, but these relationships are not strongly bonded with emotion so they can be dropped quickly. A meeting may begin with ten minutes of ice-breaking time and then get down to business promptly. However, such ice-breaking exercises rarely occur in relationship-based societies because, most likely, these ice-breaking activities happened prior to meetings through meals and golf outings, and so on. All BRIC countries belong to relationship-based societies. Consequently, fashion companies from task-based cultures need to be mindful about building trust before getting down to business.

Information-oriented vs. Relationship-oriented Cultures

There is a noticeable overlap with some of these cultural dimensions. Studies have pointed out that collectivism, high power distance cultures, and polychronic time perception are correlated and go together. Synthesizing multiple dimensions of culture, Cateora et al. (2013) effectively categorized them into two types: information-oriented vs. relationship-oriented cultures (Table 4.5). The US represents an information-oriented culture, while Japan belongs to a relationship-oriented culture. As shown in Table 4.5, although the US and Japan are both high-income countries, their cultural orientations are quite different. In relationship-oriented cultures, building and maintaining relationships is important, and is believed to save transaction costs and is thus efficient. In information-oriented cultures, efficiency is gained through competition. Face-to-face meetings are still preferred in Japan, even though the internet and emails are widely used for business purposes. This dichotomy may be too simplistic, but it can offer a basic understanding of different cultures.

Table 4.5 Information-oriented vs. relationship-oriented cultures

INFORMATION-ORIENTED (e.g., the US)	RELATIONSHIP-ORIENTED (e.g., Japan)
Low context	High context
Linguistic directness (explicit)	Linguistic indirectness (implicit)
Monochronic time	Polychronic time
Individualism	Collectivism
Low power distance	High power distance
Efficiency through competition	Efficiency through reducing transaction costs

Source: Modified by the author based on Cateora et al. (2013).

Implications of Cultural Environment on Global Fashion Marketing

Global fashion marketers who have interacted with foreign partners may have already observed cultural differences but did not know the reasons behind them. The above cultural dimensions will be a useful point of reference from which differences in consumer behaviors, business practices, negotiation, and retail and human resource management can be understood. This section further provides a couple of cautions that global fashion markets should be aware of in applying the multiple cultural dimensions to actual business settings.

Know Your Enemies and Yourself to Win

In the fifth-century Chinese classic *The art of war* by Sun Tzu, there is one particularly telling phrase: "If you know your enemies and know yourself, you will not be imperiled in a hundred battles." In doing business globally, understanding cultures, especially at the negotiation table, is critically important to win the game. Take a negotiation between Chinese and American companies for example. As illustrated above, China represents a relationship-oriented culture, while the US belongs to an information-oriented culture. Imagine how representatives from these two countries approach issues differently at a negotiation table. The Chinese partner puts forward several issues at one time and sometimes goes back to previous issues (polychronic time culture), asks indirectly (high-context culture), and seeks approval from their boss (high power distance culture). Moreover, they haggle price terms (saving from long-term orientation culture) and try to persuade by saying: "we are now friends." Americans consider such approaches ineffective and inefficient because they believe in getting to the point directly in written documents (low-context culture) and discussing one issue at a time (monochronic time culture). Americans have the authority to make a decision (low power distance), so cannot understand the other's need to consult with their boss. As a result, Americans can see Chinese negotiators as inefficient, indirect, and even dishonest, while Chinese negotiators can view American negotiators as aggressive, impatient, and impersonal (Graham and Lam, 2003). If American partners can see Chinese partners from a Chinese cultural perspective and vice versa, misunderstandings could be minimized and negotiations could be more productive. Therefore, global fashion marketers are encouraged to be exposed to cross-cultural understanding and training before engaging in important decision-making processes.

Do Not Assume All Are the Same Within a Culture

People often roughly classify the world into two cultures: Western and Eastern. However, not all Westerners are the same. For instance, Northern and Southern Europe represent different cultures. Northern European countries (Belgium, Denmark, and so on) belong to individualistic cultures, while Southern European countries (Spain, Greece, and so on) represent collectivistic cultures. Likewise, countries in North America belong to individualistic cultures, while countries in South America are largely collectivistic cultures. While located in Asia, China and India are quite dissimilar because their cultures are rooted in different religions: Confucianism in China and Hinduism in India. Positioned halfway on the individualism–collectivism continuum, Indians behave both individualistically and collectivistically at the same time. Kumar and Sethi (2005, p. 42) pointed out that "culturally speaking, India is closer to Europe and North America than it is to Confucian Asia." Similarly, while sharing the same religious beliefs, not all Muslim countries are the same. Saudi Arabia is strict, but the Emirate of Dubai, one of the United Arab Emirates, is relatively flexible in their observance of Islamic beliefs (Squadrin, 2019). Further studies are also suggested to identify the differences between Shiite Muslims (Iran for example) and Sunni Muslims (Saudi Arabia for example) (Fam et al., 2004).

A related caution is that there are still variances among consumers in a culture. This implies that not all Americans, for example, are individualistic to the same extent. As one of the largest countries in the world, the northern and the southern states of the country are quite different; the north being more individualistic than the south. In northern states, students may address a professor by their first name, while in southern states, professors expect to be addressed as Dr. or Professor and surname, similar to collectivistic countries.

In studies comparing cities in China, consumers in Beijing (Cho et al., 2010) and in coastal cities were found to exhibit more individualistic cultural values than those in inland cities (Zhang et al., 2008). Similarly, Mumbai, the most affluent city among three cities studied for India, was found to be more individualistic (Jin and Son, 2013). As these empirical studies show, global fashion marketers need to pay attention to subtle cultural differences across cities in a country, especially in countries with large purchasing power.

Triandis (1995) explains that, culturally, tightness (homogeneity) is related to collectivism and looseness (heterogeneity) leads to individualism. Several personal factors also influence the degree of individualism or collectivism in any given culture. People become more collectivistic with age because they are likely to have established social relations (tightness). High social class and more traveling and living abroad increase independence and exposure to different viewpoints (looseness), which increases the degree of individualism. This implies that cultural differences do exist at the individual level within a country. Some scholars, therefore, suggest measuring cultural dimensions at the individual level (see, for example, Triandis and Gelfland, 1998), rather than treating a whole country as having the same culture.

Does a Country's Economic Development Change the Culture? Culture Does Change but Slowly

Culture is not something that changes quickly. For example, countries become more individualistic as economic affluence increases (Hofstede, 2001; Triandis, 1995). However, only the extent changes and the original classification stays the same. For instance, Japan is still classified as a collectivism country even though the country has become more individualistic with its economic advancement. However, the degree of individualism is greater than other collectivistic countries, let's say South Korea. Simply put, a higher percentage of Japanese people may exhibit individualistic values than Koreans do.

A country's cultural dynamics should be understood with its exposure to international trade, together with economic advancement. As a country's experience with international partners increases, ways of doing business become more aligned with global standards and traditional values are reflected less. For example, establishing "guanxi" (the Chinese form of personal connection, relationship, or social network) is found to be important in doing business with Chinese businesspeople (relationship-oriented culture), and having a banquet with a Chinese partner was a common practice to establish relationships (Pearce and Robinson, 2000). However, the relevance of guanxi has gradually decreased (Fan, 2002) and Westerners' expectations of banquets were viewed as somewhat outdated as Chinese experiences with Westerners increased (Jin et al., 2013). This implies that the aforementioned cultural frameworks should not be blindly applied to business contexts, because depending on foreign partners' global experience, their own cultural orientation may be less pronounced in business settings.

On the country-level consumption side, however, cultural influence is even more pervasive when a country becomes wealthier and income is no longer an issue when making a purchase. In other words, once a country reaches a certain economic level, consumers' purchase decisions are largely based on the culture in the country, such as high consumption of expensive clothes in masculine cultures, not national wealth (De Mooij and Hofstede, 2002).

CASE STUDY 4.1

Two Boycott Cases: Muslims against Danish Brands and Chinese against Dolce & Gabbana

A boycott is a movement by which consumers assert their power by rejecting certain products or brands to express their anger or disapproval. Consumers can demonstrate their disagreement with certain conduct or decisions of brands, and brands can be significantly influenced by such protests in terms of sales and brand image (John and Klein, 2003; Sari et al., 2017). While the causes of consumer boycotts are many, the lack of cultural understanding toward targeted foreign countries is one of the prime reasons in global marketing. Two of the widely publicized boycott cases driven by cultural issues are the Muslim boycott against Danish brands in 2005 (Al-Hyari et al., 2012) and the Chinese boycott against Dolce & Gabbana in 2018.

In 2005, a Danish daily broadsheet newspaper, *Jyllands-Posten*, published 12 cartoons of the Prophet Muhammad (Jensen, 2008) that included satirical drawings and stories about him, which infuriated Muslims. A group of Danish Muslims protested by collecting 17,000 signatures and organizing a demonstration with more than 3,000 people in Denmark. Later, as the issue spread worldwide, Islamic countries in the Middle East launched a boycott against Danish products, led and encouraged by the countries' political and religious elite. Many retailers in Middle Eastern countries removed Danish items from the shelves and even terminated their contracts with Danish companies. The newspaper insisted that the protest by Danish Muslims could be considered as censorship and a restriction on freedom of expression, while the Islamic organizations believed it had mocked and ridiculed their faith (Jensen, 2008).

More recently, in 2018, a well-known Italian luxury brand, Dolce & Gabbana (D&G), officially apologized for its racist attitude when confronted with a boycott by Chinese consumers (Wildau, 2018; Wong and Jie, 2018; Zargani and Ap, 2019). The boycott began with the release of an online advertisement in which a Chinese model attempts to eat an oversized cannoli with chopsticks and the narrator asks, "Is it still big for you?" D&G missed an important point that Chinese people could feel uncomfortable with the ad as it may convey the impression that they were uncultured strangers to Western-style foods (Zargani and Ap, 2019; Xu, 2018) (see Appendix 1). Following this advertisement, D&G's co-founder Stefano Gabbana's personal Instagram messages were disclosed to the public, in which he used the "poop" emoji to describe China, along with other offensive comments (Diet Prada, 2018). This controversy led to a huge wave of anger among Chinese celebrities, models, and consumers. That same day, furious Chinese models refused to model in D&G's Shanghai fashion show, causing D&G to cancel the show scheduled for that evening. Although D&G claimed that the account had been hacked and apologized by posting on social media, saying, "We are very sorry for any distress caused by these unauthorized posts. We have nothing but respect for China," the boycott spread nonetheless among Chinese celebrities and consumers. Eventually, D&G posted one more video a few days later with an apology, in an attempt not to lose one of the brand's biggest markets. In the video, they even used the Chinese language to say: "We apologize" (see Appendix 2).

Discussion Questions

1. Why do you think Muslims and Chinese people were angry? What went wrong? Discuss the cultural elements that provoked the anger.
2. What are the implications of these two cases for global retailers in targeting countries with different cultural backgrounds? What did you learn from these cases?
3. Explore other incidences that show a lack of cultural understanding in the global fashion business.

References

Al-Hyari, K., Alnsour, M., Al-Weshah, G. and Haffar, M. (2012). Religious beliefs and consumer behavior: From loyalty to boycotts. *Journal of Islamic Marketing*, 3(2): 155–74.

Diet Prada (2018, November 20). As @dolcegabbana prepares to mount their next runway show in Shanghai this coming evening (7:30PM) and the rest of Instagram ... www.instagram.com/p/BqbTkY_FB7X/?utm_source=ig_web_copy_link

Jensen, H.R. (2008). The Mohammed cartoons controversy and the boycott of Danish products in the Middle East. *European Business Review*, 20(3): 275–89.

John, A. and Klein, J.G. (2003). The boycott puzzle: Consumer motivations for purchase sacrifice. *Management Science*, 49(9): 1196–209.

Sari, D.K., Mizerski, D. and Liu, F. (2017). Boycotting foreign products: A study of Indonesian Muslim consumers. *Journal of Islamic Marketing*, 8(1): 16–34.

Wildau, G. (2018, November 21). Dolce & Gabbana hit by racism accusation over China ad campaign. *The Financial Times*. www.ft.com/content/710f007a-ed5f-11e8-89c8-d36339d835c0

Wong, C.H. and Jie, Y. (2018, November 22). Dolce & Gabbana tripped up in China by promo deemed racist. *Wall Street Journal*. www.wsj.com/articles/dolce-gabbana-tripped-up-in-china-by-poor-taste-1542807773

Xu, Y. (2018, December 1). Dolce & Gabbana ad (with chopsticks) provokes public outrage in China. NPR. www.npr.org/sections/goatsandsoda/2018/12/01/671891818/dolce-gabbana-ad-with-chopsticks-provokes-public-outrage-in-china

Zargani, L., Ap, T. and Edelson, S. (2019, January 3). What to watch: Will Dolce & Gabbana weather the storm? WWD. https://wwd.com/business-news/business-features/what-to-watch-will-dolce-gabbana-weather-the-storm-1202940754

CASE STUDY 4.2

Why Are Secondhand Markets Not Thriving in China?

Rental and second-hand market platforms, such as Rent the Runway, The RealReal, ThredUP, and Etsy, have become widely accepted in the West, especially among younger generations. Yet buying pre-owned clothes is not a popular idea in China despite the country's tremendous purchasing power. Speculated reasons are multiple. First, the Chinese are skeptical of the authenticity of pre-owned items, especially luxury items. According to Chinese luxury goods authentication service Yishepai, 40 percent of luxury goods are appraised as fake.

Second, Chinese consumers attach social status to new goods and view buying second-hand goods as something poor people do to save money. Third, the Chinese have superstitions about wearing other people's clothes (Holland, 2020). The Chinese believe that a person's spirit resides in the person's clothes, so they burn the clothes when the person dies, although this practice is prohibited in certain places due to pollution concerns. Last, but not least, they worry about hygiene. The Chinese believe that pre-used and pre-owned items are not clean enough. These concerns explain why there are only 9 percent of luxury second-hand purchases in China in 2018, compared to 20 percent in France and Germany and 17 percent in the US.

This hygiene concern is also found in one study conducted with US consumers (Kim and Jin, 2021). Consumers preferred to shop in B2C settings with no direct contact with the previous owner rather than in C2C setting. Such concern was more pronounced when buying a shirt (greater physical contact with previous owners) than a handbag (Kim and Jin, 2021). In addition, Korean consumers were more concerned when second-hand goods were sold in C2C settings and items were owned for a longer period of time than US consumers (Kim et al., forthcoming).

Discussion Questions

1. Among Hofstede's cultural dimensions, which cultural dimension may be related to Chinese consumers' hygiene concerns about pre-owned or pre-used apparel items?
2. Between Chinese and US consumers, which consumers may have greater hygiene concerns about pre-owned and pre-used items? Do you think resale retailers should use different communication strategies for US and Chinese consumers?

References

Holland, O. (2020, August 31). Can China look past counterfeits and superstition in its burgeoning second-hand fashion market? CNN. www.cnn.com/style/article/china-second-hand-fashion-sept/index.html

Kim, N. and Jin, B. (2021). Addressing the contamination issue in fashion sharing: Does ownership type of shared goods matter? *Journal of Fashion Marketing & Management*, 25(2): 242–56.

Kim, N., Kim, T. and Jin, B.E. (2023). Negative and positive contamination in second-hand fashion consumption: Does culture matter? *International Marketing Review*, 40(6): 1509–30.

Summary

- Culture is an important aspect that needs to be comprehended fully to do business in dynamic global marketplaces. As culture distinguishes members of one category of people from those of another through its different elements (religion, color, and number symbols, as well as gift-giving culture), apparel brands and retailers need to understand those elements when entering any country.

- Many cultural dimensions help understand cultural differences. Hall's high-context vs. low-context culture is one of the most popular analyses of cultural dimensions. Communication with each other varies significantly across cultures. For example, in low-context countries (the US, Australia), messages are explicitly communicated in words, while in high-context cultures (Japan, Saudi Arabia), nonverbal messages and implicit communications are common.

- Cultures can be also classified by differing time perceptions. Hall's monochronic vs. polychronic time culture framework explains how people view time differently. In monochronic time cultures (North America, Switzerland, Germany, and Scandinavia), things are done one by one, time is viewed as linear, and punctuality is emphasized. By contrast, polychronic time cultures (Italy, Arab countries, and so on) have a loose and flexible time perception, several things are handled at once, and interruptions are acceptable.

- Hofstede classified culture according to five dimensions: individualism vs. collectivism, strong vs. weak uncertainty avoidance, high vs. low power distance, masculinity vs. femininity, and short- and long-term orientation. Hofstede's cultural dimensions have been widely utilized in international business. Fashion retailers can apply these dimensions in understanding consumers, management styles, and marketing their products in various cultures. For example, a word-of-mouth marketing strategy is more effective in collectivist cultures than individualistic cultures.

- In addition to Hofstede's and Hall's classic cultural dimensions models, other more recent frameworks (task-based vs. relationship-based cultures and information-oriented vs. relationship-oriented cultures) can also be used in understanding consumers and fashion business management in other countries.

- Global fashion marketers are encouraged to learn cross-cultural differences before engaging in important decision-making that involves people in other cultures. It is also important not to assume that everybody within a culture is the same as there are huge variations within a culture (Muslim cultures are not the same across the globe). The culture of a country does change, but only very slowly as the country evolves economically.

Class Activities

1. Understanding cultural differences takes time and experience. Travel to other countries can provide direct experience but watching movies that show cultural differences can offer indirect experience. A good example is *My Big Fat Greek Wedding* (2002). Discuss some movies you have watched that helped you understand a particular culture.

2. You may have experienced cultural differences in your own country or while traveling to other countries. Share your experience with your peers and explain the differences using the cultural dimensions you have learned about in this chapter.

Key Terms

- **Culture:** The collective programming of the mind that distinguishes members of one category of people from those of another. Culture is a learned behavior from generation to generation through socialization and acculturation processes.
- **Physical culture:** A society's tangible objects, such as clothing, tools, decorative art, and so on.
- **Nonphysical culture:** Intangible elements of a culture, such as values, beliefs, symbols, religion, norms, and language, that define a society.
- **Low-context culture:** Messages are explicitly communicated in words; thus, context or situation does not have much importance in communicating.
- **High-context culture:** Meaning is based on context or situation, not necessarily on words, and messages are implicit, so nonverbal messages are important.
- **Monochronic time culture (M-time):** Time is viewed as linear. Monochronic time focuses on doing one thing (mono) at a time and is concerned with promptness.
- **Polychronic time culture (P-time):** This culture has loose and flexible time perception and focuses on people and relationships over scheduled work. Several things (poly) are handled at once and interruptions are accepted.
- **Hofstede's cultural dimensions:** A multidimensional cultural framework Hofstede developed between 1967 and 1973, which includes four dimensions: individualism vs. collectivism, strong vs. weak uncertainty avoidance, high vs. low power distance, masculinity vs. femininity. Later on, a fifth dimension, long- vs. short-term orientation, was added.
- **Individualistic vs. collectivistic culture:** The extent to which people in a society are integrated into groups. In individualistic cultures, people are expected to see themselves as individuals who seek to accomplish their own goals and needs. In collectivistic cultures, people put greater emphasis on the welfare of the entire group to which the individual belongs, and individual wants and needs are often expected to be set aside for the common good.
- **In-group favoritism:** Also known as in-group/out-group bias, it is a pattern of favoring members of one's in-group over out-group members.
- **Strong vs. weak uncertainty avoidance:** The extent to which people feel threatened by uncertainty and ambiguity and try to avoid them. Cultures with a strong uncertainty avoidance have a lack of tolerance for ambiguity, and thus maintain rigid codes of beliefs and behavior. Societies with a weak uncertainty avoidance maintain a more relaxed attitude in which practice counts more than principles, thus deviation is not considered threatening.
- **High vs. low power distance:** Power distance refers to how well a society tolerates inequality. In high power distance cultures (hierarchical cultures), people accept inequality and a steep hierarchical order in which everybody has a place with no further justification. In low power distance cultures (egalitarian cultures), people are likely to expect equal power distribution and demand justification for power inequalities.
- **Masculinity vs. femininity:** This concerns how a society values stereotypical masculine or feminine traits. If a society emphasizes masculine-related values such as success, achievement, assertiveness, advancement, and title, it has a masculine culture. Feminine culture, in contrast, puts more value on feminine traits such as humanistic goals (caring for others, friendly working climate, cooperation, and so on).

- **Long- vs. short-term orientation:** This cultural dimension is the extent to which a society exhibits a pragmatic and future-oriented perspective. When a society values the future and is willing to delay short-term success and instant gratification in order to prepare for the future, the culture is one of a long-term orientation. In contrast, a culture with a short-term orientation focuses on the present or past and considers them more important than the future.
- **Relationship-based culture:** Trust is built through knowing each other over the long term. Business is personal.
- **Task-based culture:** Trust is built through business-related activities. Business is business.
- **Information-oriented vs. relationship-oriented cultures:** Cateora et al.'s (2013) simplified classification of culture, synthesizing multiple dimensions of culture.
- **Face-saving:** Defined as a person's place in their social network, face-saving is the most important measure of a person's social worth in Confucian collectivistic countries (China, South Korea, and Japan).
- **Guanxi:** Chinese form of personal connection, relationship, or social network. It is formed by tacit mutual commitments, reciprocity, and trust. It can also refer to the benefits gained from social connections through extended family, school friends, workmates, and members of common clubs or organizations.

Appendix 1. Dolce & Gabbana's Advertisement Accused of Racism in China

TRT World. (2018, November 22). *Dolce & Gabbana accused of racism in China* [Video]. YouTube. www.youtube.com/watch?v=dZhqW62pSeg

Appendix 2. Dolce & Gabbana's Apology

Dolce & Gabbana (2018, November 23). *Dolce & Gabbana apologizes* [Video]. YouTube. www.youtube.com/watch?v=7Ih62lTKicg

CHAPTER 5
Legal and Regulatory Environment: Playing by the Rules

Learning Objectives

After studying this chapter, you will be able to:

- Explain the various types and extent of government regulations pertaining to the retail sector and the reasons behind the regulations.
- Discern various intellectual property issues in the global fashion industry.
- Identify the extent of intellectual property protection by country and the implications of the varying protections for global fashion companies.
- Discuss the red tape, bribery, and corruption levels within a country that would affect the global fashion business and selected laws that should be adhered to when doing global fashion business.

Suppose your company is ambitiously planning to enter a country, only to find that your brand's domain has already been utilized in that country for a long time. This is exactly what happened when Victoria's Secret attempted to enter Australia in 2005. The brand discovered that its Australian domain had already been operating for five years. To make things worse, it was a brothel site. Victoria's Secret sued the company but lost the case (Mitnick, 2012). Australia follows the "first to file" system, indicating that whoever files for copyright, rather than prior use, has the right to use the copyright. As a result, Victoria's Secret had no option but to avoid the country for a significant length of time and was only able to enter the country in 2018. As this shows, not every country operates the same system. No single, uniform international law governing foreign business exists. Global fashion companies, therefore, need to understand that the laws are different and comply with the laws of each country within which they operate. It is impossible to explore the legal system of every country. Among many regulations, this chapter will examine the major laws and regulations related to the global fashion business. The implications of government regulations on the retail sector, intellectual property, red tape, bribery, and corruption issues will be illustrated with exemplary cases.

Government Regulations in the Retail Sector

The retail industry in any country accounts for a large portion of the country's employment. In the US, it is the largest private sector employer, supporting one in four American jobs (NRF, n.d.). As such, many governments regulate the sector to protect their domestic companies and consumers. Selected countries' government regulations concerning the retail sector are illustrated.

Gradual Retail Market Liberalization

Global fashion companies have both tangible (products) and intangible (brand name, management system, and so on) assets to operate successfully in foreign countries. This could be a threat to countries where those assets are insufficient to compete with global fashion companies that entered the countries. Thus to protect domestic markets, governments in emerging markets, in particular, are enforcing some regulations on the retail sector. One typical form is not allowing foreign investments until the domestic players gain some strength to compete. Here, we briefly review three countries' regulations pertaining to the retail sector. Table 5.1 summarizes the regulations in these three countries.

South Korea liberalized its sector in four stages from 1989 to 1996. Back in 1989, the government allowed foreign companies to operate only one store with a retail space less than 700 square meters. The sector was fully liberalized in 1996 with no restriction on size and number of stores (Sternquist and Jin, 1998). China followed a similar pattern from 1992 until it fully allowed 100 percent foreign investment in 2004. Prior to 1992, foreign investment in retailing, wholesaling, and other fields of business was entirely forbidden. Since 1992, China experimented with selected major cities and five special economic zones and gradually opened its market by allowing more cities, stores, and scope. With WTO (World Trade Organization) membership in 2001, China removed any restrictions on foreign direct investment (FDI), indicating that any firms can invest in China without any limits.

India also gradually allowed investment in the retail sector starting in 1997 when only a cash-and-carry wholesale format was allowed. Until 2011, the Indian government forbade foreign retailers from selling multiple products from different brands directly to Indian consumers. During this time, Walmart had to enter the country in 2007 as a wholesaler partnering with Bharti Enterprises selling under the store name of "Best Price Modern Wholesale." Later, Walmart operated as a cash-and-carry format under a wholly owned subsidiary of Walmart Inc., starting in 2013 after the government allowed 100 percent foreign investment in 2012. However, there are still detailed regulations: government requires that a single brand retailer needs to source 50 percent of its backend infrastructure (investment toward processing, manufacturing, storage) from India, multi-brand retail stores can set up their stores only in cities with a population of more than 1 million, and no FDI is permitted in e-commerce that sells multiple brands (Koppad and Hundekar, 2014; Masharu

Table 5.1 Summary of retail market liberalization in South Korea, China, and India

COUNTRY	STAGE (YEAR)	DETAILS
South Korea[1]	1st stage (1989)	Loosen the regulation of foreign investment. Permit one store under 700 square meters
	2nd stage (1991)	Selective opening for retail industry. Permit ten stores under 1,000 square meters
	3rd stage (1993)	Large reduction of restriction limit. Permit 20 stores under 3,000 square meters
	4th stage (1996)	Full liberalization of distribution market. No restriction on store number and size
China[2]	Prior to 1991	Foreign investments were forbidden in retailing, wholesaling, and other fields of business
	1st stage (1992)	Only selected experimental cities could have one or two foreign retailers. Retail stores had to be joint ventures, with Chinese partners having at least 51% ownership
	2nd stage (1992–6)	Foreign retailers could operate chain stores in Beijing. Foreign retailers could partially enter the wholesale sector
	3rd stage (1997–2000)	Foreign retailers could enter the capitals of provinces and autonomous regions. The number and scope of foreign retailers operating in China increased
	4th stage (2001–present)	In 2004, all restrictions on foreign retailers were removed, allowing 100% foreign direct investment (FDI)
India[3]	1991	FDI up to 51% allowed under the automatic route in the selected priority sector
	1997	FDI up to 100% allowed under the automatic route in cash-and-carry (wholesale)
	2006	FDI up to 51% allowed with prior government approval in single brand retail
	2008	The government proposed introducing FDI in multi-brand retailing
	2012	100% FDI in single brand and up to 51% for multi-brand retail sector was allowed. No FDI permitted in e-commerce multi-brand retail

Notes: 1. Sternquist and Jin (1998). 2. Goodwin (n.d.). 3. Koppad and Hundekar (2014); Masharu and Nasir (2018).

and Nasir, 2018). As the Walmart case shows, global companies need to work within the limitations of host government regulations. If a host government bans FDI, global fashion companies need to find a local partner, which may not be an easy task. Often, working with the wrong local partner could be a major obstacle, as the Beaucre case in Chapter 1 demonstrates.

Other Government Regulations on Retail Operations

Host government regulations are not limited to FDI. They also include various controls on retail operations such as censorship of media-related products or services, including social media and laws related to consumer privacy.

Take some examples of several governments. The Indian government only allows foreign e-commerce firms to operate marketplace platforms on which third parties sell goods to retail consumers. This means that foreign companies cannot sell their own inventory (Jay, 2020). With this restriction, Amazon helps sellers with warehousing and shipping goods, only serving as an intermediary between sellers and buyers. Further, to prevent one seller from dominating an e-marketplace, the Indian government enforces that no individual seller can account for more than 25 percent of sales in an e-commerce marketplace (Rao, 2016). Additionally, since 2019, the government restricts companies from offering exclusive deals in just one e-commerce site. This means that exclusive deals should be offered on multiple e-commerce sites.

In China, local ownership laws demanded that the Amazon website in China (www.amazon.cn) be operated by a Chinese-owned corporation. For example, to fulfill China's legal and regulatory requirements, Amazon Web Services China (Beijing) Region and Amazon Web Services China (Ningxia) Region had to collaborate with Chinese local partners to deliver a cloud service (Amazon Web Services, n.d.). Chinese law also regulated and restricted Amazon's internet content as well as its sale of any media-related products or services (Nguyen-Chyung and Faulk, 2014). Amazon closed its e-commerce business in China in 2019 after operating there for more than a decade (Weise, 2019). Shoppers at Amazon.cn can still purchase some products from the US, the UK, Germany, and Japan through the seller's global store (Dastin et al., 2019).

Censorship of marketing materials is another area of government regulation. For instance, in Saudi Arabia, women's faces or body parts are blotted out in advertisements. Out of respect for this, IKEA removed women from some of the photos in catalogs shipped to Saudi Arabia, which led to a public uproar. The opposing opinion is that such removal of women is a violation of international human rights standards (Molin, 2012). IKEA publicly apologized.

The Saudi government further enforces the segregation of sexes in nearly all business settings. Related to retail operations is "Saudization," the Saudi nationalization scheme first introduced in 2011, which requires hiring increasingly larger proportions of Saudi nationals. In the past, Saudi Arabia relied heavily on foreign workers in retail stores, but these guidelines require businesses to meet specific quotas, resulting in higher operation costs because hiring Saudi nationals means higher costs than hiring foreign workers (Jin et al., 2018). In 2020, the retail sector achieved a Saudization rate of 49 percent, up from 10 percent in 2018 (Douglas, 2023). Another law includes that foreign investors who have contracts with the Saudi government must subcontract 40 percent of the value of any government contract, including support services, to firms majority owned by Saudi nationals (International Trade Administration, 2020).

Imposing higher taxes on imported goods is a common form of regulation to protect the domestic industry, which directly influences consumer prices. As part of its "Make in India" drive, the Indian government imposes approximately 30–35 percent of import taxes on luxury products, making luxury products much more expensive in India (Jay, 2020). Relatedly, to protect small domestic firms from an influx of foreign goods via e-commerce, the Indonesian government imposed a range of taxes from 32.5 percent to 50 percent of value for foreign-produced textiles, clothes, and bags with a value equal to or higher than $3, effective from January 2020. This is a drastic increase because there were no taxes up to $75 in previous years (Jin and Kim, 2021; *Jakarta Post*, 2019). Chapter 11 will further discuss the implications of host government taxes on imported goods on consumer prices.

With the increasing popularity of the internet for retail operations, a growing number of countries have introduced regulations related to consumer privacy. Examples include the EU's General Data Protection Regulation (2016), the California Consumer Privacy Act (2018), Brazil's Lei Geral De Proteção de Dados (General Personal Data Protection Law, 2020), and China's Personal Information Protection Law (2021) (Ng, 2022). While the degree of restriction and law enforcement levels vary by country as well as states within countries, the essence of such regulations is the restriction of companies' access to consumer data that are otherwise freely available. Companies have utilized consumer data to deliver personalized marketing messages and product offerings, but such regulations reduce their ability to leverage consumer data and incur higher compliance costs.

As the above examples illustrate, the major reason behind the regulations is to protect industry and consumers. In addition, geopolitical tensions between two countries can also lead to a ban in a certain area. One good example is the recent Indian government's ban on 59 Chinese apps, including TikTok, from operating in India, which is thought to be due to escalating tensions with China (Jay, 2020). The US's strict trade embargo on imports of products containing Cuban goods starting in 1962 is another good example.

Above are several examples of numerous regulations and stipulations affecting retail operations in host countries. In addition to government-level regulations, it should also be noted that, in many countries, states have their own independent jurisdiction affecting business contracts and operations. This means that foreign companies need to follow regulations at the state level as well as the federal level. Another point to remember is that, in many mature markets, strict regulations protect consumers, so promises made in advertising must be kept. Regulations, at both the government and state level, are not permanent and may be lifted or modified from time to time. Therefore, companies need to be attentive and prepared for changes when considering their long-term strategic goals.

Intellectual Property Issues in the Global Fashion Industry

Protection of Intellectual Property: Why It Matters

When traveling to other countries, you may have encountered counterfeit handbags and watches on streets or in stores. Fashion goods including clothes, watches, sunglasses, purses, and handbags are some of the products commonly counterfeited. This is because the symbolic meanings attached to brand names and logos are huge compared to other products. These products are also small to carry and relatively simple to manufacture without complicated technologies. Counterfeit goods can be easily found in emerging countries such as China and Vietnam, but they are also found in Florence, Italy, and Canal Street in New York.

Imagine that you are the owner of a high-end brand and you found your goods are counterfeited and sold on a street in Vietnam. Firms spend millions of dollars on marketing in establishing brand names or trademarks to convey good quality and design only for products to be counterfeited and pirated. Piracy and counterfeiting not only cause losses in sales and profits for companies but also damage the reputation of brand names, which is extremely critical in the fashion business. However, a more positive aspect of counterfeiting is that it is a form of free advertising in creating brand name awareness. This is because, in many cases, consumers in emerging markets are first exposed to high-end brands through counterfeit goods.

Definition and Types of Intellectual Property

According to the World Intellectual Property Organization, intellectual property refers to "creations of the mind, such as inventions, literary and artistic works, designs, and symbols, names and images used in commerce" (WIPO, n.d.). Intellectual property is registered in each country to enable people to earn recognition or financial benefit from their creation. Intellectual property includes multiple forms as follows:

1. *Copyright*: "A legal term used to describe the rights that creators have over their literary and artistic works" (WIPO, n.d.). It establishes ownership of a written, recorded, performed, or filmed creative work ranging from books, music, paintings, and films to computer programs, advertisements, and technical drawings.
2. *Patent*: "An exclusive right granted for an invention" (WIPO, n.d.). This gives an inventor exclusive right to make, use, and sell an invention for a specified period of time.
3. *Trademark*: "A sign capable of distinguishing the goods or services of one enterprise from those of other enterprises" (WIPO, n.d.). Trademarks date back to ancient times when artisans used to put their signature or "mark" on their products. They include a distinctive mark, motto, device, or emblem used to distinguish their product from competing ones. The brand name and its logo, color, and unique patterns and shapes are all trademarks to be protected.

Infringement of Intellectual Property

There are three types of infringement of intellectual property:

1. *Counterfeiting* is the unauthorized copying and production of a product, such as counterfeit handbags.
2. *Associative counterfeit/imitation* is a little bit different from counterfeiting in that the product name differs slightly from a well-known brand, such as the use of Adidos instead of Adidas, a different shape of the Nike Swoosh, and so on (see Figure 5.1).
3. *Piracy* is the unauthorized publication or reproduction of a copyrighted work. This infringement is often found with software, movies, and so on.

by examining their stitching patterns, shapes, and so on. Multiple methods are utilized to appraise an item's authenticity. One lesser known method includes checking the metallic composition of accessories, buckles, or zippers against the manufacturer's specifications (Chan, 2017). Vast technologies, from adding RFID (radio frequency identification) chips to employing blockchains, are increasingly used to detect fake goods. With the increase of luxury second-hand retailers like The RealReal in the US, an authentication service becomes an integral part of the business platform (Nast, 2021).

You may think counterfeited goods can only be found on streets as opposed to in stores. But what if the infringement is happening at the store level across a country? Let's take an example of an associative counterfeit of New Balance in China. A Chinese company created a brand name and logo very similar to those of New Balance. The brand name was New Barlun and it added two little dashes on the "N" symbol that noticeably resembles New Balance's signature logo, which obviously confused Chinese consumers (see Figure 5.2). New Balance sued and won the case over its logo in 2020 after a 16-year battle. The Chinese company New Barlun was ordered to pay US$1.54 million damages to New Balance (Moon, 2020). This case ended up as a win, but time lost and damages to the brand reputation for the 16 years of a lawsuit cannot be minimized. The media sees this case as the Chinese government's commitment to establishing a sophisticated intellectual property system that matches other leading countries (The Fashion Law, 2021). As this case shows, it is vital for fashion companies to register relevant trademarks both in English and in languages for a host market even if a brand has no immediate plans to enter it.

Figure 5.1 Three examples of associative counterfeit goods.

Top: SIPA Asia/ZUMA Wire/Alamy Live News © SIPA Asia/ZUMA Wire/Alamy Live News. Middle and bottom: Courtesy of Shutterstock, photo by StreetVJ.

Some counterfeit goods are so well made that consumers unknowingly purchase them and even experts cannot tell the authenticity

Figure 5.2 New Barlun logo and store in China. Source: Courtesy of Shutterstock, photo by StreetVJ.

Ownership of Intellectual Property Rights: Prior Use vs. Registration

As in the case of Victoria's Secret in Australia, countries differ in judging who has the right to intellectual property. Is it the first person who used it (prior use) or the first person who filed it (registration)? Largely, two systems exist: prior use vs. registration (first to file).

Ownership of intellectual property rights used to be established by prior use in most common law countries, such as the UK, Canada, and other countries once under English influence. This indicates that even though it is not registered, the person who used the intellectual property first has ownership. Under this system, it is important to prove that the person is the first-time user. In contrast, in many civil law countries such as Germany, Japan, France, and non-Islamic countries, ownership is established by registration (first to file), rather than by prior use. Any individuals who did not necessarily create it can register a trademark. This is a rough categorization, as some countries change the ownership right system. For example, the US used to recognize the prior use system but from 2011 it also follows the first to file system (USPTO, 2011). Because ownership right is recognized differently across countries, critical intellectual property for any fashion company, its brand name and logo, may not be adequately protected in foreign countries. Let's review two lawsuit cases related to ownership rights.

Pierre Cardin, a French brand, is active in globalizing its brand, so it is often the first foreign brand that consumers encounter in emerging markets. Pierre Cardin learned that a resident in Jakarta had registered the brand earlier in 1977, and the brand name was legally used by a local manufacturer to produce the same type of goods. The Indonesian Supreme Court rejected Pierre Cardin's lawsuit against the "Indonesian-version Pierre Cardin" and also later cassation appeals— extraordinary appeals against judicial decisions (Sulistiyono, 2016).

Another example is Harmont & Blaine, an Italian brand, which discovered that its brand had been registered in China before the company actually entered the country. China applies the principle of the first to file system. Many foreign companies generally opted to pay to buy the ownership back. Harmont & Blaine chose the path of litigation instead. During ten years of legal disputes, Harmont & Blaine closed its 12 boutiques and halted agreements with its local partners to get rid of illegal Harmont & Blaine stores in China. After the brand won the lawsuit, it relaunched the 12 boutiques and reopened five mono-brand stores (Colurcio and Monia, 2017).

These two cases show that an improper understanding of ownership rights in foreign countries can severely undermine brands' reputation and revenues. Major implications from the cases include that not all intellectual property protected in one country is protected in the same manner in other countries.

Therefore, global fashion companies need to file far in advance even if there is no immediate entry intention.

Red Tape, Bribery, and Corruption: Implications for Global Fashion Companies

Global fashion companies need to be aware of a country's corruption, red tape, and bureaucracy levels. IKEA suspended further investment in Russia in 2009 because of red tape and bureaucracy in the country (Müller, 2016) and is finally closing all its stores in Russia and halting all exports and imports to and from Russia (Chopping, 2022).

The Corruption Perceptions Index (CPI) has been published annually by Transparency International since 1995 (Transparency International, 2021) (see Appendix 1 for the CPI). This index shows a country's corruption level by ranking 180 countries from 100 (very clean) to 0 (highly corrupt). Higher ranked countries in the CPI tend to have higher degrees of press freedom, greater integrity among public officials, and independent judicial systems. The lower ranked countries in the CPI (highly corrupt) indicate that public institutions like the police and judiciary groups are untrustworthy and ill functioning, and bribing government officials to expedite permissions can be commonplace. Bribery is the corrupt business practice of offering some type of consideration, typically a cash payment, with the aim of influencing a public official in the discharge of their official duties. Note that highly corrupt countries do have anti-corruption laws, but in practice they are often ignored.

Fashion companies can refer to various indexes to gauge a country's regulatory environment, including the World Bank's Ease of Doing Business Index, which collects data on ten factors. The indexes are usually at the country level but, in practice, the corruption and inefficiency level may vary even within a country. Therefore, these indexes should not be blindly used. When fashion companies enter a country where bribery is a common business practice and widely accepted, what should they do? Should they practice as locals do? The Foreign Corrupt Practices Act (FCPA) is an important act related to this.

US Foreign Corrupt Practices Act (FCPA) of 1977

The Foreign Corrupt Practices Act (FCPA) bans US companies and companies listed on US stock exchanges from paying bribes to foreign government officials. Violations result in stiff penalties for company officials found guilty of paying a bribe. This indicates that leaving the boundaries of a home country does not exempt a business from home country laws. What is illegal for an American business at home can also be illegal under US law in foreign jurisdictions for the firm, its subsidiaries, and licensees of US technology. Critics say that the FCPA puts US companies at a disadvantage when bribery is legal and even tax-deductible in some European countries. US brand Ralph Lauren wrapped up business in Argentina in 2012, and the FCPA might have provided a partial reason for the exit (more details are given in Case Study 5.1). Laws similar to the FCPA exist in other countries.

China's Anti-corruption Campaign and Its Impact on the Luxury Market

Gift-giving to business partners is common in China (see Chapter 4). However, when the gift is too expensive, such as luxury watches, it can be considered bribery and there is no clear distinction between a gift and a bribe. To eliminate potential bribery incidents, the Chinese government began an anti-corruption campaign in 2012; more than a million government officials have been disciplined as a result of the campaign. The purge weakened the sales of high-end items both in China and abroad, hurting profits for luxury goods makers. The anti-corruption crackdown in China is having a significant impact on luxury retail sales from fashion garments to shoes and watches (Moshinky, 2015; Ranasinghe, 2014).

South Korea's Improper Solicitation and Graft Act

South Korea's Improper Solicitation and Graft Act came into effect in 2016. It is popularly known as the "Kim Young-Ran Act" after the former Supreme Court justice who drafted it. The law makes it illegal for public officials, including journalists, private school teachers, and their spouses, to accept gifts of more than 30,000 won (about US$25) for treating someone to dinner, 50,000 won (about US$42) on a gift, and 100,000 won (about US$84) on a cash gift at weddings or funerals. When an employee breaks the law in performance of duties for the company, not only the employee but also the company will be punished with the same fine. This has brought about a quiet change within South Korean culture, since gift-giving and taking acquaintances out for food, drink, and other forms of entertainment had been widely accepted (Choe, 2016).

CASE STUDY 5.1

Ralph Lauren's Bribery in Argentina

Founded in 1967, Ralph Lauren Corporation is an American fashion company offering a wide range of products from apparel, footwear, accessories, and fragrances to home furnishings. The brand's global reach is extensive, with merchandise available both offline and online.

Argentina was one of the countries the company expanded into, but doing business there led to a high-profile case of a violation of US law. In 2013, Ralph Lauren Corporation was fined $1.6 million for bribing customs officials in Argentina from 2005 to 2009, which violated the 1977 Foreign Corrupt Practices Act, the US federal law that prohibits US companies and companies listed on US stock exchanges from paying bribes to foreign government officials. The bribery was discovered by an internal audit. Because the company promptly reported the violations and cooperated thoroughly with the federal investigation, Ralph Lauren was not prosecuted, although it had to pay the fine.

Facilitated by a customs clearance agency working for Ralph Lauren, the bribes were paid by the Argentine subsidiary in the form of cash and gifts such as perfume, dresses, and handbags, some of which cost as much as $14,000 (Bray, 2013). The goals were to secure the timely importation of Ralph Lauren

Corporation's products to Argentina without the required paperwork and inspection by local customs officials. The bribe payments and gifts totaled $593,000 (SEC, 2013) and were disguised as "loading and delivery expenses" and "stamp tax/label tax" on invoices (SEC, 2013).

In Argentina, where import controls are notoriously strict and corruption is routine, the temptation to bribe local officials to expedite the import of merchandise is very high (Raszewski, 2017; Salomón, 2019; Webber, 2012). This phenomenon is common in many emerging countries where import and export procedures lack transparency, which makes the movement of goods into and out of these countries time-consuming and costly (Mahajan et al., 2015). Such burdensome customs procedures led Ralph Lauren to exit Argentina in 2012, after 13 years of operation (Lattman, 2013).

Discussion Questions
1. What are the challenges of doing business in overseas markets, particularly in emerging countries?
2. What preventive measures can companies take to ensure that they comply with the Foreign Corrupt Practices Act in overseas markets susceptible to corruption?

References
Bray, C. (2013, April 22). Perfume, dresses and cash in Ralph Lauren bribe scheme: Ralph Lauren Corp. resolves U.S. government inquiries into customs payments. *The Wall Street Journal*. www.wsj.com/articles/SB10001424127887324235304578438704093187288

Lattman, P. (2013, April 22). Ralph Lauren Corp. agrees to pay fine in bribery case. *The New York Times*. https://dealbook.nytimes.com/2013/04/22/ralph-lauren-pays-1-6-million-to-resolve-bribery-case

Mahajan, R., Bansal, A. and Bhattacharya, S. (2015, July). Fighting corruption in the maritime industry: What you need to do to navigate in transparent waters. Deloitte. www2.deloitte.com/content/dam/Deloitte/in/Documents/finance/in-fa-fighting-corruption-in-maritime-industry-noexp.pdf

Raszewski, E. (2017, March 30). Argentina's Macri faces rising complaints over import policies. Reuters. www.reuters.com/article/us-argentina-economy-trade/argentinas-macri-faces-rising-complaints-over-import-policies-idUSKBN1712Y4

Salomón, J. (2019, November 27). Argentina customs "Mafia" earns millions from China imports. Insight Crime. www.insightcrime.org/news/brief/argentina-customs-mafia-dodges-millions-china-imports/

SEC (Securities and Exchange Commission) (2013). SEC announces non-prosecution agreement with Ralph Lauren Corporation involving FCPA misconduct. www.sec.gov/news/press-release/2013-2013-65htm

Webber, J. (2012, January 11). Argentina tightens import controls. *Financial Times*. www.ft.com/content/92bb2e38-3c77-11e1-8d38-00144feabdc0

Summary

- Every country regulates its retail sectors by imposing laws on foreign companies to protect their domestic companies and consumers. To do business aligning with the host country's laws, global fashion companies must understand the laws of each country within which they operate.

- To help domestic retailers gain strength to compete with foreign companies, the governments of emerging countries have gradually allowed foreign investment in multiple stages. For example, South Korea, China, and India liberalized their retail sector in various stages.

- The host country's regulations are not limited to foreign direct investment. They also impose various controls on retail operations and media-related products or services, including social media. For example, the Indian government only allows foreign e-commerce firms to operate marketplace platforms on which third parties sell goods to retail consumers. The Saudi government further enforces segregation of the sexes in business settings.

- Fashion companies need to follow regulations at the state level as well as the federal level, as states have their own independent jurisdiction affecting business contracts and operations. Regulations, both government level and state level, are not permanent and are likely to be lifted or modified from time to time. Therefore, companies need to be attentive and prepared for the changes when considering their long-term strategic goals.

- One of the threats in doing business in emerging economies is related to intellectual property. Intellectual property includes copyright, patents, and trademarks. Infringement of intellectual property includes counterfeiting, associative counterfeit (imitation), and piracy.

- Countries differ in judging who has the right to an intellectual property: the first person who used it (prior use) or the first person who filed (registration). As there are many examples of lawsuits related to intellectual property, it is vital for fashion companies to register relevant trademarks both in English and in the languages of the host market even if a brand has no immediate plans to enter it.

- Starting a business or opening a store in foreign countries involves various permissions from local and federal governments. Such a process involves paperwork and processing time, which are very different by country. Global fashion companies need to be aware of a country's corruption, red tape, and bureaucracy levels. For this, various indexes (Corruption Perceptions Index, Ease of Doing Business Index) are helpful to gauge a country's regulatory environment.

Class Activities

1. Why do governments of emerging countries enforce some regulations on retail sectors? Discuss the reasons and implications for global fashion companies.

2. Discuss the Foreign Corrupt Practices Act in the US and investigate if there are any similar laws in your country.

Key Terms

- **Government regulations in the retail sector:** Many governments regulate the retail sector to protect their domestic companies and consumers.
- **Retail liberalization:** Loosening restrictions on foreign retailers' business operations, in particular in emerging countries by its governments.
- **Intellectual property:** "Creations of the mind, such as inventions, literary and artistic works, designs, and symbols, names and images used in commerce."
- **Copyright:** A legal term used to describe the rights that creators have over their literary and artistic works.
- **Patent:** "An exclusive right granted for an invention." It gives an inventor exclusive right to make, use, and sell an invention for a specified period.
- **Trademark:** "A sign capable of distinguishing the goods or services of one enterprise from those of other enterprises."
- **Counterfeit:** Unauthorized copying and production of a product such as counterfeit handbags.
- **Associative counterfeit/imitation:** The product name differs slightly from a well-known brand, such as the use of Adidos instead of Adidas and a different shape of the Nike Swoosh.
- **Piracy:** Unauthorized publication or reproduction of copyrighted work.
- **Ownership of intellectual property rights:** Two systems exist: prior use vs. registration (first to file). Under the prior use system, the person who used the intellectual property has the ownership even though it is not registered. Prior use is prevalent in most common law countries, such as the UK, Canada, and other countries once under English influence. Conversely, in the first to file system, ownership is established by registration, rather than by prior use. Many civil law countries, such as Germany, Japan, France, and non-Islamic countries, follow the system.
- **Bribery:** Providing money, gifts, or other benefits to host countries' officials to obtain favor.
- **Foreign Corrupt Practice Act (FCPA):** This act bans US companies and companies listed on US stock exchanges from paying bribes to foreign government officials.

Appendix 1. Corruption Perceptions Index

Transparency International (2023). *Corruption perceptions index 2023.* www.transparency.org/en/cpi/2023

Assessing Global Market Opportunities

PART 3

Before entering global markets, companies need to assess market opportunities to make proper decisions. Part 3 starts with internationalization theories, followed by details of two important decisions companies need to make: market selection, and market entry mode. In Chapter 6, major internationalization theories will be explained and related to selected global fashion companies. Chapter 7 illustrates how to find a market to enter. The steps (preliminary analysis and screening, market research, and feasibility test) and factors to consider in evaluating potential markets are discussed. Once a market is chosen, the next important decision is how to enter the market. In Chapter 8, entry mode choices (export/wholesaling, licensing, franchising, joint venture, concession, flagship stores, acquisition, and wholly owned subsidiary) will be explained and the strengths and weaknesses of each mode outlined.

CHAPTER 6
Internationalization Theories

Learning Objectives

After studying this chapter, you will be able to:

- Articulate major internationalization theories: the internationalization process model, Dunning's theory of the eclectic firm, the transaction cost analysis framework, and the network model.
- Compare the assumptions, strengths, and weaknesses of each internationalization theory.
- Discuss the psychic distance paradox and its implications for fashion companies.
- Explain selected fashion brands' internationalization using the theories.

When do firms decide to enter other countries? Which country does a fashion company choose to enter? How do fashion retailers enter international markets? What factors are related to firms' internationalization behaviors? While firms do not always follow certain patterns, there are a number of patterns of firm internationalization. Firm internationalization theories explain when, where, and how retailers enter international markets. This chapter explains the major firm internationalization theories: the internationalization process model, Dunning's theory of the eclectic firm, the transaction cost analysis framework, and the network model. These theories have been developed mainly from the manufacturing perspective, thus their application to the retail sector may not be perfect. Yet the theories serve as a sound foundation in explaining retail firm internationalization. Each theory will be introduced with examples of selected fashion brands' internationalization behaviors.

Internationalization Process Model

The internationalization process model is probably one of the most referred to theories in explaining firm internationalization. It was developed by scholars at the University of Uppsala in Sweden in the 1970s, thus it is often referred to as the "Uppsala model" or "U model." Johanson and Vahlne (1977) assumed that two major obstacles for a firm to enter foreign markets are the lack of foreign market knowledge and market uncertainty, which increase risks for the firm. To minimize the risk, firms first grow solidly in their home market and then choose to expand into psychically close countries (neighboring countries). As the company's experience and familiarity with foreign markets grow, it subsequently ventures into psychically distant countries. Psychic distance is defined as "a firm's degree of uncertainty about a foreign market resulting from cultural differences and other business difficulties that present barriers to learning about the market and operating there" (O'Grady and Lane, 1996, p. 330). Consequently, the farther the psychic distance, the greater the risk. As a result, companies start by entering psychically close countries that exhibit similar economic, cultural, and political systems (Evans et al., 2000), often neighboring countries. However, entering psychically close countries does not necessarily result in great performance. This is known as the "psychic distance paradox" (see Box 6.1).

Another major strategy to minimize the risk includes investing fewer resources and choosing the entry mode with the lowest risk, such as exporting reactively for the orders received. Once firms gain foreign market knowledge through export experience (experiential knowledge), they gradually increase their resource commitments according to an established chain: no regular export activities (sporadic export), exports via overseas agent, overseas sales subsidiaries, and overseas production manufacturing (Johanson and Wiedersheim-Paul, 1975; Olejnik and Swoboda, 2012). As this model proposes stages, it is also called the "stage model." Within a foreign country, firms gradually increase their resources following these stages, while expanding to psychically distant countries as their knowledge and commitment increase (Figure 6.1). In summary, this model views firm internationalization as a gradual, incremental, and sequential process beginning with psychically close countries and transitioning to

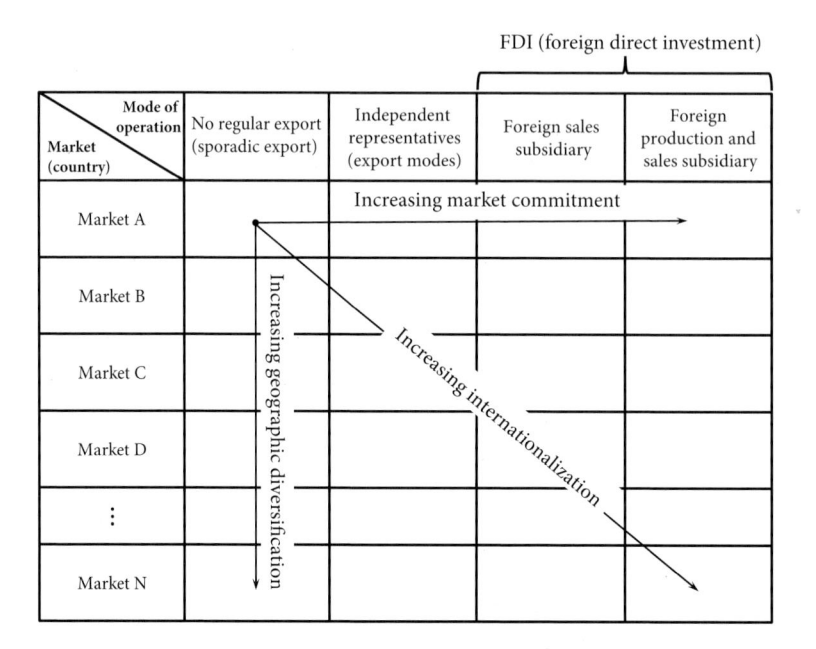

Figure 6.1 Internationalization process model: an incremental approach.

more distant nations as their knowledge and resource commitment levels increase.

This model is simple and useful to explain the internationalization of small and medium-sized organizations in volatile markets. When firms lack the knowledge of host markets, they often choose to enter countries by partnering with local companies and hiring local managers who know the market well. However, the model fails to explain a cooperative mode of entry such as a joint venture. It is also too deterministic and sequential when not every firm follows the same paths. Also, not every firm systematically enters by measuring psychic distance. One research paper analyzing the internationalization patterns of fast fashion retailers such as Zara and H&M found that, at the beginning of internationalization, the retailers choose geographically and economically close countries mirroring the Uppsala model, but no incremental patterns were observed afterwards. They rapidly expanded to countries that were culturally close to each other rather than close to the home market (Childs and Jin, 2013). Also, in practice, firms withdraw their investment if it fails to generate enough returns, but the model does not explain firms' reversible actions like going back to the previous path. Some scholars also point out that this model ignores the fact that psychic distance decreases as the world becomes more homogeneous (Andersen, 1997; Johanson and Mattsson, 1988, Johanson and Vahlne, 1997; Madsen and Servais, 1997).

Another major criticism is the model's inability to explain "born globals," also called "international new ventures." Born globals are firms that internationalize rapidly and simultaneously, at or near their establishment, into the world's leading markets, such as the US, Europe, and Japan, regardless of psychic distance (Jin et al., 2018; Oviatt and McDougall, 1994). An increasing number of fashion firms successfully enter global markets near or upon launching their brands. Gymshark, the UK fitness apparel brand, is a good example of a born global in the fashion industry (see Case Study 13.1). Established in 2012, Gymshark started its global expansion in 2018 (Turner, 2018) and now serves customers in over 230 countries across 14 online stores (Gymshark, n.d.). South Korea's cosmetic brand Dr. Jart+'s expansion into the US is another good example of born global. From the very beginning, Dr. Jart+ was created to aim for global markets. It entered the US in 2011 to build its global brand reputation in consumers' minds. This is opposite to the Uppsala model that assumes a gradual expansion into psychically close countries. The US is not a psychically close country to South Korea. The internationalization of the U model is contrasted with that of born global in Figure 6.2.

Born global scholars initially focused on small, technology-intensive firms that can enter multiple markets simultaneously with their intangible assets (software) (Rialp et al., 2005). Later, more born globals are observed in consumer goods sectors thanks to the internet. Today, many new and small startups are born globals, selling to a global audience via a centralized e-commerce website. Gymshark and many other luxury e-commerce brands (such as Farfetch) are, by definition, born global. In fact, the definition of born globals is rather vague in academic papers. In Knight and Cavusgil's (2004) criteria, internationalization within three years of firm inception (time) and a foreign sales ratio exceeding 25 percent (scale) are widely used, but no universally

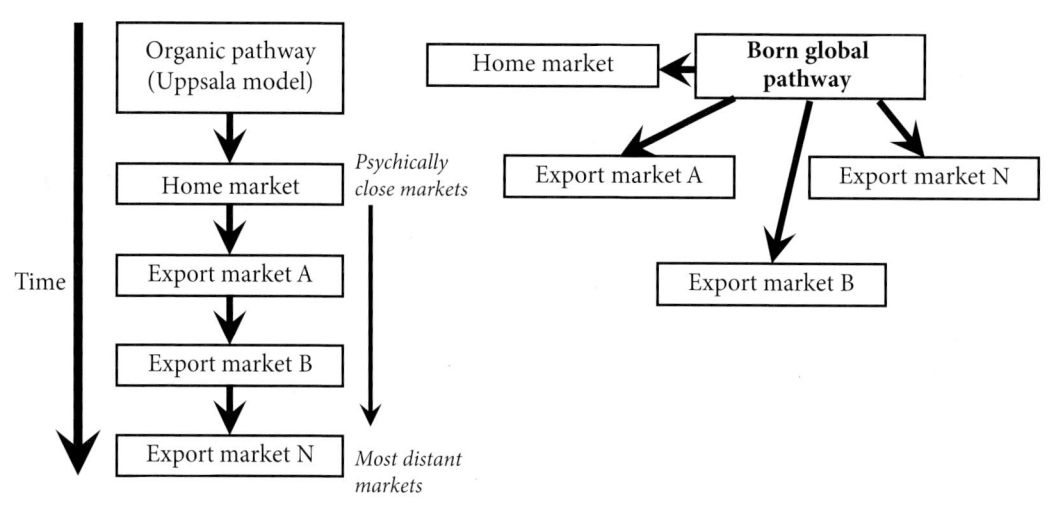

Figure 6.2 U model vs. born global's expansion pattern.

agreed definition is used in classifying firms as born globals.

The internationalization patterns of the U model and born globals can be understood with the waterfall or the sprinkler strategy (Stremersch and Tellis, 2004). The waterfall strategy involves entering one market first and then another, taking time to understand a market, whereas the sprinkler strategy involves simultaneous entry into many different markets or minimizing the time lag between market entries (Nijssen et al., 2019). The U model is similar to the waterfall strategy in that it requires relatively low investment because of gradual international market entry. In contrast, born globals use the sprinkler strategy, exposing new products to a maximum number of markets as rapidly as possible. Thus firms can fully exploit economies of scale and experience in R&D and manufacturing. US fast fashion brand Forever 21's internationalization is a good example of the sprinkler strategy. After careful internationalization at the beginning, it rapidly entered 47 countries in only six years (2001–7), which might have resulted in its withdrawal from many markets (Maheshwari, 2019). It exited the Australian market after three years of operation (Brook, 2017). Firms need to consider the tradeoff between the two strategies and evaluate the pros and cons of each approach. The waterfall strategy (U model) focuses on risk minimization by taking a sequential process, while the sprinkler strategy (born globals) pays more attention to sales maximization by entering multiple countries at the same time. Without the proper amount of managerial and financial resources and risk assessment, the sprinkler strategy is hard to pursue, as the example of Forever 21 shows. Consequently, a choice between the two approaches depends on firms' resources, short-term and long-term goals, and risk assessment.

Ownership-Location-Internalization (OLI) Model

Built on the various international production approaches, the OLI model attempts to

BOX 6.1
Psychic Distance Paradox

It is assumed that firms entering psychically close markets will likely perform better because they face fewer cultural and psychological barriers. Yet this notion turned out to not always be true. Retailers perform better in distant markets compared to close to home markets: a phenomenon known as the "psychic distance paradox." "Starting the internationalization process by entering a country psychically close to home may result in poor performance and, possibly, failure" (O'Grady and Lane, 1996, p. 310). One good example of the psychic distance paradox is Target's failure in Canada (see Case Study 6.1). More recent examples of US retailers exiting the Canadian market include Nordstrom, which announced the closure of its 13 Canadian stores (6 Nordstrom stores and 7 Nordstrom Rack stores) in late June 2023 (Martin, 2023; Repko, 2023), and Bed Bath & Beyond, which closed its 54 stores and 11 BuyBuy Baby stores in April 2023 (Howland, 2023; Punchard, 2023), resulting in 1,400 job losses. Many US brands assumed that expanding to Canada would be easy and deemed it a viable strategy to apply what had been proven successful in the American market to the Canadian market. Such views can be a barrier to a successful entry and performance, as they can lead to complacency and cause brands to be unprepared to respond to unforeseen differences.

References

Howland, D. (2023, February 13). Bed Bath & Beyond Canada is going out of business. *Retail Dive*. www.retaildive.com/news/bed-bath-beyond-canada-going-out-of-business/642619/

Martin, K. (2023, March 3). Nordstrom leaving Canada, cutting 2,500 jobs. FOXBusiness. www.foxbusiness.com/markets/nordstrom-leaving-canada-cutting-2500-jobs

O'Grady, S. and Lane, H.W. (1996) The psychic distance paradox. *Journal of International Business Studies*, 27(2): 309–33.

Punchard, H. (2023, February 14). Bed Bath & Beyond Canada's store closures are one of the largest recent retail failures. BNN Bloomberg. www.bnnbloomberg.ca/bed-bath-beyond-canada-s-store-closures-are-one-of-the-largest-recent-retail-failures-analyst-1.1883729

Repko, M. (2023, March 2). Nordstrom earnings top expectations as retailer starts winding down Canada operations. CNBC. www.cnbc.com/2023/03/02/nordstrom-jwn-earnings-q4-2022.html

explain when firms invest in foreign countries for production. According to this framework, a firm's international engagement and mode of entry depend on three advantages firms have: ownership (O), location (L), and internalization (I) advantages (Dunning, 1988). In other words, a firm needs all three advantages to successfully engage in foreign direct investment

(FDI). If one or more of these advantages are absent, a company should employ a different market entry mode. Taking the initials of the three explanatory variables, it is called the OLI model. Another name is "Dunning's eclectic paradigm," after British economist and scholar John Dunning who proposed the theory in 1979. The word "eclectic" represents the idea that several economic theories are embedded in the theory for a full explanation of the firm internationalization behaviors. Let's delve into the three variables:

1. *Ownership advantages (O)*: When a firm has certain advantages over rivals in foreign countries, it is more likely to engage in internationalization. The advantages can be asset-based or transaction-based. Asset-based ownership advantages can be tangible (factories, machinery, and so on) or intangible (brand reputation, trademark, patent, or copyright). Transaction-based ownership advantages are highly tacit and cannot easily be copied, such as a service, a sophisticated logistics system, merchandising information systems, and so on. Assets that are rare, valuable, hard to imitate, and organizationally embedded offer firms competitive advantages in host countries.

2. *Locational advantages (L)*: Locational advantages are related to how suitable the host country is with respect to the firm's strategies. From the retail perspective, Pellegrini (1991) identified locational advantages as cultural proximity, geographical proximity, competitor's moves, market size, and cost of land and labor. The more similar the cultures, the greater the chance that retail expansion will be successful (*cultural proximity*). If the host country is closer to the home market, it offers locational advantages as it reduces the costs related to transportation (*geographical proximity*). When few competitors enter the host country, the country is attractive to enter as first-mover advantages will be substantial (*competitor's move*). Additionally, if a host market size is big and the cost of land and labor is low, it gives locational advantages.

3. *Internalization advantages (I)*: When a company has ownership advantages, they do not want to share them with external partners, so they keep them internal. In other words, the greater a company's ownership assets, the more important it is to protect these assets by guarding company secrets. Consequently, if a firm has internal advantages to keep, it is likely to invest in establishing its own factories and produce internally. When a firm's secrets can be shared, other entry modes such as licensing or franchising will be chosen.

In summary, through the three explanatory factors, the OLI model provides explanations for why, where, and how. O explains *why* a company enters foreign markets, L explains *where* to enter, and I explains *how* it enters (entry mode). The OLI model is effective in explaining FDI with rich explanatory variables, but it is criticized as being too holistic and static, giving little guidance as to the dynamics of the internationalization process (Andersen, 1997; Dunning, 2001).

Transaction Cost Analysis (TCA) Framework

Any economic activities entail transaction costs. When firms expand to international markets, transaction costs include ex ante costs and ex post costs. Ex ante costs occur before entry into a country, including search costs and contracting costs. Ex post costs arise after entry into the country, such as monitoring costs and enforcement costs. Monitoring costs are incurred to detect foreign partners' opportunistic behaviors (Rindfleisch and Heide, 1997). The transaction cost analysis (TCA) framework was developed drawing on Williamson's (1985) transaction cost economics (TCE). TCE assumes that transaction costs are inevitable because of humans' bounded rationality and opportunism. That is, transaction costs occur because a decision maker's rationality is bounded due to their limited cognitive capabilities, insufficient information and time. TCE regards opportunism as human nature and defines it as "self-interest seeking with guile" (Williamson, 1981, 1985). Opportunism in international business includes misleading, distorting important business information, doing less work than agreed, and moral hazards.

TCA argues that a firm chooses the international entry mode that minimizes transaction costs after assessing its transaction costs. That is, if transaction costs outweigh benefits, firms internalize their investment and management control and integrate vertically (operate their production facilities in foreign countries) to reduce transaction costs. If transaction costs are evaluated to be low, firms can choose contractual modes such as licensing and franchising that require foreign partners. As with many other theories and models, TCA is not without weaknesses. While TCA effectively explains a firm's vertical integration decisions, its weakness lies in its static orientation, failing to consider the dynamic nature of international business. Furthermore, the framework presents an inherent difficulty of measuring transaction costs and does not consider non-transaction costs and benefits.

Network Model

Firms are connected in network relationships. The basic assumption of the network model is that an individual firm is dependent on other firms' resources, and companies can gain access to these external resources through their network positions. Describing network relationships as market assets, Johanson and Mattsson (1988, p. 296) posit that "the firm establishes and develops positions in relation to its counterparts in foreign networks." As such, the network model defines the firm internationalization process as the establishment, maintenance, and development of relations with network participants in foreign markets (Johanson and Mattsson, 1988). The literature largely classifies networks into two types: social or personal networks (informal networks), and business networks (formal networks). Social or personal networks include friends, relatives, diaspora, and so on, while business networks can be developed with suppliers, partner firms, internationally experienced managers, business consultants, and so on. Network relationships help firms, especially small companies, overcome their resource deficiencies by identifying and exploiting market opportunities, facilitating learning, and supporting international performance. Networks of business relationships provide market opportunities and knowledge, influencing initial market entry and mode of entry (Coviello and Munro, 1997). Being a part of a network, therefore, reduces the risks of foreignness in an international market.

The network model, however, does not have specific explanatory factors like the other internationalization models. The network model views internationalization as an emergent and unplanned process rather than a planned and rational development, as suggested by other models. Indeed, in the case of the market entry into Kuwait of Victoria's Secret, the selection of market and international partners was discovered serendipitously through a simple social network, in which an intern turned out to be the nephew of a major retail company owner in Kuwait (Jannarone, 2011). One aspect of the network model is the source of learning. The network approach regards the exchange of information within business networks as the source of learning about foreign markets, compared to the U model that views experience as the source of learning. The network approach is also useful in explaining international cooperation, which the U model is silent on, and can provide answers to questions such as why some companies accelerate the internationalization process and enter a number of markets at once and why others choose markets that are more distant. It is because the network can help enter far distant markets, as the Victoria's Secret case shows.

Each theory has a set of assumptions, strengths, and weaknesses. Any single internationalization theory may not adequately explain a fashion brand's internationalization in its entirety (Picot-Coupey et al., 2014). Collectively, the theories can offer a more complete picture of fashion firm internationalization (Lu et al., 2011).

CASE STUDY 6.1

Why Target's First Internationalization Failed

Founded in 1946, Minneapolis-based Target is a general merchandise retailer with 1,938 stores in all 50 US states and the District of Columbia. Target stores are so ubiquitous that about 75 percent of the US population lives within 10 miles of a Target store. With more than 450,000 employees, Target not only carries third-party brands but also launched 45 in-house brands for product categories ranging from apparel and backpacks to home décor and furniture. In 2021, Target grew comparable sales by 12.7 percent and reaped $106 billion in revenue. For Target, apparel is an important product category. Nineteen out of 45 in-house brands are apparel-related, and a significant portion of Target's sales come from the apparel category. In 2021, apparel and accessories accounted for 17 percent of Target's total revenue (Target, 2021). Given that Target has a long history with a strong foothold in the US, you may be wondering why the company has not expanded internationally. The answer is that it did make an attempt but failed badly.

In 2013, Target made their first internationalization attempt in Canada after acquiring the Canadian discount store chain Zellers in 2011. It opened 124 stores across all 10 provinces by renovating the Zellers stores. To support the 124 stores, Target built three distribution centers. The success of Target crucially depended on its ability to remodel the stores in time, build supply chain capabilities and technology systems, and hire and train qualified staff, in addition to the ability to offer the expected product assortment (Target, 2012). The company managed to do the first but failed at the rest. In January 2015, Target exited the Canadian market with a pretax loss of $5.1 billion (Target, 2014).

Most critically, the entry was hasty and too ambitious, with 124 stores opening within ten months (Dahlhoff, 2015). As a result, there was no time to test the new supply chain management system and the point of sale system, or adequately train the staff, all of which led to a serious inventory problem and poor customer experience. The rush to open stores meant that staff had to enter data for roughly 75,000 different products into the supply management system under pressure to meet the tight deadline (Castalo, n.d.). The results were many inaccurate product information entries, which hampered the movement of products from vendors to warehouses and to the store shelves. In addition, the new point of sale system kept malfunctioning. The self-checkouts gave incorrect change, items would not scan, and the system returned incorrect prices (Castalo, n.d.). What Canadian customers experienced were empty shelves and bad customer service. However, without time to address the problems before opening another wave of stores, the inventory problem that resulted in empty shelves persisted (Austen, 2015).

What is more, the product assortment and pricing were off. Many Canadians found the prices too high (Austen, 2014, 2015). The relatively high prices were not the results of an arbitrary decision but a number of factors such as the differences in Canadian packaging laws, protectionist tariffs, and exclusive wholesale arrangements that did not allow the company to use the American distribution network (Austen, 2014). Nonetheless, they were a major source of discontent for Canadian customers (scan the QR code to see why).

You may find Target's utter failure in Canada rather puzzling, given its geographic proximity, linguistic similarity, and cultural ties. Target is familiar to the many Canadians who had visited the stores in the US (Austen, 2015). However, Target was overoptimistic, evinced by its commitment to 189 store locations, and opening 124 stores, which was the company's largest, single-year store expansion in its history.

Target's failure in Canada is a classic example of psychic distance paradox, which is that running a business in psychically close countries is not necessarily easy to do because assumptions of similarity can lead executives to overlook critical differences.

Discussion Questions

1. What led to Target's exit from Canada?
2. What is the psychic distance paradox?
3. What should companies do to avoid the psychic distance paradox?

References

Austen, I. (2014, February 24). Target push into Canada stumbles. *The New York Times*. www.nytimes.com/2014/02/25/business/international/target-struggles-to-compete-in-canada.html

Austen, I. (2015, April 21). Target's hasty exit from Canada leaves anger behind. *The New York Times*. www.nytimes.com/2015/04/22/realestate/commercial/targets-hasty-exit-from-canada-leaves-anger-behind.html

Castalo, J. (n.d.). The last days of Target: The untold tale of Target Canada's difficult birth, tough life and brutal death. Canadian

Business. www.canadianbusiness.com/the-last-days-of-target-canada/

Dahlhoff, D. (2015, January 20). Why Target's Canadian expansion failed. *Harvard Business Review*. https://hbr.org/2015/01/why-targets-canadian-expansion-failed

Target (2012). *Target 2012 annual report*. https://investors.target.com/static-files/cd005867-9956-49b9-a69a-421e3f966030

Target (2014). *Target 2014 annual report*. https://investors.target.com/static-files/25786cd8-19a2-4895-938d-519c02157000

Target (2021). *Target 2021 annual report* https://corporate.target.com/_media/TargetCorp/annualreports/2021/pdfs/2021-Target-Annual-Report.pdf

USA TODAY (2015, January 15). See why Target Canada failed [Video]. YouTube. www.youtube.com/watch?v=0_O5bcq1dBw

Summary

- Firm internationalization theories explain when, where, and how retailers enter international markets. Major internationalization theories include: the internationalization process model, the ownership-location-internalization (OLI) model, the transaction cost analysis (TCA) framework, and the network model.

- Any single internationalization theory may not adequately explain a fashion brand's internationalization in its entirety. Each theory has a set of assumptions, strengths, and weaknesses; collectively, the theories can offer a more complete picture of firm internationalization.

- The internationalization process model, also known as the "Uppsala model" or "U model," posits that firms typically employ two strategies to minimize the risk of entering foreign markets: firms first expand into neighboring countries with similar or familiar cultures and business environments and then to more psychically distant countries as they gain more experience and resources, and firms choose an entry mode with the lowest risk such as export and gradually select entry modes that require more resource commitment.

- While the internationalization process model is simple and useful for explaining the early internationalization of small and medium-sized organizations in volatile markets, it has several limitations. It fails to explain cooperative modes of entry such as joint ventures, firms' reversible actions like withdrawing from a market, and born globals that internationalize rapidly and simultaneously at or near their establishment. It is also too deterministic and sequential when not every firm follows the same paths and ignores the fact that psychic distance decreases as the world becomes more homogeneous. In addition, not every firm systematically enters measuring psychic distance.

- The internationalization patterns of the U model and born globals can be understood with the waterfall or the sprinkler strategy. The U model is similar to the waterfall strategy, which involves entering one market first and then another, taking time to understand a market. Born global firms use the sprinkler strategy, which involves simultaneous entry into many different markets or minimizing the time lag between market entries.

- The ownership-location-internalization (OLI) model, also known as "Dunning's eclectic paradigm," explains when firms invest in foreign countries for production. According to this framework, a firm's international engagement and mode of entry depend on three advantages firms have: advantages relating to ownership (O), location (L), and internalization (I).

- While the OLI model is effective in explaining FDI with rich explanatory variables, it is criticized for being too holistic and static, giving little guidance in regard to the dynamics of the internationalization process.

- The transaction cost analysis (TCA) framework suggests that a firm chooses the international entry mode that minimizes transaction costs. For example, if transaction costs outweigh benefits, firms internalize their investment and management control and integrate vertically to reduce transaction costs. If transaction costs are evaluated to be low, firms can choose contractual modes such as licensing and franchising that require foreign partners.

- While the TCA framework effectively explains a firm's vertical integration decisions, it fails to explain the dynamic nature of international business. Furthermore, the framework presents an inherent difficulty of measuring transaction costs and does not consider non-transaction costs and benefits.

- The network model posits that an individual firm is dependent on other firms' resources and companies can gain access to these external resources through their network positions. According to the network model, social and business network relationships can help firms overcome their resource deficiencies by identifying and exploiting market opportunities, facilitating learning, and supporting international performance.

- While the network model is useful for explaining international cooperation, it does not have specific explanatory factors like other internationalization models, because the network model views internationalization as an emergent and unplanned process, as opposed to a planned and rational development.

Class Activities

1. Choose a brand in your country that has entered international markets and analyze its internationalization patterns. Discuss whether it followed the U model or born global.

2. Conduct your own research on other cases of the psychic distance paradox (cases where companies did not do well and ended up exiting neighboring countries). What were the failure factors? Compare the reasons with those of Target in Case Study 6.1.

3. E-commerce and m-commerce are increasingly becoming important shopping channels. How does this change influence internationalization theories? In other words, does the change affect where and how to enter other countries?

Key Terms

- **Internationalization process model:** Also known as the "Uppsala model" or "U model," it posits two major obstacles in internationalization: lack of foreign market knowledge, and market uncertainty.
- **Psychic distance:** A firm's degree of uncertainty about foreign markets, resulting from cultural differences and other business difficulties, which present barriers to learning about and operating in foreign markets.
- **Psychic distance paradox:** Argues that running a business in psychically close countries is not necessarily easy to do because the assumption of similarity can lead executives to overlook critical differences, which can lead to failure.
- **Born globals:** Firms that internationalize rapidly and simultaneously at or near their establishment.
- **Waterfall vs. sprinkler strategy:** The waterfall strategy involves entering one market first and then another, taking time to understand a market, whereas the sprinkler strategy involves the simultaneous entry into all markets or minimizing the time lag between market entries.
- **OLI model:** Argues that a firm's international engagement and mode of entry depend on three advantages: ownership (O), location (L), and internalization (I). The OLI model posits that firms need all three advantages to successfully engage in FDI. Otherwise, a company employs a different market entry mode.
- **Ownership advantages:** Can be asset-based or transaction-based. Asset-based ownership advantages can be tangible or intangible assets. Transaction-based ownership advantages are highly tacit and cannot be easily copied, such as a sophisticated logistics system. Assets that are rare, valuable, hard to imitate, and organizationally embedded offer firms a competitive advantage in host countries.
- **Locational advantages:** Relate to cultural proximity, geographical proximity, competitor's move, market size, and the cost of land and labor. High cultural and geographical proximity, slow competitor's move, big market size, and low cost of land and labor will offer advantages in host countries.
- **Internalization advantages:** The greater a company's ownership assets, the more important it is to protect these assets by guarding company secrets. If a firm has internal advantages to keep, it is likely to invest in establishing its own factories and produce internally. If a firm's secrets can be shared, other entry models, such as licensing or franchising, are chosen.
- **Transaction cost analysis (TCA) framework:** Assumes that transaction costs are inevitable because of humans' bounded rationality and opportunism. The TCA framework argues that a firm chooses its international entry mode that minimizes transaction costs after assessing its transaction costs.
- **Transaction costs:** Include ex ante costs and ex post costs. Ex ante costs occur before entry into a country including search costs and contracting costs, while ex post costs arise after entry into the country such as monitoring costs and enforcement costs.
- **Opportunism:** Foundational assumption about human nature that posits that individuals are selfish and will take advantage of others when possible. Examples of opportunism in business include misleading, distorting important business information, doing less work than agreed, and moral hazards.
- **Network model:** Defines a firm's internationalization process as the establishment, maintenance, and development of relations with network participants in foreign markets. The model posits that leveraging firms' social and/or business networks can reduce the risks of foreignness in an international market.
- **Social or personal networks:** Friends, relatives, diaspora, and so on.
- **Business networks:** Suppliers, partner firms, internationally experienced managers, business consultants, and so on.

CHAPTER 7
Where to Enter: New Market Selection Decision

Learning Objectives

After studying this chapter, you will be able to:

- Describe two approaches for selecting international markets: systematic vs. non-systematic approach.
- Discuss fashion industry-specific factors in evaluating potential markets.
- Evaluate host market and firm factors in assessing potential markets and how those factors affect international market selection.

When firms decide to enter international markets, the first important decision they need to make is to select which countries to enter. It can be multiple countries at one time or one by one, as Chapter 6 addressed. Entry mode decision, which is the topic of Chapter 8, typically occurs after a country is selected. All subsequent marketing programs are developed after market selection. Selecting the right market(s) to enter, therefore, is critical for fashion firms' success in global business. The nature and geographical location of the selected markets will condition firms' ability to coordinate the ensuing international operations. Consequently, poor market selection is one major reason for failures in international business (Martín and Papadopoulos, 2007). While many internationalization theories explain how firms choose new markets, as we learned in Chapter 6, in practice, international market selection is more complex, and a significant number of factors should be considered.

Foreign markets are highly diverse, and the attractiveness and the risks associated with doing business vary tremendously. Fashion firms also differ vastly in size, international experience, product category, home country image, brand assets, and so on. In essence, entry market selection is about finding a highly attractive country with low market risk; thus, firms can enjoy a competitive advantage, given their resources, assets, and strategic goals. This chapter outlines the approaches for international market selection decisions and the factors that need to be considered for the decision.

International Market Selection Approaches: Systematic vs. Non-systematic

The choice of which country or countries to enter is a critical decision and needs to be made with considerable care and deliberation. Multiple approaches to international market selection are discussed in the literature, such as strategically vs. opportunistically, and proactively vs. reactively (Johanson and Vahlne, 1977; Martín and Papadopoulos, 2007). Among many approaches, common international market selection approaches can be grouped into two types: systematic approach (normative model) and non-systematic approach (descriptive model) (Andersen and Buvik, 2002). Each approach is now described.

Systematic Approach

In the systematic approach, international market selection is a discrete decision based on a thorough evaluation of the different markets with reference to certain well-defined criteria, such as market attractiveness in terms of the economic, social, political, and retail environments, given the company's resources and objectives (Gomes et al., 2018). Similar to a rational decision-making process, this approach sees international market selection as structured and formalized, prescribing how decisions should be made, rather than how decisions are made.

The literature is consistent in describing the potential foreign market evaluation process. Briefly, this process involves three stages: preliminary screening, identification and in-depth screening, and final selection (Sakarya et al., 2007):

1. *Preliminary screening*: In this initial stage, based on macro-level indicators (economic, sociocultural, geographic features), companies identify potential markets as candidates for subsequent in-depth analysis and eliminate countries that do not meet the firm's objectives (Kumar et al., 1994). Macro-level indicators include GDP per capita, population size and growth, economic growth rate, average hourly wages, infrastructure, and so on.

2. *Identification and in-depth screening*: Country-level macro data cannot properly help gauge market attractiveness in a specific sector. This in-depth screening stage involves industry-specific assessment for the shortlisted countries, including industry attractiveness and forecasts of costs and revenues. The assessment is based on industry-specific market size, market growth rate, consumer product acceptance, and the level of competition and entry barriers, as opposed to macro-level analysis. Additional sector-specific indicators should also be assessed. Typically used indicators in fashion retailing include retail space per 1,000 people and the number of shopping malls per 1,000 people. Each year, Kearney, a global market consulting firm, evaluates global retail markets based on numerous factors and develops a Global Retail Development Index (see Box 7.1). When assessing industry attractiveness, the target market size is more important than the entire market size (Gaston-Breton and Martín, 2011). In addition, competition level should be assessed, which can be roughly evaluated by the number of competing brands in the market. As an example, when a denim jeans company targeting 20- to 30-year-olds is considering two international

Table 7.1 Two markets compared

COUNTRY	TARGET POPULATION: CONSUMERS IN 20–30s	ENTIRE POPULATION	NUMBER OF DENIM BRANDS AVAILABLE IN THE MARKET*
Vietnam	31,874,500	96,462,100	20
Indonesia	84,377,500	270,625,600	5

Note: * The numbers are hypothetical.

markets to enter (Table 7.1), which market is more attractive? Indonesia might suit better than Vietnam with its larger target population size and smaller number of competing brands.

3. *Final selection*: This last stage determines a country that best matches the company's objectives, existing portfolio, and available resources. A firm's goal can be profit generation or building brand image. In the example above, while Indonesia may fit better, a lack of paved roads and the approximately 17,508 islands (of which 6,000 are inhabited) that comprise Indonesia result in high distribution costs, which may be challenging. If a firm's goal is building brand image in the country and it has adequate resources to invest, it can invest in distribution systems in the country. Otherwise, Indonesia may not fit for a short-term profit because return on investment may be slow.

Firms also should consider their existing portfolio. For a firm that already operates in multiple countries, it should also take into account its current portfolio, such as to what extent a new country adds value to the existing portfolio. If the addition does not create much value to the existing portfolio, its decision can be revisited. If no Southeast Asian market has yet been entered, adding Indonesia, as in the above example, can serve as a springboard to Southeast Asian market entry. Or, although the Indonesian market may not be attractive in generating immediate profits, the firm can invest in diversifying its market presence for the long-term goal of global brand-building.

Available resources also affect a firm's final selection of countries. Larger firms with abundant resources can enter multiple countries at the same time, while resource-deficient small firms may choose a neighboring country to reduce risks. Yet small companies can aggressively enter geographically distant countries if they are backed up by large companies. Danish cashmere brand Ganni expanded beyond Nordic markets with the support of L. Catterton, an LVMH-linked private equity firm. L. Catterton acquired 51 percent of Ganni's stake (Fernandez, 2017).

In this final selection stage, more detailed insights beyond macro and industry-specific factors, such as consumers' acceptance of global brands, should be analyzed, thus employing a local market research company will be highly beneficial (Kumar et al., 1994).

Non-systematic Approach

Unlike the systematic approach, a non-systematic approach is not based on certain evaluation criteria. In a non-systematic approach, international market selection is based on subjective and contingency factors, psychic distance, and attraction to specific opportunities in the host market. For instance, firms can choose to enter psychically close countries, assuming that the risk is small and market environments are similar, without conducting a detailed evaluation, as opposed to the systematic approach. This approach mainly describes how a decision is made.

In many cases, firms choose a country to enter by reacting to specific opportunities via multiple sources. First, opportunities can come via personal and business networks (Hutchinson et al., 2009). Personal networks, characterized by a high level of trust and commitment, include close friends or family of owners/founders, diaspora, and so on. For example, a diaspora network is a good source of information. Many Singaporean firms enter Malaysia through relatives living in Malaysia. A business network is formed through partner firms, internationally experienced managers, business consultants (see Box 7.2), government institutions (embassies, chambers of commerce in host countries), and by attending trade fairs, exhibitions, and conferences (Jin et al., 2018). Both types of networks help firms initiate the internationalization process. Especially for small and medium-sized enterprises, personal networks provide more new and existing market information than formal databases (Jin et al., 2018).

Second, firms can choose a new market to enter by responding to an inquiry from a foreign company that is searching for new suppliers of a particular product, or unsolicited requests of potential franchisees (Doherty, 2009; Jin et al., 2015). A number of empirical studies have revealed that the "choice" of international markets is frequently based on unsolicited orders. In this case, market selection and entry mode decisions are taken jointly. Third, the opportunity can happen by chance. For example, a local chamber of commerce can encourage a firm to test a particular market. Another good example of reacting to chance is the entry of Victoria's Secret into Kuwait, which happened serendipitously because an intern was a nephew of a large retail firm in Kuwait (Jannarone, 2011). Fourth, a specific market can be chosen thanks to a referral by business acquaintances. Thus the non-systematic approach is opportunistic in nature, which can be successful in some cases but risky as no formal testing or market research are involved. Table 7.2 compares the systematic and non-systematic approaches.

Table 7.2 Comparison of systematic and non-systematic approaches

SYSTEMATIC APPROACH	NON-SYSTEMATIC APPROACH
Normative model	Descriptive model
How decision should be made	How decision is made
Structured, formalized process based on certain well-defined criteria	Rule of thumb procedure based on subjective and contingency factors
Typically large companies use this approach	Many small companies rely on this approach

BOX 7.1
Global Retail Development Index (GRDI)

Each year, the GRDI is developed by consulting firm Kearney based on four factors, each contributing 25 percent: country and business risk, market attractiveness, market saturation, and time pressure. Below shows how each factor is calculated:

1. Country and business risk = country risk (80%) + business risk (20%)
2. Market attractiveness = retail sales per capita (40%) + population (20%) + urban population (10%) + number of large cities (10%) + business efficiency (20%)
3. Market saturation = share of modern retailing (30%) + number of international retailers (30%) + modern retail sales area per urban inhabitant (20%) + market share of leading retailers (20%)
4. Time pressure = measured by the compound annual growth rate (CAGR) of modern retail sales weighted by the general economic development of the country

Kearney's 2021 GRDI shows China as the first country to enter, followed by India, Malaysia, Indonesia, Bangladesh, Senegal, Morocco, Egypt, Ghana, Vietnam, and the Dominican Republic (Portell et al., 2021). This index is for retail markets in general, not necessarily fashion retail, yet it is a good tool to gauge country attractiveness as it is developed based on objective criteria. For detailed GRDI rankings and how the ranking was calculated, see the report by scanning the QR code below.

Portell, G., Mukherjee, D., Warschun, M., Pathak, S., Inoue, M. et al. (2021). *The 2021 Global Retail Development Index*. Kearney. www.kearney.com/global-retail-development-index/2021

BOX 7.2
Business Consultant as an Important Network for International Market Selection and Entry

A successful Chinese garment manufacturer learned through its production experience that having its own brand can create much more value than by just producing under buyers' brand names. To create its brand name with the specific goal of entering Western markets, the firm hired a business consultant who has a good network in Western markets. With his help, a "born global" Chinese jeans company was built in 2012. The firm could expand into the US the same year it was founded, and expansion into other countries, including Canada, the UK, Germany, and Japan, occurred a year later. The brand plans to enter China after success in these Western markets. "The brand is owned by a large Chinese garment manufacturer. The brand was actually created by an American designer for the US market. [We also sell in] Canada, Japan and now in UK and Germany. It will be soon [be sold in China] because now it is on a global platform. We've invented it so that it can go international very quickly" (Jin et al., 2018, p.433). As this example shows, new international markets can be chosen by business networks brought by a business consultant. While not systematic, business networks ease entry into foreign markets by reducing perceived risks.

Reference

Jin, B., Ramkumar, B. and Chou, W.H. (2018) Identifying sources and roles of networks in international expansion among small businesses in a less-technology-intensive industry. *International Journal of Entrepreneurship and Small Business*, 34(4): 421–44.

Host Country Factors That Affect Fashion Firms' Market Entry Decision

In addition to the factors mentioned above, a fashion company needs to assess the conditions of a potential country. Especially when considering entering a country with a different level of economic development status (say, the US entering Vietnam), compared to entering a country with the same level of economic development status (say, the US entering the UK), fashion firms need to thoroughly understand the conditions of the target host country. The challenges resulting from the differing levels of economic development are huge, in addition to the other challenges inherent in the global fashion business. Therefore, host country factors more relevant to developing countries, such as consumer demands for apparel branded goods and consumer acceptance of global brands, are reviewed.

Consumer Demand for Branded Apparel Goods

Most clothes consumed in economically advanced countries are branded goods, so branding and marketing are major activities of fashion companies. However, the opposite is true in developing countries. The brand concept is not there yet, so branding and marketing activities are new to them. As non-branded clothing is readily accessible in developing countries, consumer demand for branded apparel, despite being more expensive than unbranded items, arises with the emergence of a substantial numbers of middle-income consumers. According to one study on evolution patterns in the Asian apparel industry, consumer demand for branded apparel goods appears roughly from the golden age, when apparel production for the global supply chain is actively growing. In the case of South Korea, international brands were introduced when the country reached the golden age in the early 1980s before South Korea's national apparel brands emerged (Jin et al., 2013). A similar pattern is currently happening in Vietnam. Vietnam is the world's second largest apparel exporter (WTO, 2021), and more than 200 foreign brands have their official stores in Vietnam (Le, 2019).

This means that global fashion companies need to assess the right timing to enter developing countries. For the successful introduction of global fashion brands, a significant demand for branded apparel among middle-income consumers is essential. It is not desirable to enter too early when consumer demand for branded apparel goods is low. Neither is late entry desirable, because there will already be too much competition. China is now the world's biggest apparel market, so competition is at an all-time high. Many global brands' failures can be largely explained by fierce competition in the market: in 2018 alone, two UK brands, New Look and Topshop, as well as Amazon exited China (Cebeci, 2020). This contrasts with Zara and H&M's increasing revenues in Vietnam (Le, 2019).

Consumer Acceptance of Global Brands

Global apparel brands may not always find a warm reception in developing countries. This reluctance is not because of high prices or competition but often rooted in consumer resistance towards global brands in general, or those originating from a specific country. Accordingly, global fashion companies need to consider consumer acceptance of global brands in the host market. Three concepts have been examined to explain consumer receptiveness or resistance to global brands: ethnocentrism, xenocentrism, and cosmopolitanism.

Ethnocentrism refers to the "obligation to protect national industries from foreign competitors" (He and Wang, 2015). Consumers with high ethnocentrism, therefore, reject foreign brands in general as they believe that consuming foreign products and brands is harmful to the economies of their countries. On the other hand, xenocentrism and cosmopolitanism result in a favorable reaction toward global brands. *Xenocentrism* is "the belief that what is foreign is best, that our own lifestyle, products or ideas are inferior to those of others" (Eshleman et al., 1993, p. 109). This helps consumers welcome foreign brands from countries that are believed to be superior. *Cosmopolitanism* is defined as "a personal tendency to orient oneself beyond the boundaries of the community one belongs to" (Han and Won, 2017). Hannerz (1990, p. 239) also opined that "a more genuine cosmopolitanism is first of all an orientation, a willingness to engage with the other." This explains consumers' open-mindedness to foreign brands and appreciation of the diversity of products (Riefler and Diamantopoulos, 2009). Therefore, consumers with high cosmopolitanism have a greater intention to purchase global fashion brands (Riefler et al., 2011; Srivastava et al., 2021; Strizhakova et al., 2011).

Firm Factors That Affect Market Entry Decision

The above two market selection approaches generally suggest how a firm selects a country to enter. However, firms have different goals, resources, and experiences that affect their decisions concerning which markets to enter. The influence of firm factors, such as firm size, brand image, home country image, and internationalization experience, on fashion firms' market choices and their market selection approaches are outlined.

Firm Size

The systematic approach to selection requires resources to assess the various criteria, and so is often used by large companies that have more resources than by resource-deficient small companies. Thus small companies and firms that are at the beginning of their internationalization process are more likely to enter neighboring countries, where psychic distance is small, or other types of rule of thumb procedures exist, than larger firms with international experience (Johanson and Vahlne, 1990; Papadopoulos and Denis, 1988).

Brand Image and Home Country Image

In the fashion business, brand image and the origin of the brand (home country) serve as a cue for consumers to gauge product quality and help their purchase decision. As a result, fashion firms with a strong brand image such as Nike need less time and effort convincing consumers to try their products and thus can aggressively enter culturally distant countries (Wong and Merrilees, 2007). Likewise, brands from a country with a strong fashion image (such as France and Italy) have advantages over brands from a country with a weaker fashion image (such as Singapore). French and Italian fashion brands, therefore, have more freedom to choose which new markets to enter, as they will be well regarded in international markets thanks to the brand power granted by their country image. In contrast, brands from a country with a weaker fashion image will need to be strategic in choosing which foreign markets to enter.

Recent anecdotal examples show that a brand from a country with a weaker fashion image often enters economically advanced nations, such as the US, in order to build brand reputation in the early stage. For example, Brazilian fashion brand Farm Rio, established in 1997, chose the US as its first international market to enter in 2019 after successful partnerships with Adidas, Shopbop, and Anthropologie (Fisher, 2019). Havaianas, another Brazilian brand, entered Spain, Portugal, and Italy after entering a couple of countries in South America (see Case Study 7.1). South Korean cosmetic brand Dr. Jart+ strategically entered the US in 2010 via Sephora and the UK in 2012 via Boots to establish its global brand recognition after its initial entry into several neighboring countries (Jin et al., 2015, 2018). These examples show that fashion brands with less global reputation or brands from a country with a weaker fashion image can strategically choose a country where they can build global reputation, regardless of psychic distance.

International Experience

As the U model specifies (see Chapter 6), many fashion firms enter psychically close countries at the beginning and then become strategic and choose markets more aggressively. In their early stages, Zara and H&M both entered geographically and culturally close countries (Childs and Jin, 2014; Lopez and Fan, 2009). For Zara, Portugal was the first country to enter after focusing on its domestic market in Spain for the initial 15 years. Afterwards, Zara made a careful expansion into geographically or culturally distant countries (Lopez and Fan, 2009). Japanese brand Uniqlo shows a similar pattern. The brand initially entered psychically close countries (China, South Korea, and Hong Kong) and then moved to enter far distant countries strategically (the US, France, Russia, and India) (Woo and Jin, 2014).

Deciding which market to enter is critical because an exit from the market results in a huge financial loss to fashion companies. Yet no concrete approaches are used and firms may use a mixture of market research (systematic approach) and networks or relationships (non-systematic approach). Moreover, while on the surface level, countries may be similar in macroeconomic factors such as the level of economic development, a deeper analysis of a country may reveal huge regional, cultural, and retail infrastructure variances (Douglas and Craig, 2011). Accordingly, companies may also need to analyze at a city or regional level after the country-level analysis. This is especially true in huge countries, such as China, India, Russia, and Brazil.

CASE STUDY 7.1

Havaianas's Flip Flops: From a Commodity to a Premium Product

Headquartered in São Paulo, Havaianas ("Hawaiians" in Portuguese) is a Brazilian sandal company founded in 1962. The inspiration for the brand's signature rubber flip flops came from Japanese zōri, flat, thonged sandals made from rice straw (Angelopoulou, 2020). Priced at around $2, the flip flops quickly became a staple for Brazilians, alongside rice and beans (Chitrakorn, 2015).

Today, with over 250 million pairs sold every year in over 100 countries, Havaianas is a global leader in the sandals category. Havaianas's biggest market is Italy, followed by the UK, France, Spain, and Portugal. What's more, Havaianas is now considered a premium brand, carried by major luxury retailers, including Selfridges and Harrods in the UK, Saks Fifth Avenue and Neiman Marcus in the US, and online luxury retailers, such as Net-a-Porter (Chitrakorn, 2015). Similar to global luxury brands like Gucci, Havaianas has been battling against counterfeits, which attests to the brand's coveted standing in the market (Limos, 2019). How did the brand manage to reposition itself as a global premium brand?

By the late 1980s, Havaianas was selling 100 million pairs a year, accounting for 90 percent of the domestic flip flop market (Chitrakorn, 2015). However, in the mid-1990s, changing consumer wants and needs amid an economic boom led to Havaianas's downturn. At the time, Havaianas produced only one model, the tradicional, which had a white sole and a blue strap. As they became wealthier, Brazilian consumers increasingly sought aspirational brands, and Havaianas's flip flops were seen as a cheap commodity. Over the decade, sales decreased by 35 percent.

To reposition its flip flops as an aspirational fashion product, Havaianas launched new models with more colors and printed designs. These new models had higher price tags. Havaianas also launched a nationwide advertising campaign featuring some of the most popular Brazilian celebrities (Baker, 2017; Jani, n.d.). Havaianas solidified its premium status through premium marketing in international markets.

Havaianas's globalization efforts began around 1999. Prior to 1999, Havaianas exported to a few neighboring countries like Bolivia and Paraguay. Since 1999, the brand has internationalized to countries farther away from the domestic market, such as Australia, Spain, Portugal, Italy, France, the UK, the US, the Dominican Republic, and Japan (Havaianas, n.d; The Fashion Law, 2017). While some of the overseas markets were culturally similar to Brazil (Portugal), many of them were economically more advanced. Although Havaianas originated from a country with a less developed economy, the brand successfully established a premium image in the more economically advanced markets. For example, when Havaianas entered the US in 2007, distribution was restricted to luxury channels, such as Saks Fifth Avenue. The brand opened its first retail store in Huntington Beach, California, one of the cities with the highest cost of living in the country. In addition to celebrity marketing, Havaianas has continually collaborated with numerous luxury fashion brands, such as Missoni (2011), Valentino (2014), Manolo Blahnik (2017), and Saint Laurent (2019), all of which contributed to international recognition (Khalpada, 2012).

Discussion Questions

1. How did Havaianas reposition itself as a premium brand?
2. Why do you think Havaianas chose economically advanced countries to enter, such as Australia, Spain, Portugal, Italy, France, the UK, and the US, when it repositioned its brand?

References

Angelopoulou, S.L. (2020, June 10). Havaianas collaborates with mastermind JAPAN on square base tradi zori flip flop. *Designboom*. www.designboom.com/design/havaianas-collaborates-mastermind-japan-flip-flop-06-10-2020/

Baker, V. (2017, July 16). Havaianas: How a Brazilian flip-flop took over the world. *BBC*. www.bbc.com/news/world-latin-america-40610739

Chitrakorn, K. (2015, July 30). Will Havaianas' product extensions work? *Business of Fashion*. www.businessoffashion.com/articles/intelligence/will-havaianas-product-extensions-work

Havaianas. (n.d). Havaianas history. www.havaianasaustralia.com.au/About-us/Havaianas-History

Jani, J. (n.d.). The story of Havaianas: How flip flops became a thing. *Highsnobiety*. www.highsnobiety.com/p/havaianas-ultimate-flip-flop-brand

Khalpada, N., Lakhanpal, R., Moreira, L., Singhand, J. and Sontakke, Y. (2012, September 2). The world at its feet. *Business Today*. www.businesstoday.in/magazine/lbs-case-study/havaianas-case-study/story/187012.html

Limos, M.A. (2019, December 16). Bye, fake flip flops: P10 million worth of fake footwear confiscated. *Esquire*. www.esquiremag.ph/politics/news/bye-fake-flip-flops-p10-million-worth-of-fake-footwear-confiscated-a00293-20191216

The Fashion Law (2017, December 6). Havaianas: How a simple sandal took over the globe. www.thefashionlaw.com/havaianas-how-a-simple-sandal-took-over-the-globe/

Summary

- Selecting the right market(s) to enter is critical for fashion firms' success in global business.

- In practice, international market selection is complex, and a significant number of factors should be considered. In essence, the selection is about finding a highly attractive country with low market risk.

- General international market selection approaches can be classified into two categories: the systematic approach (normative model) and the non-systematic approach (descriptive model).

- In a systematic approach, market selection is a discrete decision based on a thorough evaluation of different markets with respect to specific, well-defined criteria, such as market attractiveness in terms of economic, social, political, and retail environments, given the company's resources and objectives.

- In the systematic approach, the potential foreign market evaluation process comprises three stages: preliminary screening, identification and in-depth screening stage, and final selection.

- In the preliminary screening stage, firms identify potential markets as targets for future in-depth analysis and eliminate countries that do not satisfy the firm's goals according to macro-level indicators. The identification and in-depth screening stage includes an industry-specific assessment of shortlisted countries, involving analyses of industry attractiveness and cost and revenue prediction. The final selection stage decides which country best fits the company's objectives, existing portfolios, and available resources.

- The non-systematic approach refers to a market selection approach based on subjective and contingent factors, psychic distance, and attractiveness to specific opportunities in the host market, rather than on specific evaluation criteria.

- In the non-systematic approach, firms choose a country to enter, reacting to specific opportunities via personal and business networks, an inquiry from a foreign company searching for new suppliers of a particular product, or unsolicited requests of potential franchisees.

- Fashion companies further need to assess the host country factors that affect fashion firms' market entry decisions. Entry into a country with a different level of economic development status requires a more thorough understanding of the conditions of the market than entry into a country with the same level of economic development status. Host country factors that are more relevant to developing countries include consumer demands for apparel branded goods and consumer acceptance of global brands.

- Consumer demand for branded apparel products appear from the golden age when apparel production for the global supply chain is actively taking place, requiring a significant group of middle-class consumers who can afford global apparel brands.

- Since global apparel brands may not always find a warm reception in developing countries, global fashion companies need to consider the receptiveness or resistance to global brands by assessing host market consumers' ethnocentrism, xenocentrism, and cosmopolitanism levels.

- Firms have different goals, resources, and experience. Firms' market entry decisions and their market selection approaches differ by firm factors, such as firm size, brand image, home country image, and internationalization experience.

Class Activities

1. Discuss how companies can overcome ethnocentrism.
2. Conduct your own research on how small fashion companies in your country find an international market to enter.
3. Evaluate the pros and cons of using non-systematic or network approaches in finding an international market to enter.

Key Terms

- **Systematic approach:** An international market selection approach that refers to a discrete decision based on a thorough evaluation of different markets, with respect to specific, well-defined criteria such as market attractiveness in terms of economic, social, political, and retail environments, given the company's resources and objectives.
- **Foreign market evaluation process:** The process involving the preliminary screening stage, identification and in-depth screening stage, and final selection stage. In the preliminary screening stage, firms identify potential markets as targets for future in-depth analysis and eliminate countries that do not satisfy the firm's goals according to macro-level indicators. The identification and in-depth screening stage includes industry-specific assessments of the shortlisted countries, involving industry attractiveness and costs and revenue analyses. The final selection stage decides which country best fits the company's objectives, existing portfolios, and available resources.
- **Non-systematic approach:** Market selection approach based on subjective and contingent factors, psychic distance, and attractiveness to specific opportunities in the host market, rather than on specific evaluation criteria.
- **Personal network:** Close friends or family of owners/founders, and diaspora; characterized by a high level of trust and commitment.
- **Business network:** A network formulated through partner companies, internationally experienced managers, business consultants, government institutions including embassies and chambers of commerce in host countries, and by attending trade fairs, exhibitions, and conferences.
- **Global Retail Development Index:** Developed by Kearney each year, it assesses the attractiveness of the world's retail market based on four factors: country and business risk, market attractiveness, market saturation, and time pressure.
- **Host country factors:** The conditions that need to be understood and assessed when considering entry into a potential host country.
- **Ethnocentrism:** A consumer's sense of obligation to protect national industries from foreign competitors.
- **Xenocentrism:** A consumer's belief that what is foreign is best and that their own lifestyle, products, or ideas are inferior to those of others.
- **Cosmopolitanism:** A personal tendency to orient oneself beyond the boundaries of the community one belongs to; explains consumers' open-mindedness to foreign brands and appreciation of the diversity of products.
- **Firm factors affecting market entry decision:** The factors that influence firms' specific market entry choices and their market selection approaches: firm size, brand image, home country image, and internationalization experience.
- **Home country image:** A brand's country of origin image that serves as a product quality cue to help consumers make purchase decisions.

CHAPTER 8

How to Enter: Entry Mode Decision

Learning Objectives

After studying this chapter, you will be able to:

- Explain the various entry modes a company can choose when entering a foreign market.
- Describe the entry modes by their risk and resource commitment levels and corresponding control.
- Compare the pros and cons of each market entry strategy.
- Explain preferred entry modes by retailer format or brand level and why these modes are the most effective.
- Discuss the factors related to the entry mode choice.
- Identify possible alternative entry modes to test out market entry feasibility.

After choosing an international market to enter, the next important decision a company needs to make is how to enter the market (entry mode decision). Companies have a range of entry mode options, starting with exporting and extending to wholly owned subsidiaries. This decision is critical because it specifies the level of resource commitment a company should make and the level of control the company can have in return (Lu et al., 2011; Picot-Coupey et al., 2014). It also reflects the strategic flexibility the company can retain. For example, exporting requires the lowest level of risk and commitment because it only involves products, overseas, not people, factories, or stores, but it gives a firm the least amount of control because the importers determine the pricing and distribution of the products. In addition, the return tends to be minimum, compared to other higher commitment entry modes such as a joint venture. Foreign direct investment, however, is entirely opposite in terms of resource commitment, risk, and control. Basically, the higher the level of commitment, the more control firms have (Lu et al., 2011; Picot-Coupey et al., 2014). However, companies need to assess the various risks (cultural differences, degree of retail market development in host country, and so on) and market potential before making such a commitment (Lu et al., 2011; Picot-Coupey et al., 2014).

In this chapter, various entry modes will be introduced first with actual examples of global apparel brands, followed by factors related to deciding on the entry mode, and implications for retailers. Fashion companies can have multiple distribution channels in one country. For example, Mulberry has a flagship store in Tokyo, two concession stores, a wholesale agreement, and an e-commerce platform to reach Japanese consumers (Hendriksz, 2017). Here, we focus on the initial market entry mode with which a firm chooses to enter a foreign market. Firms' selection of diverse distribution channels in a country subsequent to entry will be discussed in Chapter 12. An increasing number of fashion companies enter other countries via online, which will be also handled in Chapter 12.

Market Entry Choices

Traditionally, a company has three groups of entry modes from which to select:

1. *Export*: indirect export, direct export, and export via e-commerce platforms
2. *Contractual entry*: licensing and franchising agreement
3. *Investment entry*: joint venture, acquisition, and wholly owned subsidiary.

In addition to these entry modes, this chapter includes two more investment entry modes in order to reflect fashion industry practices. Those are concessions and flagship stores (Alexander and Doherty, 2009; Moore et al., 2010; Picot-Coupey et al., 2014).

The entry mode decision entails two major implications. First, the amount of equity and commitment required by the company differs according to the chosen entry mode. Second, different modes affect the risk, return, and control levels for firms. Figure 8.1 presents a summary of the levels of risk and commitment, and firms' corresponding control and involvement levels, according to their choice of entry mode.

A brief description of each entry mode and an example are shown in Table 8.1. In the next section, each entry mode and its pros and cons are explained in detail.

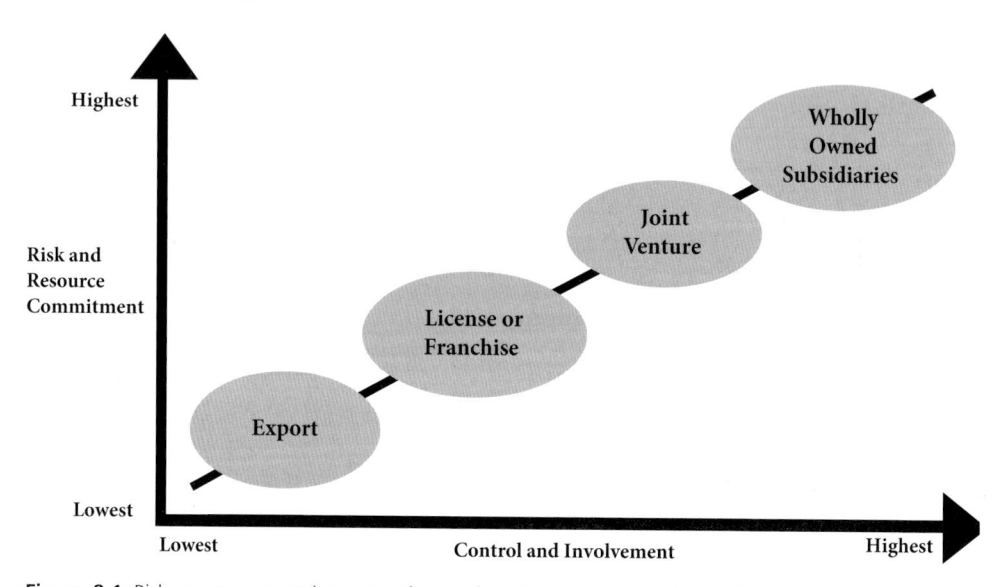

Figure 8.1 Risk, resource commitment, and control and involvement level by entry mode.

Table 8.1 Brief description of each entry mode and fashion industry examples

ENTRY MODE	EXPLANATION	EXAMPLE IN THE FASHION INDUSTRY
Exporting	Sending goods or services to an international market for sale without establishing an offline or online retail presence	Tiffany & Co. entered the Japanese market via export in 1972
Licensing	A contractual entry mode in which a licensor (a company that owns intangible property) grants a licensee (a company in a foreign country) the right to use the property (e.g., brand name) for a specified period	Burberry entered Japan with a licensing agreement with Sanyo Shokai Ltd in the 1970s, which was terminated in 2015
Franchising	A contractual entry mode in which a franchisor supplies a franchisee in a foreign country with its retail format and provides other assistance (i.e., operations) over an extended period	Zara entered Saudi Arabia via a franchise agreement with Fawaz Al Hokair Group in 1999
Joint venture	The establishment of a new firm combining a firm in a company's home country with a firm in a host country to achieve a common business objective. Both companies share ownership	Bloomingdale's department store entered the United Arab Emirates by establishing a joint venture with Al-Tayer Group in 2010
Concessions	Establishment of a shop within a shop, usually a department store in a foreign country	J.Crew entered China by opening a corner in Lane Crawford department store in Hong Kong in 2012
Flagship store	A company-owned, large-scale store designed to showcase its brand, typically established in a prime location in a metropolitan city	Uniqlo entered the US by opening a flagship store in New York in 2006
Acquisition	Acquiring control over a firm in the international market	L'Oréal entered China by acquiring 3CE in 2017, a cosmetic brand of the Korean firm Stylenanda
Wholly owned subsidiary	A subsidiary in a foreign country that a parent company entirely owns	Uniqlo entered India through a wholly owned subsidiary by opening its first store in New Delhi in 2019

Exporting

Exporting means sending products to a foreign market for sale without establishing a store in the market. Exporting involves the lowest resource commitment of all the entry mode options because it only involves products, without making a financial investment in the host countries. Low resource commitment means low financial risk. Thus, fashion brands often choose this mode as their first international step. Exporting can be either indirect or direct.

Indirect exporting means that the company sells its products to intermediaries who then resell to buyers in a foreign market. The intermediaries include an export trading company, export management company, buying office, and others that buy to supply customers abroad. In indirect exporting, a firm's main task is to find a suitable intermediary firm and then let the intermediary handle most of the details of the exporting process, such as shipping and finding distributors. Thus, this mode entails the lowest risks and complexities and is chosen by companies with little experience and few resources and contacts.

Direct exporting occurs when fashion firms sell their goods directly to buyers in target countries without owning either an online or an offline store in those countries. As a seller or direct exporter, fashion firms take full responsibility for getting their goods into the target market by directly selling to local buyers. Here, buyers are not necessarily defined as the final consumers in the target countries. Local buyers typically include buyers from department stores and specialty stores, distributors, and sales representatives.

Fashion brands can sell to *international buyers* from department stores and specialty stores by attending trade shows overseas. That is, they present their merchandise at trade shows, foreign buyers select the styles to be sold at their stores, and then place orders before the fashion season. This arrangement is also called *wholesale*. Popular trade shows include MAGIC Las Vegas (Las Vegas), Liberty Fairs, and Coterie (New York), Who's Next (Paris), Pitti Immagine Uomo (Florence), and Momad (Madrid). Table 8.2 presents trade shows and their specialty areas. The task of the fashion companies ends when they ship the ordered goods to the buyers who then handle the rest of the selling process in their respective countries.

Table 8.2 Fashion trade shows and their specialty areas

FASHION TRADE SHOWS	LOCATION	SPECIALTY AREAS
MAGIC Las Vegas	Las Vegas	Women's young contemporary, sportswear, trend, footwear, and accessories www.magicfashionevents.com/en/home.html
Liberty Fairs	New York Las Vegas	Contemporary menswear trade show https://libertyfairs.com
Coterie	New York	Contemporary and advanced contemporary women's apparel, footwear, and accessory brands https://coteriefashionevents.com
Who's Next	Paris	International fashion trade show for womenswear in Europe https://whosnext.com
Pitti Immagine Uomo	Florence	Men's clothing and accessories/tailored street style https://uomo.pittimmagine.com/en
Momad	Madrid	International fashion, footwear, and accessories exhibition www.ifema.es/en/momad

Figure 8.2 Licensing agreement.

The main advantage of exporting is that it allows companies to sell goods to international markets without significant financial investment. As firms begin to understand the market and its consumers and gain confidence, they can gradually increase their resource commitment, as the U model explains (see Chapter 6). The main disadvantage of exporting is that it offers fashion firms least control, which means fewer opportunities to learn about foreign markets and their consumers and properly handle their brand image. As fashion companies' most important asset, once brand image is damaged in their host countries, it takes a long time to recover. Therefore, firms need to conduct adequate market research before entering foreign markets. Since the resource commitment involved is low, firms can devise their exporting strategies quickly, and vigilant monitoring should follow. The next level of resource commitment is a contractual entry that includes licensing and franchising agreements.

Contractual Entry: Licensing and Franchising Agreements

Fashion companies can enter international markets through contractual agreements. Licensing and franchising agreements are the two main types of contractual entry.

Licensing Agreement

Licensing is popularly used for accessories of many high-end designer brands, such as Gucci sunglasses, Prada perfume, Salvatore Ferragamo eyewear, watches, fragrances, and so on. A luxury brand can create multiple licensing agreements for their accessories. For example, Italian luxury brand Ermenegildo Zegna licenses with Marcolini Group for its sunglasses and optical frames and with Estée Lauder to develop and market new fragrances and grooming lines. As this example shows, in a licensing contract, a licensor (say, a US fashion company) allows a licensee (a manufacturer or retailer in a foreign market) to use the licensor's know-how and intangible assets, such as brand name, trademarks, patent rights, and the rights to use technological processes for a specified period. In return, the licensee pays a fee or royalty (usually 5 percent of sales) or other type of payment to a licensor as agreed in the contract. Figure 8.2 depicts a typical licensing agreement.

One typical scenario is when a manufacturer allows a manufacturer or retailer in a foreign country to produce products under its name. Licensing is a fast means of establishing a presence in a foreign market and making a profit without an actual investment. Therefore, it works well when a company has scarce capital and the host country is sensitive to foreign brand name ownership. However,

Figure 8.3 A Pierre Cardin lingerie corner in a Vietnamese department store.
Source: Courtesy of B. Ellie Jin.

licensing provides the least amount of managerial control. In the case of Zegna above, Zegna has no control over the Marcolini Group and Estée Lauder's production, marketing, and distribution of the licensed products. As far as consumers know, they are purchasing Zegna fragrances. They do not know that Estée Lauder produces for Zegna. So, if Estée Lauder performs poorly, that is, the quality is not good, the price is not right, they distribute via improper channels, and so on, this may ruin Zegna's reputation. Thus, finding the right licensing partner is extremely important. Since licensing provides the least amount of control, if the brand's image is heavily used, it may become diluted and inconsistent.

Pierre Cardin is probably the world's most extensive licensor: it has more than 350 active licenses worldwide, from clothes to cigarettes, frying pans, floor tiles, toilet seats, and hospital mattresses. The number of licenses is currently down from about 800 in the 1990s (Diderich, 2016). The brand is quick to enter emerging markets; thus, it is often one of the first brands that consumers in an emerging economy encounter. In 2010, Pierre Cardin was one of the few global brands available in Vietnam (Figure 8.3). With its licensing agreement, the brand can reach consumers quickly in many different countries across multiple product categories without much financial investment; however, this may confuse global consumers about the identity of the Pierre Cardin brand (Okonkwo, 2007). Thus, its fame from the 1960s has been seriously challenged.

To protect brand image, many luxury brands that have entered a foreign market with a licensing agreement decide to terminate or not renew the agreement. As a good example, Burberry terminated its licensing agreement in Japan in 2015, even though it had generated $800 million in sales and $80 million in royalties annually at that time (see Case Study 8.1).

Franchising Agreements

While a licensor allows a licensee the use of its brand names (or other intangible assets), the franchisor allows the franchisee the right to use a proven way of doing business (operating a retail store) by providing a standard package of products, systems, and management services. In return, the franchisee who buys the right pays an initial fee and a royalty percentage of total sales to the franchisor, just as a licensee pays a fee and royalties to the licensor.

Franchising agreements can be a win–win scenario for both franchisor and franchisee. For the franchisor (say, a global fashion brand such as Benetton), because the franchisees provide capital to open stores across the globe, this allows rapid expansion to the global marketplace while keeping the brand image consistent. Most Starbucks and McDonald's restaurants are franchised stores; wherever you go in the world, the stores' atmosphere and product offerings are the same. The franchisee also provides the franchisor with local knowledge and an entrepreneurial spirit. For the franchisee, it allows them to operate a branded retail store without establishing a brand name, retail operation knowledge, and a proven system. This combination of skills permits flexibility in dealing with local market conditions

and yet provides the parent firm (franchisor) with a reasonable degree of control (Picot-Coupey et al., 2014). Therefore, franchising is the fastest growing market entry strategy even in times of economic downturn (Alon et al., 2017). Adidas entered India in 1995 through a franchising agreement (Mitra, 2015).

Two types of franchising arrangements can create business opportunities in different ways: direct franchise and master franchise. While a *direct franchise* involves an individual contract for a franchisee, a *master franchise* contract grants the franchisee the right to sub-franchise the concept to others within an exclusive territory (a particular state, country, or region). Under a direct franchise, a franchisor can contract three ways: as a single unit, as multiple units, or as an area developer (Figure 8.4). A single unit is the traditional franchise contract: a direct contract between a franchisor and a franchisee. Under the multi-unit franchise and area developer contracts, a franchisor permits the franchisee to open and operate more than a single unit store within a specific period (FranCity, 2015). The main difference between a multi-unit franchise and an area development franchise is that an area development grants the franchise exclusive rights to a territory and requires the franchisee to open and own a specified number of outlets (Lee et al., 2012). Typically, area developers should pay a development fee and are responsible for developing the business units in that area unless the franchisor wants to retain its rights for units in special locations, such as airports, train stations, bus stations, and amusement parks. The area developer can expand the business quickly because there is no need to negotiate with multiple franchisees, but at the same time, the franchisor holds less control (Lee et al., 2012).

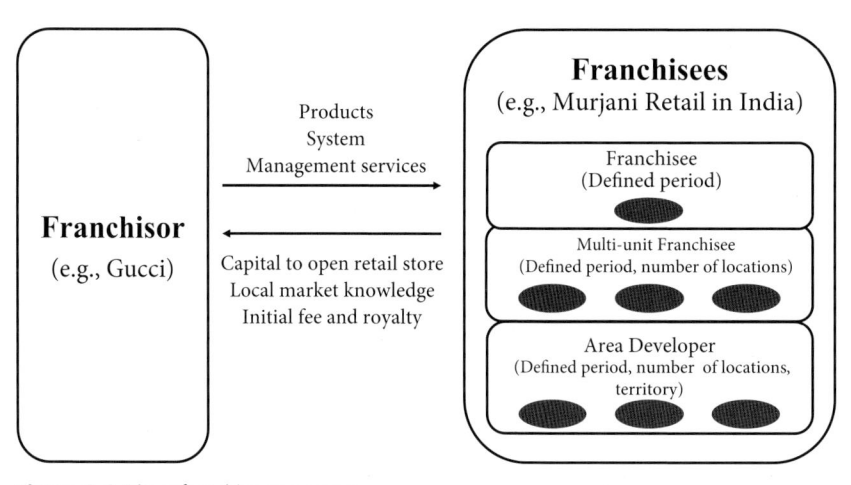

Figure 8.4 Direct franchise agreement.

In a master franchise contract, the franchisor allows a master franchisee to manage the full range of products and services through sub-franchising within a specific country, region, or continent. As shown in Figure 8.5, the master franchisor becomes a sort of a franchisor to those sub-franchisees because of the sub-franchisees' contract with the master franchisor, who negotiates between the franchisor and sub-franchisees. The master franchisee's royalties to its franchisor includes both payment received for every unit set up by the sub-franchisee and that collected from units operated by the master franchisee. The master franchisee can build its own units first in order to test potential franchisees in the region (Lee et al., 2012). One good example of a master franchise agreement is the contract between Zara, a franchisor, and Fawaz Al Hokair Group, a master franchisee, in entering the Saudi Arabian market in 1999. Under the master franchise agreement, the Fawaz Al Hokair Group has the right to sub-franchise Zara stores in Saudi Arabia (Baena, 2012).

The key issue in franchising agreements is finding a suitable local franchise partner because the brand image and uniformity of the brand's offerings in the host country are entirely up to the local partner. An ideal franchise partner can be either an individual or retail company that has good local knowledge, is financially secure, and has good business know-how. While a franchising agreement provides various advantages, it carries the risk of the concept being copied by the franchisee, thus becoming a competitor later on (see Table 8.3).

Investment Entry: Joint Venture, Concession, Flagship Store, Acquisition, and Wholly Owned Subsidiary

After the export and contractual entry modes explained above, the investment entry mode is the next level of commitment a fashion company can make. Compared to the two previous entry modes, this mode involves an actual investment.

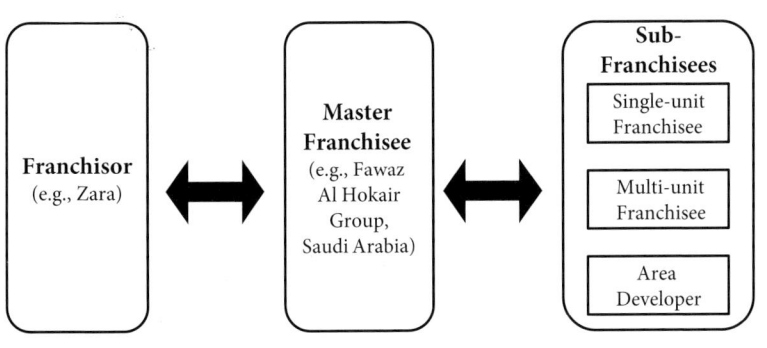

Figure 8.5 Master franchise agreement.

Table 8.3 Advantages and disadvantages of the franchise system

ADVANTAGES	DISADVANTAGES
• Low initial investment for franchisors • Rapid chain development • Faster entry and growth because various resources will be acquired from franchisees • Franchisees (independent entrepreneurs) are more motivated than salaried employees • Less administrative control • Gain better knowledge of local markets	• Limited individual financing capability • Risk of former franchisees copying the concept and creating a competitive chain • Presence of different franchisees in the same city can lead to market saturation • Incomplete information available on performance • Difficult to control recruitment standards for franchisee employees • Training and control of franchisees may require more effort, especially in emerging countries

Source: Developed by the author based on Durand (2019); Filieri (2015); Gauzente and Dumoulin (2010).

Joint Venture

A joint venture (JV) is formed when two or more retailers come together to create a new enterprise. One example is Samsung Tesco, a joint venture established in Korea by a 50/50 investment between the Korean company Samsung and the UK retailer Tesco (Computer Business Review, 2006). The joint venture existed under the name Homeplus until 2008 when it was acquired by the local retailer E-land (Vitorovich, 2008). Compared to export and contractual agreements, JVs require a significant resource investment. Joint ventures are chosen for two main reasons.

First, a JV is often formed for entry into a country with distinct cultural differences or with high competition. Gucci entered the United Arab Emirates (UAE) by establishing a joint venture with Al Tayer Insignia, the largest UAE-based luxury retailer in the Middle East (Korukcuoglu, 2012). Dubai Bloomingdale's, the first Bloomingdale's store outside the US, opened in the Dubai Mall in 2010 and was also a joint venture between Macy's and Al Tayer Insignia (Bladd, 2010; Business Insider, 2010). In this case, Al Tayer already knew the market and could help both Gucci and Macy's to achieve their goals. The Japanese lifestyle brand Muji entered India in 2017 by establishing a joint venture with Reliance Brands, which sells an array of global brands, including Kenneth Cole, Steve Madden, Diesel, and Brooks Brothers (Bailay, 2017). In this instance, Muji could have chosen to be 100 percent wholly owned, as government regulations in India eased in 2012; however, as the retail market in India is growing, Muji might have seen the Indian market as having high competition, and therefore sought a JV partner.

Similar to the franchising agreement, these JV partners help each other like a married couple. A JV is often compared to a marriage because both partners share responsibilities and goals. Global retailers provide their expertise about the supply chain, product development, and store operations, while local partners assist with extensive knowledge about their consumers, markets, and operating expertise, as shown in Figure 8.6.

The second reason to choose a joint venture is that in many emerging countries, foreign direct investment is banned, thus having a local partner (a joint venture partner) is required to enter the market until the host government's stipulation is lifted. China had this regulation until 2001, and India until 2012 (Long, 2005; Sharma and Sahu, 2012). However, the Indian government allowed foreign companies to establish wholly owned entities operating only single-brand retail stores, but it still bans multi-brand stores from operating (Sharma and Sahu, 2012). This means that, until 2012, many retailers entered India after forming a joint venture with a local partner. Walmart established Walmart-Bharti in 2010 (Walmart, n.d.) and Zara established Zara-Trent (a subsidiary of Tata Group) in India in 2010 (Shamnani, 2018).

Although joint ventures bring substantial benefits to both parties, the impact of their failure is significant because both companies invest to establish a company. Case Study 2.1 shows how Macy's exit from a JV in China resulted in a $19 million loss over three years. There are many cases of failure in the global fashion industry. The Italian jeans brand Replay exited India in 2008 because its JV with the Future Group did not work well (Bailay, 2018). The Korean brand On & On's joint venture, established with a Chinese partner in 2004, failed after a nine-month-long legal trial, which resulted in the closure of the majority of its established stores. The partnership ended because each partner had different goals: the Chinese partner pursued aggressive expansion for a fast profit generation, while On & On valued establishing a prestigious image even though that might take more time (Jin and Chung, 2016). As this case shows, just like married couples, joint venture partners should share the same goals and vision in order to achieve their common goals.

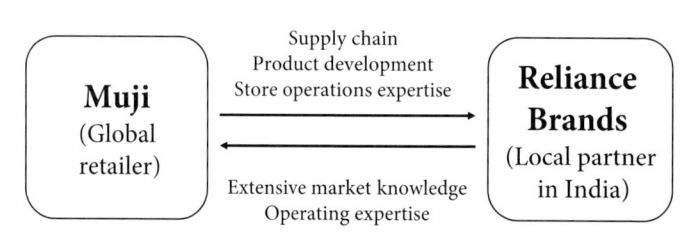

Figure 8.6 Joint venture between Muji and Reliance Brands in India.

Concessions: A Store within a Store

Fashion companies can also enter a foreign market by having a concessions corner within a department store. For example, J.Crew entered China by opening a corner in Lane Crawford department store in Hong Kong in 2018, which is the Asian version of Barneys New York (Ng and Sanchanta, 2012). In this case, J.Crew was still responsible for providing stock, staff, and merchandising, but the financial risk and commitment was limited because it was just renting a small space within a large store. Without strong brand recognition, the concessions corner may not appeal to consumers in the host country. Thus, this mode is appropriate for fashion companies with strong brand recognition. Luxury retailers often use this entry mode to research a market and test opportunities before making a larger commitment, often combined with a flagship operation.

Flagship Store

A flagship store is a large-scale company-owned store designed to showcase a brand (Kozinets et al., 2002). It extends to four sales floors, as opposed to just two floors, and is five to eight times larger than standard retail stores (Moore et al., 2010). It is typically located on a major fashion street in a metropolitan city such as Madison Avenue in New York, Via Monte Napoleone in Milan, Avenue des Champs-Elysées in Paris, Oxford Street in London, and Ginza shopping district in Tokyo (Moore et al., 2010). Since the space in those major shopping districts is astronomically expensive, a fashion company cannot afford to maintain many flagship stores in a given country. In many cases, owing to such high rental costs, flagship stores may not generate much profit. Still, many luxury brands choose to enter a country by first opening a flagship store with the main intention of building their brand image (Moore et al., 2010). Brand image is of the utmost importance for luxury brands; therefore, the flagship store is invested in as a communication and publicity tool rather than a store where there is an expected return on investment (Fernie et al., 1997; Moore et al., 2000). In addition to introducing, reinforcing, and enhancing a fashion retailer's position and status, its second strategic function is to use its space to develop and introduce new business propositions, such as cafés, restaurants, and home furnishings (Moore et al., 2010). Its third function includes providing a venue to develop relationships with distribution partners, fashion media relations, and customer relations. A flagship store further serves as a model to educate franchise partners (Moore et al., 2010).

Mass-market brands also invest in flagship stores to boost their brand recognition more quickly. Uniqlo, a Japanese apparel brand, strategically established its flagship stores in major fashion cities: New York (2006), London (2007), Paris (2009), and Shanghai (2010). This contrasts with Giordano, another Asian mass-market brand, that has mainly focused on standalone stores in duty-free shops at airports or in central shopping districts (Woo and Jin, 2014). Similarly, Zara chose to enter China by opening a flagship store in Shanghai in 2006 (The Corner, 2012) and Abercrombie & Fitch did the same in 2014 (Doland, 2014). While opening flagship stores is still a prevalent mode of entry among luxury brands, its popularity has waned slightly due to the omnipresence of online shopping worldwide (King, 2017).

Acquisition

Another investment method through which firms can enter a country is by acquiring an existing fashion or retail organization in a host country. This method is commonly chosen by big-box retailers such as Walmart, especially when entering developed economies. In the domestic market, big-box retailers often expand gradually by adding multiple stores. This is called "organic growth." However, in developed economies, gradual expansion is often impossible because desirable locations have already been occupied by local competitors, and adding stores, which entails government permissions and construction, may be a lengthy process. Walmart, for example, made multiple foreign market entries by acquiring existing local retailers. It entered the UK in 1999 by acquiring 229 Asda stores, Germany in 1998 by acquiring 21 Werthauf stores, Japan in 2002 by acquiring Seiyu, and India in 2018 by acquiring Flipkart (Russell, 2018a, 2018b). For a similar reason, US online retailer Amazon bought the Dubai-based online retailer souq.com in 2017 with the intention of entering the Middle Eastern region. Amazon paid $580 million for the acquisition, the priciest international acquisition by Amazon to date (Kim and Levy, 2019). Amazon entered Germany by acquiring the online bookstore Telebook, Inc. and the UK by acquiring Bookpages, both in 1998, and China by acquiring Joyo.com in 2014 (Nguyen-Chyung and Faulk, 2014). In 2017, L'Oréal acquired 3CE, a cosmetic brand of Korean firm Stylenanda with a turnover of $152 million. L'Oréal intends to enter the Chinese market by leveraging the popularity of 3CE in China bolstered by the popularity of Korean pop culture (Well, 2018; White, 2018).

Acquisition allows firms to start operating a number of existing stores immediately upon entering a country, which ensures swift market penetration and immediate cash flow. Firms can also quickly add subsequent organic growth based on established operations. For example, Walmart added 74 Interspar stores after the acquisition of 21 Werthauf stores in Germany. The acquisition typically takes over management teams and employees, which facilitates faster expansion into the country; however, this can cause conflicts with existing teams owing to cultural differences. Another potential challenge of acquisition comes when an acquiring company presents with an excess of confidence over the acquired company. Acquired companies may decide to sell because of their inability to solve certain challenges they may have. Acquiring companies sometimes make acquisitions decisions with the assumption that they could solve these challenges. However, such challenges may persist, and other challenges related to foreign operations may also present themselves, which can seriously deter the acquired firm's growth. This may eventually cause firms to withdraw from the market. Walmart withdrew from the German market in 2006, which was a hefty divestment decision. Compared to domestic acquisitions, cross-border acquisitions carry more complicated regulatory and legal issues. Due to the potential for different cultural and business practices, the merging of a new firm into an acquiring international firm is often more challenging (Hitt et al., 2019).

Wholly Owned Subsidiaries

A wholly owned subsidiary requires a 100 percent investment in a foreign country, either by building manufacturing facilities or by opening retail stores; thus, it is the highest level of resource commitment. It is a pricey decision, particularly in the early stages, because sales are small relative to the overhead costs. As shown in Figure 8.1, this entry mode allows firms the highest operational control. That is, firms can control many different aspects of brand and store management, including decisions regarding store location, merchandise assortment, price, sales associates, and so on. For luxury brands, brand image is the most important asset compared to other fashion brand levels; thus, a wholly owned subsidiary is often chosen in order to control every aspect of its operations in foreign countries. In each country a luxury brand enters with a wholly owned subsidiary, it basically establishes a separate company, such as Ermenegildo Zegna China, Co., Ltd, Ermenegildo Zegna Korea, Co., Ltd, and Ermenegildo Zegna Canada, Co., Ltd. Through the separate company, luxury brands directly operate their stores, including flagship stores, stores within department stores, and so on. Firms establish wholly owned subsidiaries in a market where growth potential is high and country risk is perceived to be low. Japanese retailer Uniqlo, for example, opened its first store in India in New Delhi in 2019 through a wholly owned subsidiary (Tandon, 2018).

Factors Related to Entry Mode Decisions

Fashion firms' decision on which market entry mode to pursue is complicated, as there are many factors to consider. The traditional internationalization theory, and the U model in particular, posits that firms feel risk from their lack of host market knowledge, thus choosing to gradually increase their financial commitment from exporting to directly investing, as their knowledge of the market increases.

However, in practice, firms must consider the degree to which they desire to control their products, as well as market-specific factors (market size, market growth potential, market competition) and country-specific factors (cultural distance, government regulations in host countries), together with assessing their risk and commitment levels (Agarwal and Ramaswami, 1992; Lu et al., 2011). For example, if a fashion firm prefers to maintain greater control over their operations, as in the case of luxury brands, the firm may choose the wholly owned subsidiary or flagship store as an entry mode. However, if the host country prevents foreign firms from making a 100 percent investment, the firm needs to choose a local partner, so a joint venture or franchise agreement would be the maximum investment they could make. For example, the Indian government did not allow the establishment of wholly owned subsidiaries until 2012. Therefore, to enter the Indian market prior to 2012 (Business Standard, 2013), Burberry made a franchising agreement with Media Star in 2004 (Oxberry, 2009), Gucci with Murjani Retail in 2006, and Ferragamo with Sports Station India in 2006 (Rai, 2007).

To enter culturally distant countries, many firms prefer to work with local partners via franchising agreements, even though there are no government regulations and firms' desire for operational control is high. Fast fashion brand Zara's entry into the Middle Eastern market is an example. Since Zara perceived the Middle Eastern market as culturally distant from its home country, entering this market was risky. Firms can mitigate this risk by having a joint venture partner. American athletic footwear brand Skechers entered India in 2012 through

```
High growth potential
Low risk
Want to control
Have resource to commit
```
↓
Wholly owned subsidiary

```
Large, competitive markets
Good location is difficult to acquire
Host government's regulation
```
↓
Joint venture

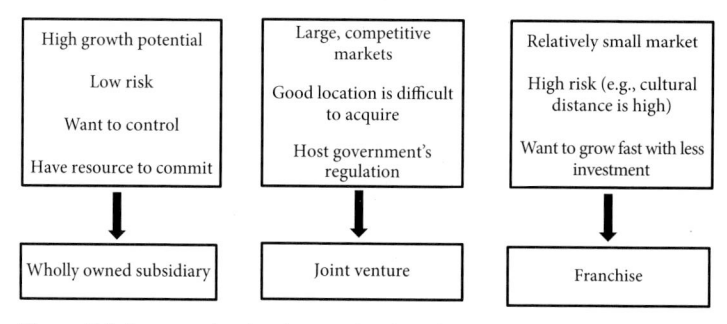

```
Relatively small market
High risk (e.g., cultural distance is high)
Want to grow fast with less investment
```
↓
Franchise

Figure 8.7 Factors related to international market entry mode decisions.

a joint venture with Future Group (ET Retail. com, 2017).

Certain entry modes are favored according to store format. While big-box retailers prefer FDI or acquisition, luxury fashion brands tend to favor flagship stores or wholly owned subsidiaries to control their operations and protect their brand image. A fashion firm can have a wide range of entry modes as part of its internationalization strategy. That is, a fashion brand should not choose the same entry mode for every international market, and the entry mode decision should be a strategic decision considering diverse factors. For example, Zara favors its own network of international stores to fully control its design, manufacturing, and retailing. Yet it often chooses to pursue a JV when it enters large, competitive markets where it is difficult to acquire property to set up retail outlets, or where there are other kinds of obstacles that require cooperation with a local company. Zara's entry into Germany, Italy, and Japan are such examples. For high-risk countries that are culturally distant or have small markets with low sales forecasts, such as Saudi Arabia, Kuwait, Andorra, or Malaysia, it chose a franchise agreement, even though it usually prefers organic growth (Lopez and Fan, 2009). Figure 8.7 summarizes the factors related to selected entry mode decisions.

Implications for Fashion Companies

Entry mode decisions are strategic decisions that firms should make carefully when entering a foreign country. These decisions cannot be easily reversed or divested from once a resource commitment has been made. Therefore, firms should be aware of several points before making such important decisions.

First, fashion companies have many alternatives they can utilize to test out their feasibility in an international market. Exporting is one option, but establishing a concession store, selling online, and even launching a pop-up store can be employed for testing purposes. A growing number of fashion brands are testing international markets via online sales. The Dutch brand Scotch & Soda initially tested the Indian market online by working with Myntra.com before opening a physical store by partnering with Reliance Brands. The UK's Dorothy Perkins is now seeking to open physical stores in India after four years of online retailing with Jabong.com. The use of e-commerce as a testing ground can occur in multiple ways. Small firms can export via a large online shopping mall such as Amazon.com and Aliexpress.com in China. The firms can then further develop websites in different languages to specially target consumers in host countries. For example, UK e-tailer Asos.com developed asos.cn in China in 2013 after selling via its own website in the UK for several years (Butler, 2013). However, Asos.cn exited China in 2016 after three years of operations (*Financial Times*, 2016; for more on this, see Atwal and Bryson, 2017). While the idea of testing an international market online in a firm's home country first and then establishing an online presence in the local language is valid, this method does not guarantee success. This is because online operations in any country still require merchandising strategies: meeting customers' needs with the right products at the right prices at the right place, and in the right quantities.

Establishing a pop-up store can be another way of testing an international market. In 2013, Zalando, a Berlin-based fashion e-commerce company, opened its first pop-up store in Milan, Italy to test the possibility of opening offline stores because Italian consumers are strongly brand driven and prefer physical stores (Alexander et al., 2018; Pavarini, 2013; Fashion United, 2013).

Second, while the initial entry mode decision is important, this decision is not permanent. As a firm becomes more familiar with the market, culture, and consumers, it can gradually increase its commitment. As depicted in Figure 8.8, Tiffany & Co. and Ralph Lauren have gradually increased their resource investments in Japan from exports or licensing to wholly owned subsidiaries (Cho and Jin, 2012).

Firms can also increase their commitment when the host government lifts its stipulations on foreign investments. Nike entered India through a seven-year licensing agreement with Sierra Industrial Enterprises, and then established a fully owned subsidiary, Nike India, after India's Department of Industrial Policy and Promotion granted permission for 100 percent foreign investments in 2012 (Business Standard, 2014). Figure 8.9 presents the examples of Puma and Adidas, both of which switched to direct investments after the stipulation was eased (Kumar, 2016).

Third, fashion companies can reenter a market following a divestment decision. While the U model views the incremental resource commitment from export to wholly owned subsidiaries, in practice, fashion companies could exit and then reenter the market later on. That is, the process does not always move linearly through gradual investment. A firm's

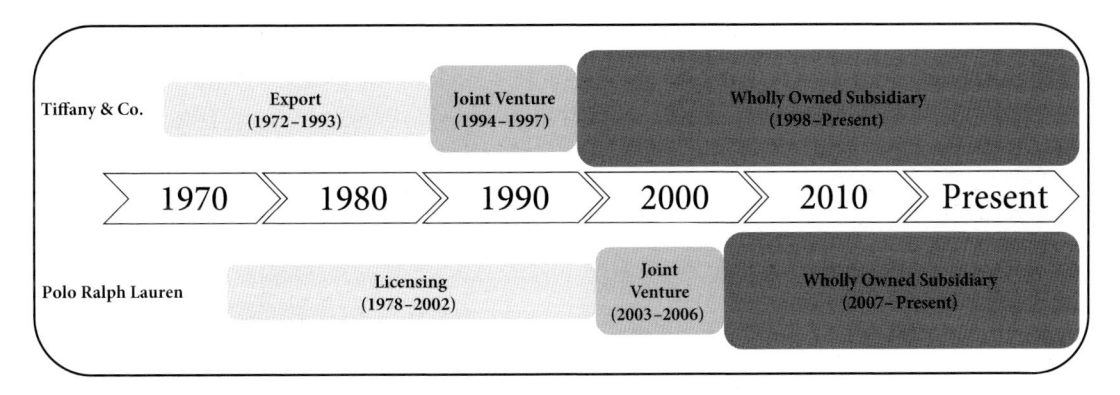

Figure 8.8 Resource commitment increase within a country: Tiffany & Co. and Ralph Lauren in Japan.
Source: Modified based on Cho and Jin (2012).

2012

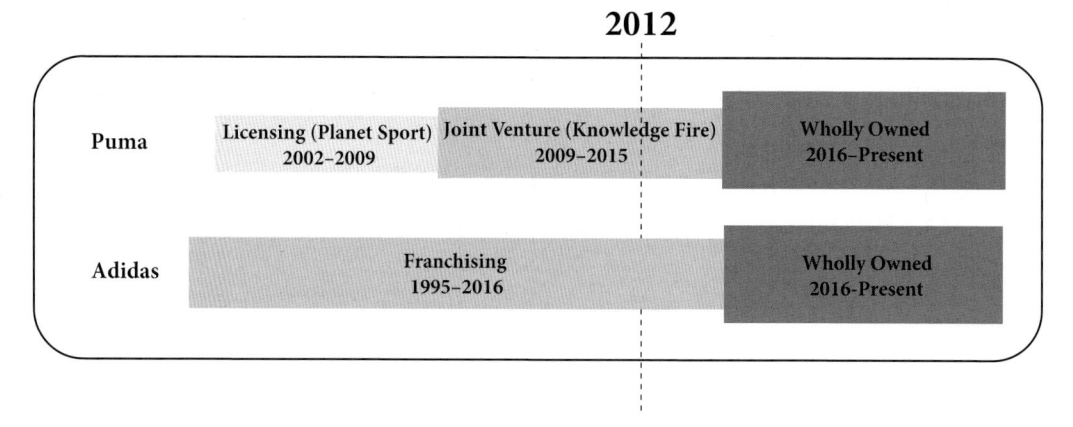

| Puma | Licensing (Planet Sport) 2002–2009 | Joint Venture (Knowledge Fire) 2009–2015 | Wholly Owned 2016–Present |

| Adidas | Franchising 1995–2016 | | Wholly Owned 2016–Present |

Figure 8.9 Fashion brands' resource commitment increase after 2012 lifting of Indian government regulations.
Source: Developed by author based on Bhushan (2005); *The Economic Times* (2009).

entry, divestment, and reentry decisions should be made strategically, based on a thorough analysis. With the growing popularity of online retailing, fashion brands can choose to reenter a market only online. For example, American casual wear brand Gap Inc. reentered the German market only online, partnering with Zalando, after two attempts with its traditional mono-brand brick-and-mortar store strategy, with retreats in the 1980s and 1990s and a final withdrawal in 2004 (Clifford and Alderman, 2011; Tran, 2015). Italian jeans brand Replay reentered India online through Flipkart and Myntra in 2014 eight years after its exit (Bailay, 2018). Replay's initial entry into India was through a JV with the Future Group.

Fourth, fashion brands can choose to pursue multiple entry modes at the same time. For example, Gap Inc. entered China in 2010 by opening wholly owned Beijing and Shanghai stores and simultaneously operating online (Gap Inc., 2010). Just as many fashion brands choose an omnichannel strategy to provide consumers with diverse venues, firms can also choose a multichannel entry strategy for an international market. However, multichannel entry requires a significant level of investment; firms should make the decision after obtaining a comprehensive understanding of the market and their growth potential in that market (Lu et al., 2011).

Fifth, the choice of entry mode should be determined by considering its long-term impact on a fashion brand's equity. After all, the most important asset a fashion company has is brand equity, which takes some time to establish, but once lost, it is not easy to recover. As shown in the Pierre Cardin example earlier and the Burberry example in Case Study 8.1, firms' entry mode decisions should not be driven solely by the short-term goal of profit-making.

CASE STUDY 8.1

Two Sides of Licensing: The Case of Burberry in Japan

Burberry entered Japan in 1970 via a licensing agreement with Sanyo Shokai Ltd, which initially imported Burberry coats to Japan beginning in 1965. Entering Japan with a licensing agreement made sense at the time because this gave Burberry a foothold in a foreign market where it lacked distribution networks or local expertise, not to mention the considerable financial gains incurred from the royalties collected from each sale. Under the licensing agreement, Sanyo Shokai built Burberry brand's business in Japan by independently opening physical outlets and developing products. Fully capitalizing on the autonomy endowed by the licensing agreement, Sanyo Shokai created two labels tailored to local preferences to be marketed and sold exclusively in Japan: Burberry Blue Label brand for women and Burberry Black Label for men (Fasol, 2015). The products were much more affordable than those in the global Burberry collection. Women's shirts were priced as low as $70, compared with around $250 for a cotton blouse from the global Burberry collection (Chu and Megumi, 2015).

The licensing deal generated about $800 million in sales and brought Burberry $80 million in royalties annually (Chu and Megumi, 2015). Thanks to the licensing deal, Burberry could achieve exceptionally high brand awareness and growth in a market where many other luxury brands were seeing tepid growth, relative to China. The products sold at more affordable price points were, however, at odds with the brand's luxury positioning. By 2006, Burberry had 23 licensees around the world and was already suffering from brand dilution due to these extensive licensing deals. Burberry's years of licensing agreements in foreign markets resulted in disparately branded and priced products, from dog outfits to Scotch whisky (Chu and Megumi, 2015). In 2009, as part of its efforts to regain control of its image as a luxury brand, Burberry opened its first directly operated standalone store in Tokyo, Japan, that offered its global collections (Burberry Prorsum, London and Brit), alongside the Black and Blue labels (Imran, 2015).

Six years later, Burberry decided to completely transform its business model in Japan into a direct model by discontinuing the licensing deal altogether and directly operating its standalone stores and concessions. In June 2015, Burberry prematurely terminated its licensing agreement with Sanyo Shokai that was meant to expire in 2020 (Fasol, 2015), even though the termination of the licensing deal would shrink Burberry's presence in Japan from nearly 400 stores to about two dozen (Chu and Megumi, 2015). In the short term, Burberry saw some loss in revenue, but in the long term the brand expects to achieve its creative and commercial potential by delivering consistent global product offerings and branding.

Discussion Questions

1. Why did Burberry terminate its licensing contract with Sanyo Shokai Ltd. five years before the expiration date?
2. What are the gains and losses involved for Burberry in its licensing agreement in Japan?

3. What can brands do to reap the benefits of licensing while minimizing the risks?
4. Is licensing a riskier strategy for some brands more than others? If so, what are the characteristics of brands that need to be particularly wary of the potential risks?

References

Chu, K. and Megumi, F. (2015, August 14). Burberry revamps its image in Japan. *The Wall Street Journal.* www.wsj.com/articles/burberry-revamps-its-image-in-japan-1439547804

Fasol, G. (2015, August 18). Burberry solves its "Japan problem", at least for now. Japan Strategy. www.japanstrategy.com/2015/08/18/burberry-mackintosh-san-yo-shokai

Imran, A. (2015, July 27). How Burberry is rebuilding its Japan business. Business of Fashion. www.businessoffashion.com/articles/bof-exclusive/bof-exclusive-how-burberry-is-rebuilding-its-japan-business

Summary

- After the market to enter is chosen, firms need to decide how they will enter the country. Firms can choose from various entry modes: export, contract entry (licensing and franchising), or investment entry (joint venture, concession, flagship store, acquisition, and wholly owned subsidiary).

- In making the decision, firms should consider the level of resources they can commit, the level of control they desire, and how much strategic flexibility they want to retain. For example, exporting is the least resource commitment a firm can make to enter a market, but in return it brings the least control to the company.

- Each entry mode has its pros and cons, which should be considered. Firms should make any entry mode decision carefully because once resources are committed, the decision becomes difficult to change, and a divestment decision may result in a huge loss to the company and brand image. Thus, firms are encouraged to test an international market before making a significant investment. Internet sales and pop-up stores can be feasible ways through which to test a market.

- Along with the risk and resource commitment involved, firms should also consider the host government's control over foreign investments, the market potential for their products, and the level of competition in a host country. Because of these varying factors across countries, firms do not employ the same entry modes for every country they enter.

- Firms may increase their resource commitment within a country as they gain knowledge about consumers, culture, and market. It also depends on the company's strategic direction and a host government's lifting of regulations.

Class Activities

1. Discuss how a fashion firm can test a foreign market prior to entry.
2. Discuss the criteria for selecting an ideal partner for licensing, franchising, and joint ventures. (Hint: Why does a fashion firm choose each of the entry modes?)

Key Terms

- **Exporting:** Sending goods or services to an international market for sale without establishing an offline or online retail presence. Involves the lowest resource commitment among all entry options. Exporting can be either indirect or direct.
- **Indirect export:** A fashion firm sells its products to intermediaries who then sell to buyers in a foreign market.
- **Direct export:** A fashion firm sells its goods directly to buyers in target countries.
- **Contractual entry mode:** An entry mode that requires a contract. Licensing and franchising are contractual entry modes.
- **Licensing:** Contractual entry mode in which a licensor (a company that owns intangible property) grants a licensee (a company in a foreign country) the right to use the property (brand name) for a specified period.
- **Franchising:** Contractual entry mode in which a franchisor supplies a franchisee in a foreign country with its retail format and provides other assistance (operations) over an extended period.
- **Joint venture:** Establishment of a new firm combining a firm in a company's home country with a firm in a host country to achieve a common business objective. Both companies share ownership.
- **Concessions:** Establishing a shop within a shop, usually a department store in a foreign country.
- **Flagship store:** A company-owned, large-scale store designed to showcase its brand, typically established in a prime location in a metropolitan city. An investment entry mode.
- **Acquisition:** An investment entry mode in which a firm acquires control over a firm in the international market.
- **Wholly owned subsidiary:** A subsidiary in a foreign country that a parent company entirely owns: highest level of resource investment a fashion firm can make.
- **Big-box retailer:** Offers a large variety of products in a huge space, such as Walmart and Tesco. Typically, mass retailers that focus on high volume at low price.
- **Organic growth:** A firm expands gradually by adding new stores within an existing framework or integrated into an organization.

Developing Global Marketing Strategies

PART 4

Subsequent to two major decisions—where to enter (market entry decision) and how to enter (entry mode decision)—fashion companies then need to develop their marketing mix accordingly. Part 4 consists of five chapters, starting with brand management for global markets and then moving on to the discussion of global marketing strategies as outlined by the marketing 4Ps: product development (Chapter 10), price (Chapter 11), place of distribution (Chapter 12), and promotion (communication, Chapter 13).

CHAPTER 9
Brand Management for Global Markets

Learning Objectives

After studying this chapter, you will be able to:

- Articulate the types and benefits of global brands and consumer proposition of each type of global brand.
- Explain the strategic global brand management process.
- Describe the consumer culture positioning options available to global fashion companies.
- Discuss country of origin (COO), country image, and the relevance of each for global fashion brand management.

Global brands have a power over local brands in many aspects. Consider some well-known global brands such as Coca-Cola, Apple, and Starbucks. Everywhere you see the same product, the same store atmosphere, and the same service. At Starbucks, you can expect the same cup of coffee you enjoy in the US in all other countries you visit. Similarly, for global fashion brands such as Levi's, Nike, and Louis Vuitton, you see the same products in other countries. By having consistent brand images across the countries, global brands have numerous advantages; so it is a desirable goal for many fashion companies to develop strong global brands.

This chapter is devoted to understanding the process of global fashion brand management. Consumers expect the same brand image across countries. Therefore, brand management at the global level—seeing the global market as one—and developing marketing strategies through segmentation (S), targeting (T), and positioning (P) are critical processes. While brand image consistency across countries is emphasized, brands may adapt different positioning strategies according to the market competition and economic development status of host markets (developed vs. developing countries). This chapter explains the STP marketing strategies and a particular positioning strategy—consumer cultural positioning—with examples of global fashion brands. Lastly, in global brand management, the origin of brands is crucial. The country effects, specifically the Country of Origin (COO) effect and country image effect, have been extensively studied in the literature. Although the relevance of the COO effect may be weaker in today's global marketplace, consumer perceptions of the notion are still relevant, so it will be discussed.

Types and Benefits of Global Brands

Global vs. Local Brands

If you see a certain brand only in one country, that brand is a local brand. A local brand achieves success in a single national market. It presents the lifeblood of domestic companies and established local brands serve as a significant competitive critical hurdle to global companies. In contrast, if a particular brand operates in many countries, that brand is a global brand. A global brand has the same name and similar image worldwide. Having a market presence in two countries as opposed to fifty-five countries will definitely create a different consumer perception toward the brand. That is, the more countries in which you see the brand, the stronger brand globalness the brand presents. Luxury brands are mostly global brands targeting the same segment with the same positioning and pricing strategies across the world, although there may be a certain level of localization.

Global brands have concrete advantages over local brands in the global marketplace in terms of consumer preference, marketing, and operations. More and more companies are moving toward global brand positioning because consumers seem to exhibit a certain fondness toward global brands over local competitors, even though quality and values may not be objectively greater (Steenkamp et al., 2003). It is because global brands confer a sense of status and prestige for consumers that signal quality and convey the image of being a part of global culture. When you consume Nike products, you feel like you are part of a global culture, as many consumers in other countries will use the same products.

Fundamentally, global brands extend the products and services proven to be successful in a domestic market into other countries, thus saving the many costs associated with marketing and operations. Although some modifications may be needed, global brands are more likely to use the same marketing campaigns. Moreover, development costs can be saved as the same products and services apply to other markets. With strong global brand name recognition, it is easy to build brand awareness in other countries, which enhances efficiency and saves introduction costs (Steenkamp, 2017).

Types of Global Brands

Most luxury brands are global brands, but this does not mean that global brands are always high-end. Mass brands such as L'Oréal Paris are also global brands. Global brands can be classified into five categories from the lowest to the highest price points. Each brand has different targets, value positioning, and challenges (Steenkamp, 2017). The distinction between a value brand and a fun brand may be unclear, because of similar target consumers and price points. However, the major difference between the two is "brand appeal"; a fun brand appeals with fun and stimulation while the value brand focuses on acceptable quality at the lowest price. The five categories are as follows:

1. *Value brands* (e.g., Uniqlo and IKEA)
   - Value positioning: Acceptable quality at lowest price
   - Challenges: Customer loyalty and low price positioning are factors that may not work well globally.
2. *Fun brands* (e.g., Zara, H & M and swatch)
   - Value positioning: Lifestyle, enjoyment, and stimulation targeting global youth
   - Challenges: Popularity declining in many countries because of concerns around corporate social responsibility and environmental sustainability.
3. *Mass brands* (e.g., Levi's and L'Oréal Paris)
   - Value positioning: High quality with above-average pricing targeting the middle classes (but note that Levi's is positioned as high-end in some countries)
   - Challenges: This middle position makes them vulnerable to attacks from the brands priced above and below.
4. *Premium brands* (e.g., Lululemon Athletica and Patagonia)
   - Value positioning: Top-notch quality tailored for highly engaged consumers, delivering emotional benefits at a premium price point.
   - Challenges: Sustained breakthroughs in research and development are essential to uphold a premium status.
5. *Prestige brands* (e.g., Hermès and Loro Piana).
   - Value positioning: Social distinction and scarcity targeting the global elite with very high prices
   - Challenges: Maintaining scarcity.

Strategic Global Brand Management Process

Brand management for the global market starts with the registration and establishment of the brand name, then the identification and establishment of brand positioning and values. The next step is to plan and decide the level of standardization and localization and, lastly, to implement brand marketing programs (Figure 9.1). Major points of difference from domestic branding include the establishment or development of a new brand name in foreign countries and deciding on the degree of standardization and localization. While it would be ideal to use the same brand name across countries, any concerns around legality and meaning may require the development of a new brand name. In addition, the extent to which the marketing mix should be localized is a critical decision a fashion firm should make.

Global Brand Naming

As Chapter 5 specified, it is important to register brand names across countries even without an immediate entry plan. The same

Register and establish brand name for global markets
⬇
Identify and establish brand positioning and values
⬇
Plan and decide the level of standardization and localization
⬇
Implement brand marketing programs

Figure 9.1 Global strategic brand management process.

brand name can be registered in other countries unless there are legal and meaning issues. If the existence of the same or similar name in a host country, either in the same category or in different categories, confuses consumers, it needs to be changed, considering the nuances in local language. For example, T.J. Maxx, US-based off-price retailer, modified its name to T.K. Maxx when it entered the UK in 1994 to avoid confusion with a discount department store chain in the UK, T.J. Hughes, whose product offering—premium brands at discounted prices—was similar to T.J. Maxx. Now T.J. Maxx uses the T.K. Maxx name across Europe and Australia (Hanbury, 2018). Irish fashion retailer Primark's original name was Penneys but it had to change its name to Primark in the UK because JCPenney, the US department store, was already registered there (Hanbury, 2018). When Spanish fast fashion brand Mango launched in Australia in 2004, the brand name Mango already existed as a children's wear label owned by local company Best & Less (*Inside Retail*, 2013). Therefore, it was legally impossible to use the name Mango there; so Mango changed its brand name to MNG.

In non-English speaking countries, a brand name is written in the local languages, typically using phonetic equivalent. In Chinese, however, each word has its own meaning, so there could be about 200 characters that resemble the sound of each syllable. As a result, a new brand name should be created, considering both meaning and phonetic sounds in Chinese. This indicates that the Chinese brand name sounds like the original brand name, while its meaning conveys what the brand is offering. Good examples include:

Benetton (贝纳通): Bei na tong
贝: valuable
纳: meaningless (connector)
通: though

Clinique (倩碧): Qian bi
倩: Beautiful, elegant
碧: a color-bluish-green

Nike (耐克): Nai Ke
耐: endurance
克: overcome, subdue

The Face Shop (菲诗小铺): Fei shi xiao pu
菲: luxurious
诗: poetry
小: small, little
铺: shop

Chanel (香奈儿): Xiang nai er
香: scented, perfumed, fragrant
(others are meaningless)

Vetement (维特萌): Wei te meng
维: unique
特: special
萌: cute

If the company were careless in translating its brand name, it might have been translated into absurd phrase. High-end Italian brand Bottega Veneta's initial translation "Baotijia" (宝缇嘉) was already registered in mainland China, so the brand had to officially change its name to "Baodiejia" (葆蝶家) in 2013. However, this didn't sit well with its customers, as it could mean "a steep drop in price," which contradicted the brand's high-end image. Bottega Veneta stopped using the Chinese name on its official Chinese website and its social media channels in China (Chitrakorn, 2017). In order to present a unified brand image, some luxury brands avoid rebranding their names in China entirely. Similarly, global fashion brands such as Chanel and Nike mainly use their original English names to convey their global image even though they both have Chinese brand names.

Global STP Strategy

After the registration of a brand name in a host country, the next task is to establish the marketing strategy: segmentation (S), targeting (T), and positioning (P). The same STP strategy applies to global branding, but companies can choose a different segment yet position it as the same. With two target market options (similar or different) and two positioning appeals (similar or different), fashion companies have four possible scenarios (see Figure 9.2):

1. *Similar targets and similar positioning*: This case is truly global as it targets similar segments across countries with similar positioning themes. Nike is a good example of this strategy. It targets aspiring athletes using high-performance positioning across countries. Consequently, you will see similar products and advertisements wherever you go.
2. *Similar targets but different positioning*: This strategy keeps similar targets, while modifying the also positioning strategy. In the case of Levi's, while it maintains similar segments/targets (youth) across countries, it positions itself differently. In many countries, Levi's is positioned as high-end denim jeans and even perceived as a status symbol (see Chapter 11 for more comparisons). In contrast, in the US, it is positioned as casual denim jeans, not as a status symbol (Vrontis and Vronti, 2004). American jeans brand Lee also positions differently, offering high-quality products at higher prices in China. It is positioned with a cosmopolitan European image. For this, advertising campaigns feature major European cities such as Paris, London, and Rome, and products are distributed via luxury malls and standalone stores, as compared to Kohl's and JCPenney in the US. Lee designs totally different products for Chinese consumers in its Hong Kong office. For example, Jade Fusion, cool denim jeans for the summer time, is an innovation specifically developed for Chinese consumers. Similarly, American denim jeans brand Wrangler uses a very different positioning strategy in Europe. A pair of Wrangler jeans is about $160 in Europe, compared to $24 in the US. It offers much better quality in Europe, with W sign on the back pocket in Europe vs. no W sign in the US (Edmond Villano, 2020, November 4, personal communication).
3. *Different targets but similar positioning*: In this strategy, companies target different segments but use the same positioning. For example, IKEA primarily targets singles in the US, while newly married couples are the prime target in Europe (Johansson, 2009). In terms of positioning, IKEA offers affordable modern furniture pieces with an assemble yourself concept across all countries.
4. *Different targets and different positioning*: This strategy utilizes a true localization concept employing different targets and differing positioning in other countries. Levi's has developed a new brand, dENiZEN, for the Asian market, targeting a younger demographic with lower price points.

While the global STP strategy should be developed based on thorough research, its positioning could be changed later on if the initial positioning strategy is not working in the host country, which might be a costly decision.

		Target market	
		Similar	Different
Positioning	Similar	Nike	IKEA
	Different	Levi's, Lee, Wrangler	Levi's dENiZEN

Figure 9.2 Global STP strategy.

Global Marketing Mix Strategy Options

Once the global STP strategies are developed, the next step is to develop marketing mix strategies. As stated in Chapter 2, one of the important decisions for a fashion firm in doing global business is to decide the extent to which its marketing mix is to be modified. It is not a dichotomous decision, modify or not modify; it is about what marketing mix elements need to be modified and to what extent. As shown in Figure 2.3 (see p. 31), firms have several options and strategically choose the degree of modification. In theory, a globally standardized strategy is the best approach to consistently delivering the global value propositions to the target segment. It also saves time and resources by applying the same marketing mix across countries, thereby keeping the brand image consistent. However, in practice, standardization of the marketing mix (keeping all marketing elements the same) is often unrealistic. Consumers' body physique, taste regarding design and color, as well as attitude toward various advertising campaigns vary across countries, so fashion firms need to analyze these elements before deciding on the strategies. Chapters 10, 11, 12, and 13 are devoted to each of the four marketing mix elements in more detail.

Consumer Culture Positioning Strategy

Positioning is about locating a brand in consumers' minds over and against competitors with all the attributes and benefits the brand offers. So the key is to develop strong value propositions to distinguish the brand from competitors. Product attributes, such as use of sustainable materials (Patagonia), brand symbols (Burberry), unique services (Stitch Fix), and affordable quality at a reasonable price (Zara), are usually used to position themselves against competitors. Also, relevant to global fashion brand positioning is consumer culture positioning (CCP) strategy: the positioning of a brand as a symbol of a global, foreign, or local culture (Alden et al., 1999). The approach makes sense, in that, with globalization, there are global consumer segments that associate similar meanings with certain places and people. In other words, with common symbols and meanings, a fashion company can position their brand as global, foreign, or local. Possible tools to position a brand as global, foreign, or local include, for example, the pronunciation of the brand name, symbols used and/or spelling of visually displayed brand name, symbols used for brand logo, central themes, and appearance of spokesperson(s):

1. *Global CCP* identifies the brand as a symbol of a global culture or segment. Nike and Benetton use global CCP positioning. With the slogan, "United Colors of Benetton," Benetton emphasizes the unity of humankind, positioning the brand as a global culture. Benetton was an iconic Italian brand in the 1980s and 1990s, yet mainly uses English in its written and spoken communications worldwide to convey the global image. Italian culture and images were never emphasized in its communications. Similarly, Nike does not use its country's image; instead it emphasizes athletic bodies and features high-profile athletes and celebrities, and does not connect the brand with the American image although consumers may connect it with American culture. In this sense, global CCP may be more effective in developing countries because global image connotes enhanced status for them.

2. *Foreign CCP* is defined as a strategy that positions the brand as a symbol of a specific foreign consumer culture. It associates the brand's users, use occasions, or product origins with a particular foreign country or culture. IKEA emphasizes its Swedish origin to position the brand as Swedish (foreign). Its brand logo has the same colors as the Swedish flag and it offers Swedish cookies and dishes at IKEA stores. The Chinese luxury fashion brand Shang Xia—the name literally means "up-down" in Chinese—also uses foreign CCP, with its brand name sounding Chinese and its logo composed of two Chinese characters "up-down." In this way, the brand positions itself as Chinese (foreign).

3. *Local CCP* associates the brand with local cultural meaning, reflects the local culture's norms and identities, and portrays it as consumed by local people. It uses local culture and history in brand naming and positions it as locally produced with local ingredients and artisan techniques in product development. Good examples of local CCP include L'Occitane en Provence, Acqua di Parma, and Bottega Veneta, where a local language emphasizes a particular local name. The name of the French luxury body and skin care brand L'Occitane en Provence means "the Occitan women in Provence" in French. Occitania existed during the Middle Ages and Provence is a geographical region and historical province of southeastern France. The brand stresses the use of sustainably sourced, local ingredients providing high quality. The name of the Italian fragrance brand Acqua di Parma means "water from Parma" in Italian, the name emphasizing the northern Italian city of Parma, where the brand originated in 1916. The brand range now extends to candles, bathrobes, and leather accessories, all exclusively made in Italy. To emphasize its localness, the brand's logo is the coat of arms of Marie Louise, Duchess of Parma, who ruled from 1816 to 1847. The name of Italian luxury brand Bottega Veneta means "Venetian shop" in Italian, and it was founded in 1966 in Vicenza, Veneto, a region in Italy of which the capital is Venice; thus its origins are echoed in its name. It prides itself on its craftmanship, and its popularity (and high price) is derived from its leather weaving technique called *intrecciato* (meaning "braided" in English).

All the examples cited above are global brands. Yet they position themselves with either global, foreign, or local consumer cultures in the global marketplace, utilizing the pronunciation of the brand name (Shang Xia, L'Occitane en Provence, and Acqua di Parma), symbols used and/or spelling of visually displayed brand name (color of IKEA brand logo), symbols used for brand logo (coat of arms in Acqua di Parma), and central themes (United Colors of Benetton).

Country of Origin and Country Image for Global Fashion Brand Management

Country of Origin (COO)

In managing brands in the global marketplace, the brand's country of origin often influences the image of the brand and serves as a quality cue, especially when consumers are unfamiliar with the brand name. For example, Italy is known for its fashion image, so apparel products bearing the words "Made in Italy" create a favorable image among global consumers when the brand is unknown. This is called the country of origin (COO) effect. Originally, COO indicated the country where the product was made, so the COO effect is defined as any influence that the country of manufacture has on a consumer's positive or negative perception of a product. This is because a manufacturing country has been the same as the brand's country of origin, such as Prada products made in Italy. The COO effect is more pronounced if a product is more expensive, durable, or involves some type of risk (health, social). The COO effect changes as the country advances economically. For example, apparel items bearing the words "Made in Korea" were considered to be low quality in the 1970s and 1980s in the US, but they are rarely available in the US apparel market today. If it exists, it is least likely to be associated with low quality.

Country Image: How It Is Different from Country of Origin

Today, with the widespread practice of global sourcing, the COO effect becomes less relevant in evaluating a product than before. This is because Prada products, for example, are often made in China. Made in a country (such as China) is not the same as brand origin (such as Italy). Thus, studies started to distinguish the country image effect from the COO effect, while some studies still use COO and country image interchangeably. Country image is defined as consumers' overall beliefs regarding a particular country's various features, such as economics, society, people, and products (Josiassen et al., 2013). Country image has two dimensions: macro and micro country image. Macro country image is the overall perception of the country in terms of economics, people, or technology, while micro country image accounts for the perception about a country for a specific product category (Pappu et al., 2007); thus, micro country image varies by product category. The micro country image effect is potentially great in a product category for which the country is known, such as French perfume, Italian leather, and Chinese silk. One study found that the effects of macro and micro country images differ by product category. In symbolic goods such as handbags, both macro and micro country images are equally important to the purchase intention, while only micro country image plays a greater role in the purchase intention of functional goods (cell phones) (Jin et al., 2018). This denotes the overarching influence of country image for fashion products.

Traditionally, one brand had only a single country image because, for example, an Italian brand was owned by an Italian company and manufactured in Italy. However, as cross-border merger and acquisition and offshoring practices become more common, one apparel item may involve multiple country images. Take a Valentino dress as an example. It has the images of three countries: Valentino's brand origin is Italy (COB, country of brand), but it is owned by a company in Qatar (COC, country of company) and made in China (COM, country of manufacturing). Which country image will be stronger in evaluating an apparel item: COB, COM, or COC? The former COO effect is, in fact, now the COM effect, which is seen to be less strong than before, thanks to the now ubiquitous practice of global sourcing. This notion is graphically described in Figure 9.3. The place of manufacture (that is, COO or COM effect) still affects purchase decision and may be stronger in emerging markets where products or brands from industrialized countries are preferred (Batra et al., 2000; Pappu et al., 2007; Wang and Chen, 2004).

Foreign Branding

Because of the overarching effect of country image, fashion companies often employ foreign branding to reap the benefits from a certain country (see Box 9.1). You will probably be surprised to learn that the actual brand origin country is not what you think. Because of the effect of country image on product evaluation, fashion companies intentionally create brand names to associate with a certain country. This strategy is called "foreign branding"—the use of foreign or foreign-sounding brand names to imply that they are of foreign origin to gain specific effects from the country image (Aichner et al., 2017; Leclerc et al., 1994). Foreign branding can affect consumers' perceptions and attitudes (Leclerc et al., 1994), serving as a popular tool in both developed and emerg-

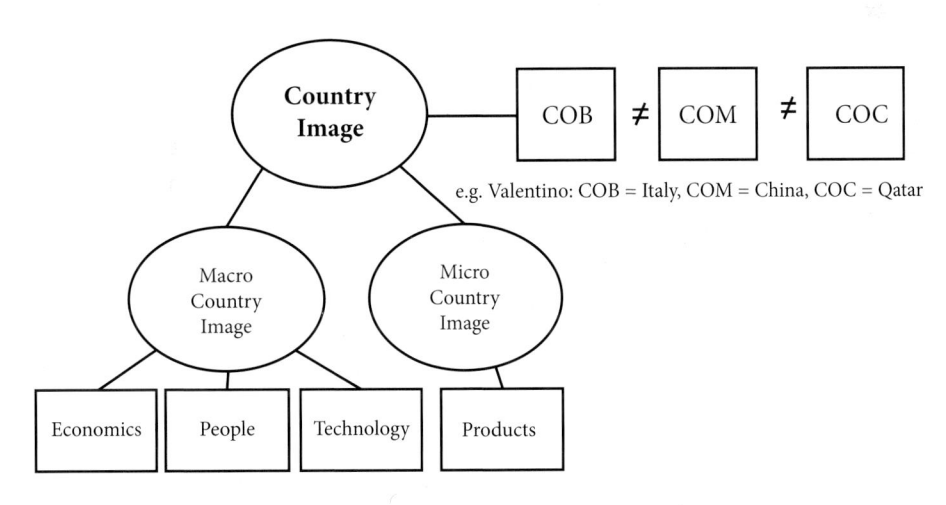

Figure 9.3 Country image: its concepts and dimensions.
Source: Modified by the author based on Woo (2016).

ing countries that propose a certain country to evoke specific product qualities (Melnyk et al., 2012). In particular, companies in emerging countries increasingly develop brand names in foreign languages with the hope that this foreign image can create the perception of higher brand quality and a greater social status (Melnyk et al., 2012). Products were perceived to be much more hedonistic when the brand name was pronounced in French as opposed to English (Leclerc et al., 1994). It is not uncommon to see many fashion and cosmetic brands use French- or Italian-sounding names. For example, Japanese fashion brand Issey Miyake uses French names for its perfume lines, such as L'Eau Bleu and La Crème de L'Eau, to emphasize hedonic elegance and seductive characteristics by leveraging certain associations with French brands (Melnyk et al., 2012).

BOX 9.1
Foreign Branding Quiz

From brand names and logos, we often associate a brand with a certain country. From which country do the following brands originate? Discuss what makes you think the brand is from that country.

Tod's: _____
Descente: _____
Dr. Jart+: _____
Giordano: _____
Le Tigre: _____
Tumi: _____

CASE STUDY 9.1
Tommy Hilfiger's Different Positioning across Countries

US fashion brand Tommy Hilfiger is a globally recognizable brand dedicated to classic American style, with a modern twist. Its product range includes womenswear, menswear, kids wear, cosmetics, accessories, and perfumes. By 2022, Tommy Hilfiger had approximately 2,000 retail stores in 100 countries around the world.

Once considered a premium American brand, Tommy Hilfiger has lost its cachet in the US over the past decade. The principal designer Tommy Hilfiger acknowledged that the brand grew so quickly that the US market was oversaturated and diluted the brand. The brand sees expansion to Europe and Asia as an opportunity to build a premium fashion label (Hall, 2018). To build the premium image, for example, in Singapore, the brand strategically chose high-end locations next to Saint Laurent and Ted Baker (Segran, 2016). In China, the brand offers higher quality and is sold in standalone stores and department stores at higher prices than in the US (Allison, 2021). The premium positioning strategy continues in Europe. The brand can be seen at high-end department stores such as La Rinascente in Italy and it has a flagship store in a prime location in London.

As a comparison, in the US, the brand is widely available through Macy's and outlet stores at an affordable price. With its global strategy, the brand's growth comes from international sales, which accounted for 4 percent overall year-on-year growth. Asia contributed 9 percent of its revenues in 2017 (Hall, 2018), while North American revenues decreased by 5 percent (Segran, 2016).

Discussion Questions

1. How is Tommy Hilfiger positioned differently across the globe? What strategies does the brand use to position the brand differently?
2. Evaluate Tommy Hilfiger's global positioning strategy. Do the premium strategies in Asia and Europe continuously work? What does the brand need to do to keep the premium image in global markets?

References

Han, A. (2021, November 18). Tommy Hilfiger in China: Digital marketing and celebrity endorsements. *Daxue Consulting*. https://daxueconsulting.com/tommy-hilfiger-in-china/

Hall, C. (2018, September 3). Tommy Hilfiger's pivot to Asia. *Business of Fashion*. www.businessoffashion.com/articles/china/tommy-hilfigers-pivot-to-asia/

Segran, E. (2016, October 27). How Tommy Hilfiger is reimagining this brand. *Fast Company*. www.fastcompany.com/3064125/how-tommy-hilfiger-is-reimagining-his-brand

Summary

- Global brand refers to a brand known and sold in many parts of the world, typically with the same name and similar brand image, whereas a local brand is only available locally.
- Global brands achieve various benefits by keeping brand image consistent across countries.
- The global brand management process starts with the registration of brand names in a host country, then establishes a target market strategy including segmentation (S), targeting (T), and positioning (P) plans and determines the level of standardization and localization, and, lastly, implements brand marketing programs.
- It is important to register brand names across countries even without an immediate entry plan because, once taken, different brand names should be used. Spanish brand Mango operates under the name MNG in Australia, as the brand name Mango already existed there.
- The STP strategy applies to global branding, but companies can choose to segment and position it differently or target a different segment but position it as the same.
- In theory, a globally standardized strategy is the best approach to consistently delivering the global value propositions to the target segment. It also saves time and resources by applying the same marketing mix across countries, thereby keeping the brand image consistent. However, in practice, standardization of the marketing mix (keeping all

marketing mix elements the same) is often unrealistic. One of the important decisions for a fashion firm in doing global business is to decide the extent to which its marketing mix is modified.

- One of the global brand positioning strategies, consumer culture positioning (CCP) strategy identifies a brand as a symbol of global, foreign, or local culture by using common symbols and meanings. This CCP strategy includes three positioning levels: global CCP, foreign CCP, and local CCP. Global CCP identifies a brand as a symbol of global culture or segment without using the particular country's culture or image. Foreign CCP positions the brand as a symbol of a specific foreign consumer culture, while associating the brand with a particular foreign country or culture. Local CCP links a brand to localness by relating the brand to a particular local culture or history.

- In managing global brands, the brand's country of origin is important because it affects the brand image and serves as a quality clue. However, the country of origin (COO) (made in country image) effect has weakened due to extensive global sourcing practices.

- The country image effect has more relevance in product evaluation than the COO effect. Leveraging the country image effect, fashion companies often use foreign branding.

- Foreign branding is a strategy that uses foreign language or foreign-sounding brand names to connect to a country image to create positive product evaluation. The use of French- or Italian-sounding names is common in the fashion industry. An example includes Issey Miyake's L'Eau Bleu for his perfume line.

Class Activities

1. Find examples of *foreign* consumer culture positioning among global fashion and beauty brands and discuss how the brands position their brands as foreign.

2. Find examples of *local* consumer culture positioning among global fashion and beauty brands and discuss how the brands position their brands as local.

3. Search for local fashion companies in your country that utilize a foreign branding strategy and discuss the pros and cons of the strategy.

4. Global fashion brands often use different positioning strategies in other countries. Discuss the pros and cons of this approach.

Key Terms

- **Global brand:** A brand known and sold in many parts of the world typically with the same name and brand image.
- **Local brand:** A brand that operates only in a single country.
- **Global brand management process:** Process of managing a brand globally. The process starts with registering brand names in a host country, establishing brand positioning and values, planning and determining the level of standardization and localization, and implementing brand marketing programs.
- **Global brand naming:** Means changing the name in consideration of local linguistic nuances and meanings to prevent consumer confusion.
- **Consumer culture positioning:** Positioning a brand as a symbol of global, foreign, or local culture.
- **Global consumer culture positioning:** Identifies a brand as a symbol of global culture or segment without using the culture or image of a specific country.
- **Foreign consumer culture positioning:** Positions a brand as a symbol of a specific foreign consumer culture.
- **Local consumer culture positioning:** Relates the brand to a particular local culture reflecting the local culture's norms and identities.
- **Country of origin (COO) effect:** A country where the product was made, defined as any influence the country of manufacture has on a consumer's positive or negative perception of a product. The COO effect is more pronounced when it is an expensive product, durable, or accompanied by health or social risks.
- **Country image:** Consumers' general beliefs about diverse features of a specific country, including economics, society, people, and products. Country image has two dimensions: macro and micro country image. It is different from the COO effect but often used interchangeably.
- **Country of manufacturing:** The country where the brand's products are manufactured.
- **Country of brand origin:** The country from which a brand originates.
- **Country of company:** The country where the company that owns the brand is actually located.
- **Foreign branding:** Branding strategy that uses foreign or foreign-sounding brand names in order to achieve a specific effect from a certain country's image.

Answers to Box 9.1 Quiz

Tod's: *Italian* luxury shoes and handbags
Descente: *Japanese* sports clothing and accessories
Dr. Jart+: *Korean* cosmetics

Giordano: *Hong Kong* casual wear brand
Le Tigre: *American* sportswear brand
Tumi: *American* brand of high-end suitcases and bags for travel

CHAPTER 10
Product Development for Global Markets

Learning Objectives

After studying this chapter, you will be able to:

- Explain the importance of offering products and services suitable for the global market.
- Illustrate why the same products for domestic markets are not selling well in other countries and possible reasons and occasions for product adaptation.
- Articulate the significance of developing culturally appropriate products.
- Discuss multiple approaches of product localization for global markets.

Unlike other consumer goods, consumer tastes regarding fashion items are very different even within the domestic market. Imagine satisfying the fashion needs of global consumers who live in different economic, cultural, geographic, and religious environments. Offering the same products (standardization) works to a certain extent but global consumers expect fashion brands to pay attention to their particular needs and tastes. After introducing the importance of offering products suitable for the global market, this chapter highlights offering culturally appropriate products, with examples of prior failures. The extent of product adaptation can be wide, from adding care instructions and size labels in the language of the host country to developing entirely new products for the market. The extent will be detailed with actual examples.

The Importance of Offering Products and Services Suitable for Global Markets

For global fashion marketers, whether a firm's products can be sold in their present form or whether they need to be adapted to foreign markets is an important decision to make. If the same products designed for domestic consumers sell well in foreign markets without any modifications (standardization), it can save time and resources leveraging economies of scale (see Chapter 2 for the benefits of standardization and adaptation). In practice, however, something has to be changed to be relevant for foreign markets, even small changes such as size and care labels in the language of host countries.

Some products cannot be sold at all in foreign markets without modification, known as "mandatory adaptation." An example of mandatory adaptation is ensuring the electronic goods have the correct voltage for the specific location where they are sold. In the fashion industry, one good example of mandatory adaptation is alcohol-free perfumes for Muslim countries as the Quran bans alcohol consumption. However, some Muslim countries may allow perfumes containing a small quantity of alcohol.

Discretionary adaptation, in contrast, occurs when fashion companies choose to tailor their products specifically to market needs in order to gain greater acceptance. In this case, firms can choose to make certain adaptations or not to do so. In the fashion business, most adaptations are discretionary, so this section focuses on discretionary adaptation. Discretionary modification includes modifying product design or choosing the right products for the local market, according to culture, season, religion, and economic development level.

Modification Addressing Culture

Addressing host countries' culture with product changes or new development, fashion companies can effectively appeal to the consumers. Certain objects and symbols have cultural connotations. One Danish jewelry company found that amber is an auspicious gem believed by Chinese consumers to bring luck, happiness, health, and security. Based on this understanding, the company developed more products with amber achieving remarkable success (Jin et al., 2018). Cosmetic companies can better address the needs of Muslim consumers or even create demand if they develop products with halal certification. Halal (meaning "permissible" or "lawful" in Arabic) certification is strictly required for food categories, but it is not universally enforced in cosmetics. To be halal certified, cosmetics must not contain any parts of forbidden animals, such as pigs and dogs, must be handled with clean utensils, and must be made with materials not harmful to humans. These requirements necessarily increase development costs. Yet Japanese cosmetic brand Shiseido modified its product offering in Malaysia by creating a sub-brand, Za, and selling 28 halal skincare products. US cosmetic brand Estée Lauder listed several halal products on the Muslim consumer group website (Chitrakorn, 2015).

Cultural sensibilities toward sexual images vary as well. While the sexual images of US lingerie brand Victoria's Secret are accepted in the domestic market, the same products were perceived as too sexy when it first tried to enter China in 2014. Chinese consumers initially viewed Victoria's Secret products as "not good wife material." Consequently, Victoria's Secret only carried accessories and beauty products, and lingerie was not sold until 2018 when sexuality was more accepted. In addition, the brand only aired its TV commercials in the middle of the night to limit exposure to customers (Chen, 2018). In this case, companies need to understand how their current products will be viewed and interpreted in host countries and either modify or select more appropriate products for their culture, as Victoria's Secret did.

Modification Addressing Season

Products developed for domestic markets may not be suitable for a season in host countries. For example, the seasons in the Southern hemisphere are opposite to those of the Northern hemisphere, so fashion brands need to carry the right products for their seasons. Forever 21 exited the Australian market after only three years of operation there. One reason was offering the same seasonal clothes as in the US, resulting in Australian consumers finding summer clothes in stores during their winter. In contrast, Zara developed different seasonal products especially for the Australian market (Dishman, 2012). Likewise, when Brazil's women's clothing brand Farm Rio entered the US market, it had to diversify its product line to include fall, winter, and spring collections since Brazil experiences year-round summer, and the brand initially only offered summer products (Chen, 2022).

Modification Addressing Religion

In Muslim countries, it is the norm for women not to expose their arms and legs, so modest clothes that cover their bodies are needed, including hijabs. However, it would be a mistake to assume that all Muslim countries are the same. Indonesia, home to the world's largest Muslim population, has little in common with the fashion preferences of women in Saudi Arabia and the United Arab Emirates (UAE). While covering the body is the same, Indonesian women wear colorful dress while women in the Gulf region wear darker monotone dress (Palmer, 2018). Fashion companies have to carefully study the diversity found in Muslim countries and connect with them when modifying products to satisfy the modest fashion needs of this growing demographic.

Modification Addressing Economic Development Level

The needs of consumers in economically advanced countries are different from those in less developed countries. Consumers in mature economies tend to be fickle and expect more for their money; it is also hard to satisfy them with good design and function alone. Product innovation with new materials, such as Nike's breathable Dri-Fit sportswear range, and innovative services, such as Stitch Fix and The RealReal, create major competitive advantages. Consumers' expectations continue to rise, and they demand ever-higher quality and improved service at competitive prices. Much of the real satisfaction in mature markets, which is essential for customer loyalty and positive word of mouth, comes with emotional or hedonic factors. Many reputable global brands, therefore, focus on creating an enjoyable shopping experience, such as Nike and REI (Recreational Equipment Inc.). In the US, Nike's flagship store in New York city offers a customized experience such as adaptable lighting in the fitting room to simulate the environment for various athletic endeavors such as a night run or a yoga studio (Childs and Jin, 2017). Nike's newest retail concept, Nike Style, opened in Seoul in 2022, offering blended physical and digital experiences such as augmented reality experiences (Fitzgerald, 2022). Meanwhile, in the REI Seattle and Denver stores, consumers can test climbing gear in a real rock-climbing facility in the store (www.rei.com).

In contrast, consumers in emerging markets are more likely to pay attention to well-known brand names. Unlike more mature markets, domestic products tend to be seen as less desirable, even though their functional performance may be superior. Foreign brands are preferred and viewed as a status symbol. Therefore, to satisfy their needs, products can be developed with more symbolic features for those markets. In terms of service, probably because of abundant labor, a greater number of sales associates assist customers in retail stores in emerging markets. Similarly, the do-it-yourself concept is not common. When IKEA entered India in 2018, it modified its service level and started to offer on-site assembly services, a first for IKEA, because the do-it-yourself concept was new to Indian customers (Shoulberg, 2018). In less developed economies, consumer needs tend to be basic and easy to identify. For global fashion brands, therefore, the less economically developed a market is, the greater degree of product change may be needed for consumer acceptance.

Developing Culturally Appropriate Products

Now that we have learned the importance of developing products and services suitable for global markets, we turn to examine possible pitfalls for global brands resulting from a lack of cultural understanding. Such pitfalls have resulted in boycotts and protests and global brands have had to take action to remedy their mistakes. The essence is that products for global consumers should not create any bad associations with any cultural symbols.

Use of National Flag in Product Design: Not Suitable for Some Countries

While designing with flag themes or colors is acceptable or even desired to celebrate certain days such as Independence Day (July 4) in the US, the same does not apply to all countries. Puma created limited edition sneakers in the colors of the UAE flag to celebrate the country's 40th National Day in 2011. However, the shoes were perceived as an insult and disrespectful to UAE consumers, because the flag is a sacred symbol for them, so should not be trivialized by putting it on shoes, which are considered as dirty, being on the ground. All in all, it was poorly thought-through, and a culturally insensitive blunder. Puma apologized to UAE consumers and removed the shoes from all stores (see Further Reading) (Elwazer, 2011; George, 2011).

Slogans on a Hooded Sweatshirt Perceived as Racism: Interpretation May Differ by Countries

People wear T-shirts or hoodies with a short phrase that conveys important messages or just fun phrases. Some phrases, however, can result in unexpected reactions in certain markets. One of the images on the H&M website in South Africa showed a Black child wearing a hooded sweatshirt that said: "Coolest Monkey in the Jungle" (see Further Reading). South African consumers were outraged, viewing it as racism because they thought H&M was intentionally comparing Black people with monkeys. This resulted in serious protests at various

H&M stores in the country. Mannequins were toppled, racks overturned, and merchandise scattered. H&M closed all its stores temporarily to protect its employees and prevent further damage (Kaye, 2018). As seen in this case, people do not always attach the same meaning to the same phrases.

Graphics Could Resemble Important Symbols: Be Aware

Creative graphics on products can accidentally resemble important symbols or words, which can cause big problems. This happened to Nike regarding a pair of shoes. The 1997 incident happened when the word "air" written in flaming letters on Nike's basketball (Air Bakin) shoes resembled the Arabic word for Allah or God. The graphic offended Muslims in America who boycotted the shoes. Nike apologized and recalled 38,000 pairs of shoes worldwide, discontinued the line, and introduced a review panel into its development process to prevent any similar problems in the future (Jury, 1997). Yet another similar mistake happened in 2019. This time, the words "Air Max" spelled out on the sole of the Nike Air Max 270 shoe looked like Allah in Arabic. In Muslim culture, showing the sole of a shoe is seen as disrespectful and shoes are considered dirty. Nike was accused of blasphemy. A petition was launched, claiming that Nike was allowing God's name to be "trampled, kicked, and become soiled with mud or even filth"; it gained 6,000 signatures in a few hours. Responding to this, a Nike spokesperson said: "Nike respects all religions and we take concerns of this nature seriously" (Boyd, 2019)

(see Further Reading). Once again, stricter scrutiny of products at the development stage would seem to be called for, to test for cultural sensitivity. Nike is a famous global brand so it receives more media attention for these types of incidents, but the brand is not the only one that makes such mistakes.

As the above cases show, product development and marketing teams should study whether their products might convey unwanted meanings in other cultures and should examine if any parts of products could have negative connotations before selling their products globally. This is all essential in order to maintain brand reputation in the global marketplace.

Product Localization Approaches for Global Markets

In Chapter 2, we learned that adaptation or localization is not a yes or no question. It is a matter of degree, how much and what aspects need to be changed in which countries. Below, the degrees of product adaptation are introduced from smallest changes (a size or term modification) to the greatest changes (new brand development for certain markets). As addressed in Chapter 2, the terms "localization" and "adaptation" are used interchangeably in this book.

Localizing Size

Consumers cannot buy clothes that do not fit, even though the style, quality, and price are all good. Accordingly, if global fashion brands are able to modify just one aspect of a product, that should be size. This is because, without correct sizing, it will not sell. Body physiques vary greatly country to country. Asian body frames are much smaller than those of Americans, so the clothes designed for the shape of US consumers do not fit well for Asian consumers. Offering the right sizes to consumers in host countries is fundamental, yet many brands' failures in foreign markets are associated with sizing issues. US brand Banana Republic's failure in the UK market is ascribed to not offering UK sizing options. British fashion retailer Topshop filed for bankruptcy in 2019 after closing its 11 offline stores in the US because of not offering a plus-size line whereas its competitors like ASOS and Boohoo offer an extensive selection for plus-size consumers. British multinational retailer Marks & Spencer exited China in 2018 after ten years of operation there. Among the reasons cited was that its offerings were simply too big for smaller Chinese frames and that it did not include a Chinese sizing system on the label so consumers had a hard time finding the right size.

As seen in these cases, when it comes to localizing sizes, two aspects should be noted: offering sizes that fit consumers in host countries and communicating the right sizes so consumers can pick their sizes easily.

1. *Offering the right sizes for consumers in host countries*: Developing totally new clothes to accommodate different body physiques is costly, so one easy way is to add more sizes or not offer sizes that have only a low chance of being selected. For example, in Japan, Gap offers XXS, XS, S, M, and L to address smaller body frames, but it offers XS, S, M, L, XL, and XXL in the US. That is, size XXS is added to fit Japaneses consumers' smaller body shape and XL and XXL are not offered. American brand J.Crew added 000 and XXXS sizes in response to the requests of petite Asian consumers, especially in new stores in Hong Kong (Lee and Wang, 2014). Fashion brands may also need to modify their designs to cater to the shapes of consumers' feet in host countries. A leading Italian shoe manufacturer learned that Americans have thicker ankles and narrower, flatter feet than Italians. So it made appropriate changes in its designs to develop comfortable shoes for US customers.

2. *Communicating right sizes*: Another layer of complexity related to sizing is that each country has their own sizing systems. When an American, who typically wears a size 6, shops in Italy where sizing starts at 38, it can be puzzling to determine which size to try since there is no size 6. Table 10.1 shows the size comparison. If an American women's brand sells in Italy with its own size label (0, 2, 4, 6, 8), Italian consumers have no idea what sizes they need to pick. Therefore, many global fashion brands offer multiple size measurements on their labels covering major markets, as shown in Figure 10.1. Communicating size equivalence is even more important for online companies as consumers cannot try goods on.

Localizing Clothing Terms

Terms referring to clothing items are different even in countries using the same language. For example, athletic footwear has a variety of names, such as sneakers in the US and

Table 10.1 Women's apparel size conversion chart

S-M-L	USA	UK/AU/NZ	ITALY	FRANCE	GERMANY	JAPAN
S	2	6	38	34	32	7
S	4	8	40	36	34	9
M	6	10	42	38	36	11
M	8	12	44	40	38	13
L	10	14	46	42	40	15
L	12	16	48	44	42	17
XL/1X	14	18	50	46	44	19
1X/2X	16	20	52	48	46	21
2X	18	22	54	50	48	23
3X	20	24	56	52	50	25
3X	22	26	58	54	52	27
4X	24	28	60	56	54	29

Source: Sizeguide.net. (n.d.).

trainers in the UK, while in Australia and Canada runners is the commonly used term. A sweater is called a jumper in the UK (see Table 10.2). In this case, the signs in the store and on websites and hangtags should also be modified. Imagine how odd it may feel for UK consumers when they read "sweater" on the website when "jumper" is commonly used in the UK. These small modifications may not seem important, but using terms that are not used in the host market gives the impression that the brand does not pay enough attention to the consumers in that particular market.

Localizing Colors

Consumers' color preferences vary greatly even within a country. In the US, consumers in metro cities tend to wear monochromatic colors, whereas consumers in the Midwest seem to like bright colors. Fashion companies develop products accordingly, and retailers carry colors that their target consumers prefer. This notion continues in foreign markets. German consumers like darker colors than consumers in Spain (Segran, 2016). Chinese consumers are fond of red as it symbolizes luck, happiness, and joy in China (see Chapter 4), so more products with red color are offered to cater for their preferences. Together with the colors red and gold, the double happiness Chinese character and dragons are also used on products targeting consumers in China. However, the use of such traditional symbols is seen as clichéd and outdated among young Chinese consumers (Solca and Zhu, 2021). When Bulgari reentered India in 2014, nearly 20 percent of the products were tailored to local tastes, so they had more yellow gold as opposed to pink gold, which is popular in Western markets (Atwal and Bryson,

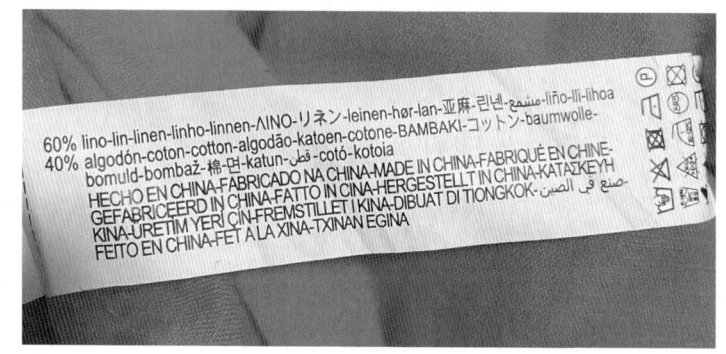

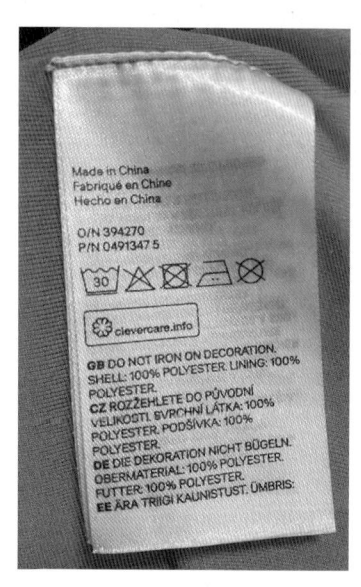

Figure 10.1 Sizes and care labels in multiple languages.
Source: Courtesy of B. Ellie Jin.

166 Part 4 Developing Global Marketing Strategies

Table 10.2 Different clothing terms in selected English-speaking countries

AMERICAN ENGLISH	CANADIAN ENGLISH	BRITISH ENGLISH	AUSTRALIAN ENGLISH
Pants	Pants	Trousers	Pants, Daks
Sweater	Sweater	Jumper	Jumper
Sneakers	Runners	Trainers	Runners
Swimsuit/bathing suit	Swimsuit	Swimming costume	Bathers
Bath robe	Housecoat	Dressing gown	Dressing gown

2017). Dior launched the "Dior Or" capsule collection in order to celebrate the holy month of Ramadan by imbuing the color gold into the apparel, shoes, and accessories (McClelland, 2022). In Islam, gold is a symbol of prosperity and success (Arab America, 2019). Conversely, fashion companies also need to be careful of not offering culturally irrelevant colors (refer to Chapter 4 for more examples). In Malaysia, for example, green is an unpopular color as it is associated with the jungle and illness, so global fashion brands operating there may have products with less green because it is unappealing to them.

Developing Limited Editions

The next level of product localization includes developing limited editions for certain occasions. This approach is effective in that it can appeal to consumers in host countries, thus creating positive images toward the brand without too much time or resource investment. This is because establishing a new product line, representing the next stage of localization, demands a sustained commitment involving increased resources, investment, and effective management.

To cater to Chinese consumers' gift-giving culture on New Year's Day, many brands develop limited editions for Chinese consumers mostly using Chinese Zodiac signs. For example, 2011 was the Year of the Rabbit, which began on February 3. Nike developed a limited edition of Air Jordan to celebrate the fact that Michael Jordan was born in 1963, the Year of the Rabbit. The shoes were accented with red and gold colors following the Chinese tradition of giving cash gifts in red and gold envelopes. The shoebox was also in red with a traditional Chinese pattern on it. Kate Spade offered a fuzzy clutch with the shape of sheep in the Year of the Sheep in 2015. Similarly, Salvatore Ferragamo created goat and sheep printed scarves in red and black for Chinese consumers celebrating the Year of the Sheep. Burberry also modified its scarf for Chinese consumers by adding the Chinese character for "prosperity" to its classy color block design. It quickly sold out in many cities. Italian luxury brand Bottega Veneta also developed a limited edition clutch for the Indian market combining its *intrecciato* weave with an Indian knot.

Luxury brands also utilized the Chinese lucky number eight to design a limited edition. In 2009, Montblanc offered a limited edition fountain pen in gold lattice interlocking the number eight with a diamond stud on the clip. Hermès launched a limited edition Indian sari, targeting the Indian market. The sari is a traditional garment that ranges from 3.5 to 9 yards in length with many different ways to drape it.

Most Indian women wear a sari at special occasions such as weddings and formal occasions (Tulshyan, 2011).

Developing a Product Line for Certain Markets

Developing a new brand for certain consumer groups may be ineffective, given the time and resources needed for the effort. One effective approach is to develop a product line that addresses the needs that clearly exist within a brand. In this case, the size of the market to be catered for should be big enough to justify the addition of a product line. A good example is Nike's Pro Hijab, which came onto the market in spring 2018, specifically designed for Muslim women athletes. The head cover is a single-layer pull-on design made from lightweight polyester in dark, neutral colors, designed to solve the performance constraints of the traditional hijab in sport and also enhance Nike's market expansion efforts in the Middle East (Alkhalisi, 2017; Palmer, 2018). Similarly, Dolce & Gabbana created a hijab and abaya collection in 2016 featuring black and beige items. The abaya is a full-length dress worn by Muslim women covering the whole body except the head, feet, and hands. Tommy Hilfiger launched its first Ramadan capsule collection in 2016 consisting of 15 modest designs, featuring maxi dresses, skirts, boleros, and accessories in rich colors and featuring lace, chiffon, and crepe fabrics. The collection was sold through stores in Bahrain, Kuwait, Qatar, Saudi Arabia, the UAE, and Egypt. The collection was well received so the brand decided to continue. Following its success, DKNY, Oscar de la Renta, and Zara also launched Ramadan collections (Segran, 2016).

When it entered India in 2019, Uniqlo concurrently launched a line of kurtas (loose collarless shirts) for men and women designed by a local designer in India, together with its regular offering. This was well received among Indian consumers because two-thirds of the womenswear market comprises traditional Indian attire (Hall and Jay, 2021). Thus, if Uniqlo only carried the same items as it sold in other countries, it would lose two-thirds of the market in India. In sum, creating a product line within a brand is an effective modification if there is a clear need (or if there is sufficient demand), thus the product line can be efficiently marketed with the established brand image.

Developing a New Brand for Certain Markets

After creating a product line within a brand, the greatest modification effort is developing a new brand for certain markets. While the localization effort requires time and resources, it is worthwhile if the new development creates demands and addresses the needs of local consumers. Levi Strauss and Co.'s launch of dENiZEN for the Chinese consumer in 2010 is a good example. This is unique, as the brand was developed with Chinese consumers in mind and was the company's first brand launched outside the US. The target, price, and design are different from those of original Levi's. The brand dENiZEN targets 18- to 29-year-old consumers, comes in various fits including the slim fit favored by many Asians, and is priced at a low-middle point at $40–60, half of Levi's jeans in China. The new brand was successful and entered the US with a new line of jeans available exclusively at Target (Waldmeir, 2010).

Products that are successful in a firm's home market may not sell well because of environmental differences between markets. Global marketers therefore must find the balance between standardizing products and services and adapting them to specific markets. The above discussion described various levels of product localization. Those levels are not mutually exclusive; both color and size localization can be developed together with offering limited edition products. Here, the essence is that localization efforts should create demands that address the needs of local consumers and without which brands cannot effectively serve the market. Each localization requires time and resources. Thus, global fashion brands need to do market research to see if localization is needed, identify which aspects of localization guarantee their investments, and plan early for the necessary adaptation. With well-planned integration, localized products and services can be applied to many other markets, bringing more success to brands.

CASE STUDY 10.1
How Gentle Monster Achieved Its Wild Success

Gentle Monster, founded in 2011, is a luxury eyewear brand based in Seoul, South Korea, known for its avant-garde designs and experimental retail concept. Gentle Monster saw a surge in popularity in the domestic market and its neighboring country China after South Korean actress Jun Ji-hyun wore its sunglasses in *My Love from the Star*, a popular Korean TV drama aired between 2013 and 2014 (Reuters, 2017). Since then, the brand's popularity has expanded beyond Asia. Gentle Monster became the first and only global eyewear brand originating from Korea. The brand has presence in about 19 countries, including overseas flagship stores in major metropolitan cities, such as New York and Shanghai, as well as leading fashion retailers, such as Opening Ceremony and Beakers (L Catterton, 2017). The brand's appeal is further attested by a major investment from L Catterton, the largest consumer-focused private equity firm, formed through the partnership of Catterton, LVMH, and Groupe Arnault (L Catterton, 2017).

At its inception, Gentle Monster sought to close a gap in the Asian eyewear market, dominated by Western brands (Im, 2018). These Western brands' products are made to accommodate Western facial features, therefore not many meet Asian consumers' preferences for fashion products that help achieve their ideal beauty standard of having a small face. Keenly aware of the unmet needs, Gentle Monster developed ultra-oversized eyewear with a low-bridge fit (Sherman, 2016). The brand produces three generations of sunglasses, each with a different purpose and concept. Most of the sales come from the first-generation products, designed to appeal to the mass market. The second-generation products are more fashion-forward, and third-generation products are like unique runway pieces, epitomizing fun and experimentation (Im, 2018).

The brand maintains the newness and solidifies its global reach through collaborations with high-profile brands, designers, and celebrities, such as Alexander Wang, Fendi, and Jennie of Blackpink, a K-pop girl group with a global fanbase (Gentle Monster, n.d.). The brand's experimental spirit extends to other aspects of retailing, from store design to marketing editorials and campaigns (Im, 2018). For example, Gentle Monster redesigns its flagship stores every 25 days with creative installations that push the boundary of retail space, through collaborations with diverse artists and brands (Gentle Monster, n.d.).

Discussion Questions

1. How are the eyeglasses of Gentle Monster different from traditional ones? Why is this appealing to Asian consumers?
2. Why do you think Gentle Monster collaborates with high-profile brands? Why do you think Gentle Monster redesigns its flagship store every 25 days? What are the consequences of these two efforts?
3. Assess the three tiers of offerings with different purpose and concept. Is the strategy effective? Why/why not?

References

Gentle Monster (n.d.) Recent project. www.gentlemonster.com/project

Im, E.-B. (2018, June 10). Gentle Monster looks beyond sunglasses: Local sunglasses brand eyes bigger future with LVMH. *The Korean Herald.* www.koreaherald.com/view.php?ud=20180610000182

L Catterton. (2017, September 8). L Catterton Asia announces new partnership with Gentle Monster. www.lcatterton.com/Press.html#!/LCAsia-partners-with-GentleMonster

Reuters (2017, September 7). LVMH-backed PE fund buys a piece of South Korean style. www.reuters.com/article/us-gentlemonster-lvmh/lvmh-backed-pe-fund-buys-a-piece-of-south-korean-style-idUSKCN1BJ009

Sherman, L. (2016, July 17). How Gentle Monster rode the K-pop wave to $160 million. Business of Fashion. www.businessoffashion.com/articles/intelligence/how-gentle-monster-road-the-k-pop-wave-to-160-million

Summary

- Fashion brands need to modify their products for global markets. Determining to what extent is an essential part of product development in the global market.
- Global brands have to change something to be relevant in foreign markets, including mandatory adaptation without which products cannot be sold and discretionary adaptation for greater acceptance.
- Discretionary modification involves modifying product design or selecting products suitable for the local market considering culture, season, religion, and economic development level.
- Fashion companies can effectively appeal to consumers through modifications by addressing host countries' culture with product changes or new development.

- Fashion companies can implement modifications that address the seasons because products developed for domestic markets may not be suitable for a season in host countries.
- Modifications addressing religion mean that fashion companies should carefully study diversity among countries, even if they are of the same religion, and follow them when modifying products.
- Products for global consumers should not make any bad associations with any cultural symbols. For example, use of the national flag in product design may not be acceptable in some countries, interpretation of slogans on products may differ by country, and graphics on products can accidentally resemble important symbols or words, causing huge mistakes. Therefore, fashion companies should study whether their products can convey unwanted meanings in other cultures and examine what parts of their products may create negative connotations before selling their products globally.
- Product localization approaches for global markets include localizing size, clothing terms, and colors, developing limited editions, a product line, and new brands for certain markets.
- When it comes to localizing sizes, firms should note two aspects: providing sizes that fit consumers in host countries, and communicating the right sizes so consumers can choose their sizes easily.
- Even in countries that use the same language, the terms for clothing items are different. Careful attention should be paid when firms localize clothing terms according to the terms used in the host market.
- Regarding localizing colors, consumers' color preferences vary greatly from country to country and even within a country. Thus, fashion companies must provide colors preferred by consumers while being cautious to avoid culturally irrelevant choices.
- Developing limited editions for specific occasions is an effective approach to appeal to consumers in host countries by creating positive images toward the brand without too much time and resource investment.
- Creating a product line tailored for certain markets is an effective modification, provided there is sufficient demand. The newly created line is within the brand, so can be effectively marketed leveraging the established brand image.
- The main essence for fashion companies is that localization efforts should create demands addressing the needs of local consumers and without which brands cannot effectively serve the market. With well-planned integration, localized products and services can be applied to many other markets, bringing more success to brands.

Class Activities

1. Have you ever felt that some apparel items from other countries do not suit your needs? Was it because of the colors, styles, or sizes of the products? Discuss how it did not fit your needs and how the company could modify its products to better fit your needs.

2. Discuss any product localization needs that guarantee a product line development, such as the hijab example.

3. When you shop for apparel and accessories from foreign online websites, do you encounter any difficulties? Discuss the difficulties and how you could fix them if you worked for the online company.

Key Terms

- **Mandatory adaptation:** Adaptation to modify a product compulsorily because it cannot be sold in a foreign market without a change or modification of the product.
- **Discretionary adaptation:** Adaptation that occurs when a company chooses to specifically tailor its products to market needs for greater acceptance. Involves modifying product design or selecting products suitable for the local market, considering culture, season, religion, and economic development level.
- **Product localization:** Refers to approaches for global markets including localizing size, clothing terms, and colors, developing limited editions, a product line, and a new brand for certain markets.

Further Reading

UAE flag colors on Puma shoes

Source: Elwazer, S. (2011, November 28). UAE flag colours on Puma shoes anger nationals. CNN. http://edition.cnn.com/blogarchive/insidethemiddleeast.blogs.cnn.com/2011/11/28/uae-flag-colours-on-puma-shoes-anger-nationals/#:~:text=%22Puma%20have%20launched%20a%20pair,about%20their%20reputation%20when%20he

Slogan on a hooded sweatshirt of H&M

Source: Kaye, L. (2018). H&M struggles repairing a battered reputation in South Africa. TriplePundit. www.triplepundit.com/story/2018/hm-struggles-repairing-battered-reputation-south-africa/13616

Nike Air Max 270 shoe looks like Allah's name in Arabic

Source: Boyd, C. (2019, January 28). "Just don't do it!" Thousands of Muslims demand Nike withdraw "insulting" Air Max trainers "that have Allah written on the sole". Dailymail.com. www.dailymail.co.uk/news/article-6640481/Muslims demand-Nike-withdraw-insulting-Air-Max-trainers-Allah-written-sole.html

CHAPTER 11
Pricing for Global Markets

Learning Objectives

After studying this chapter, you will be able to:

- Discern the differences among tariffs, duties, and taxes and how these affect consumer prices in a country.
- Understand the tariffs levied on imported goods that vary by countries and their impact on the prices of the same products across countries.
- Discuss the factors related to price escalation when crossing borders and how to minimize its effect.
- Compare different approaches to pricing for the global marketplace.
- Articulate several factors that affect pricing decisions for global markets.
- Explain parallel importing and gray goods and their implications for global fashion companies.

While decisions related to all the 4Ps of marketing are important, setting prices for the global marketplace is a key strategic marketing decision. This is because price often serves as a major factor in consumers' purchase decisions, which determine companies' profitability. Therefore, of all the tasks facing global marketers, determining what price to charge is one of the most difficult, as pricing is usually more localized than product or advertising decisions. Pricing is much more than just adding markups to the cost of goods sold. Price serves as a quality cue. Thus, price should reflect the quality and value the consumer perceives in the product. Moreover, the price sensitivity of local consumers and the prices of competing products and services vary country to country. Consequently, research about prices for competing brands and local brands is of great importance for an adequate pricing strategy.

When moving goods to another country, some expenses such as tariffs and transportation costs occur. Naturally, price becomes more expensive in other countries than in domestic markets (price escalation). This chapter starts with the concepts of taxes, tariffs, and duties that affect consumer prices in other countries and then moves on to price escalation and the elements that contribute to price escalation. Those factors will be dissected to learn how we can lessen price escalation. After learning the basic factors related to heightened price in international markets, a couple of approaches to pricing for global markets will be reviewed, followed by several factors that need to be taken into account for the international pricing decision. The chapter will end with parallel importing and its influence on the global fashion business, especially in the luxury brands sector.

Taxes and Tariffs on Imported Goods

Each country imposes tariffs and taxes for exported and imported goods. These are the costs that companies must pay that increase the price of products in host countries. Tariffs and duties are a form of taxation. The two terms are used interchangeably, but there is a difference between the two. Tariffs are taxes the government imposes on goods when they cross borders. Tariffs are levied on both imported and exported goods. Import tariffs are imposed on imported goods from other countries, while export tariffs are imposed on exported goods. Import tariffs are normally assessed as a percentage of the landed cost of a product. Landed cost is the price after a product has landed in host countries, typically calculated by adding shipping and/or insurance costs to the product cost (Coyle et al., 2003). In contrast to tariffs on imported or exported goods, duties are indirect taxes levied on the consumer of imported goods. Here, indirect means that the taxes paid by the consumer are passed on to the government by the seller. So, as a consumer, we pay duty, not tariff. That is why we often see "duty free" stores, not "tariff free" stores at airports. Both tariffs and duties are imposed to protect domestic industry by making imports more expensive and to increase government revenues.

In addition to tariffs and duties, other forms of taxes could also affect the final cost of products. One of the most common taxes is value-added tax (VAT), which is added to a product at every point of the supply chain where value is added to it, assuming there is an increase in value of the goods each time it passes to the next member in the supply chain. Most EU member countries have VAT, while the US does not. Sales tax collected by the state governments in the US is similar to the VAT. The next common form of tax associated with imported goods is excise tax, which is levied on certain product categories such as fuel, alcoholic beverages, tobacco, and luxury goods. Excise taxes are also called "sin taxes," as they are largely imposed on goods that have a high social cost, such as alcohol and tobacco. If a government wanted to discourage the consumption of luxury goods, they could impose high excise taxes on luxury goods.

Different taxes are applied on different products by different countries. In other words, percentages of tariffs, VAT or excise taxes imposed on products vary greatly. Table 11.1 shows taxes on imported goods by selected countries. Notably, Brazil imposes various taxes on imported goods, which naturally increases their price in the country. Tariffs and taxes are two of the elements that increase the price in host countries, although there are other reasons. As a result, fashion items can cost 50 percent more in Brazil than they do in the US (Gillespie and Hennessey, 2016). This leads Brazilian consumers to shop in the US or Europe. For example, Brazilian consumers shop at Woodbury Common Premium Outlets near New York City and fill their suitcases with luxury items (see Case Study 11.1).

Table 11.1 Taxes on imported goods by country

BRAZIL	CHINA	FRANCE	SOUTH KOREA
VAT 7–18% (per state) Duties 10–35% COFINS Tax 13.57% IPI Tax 0–20% PSI Tax 2.62%	VAT 17% Duties 0–35% (motor vehicles 34.2%) Consumption Tax 5–10%	VAT 20% Duties 5–17%	VAT 10% Duties 7.9% Excise Tax 10–20%
	SWITZERLAND	THAILAND	UNITED KINGDOM
	VAT 8% Duties 3.2% (avg.) Statistical/Environmental Tax 3% (CO_2 Emissions)	VAT 7% Duties 0–80% Excise Tax 25–80%	VAT 20% Duties 0–15% (avg. 4.2%)

VAT = Value added tax
COFINS = Contribution for the Financing of Social Security
IPI = Tax on industrialized goods
PIS = Program of Social Integration

Source: USCIB (2016).

This heavy import duty and tax system is similar in most Latin American countries. As a result, one major reason why Colombian consumers visit the US is shopping and enjoying the price differentials (Ceballos et al., 2018). This is referred to as "cross-border shopping" or "international outshopping." These concepts are not new, as consumers living on the borders of countries cross the border, typically by car, to reap the benefits of price differentials, but now consumers can do this by air. Moreover, cross-border shopping has been extended to online shopping, meaning that consumers outshop at overseas e-commerce sites without leaving their countries (US consumers shop at Asos.com in the UK, and Korean consumers shop at aliexpress.com, a Chinese e-commerce website).

While this kind of shopping requires the payment of international shipping charges and duties, the duties are often exempted if the price of products is below a threshold the government set. This is the concept of "de minimis tax," a tax imposed by an importing country for cross-border e-commerce activities. The International Chamber of Commerce Custom Guideline #11 (ICC, 2012) defines de minimis as "a valuation ceiling for goods, including documents and trade samples, below which no duty or tax is charged and clearance procedures, including data requirements, are minimal." Formulating a meaningful minimum level will have a positive impact especially on small and medium-sized enterprises and provide opportunities to increase e-commerce transactions (ICC, 2012). Box 11.1 compares the de minimis tax thresholds of Canada and the US and the implications for international consumers.

BOX 11.1
De Minimis Tax Thresholds and Cross-border E-commerce

De minimis means "smallest" in Latin, concerning things that are so minor as to be negligible. Each government sets a de minimis tax threshold, below which level no duty is imposed, as it is trivial. The de minimis tax thresholds vary by countries. In the US, the threshold is quite high, $800, meaning that no duties are imposed on a consumer who purchases an item costing less than $800 from a cross-border e-commerce website (ITA, n.d.). In Canada, the threshold is C$20, indicating that duties are levied on most items purchased (Ju and Chang, 2022). Obviously, the low threshold in Canada provides less incentive for Canadian consumers to order from international e-commerce websites. The opposite is true for US consumers. Buying from international e-tailers gives them a benefit, as duties are waived as long as an item costs less than $800. Depending on the threshold, the amount of goods imported via online can be controlled; the higher threshold means fewer restrictions, while a lower threshold results in more control on consumers' buying from foreign e-tailers. The de minimis tax thresholds are a subject of interest thanks to increasing transactions at international e-commerce websites (Ju and Chang, 2022).

References

ITA (International Trade Administration) (n.d.). De minimis value: Express shipment exemptions. www.trade.gov/de-minimis-value

Ju, J. and Chang, K.C. (2022, April 14). De minimis tax thresholds and cross-border e-commerce. GEODIS India. https://geodis.com/in/blog/customs/de-minimis-tax-thresholds-and-cross-border-e-commerce

Price Escalation and How to Minimize Its Effect

Price Escalation: Definition and Contributing Elements

Elements That Escalate Price

Moving goods overseas requires additional expenses that are not incurred in domestic markets, which increases the price of exported products substantially above their domestic price. This is called "price escalation," defined as added costs incurred as a result of exporting products from one country to another. As seen from the hypothetical case in Table 11.2 two expenses that are not incurred in domestic pricing increase the final price: sea freight and insurance, and import tariff. Because of these expenses, the final export price ($27.45) is about 20 percent higher than the domestic price ($22.50).

The freight and insurance cost can be lowered if the price is quoted FOB (Free on Board) rather than CIF (Cost, Insurance and

Table 11.2 An example of escalation of costs through exporting

COSTS	EXPORT PRICE ($)	DOMESTIC PRICE ($)
Manufacturer's price	10.00	10.00
Sea freight and insurance	1.20	
Landed cost (CIF)	11.20	
Import tariff: 8% on CIF value	0.90	
CIF plus tariff	12.10	
17.5% VAT	2.12	1.75
Distributor purchase price	14.32	11.75
Distributor markup (15%)	2.15	
Retailer purchase price	16.47	13.50
Retail margin (40%)	10.98	9.00
Consumer purchase price	27.45	22.50

Freight). The main difference between CIF and FOB is the point at which responsibility and liability of goods transfer from the seller to the buyer. FOB means that as soon as goods reach the port of origin, the seller is free of responsibilities and liability. The buyer is responsible for the costs of loading, shipping, and insuring the products. If the price is quoted on a CIF basis, the seller pays the insurance as well as freight and assumes liability until the goods reach the port of destination chosen by the buyer. Since the seller pays insurance, the CIF quote is higher than FOB. So, when quoting prices for overseas buyers, you will need to ascertain whether the quote is on an FOB or CIF basis.

Table 11.2 is a simple illustration showing how freight, insurance, and import tariff increase the final price. Additional costs, such as packing, intermediaries' margins, special taxes, and administrative costs, also contribute to escalating the final price. Here, the longer the channel, the greater the intermediaries' margins because each intermediary charges their own margins.

Environmental Influences on Price Escalation

Fashion companies also need to be aware of environmental influences on price escalation. That is, other than costs incurred for moving goods, three environmental situations also affect price escalation: exchange rate fluctuations, inflation, and deflation. Companies can gain or lose their profits just from severe exchange rate fluctuations, especially when there is a significant time lapse between signing the order and delivery of the goods. When the author traveled to France several years ago, the euro was strong, so US$1 was valued only at €0.70. This means that exchanging US$100 gave me only €70, so I could not buy much in France. Conversely, if the euro is weak and US$ is strong, exchanging US$100 could realize €150. Then I could buy more in France.

This is a simple calculation but imagine a large fashion company that deals with millions of dollars' worth of orders. If their order is worth US$10 million after six months, this could be only US$7 million or US$12 million instead of US$10 million, depending on the exchange rate. Exchange rates fluctuate so currency values swing daily, which may make it necessary to increase prices to absorb any price differentials resulting from exchange rate changes. Inflation causes consumer prices to escalate and the consumer is faced with rising prices that eventually exclude many consumers from the market. Deflation results in the opposite consequence. It leads to decreasing prices, creating a positive result for consumers, but companies need to put pressure on supply chain partners to lower costs in order to achieve decreasing prices. These three environmental situations are beyond the control of companies; therefore, companies need to be proactive to compensate for possible losses resulting from environmental influences.

Approaches to Lessening Price Escalation

Having explored the elements that escalate price, let's review how companies can reduce the escalated price. The basic idea is to find a way to pay less in each element that escalated the price. There are three general approaches: lowering the cost of goods sold, lowering tariffs, and lowering distribution costs.

1. *Lowering the cost of goods sold*: Cost of goods sold is a big portion of any price. If the manufacturer's price can be lowered, the effect will hold throughout the chain. One effective way of lowering the cost of goods sold in the fashion industry is manufacturing in countries where labor costs are cheaper. Further, firms can choose to manufacture products in free trade zones in a country where local taxes, surcharges, and so on are waived, reduced, or deferred, so that the final price can be more competitive. Some countries have foreign or free trade zones or free ports. For example, in Bangladesh, there are eight export processing zones (EPZ), similar to the free trade zone concept. In those eight EPZ, no taxes are imposed for the first two or three years and then 50 percent for the next three years and 25 percent for another year (Huda et al., 2017).

   However, a decision of sourcing from a low-wage country should be made considering other factors. For example, being agile (being closer to the market) may help increase profit more than just lowering manufacturing cost.

2. *Lowering tariffs*: Tariff rates vary by product categories. By finding a category that imposes lower tariffs, firms can save on costs. For example, boys' cotton pants can be classified as children's wear or cotton products. If tariffs imposed on cotton are cheaper than children's wear, the product can be reclassified as a cotton product rather than boys' pants. The classification of products, however, varies by country, along with tariff rates. This means that the opposite may apply in another country. Then, reclassifying boys' cotton pants as children's wear can lower tariffs in another country. Companies need to thoroughly investigate tariff rates and classification criteria to lower tariffs, which can help lessen price escalation.

3. *Lowering distribution costs*: Intermediaries (export agents) are one of the elements that escalate price. Thus, by paying a lower intermediary margin, price escalation can be lessened. The best way to lower middlemen's margin is by having less or even no middleman, because each time goods pass

through an intermediary, margin can be added up. Most e-commerce companies use a D2C model, meaning there is no intermediary. The cost saved by not having a middleman can help lower the price, which is directly translated into competitive price. Chinese fast fashion brand Shein is a D2C e-tailer, shipping directly to consumers overseas. This company can save on middlemen's margin as well as de minimis tax imposed by an importing country (see Box 11.1).

Approaches to Pricing for Global Markets

As with other marketing mix elements, companies need to decide to what degree they adapt price. The pricing decision reflects actual costs as well as a company's short- and long-term goals in the host market. There are four approaches to international pricing:

1. *Cost-plus pricing*: This approach is basic in that it adds all costs incurred when goods cross national borders. Total cost, therefore, depends on destination (travel distance, how far a host country is from a country where products are shipped), mode of transport (by air or by sea), tariffs, various fees, handling charges, and documentation costs.
2. *Flexible cost-plus pricing*: This is a variation of cost-plus pricing. It ensures that prices are competitive in their particular market environment. Thus, it adjusts the price by analyzing competitors' prices and other factors.
3. *Penetration pricing*: This approach is used to stimulate market growth and capture market share by deliberately offering products at low prices.
4. *Skimming pricing*: The opposite to penetration pricing, this approach charges a premium price. It is effective at the introductory stage of the product life cycle. Similarly, it works well when brands or product categories are new enough thanks to first-mover advantage. Many fashion brands use this approach to maximize their profits until competition forces a lower price. Good examples are Tommy Hilfiger and Reebok in India. When Tommy Hilfiger was introduced in India in 2004, there were limited brands like Tommy Hilfiger. Even with the skimming price, the brand sold well as it was perceived as a good quality global brand, thus serving as a status symbol.

Factors That Affect the Pricing Decision

It would be ideal to set the same price across all the countries a fashion firm enters. In practice, however, the same pricing across countries is infeasible. This is because there are diverse factors, which vary by country, to consider when setting prices. Even luxury brands that mainly employ standardization strategies command differing prices country by country. We review the factors at two levels: cost and company goals, and market factors.

Costs and Company Goals That Affect Pricing Decision

Firms need to be deliberate in their internal goals and cost structures for pricing decisions,

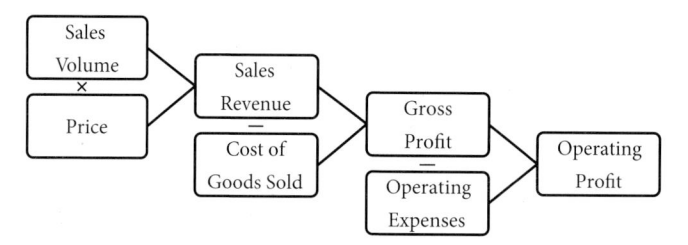

Figure 11.1 Drivers of global brand profitability.

which requires understanding the various elements related to profitability. Figure 11.1 presents how a firm achieves operating profit. Sales revenues can be maximized by increasing both sales volume and price or either of these two. This means that even though price is low, higher sales volumes can contribute to high sales revenue. Likewise, with small sales volumes, companies can reach the same level of sales revenues if the price is set high. Gross profit is achieved by subtracting the cost of goods sold from sales revenue. Therefore, the cost of goods sold should be lowered for a higher gross profit. Operating profit is gained after subtracting operating expenses from gross profit; thus, it can be maximized by lowering operating expenses such as rent.

Now, let's review company costs and goals and how they affect the pricing decision:

1. *Company costs*: Price should cover at least all costs needed to make and sell products in other countries. Several costs arise that are not incurred in the domestic market. These include tariffs, VAT, and so on imposed by the host government, which varies drastically country to country as described earlier in this chapter. Another cost for global markets is the one for intermediaries and transportation either by air or by sea. Any company costs should be lowered in order to increase profits.

2. *Company goals*: Fashion companies' goals may differ by country. In some countries, fast penetration of the market may be a priority, whereas in other countries building brand reputation may be the prime goal. Consumers may associate quality with price, a relationship that is an important facet of brand positioning. To increase market share, a fashion company may offer products at low prices. In this case, consumers may associate the brand with low quality, a perception that will be very difficult to change once it is formed. On the other hand, firms can project a premium image with high prices. These goals may vary from market to market. Therefore, firms need to reflect their strategic goal for each market when deciding pricing.

Market Factors That Affect Pricing

The pricing decision is challenging in global markets because a significant number of local factors need to be considered, in addition to cost and company goals. Among many market factors, four factors that are particularly related are analyzed here: customer demand, competition level, product life cycle stage, and economic conditions of the host market.

Customer Demand

Price should be good enough to create demand. Commanding too high a price without justifying the value of the goods often fails to create demand and results in failure in the market. The closing of all 81 Gap, Inc. stores in the UK and Ireland in 2021 is attributed to overpricing (BBC, 2021). Gap's Banana Republic also closed all eight of its stores in the UK in 2016, which was also attributed to poor pricing. According to a source: "the brand failed to justify its premium price points, leaving consumers with little encouragement to shift their spending from rivals" (Geohegan, 2016). In contrast, high prices can entice consumers to buy. High price paired with limited supply, such as the iconic Hermès Kelly and Birkin handbags, create a sense of scarcity so the value does not fade away even in the resale market. Chanel recently had a similar pricing strategy, and Korean consumers' desire to buy their classic handbag increased hugely with the expectation of selling it in the resale market at an even higher price and enjoying the price gap. However, consumers' enthusiastic demand eventually weakened as the scarcity effect declined, with many people having the same handbag in Korea (see Case Study 11.2 for details). As shown in these cases, fashion companies need to assess if their pricing is right for the target market and the effect of their pricing strategies in the host market.

Competition

The intensity of competition can also significantly affect price levels in any given market. A firm that introduces innovative products or services for the first time in a host country can command a higher price by leveraging first-mover advantages. Korean apparel brand On & On was able to set a premium price when it first entered the Chinese market in 1999. This was mainly because there was limited competition (Jin and Chung, 2016). On the other hand, if there are many competing international or local brands, firms should be mindful to set the price right so as to create demand. Therefore, the number and the extent of competitors greatly influence pricing strategy in any market. In Australia, fast fashion brand Mango's initial price was set high to cover the high cost of living there. Consumers complained that the high prices did not match the quality of the products (Blake et al., 2013; Redrup, 2013), which may explain the closure of two out of three stores.

Product Life Cycle Stage in the Host Market

If a firm entering a market in the early growth stage can possibly maintain a relatively high price, it can charge what the market can bear. In the introductory stage of the product life cycle, customers are relatively insensitive to price, as there are limited brands or products with which to compare. Similarly, if a brand concept or product category is new to the market, it can be positioned with a high price point.

Economic Conditions of the Host Market

A country's income level should be also considered in the pricing decision. It may be assumed that consumers in developed countries can pay higher prices thanks to their higher incomes. In a mature market, however, competition is so fierce that pricing and discounts, such as buying one pair of shoes and getting the second pair half price, often become an important competitive tool. Contrary to our perception, higher prices, especially for status goods, can sometimes work well in emerging markets because of an increasing need for status goods that show off consumers' recently gained wealth. In addition, a growing middle-class in emerging markets tend to view global fashion brands as status symbols and are thus willing to pay higher prices.

However, the high pricing strategy may not work well for medium-priced and low-end apparel items since there are many local products at a lower price. Disposable income, not actual income, may be more important as it is more related to purchase decisions. In many Asian countries, people live with their parents until they marry, which means that all their incomes are discretionary. This is in contrast to the US, where children start to live independently from their parents when they become a college student, which leaves less disposable income for fashion goods and services. The implication of this is that even if income levels in advanced economies are higher, the actual disposable income for clothes items might not be big enough.

In summary, the price of an item may differ greatly across countries. For example, Zara products were found to be most affordable in Spain (home country of Zara) but were the most expensive in Japan, while the US fell somewhere in the middle (Musco, 2017). Box 11.2 shows the different prices of classic Levi's 501 jeans across countries. The pricing decision is often made based on a mix of costs, goals, and other factors described above. As price affects both sales and the perception in the local market, it should be strategically decided with thorough research.

BOX 11.2
Levi's 501 Jeans Price by Country

Levi Strauss is a truly global brand having a presence in 110 countries. It is probably one of the most well-known apparel brands. How much are Levi's 501 jeans in your country? According to a study (Son and Jin, 2012), the price differs drastically from country to country. The study compared the same Levi's jeans style (501) posted on the official Levi's website in each of the 47 countries studied. As the table below shows, the cheapest price was found in Pakistan ($33) and the most expensive in Korea ($194), being six times more expensive than that of Pakistan. The price gap between the cheapest and the most expensive jeans was about $160, which could be more than one person's monthly salary in a developing country.

To analyze what the price means given consumers' income level, the study further converted the price as a percentage of monthly GDP per capita. The figure below shows that while 501 jeans are most expensive in Korea ($194), the cost is about 20 percent of Koreans' monthly GDP per capita at the time of research (2012). Consumers in India have to pay about 70 percent of their monthly income to buy a pair of Levi's jeans. This means the most expensive country is India, not Korea, according to income level. As this example shows, the price should be aligned well with a brand's positioning strategy in the country.

Levi's 501 jeans price by country

Country	Price	Country	Price	Country	Price
Pakistan	$33 (Rs2,975)	India	$90 (INR4501.00)	Brazil	$116 (R$209)
Vietnam	$43 (VNĐ900.000,00)	Ecuador	$92 ($92)	Belgium	$118 (€90)
Mexico	$55 (MEX$694)	Hungary	$92 (Ft20,214)	UK	$119 (£75)
Canada	$61 (C$60)	Colombia	$99 (COL$174,671)	Greece	$120 (€91)
Peru	$62 ($165)	Hong Kong	$99 (HK$769)	Denmark	$121 (kr682)
US	$64	Germany	$102 (€77)	France	$123 (€94)
Chile	$67 (CH$32,444)	Ireland	$102 (€78)	Australia	$124 (AU$117)
Thailand	$68 (THB2,089)	Poland	$102 (zł319)	Taiwan	$125 (元3680)
Philippines	$72 (php3,110)	New Zealand	$103 (NZ$125)	Netherlands	$136 (€103)
Venezuela	$73 (Bs620)	Spain	$105 (€80)	Russia	$143 (py64,173)
Indonesia	$76 (Rp693,900)	Portugal	$106 (€80)	Sweden	$147 (kr993)
Turkey	$79 (₺142)	Austria	$108 (€82)	Switzerland	$148 (CHF136)
South Africa	$81 (R616)	Finland	$110 (€83)	Norway	$154 (KR885)
Malaysia	$83 (RM254)	Czech Rep.	$112 (Kč2,093)	China	$158 (元999)
Argentina	$88 (ARS$382)	Italy	$112 (€85)	Korea	$194 (₩218,000)
Singapore	$90 (SGD$113)	Japan	$114 (¥ 9.500)		

Levi's 501 jeans price by share of monthly GDP per capita across countries

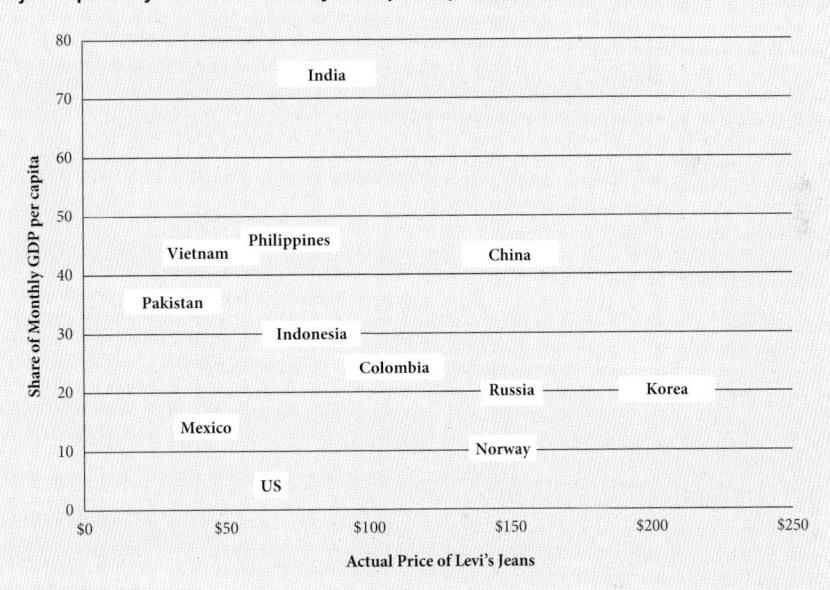

Reference

Son, J. and Jin, B. (2012, November). The price of Levi's jeans across countries: Why and how they are different? Paper presented at the annual conference of International Textile and Apparel Association, Honolulu.

Parallel Importing and Its Implications for Global Fashion Companies

Price variances occur among most fashion brands, yet their implications are significant for luxury brands. According to McDowell (2019), Balenciaga, Gucci, and Louis Vuitton's prices vary geographically by more than 35 percent on average, while Dior is one of the most consistently priced brands, with price variances of 14 percent. The luxury prices tend to be highest in the Asia-Pacific region, especially Japan, while, on average, the UK is the lowest. This is a result of most luxury brands harmonizing their prices across countries.

One managerial issue resulting from the price variance is parallel importing, which is common in the fashion industry. This happens when an unauthorized middleman imports identical products and brands from countries where prices are lower and diverts them to countries where the price is higher. It is possible because of price gaps that are large enough for the middleman to make a profit. Those products are often referred to as "gray products." To be clear, gray goods are authentic products, not counterfeit or fakes, that are imported from another country without the permission of the brands. The gray market issue is more severe in luxury sectors because price differentials can be high and moving products is relatively easy as fashion items are not heavy or bulky to import. It is estimated that the gray market accounts for 5–10 percent of luxury good sales (Shannon, 2018).

Parallel imports of luxury goods occur when an authorized retailer or distributor sells goods (excessive stocks or overordered items) at a wholesale price to unauthorized retailers in other countries where prices are higher. Many major luxury brands ignore such sales, or even sell directly to gray market players themselves to boost their short-term sales (Shannon, 2018). For consumers, buying luxury goods from an unauthorized retailer is cheaper than buying them from authorized boutiques, so it could be beneficial for them. However, it creates multiple issues for luxury brands. First, it dilutes exclusivity because of wide availability through multiple distributors. Second, it can damage the channel relationship because authorized distributors attempt to cut costs or complain to luxury brands. Lastly, it can also hamper luxury brands' local pricing strategies. This gray market is not limited to offline. Recent growth in the digital gray market is becoming a substantial concern for luxury brands (Paton, 2021). Consumers can find luxury items 30 percent cheaper at Italist.com, a digital gray website, than at the brand's official website (Shannon, 2020). Approaches to this issue vary by luxury brand. Chanel is harmonizing prices globally, while other luxury brands limit supply to wholesale partners and selected distributors who have the capabilities and resources to keep the image of the luxury brands (Shannon, 2018).

Customers are becoming increasingly price savvy, and price is becoming more transparent than ever before. Thanks to online searches, global fashion consumers can easily compare prices. If prices are excessively high in their country, consumers can fight against fashion brands via social media. In 2010, when Zara was introduced in Korea, Korean consumers exercised consumer power by posting the excessive prices on social media, and Zara then lowered the prices after listening to the complaints (Choi, 2010). Further, if prices in their countries are higher than other countries, global consumers can order from the brand directly or through an international e-commerce site. Chinese fast fashion brand Shein and the UK's ASOS are examples of this. These overseas e-commerce companies can directly ship to international consumers even without paying duties if these are below the de minimis tax threshold of the destination country. Global fashion brands need to be mindful of making the right pricing decisions (Bloomberg, 2021).

CASE STUDY 11.1
Cross-border Shopping and Luxury Fashion

Cross-border shopping is attractive because people can buy the same items at a cheaper price than they would in their home country and can shop for products unavailable in their home country. Cross-border shopping is active between neighboring countries like Canada and the US where there are big price differences. Canadians pay higher prices—more than double in some cases—for the same retail goods (CBC, 2013). Canadians account for about 30 percent of all international visitors to the US, and shopping is the most popular activity, surpassing sightseeing and visiting relatives and friends (ITA, 2016, 2019).

Globally, luxury fashion items are among the popular items for cross-border shopping because of the price differences between countries. Most luxury fashion brands are European. This means that luxury fashion goods are imported. In non-European countries, imported goods are often more expensive because there are additional costs typically borne by the importer, which are passed on to the consumer. These include tariffs, customs fees, currency fluctuations, and VAT; all can add substantially to the final price (ITA, n.d.).

Chinese consumers, the biggest consumers of luxury goods, are facing a large price gap due to differences in currency exchange rates and hefty Chinese import duties. For example, Louis Vuitton is 21 percent more expensive in China than the global average, meaning that Chinese consumers are paying US$420 more for a $2,000 handbag. In France and Italy, the price is 22 percent less than the global average, meaning that Chinese consumers can buy the same handbag for US$860 less (Duncan, 2019). The prices of brands like Balenciaga, Gucci, and Louis Vuitton vary by more than 35 percent across markets.

The price gap has boosted tourism and cross-border shopping when Chinese consumers travel to other countries where luxury goods are less expensive. It has also given rise to "daigou," or overseas personal shoppers who buy and send luxury goods to customers in China. In 2014, 70 percent of luxury brands bought by Chinese consumers were purchased abroad or through daigou (Bain & Company, 2015). Daigou agents are usually Hong Kong residents who move luxury goods between Hong Kong and mainland China. They also operate internationally from cities like New York, London, Paris, Tokyo, and Seoul, procuring luxury goods at lower prices or items that are unavailable in China (Chitrakorn, 2014).

In Latin America, where import tariffs are very high for clothing and footwear, ranging from 15 percent to 50 percent, many luxury consumers shop elsewhere for better prices and product selection (CPPLUXURY, 2018). The price of a luxury product can be more than double after all the taxes are added on. About 80 percent of Brazilian consumers' spending on luxury goods occurs abroad, mostly in the US and Europe. Brazilians spend more on luxury goods in the US than visitors from any other country (Mazza, 2014).

Recent actions by national governments and luxury brands, however, have decreased the appeal of cross-border shopping. For example, the Chinese government's reduction in import duties and stricter controls over gray markets have led more Chinese consumers to make their luxury purchases in China.

Discussion Questions

1. Why do the prices of luxury fashion goods vary across markets?
2. What are daigou shoppers and how did they come about? Who benefits from them and who is hurt by them?
3. Should the luxury global brands set different prices or harmonize across markets? What are the advantages and disadvantages of each strategy?

References

Bain & Company (2015). China's luxury market shrinks in 2014 as luxury brands adapt to shifting consumer preferences. www.bain.com/about/media-center/press-releases/2015/chinas-luxury-market-shrinks-in-2014-press-release

CBC (2013, February 8). "Country pricing" a cause of Canada-U.S. price gaps. www.cbc.ca/news/canada/country-pricing-a-cause-of-canada-u-s-price-gaps-1.1405894

Chitrakorn, K. (2014, April 9). "Daigou" agents help Chinese get luxury goods for less. Business of Fashion. www.businessoffashion.com/articles/global-currents/daigou-agents-help-chinese-consumers-get-luxury-goods-less

CPPLUXURY (2018, Novermber 19). Understanding the potential of Latin America's luxury markets. https://cpp-luxury.com/understanding-the-potential-of-latin-americas-luxury-markets

Duncan, T.A. (2019 October 9). Why luxury goods are so expensive in China. CNBC. www.cnbc.com/2019/10/09/why-luxury-goods-are-so-expensive-in-china.html

ITA (International Trade Administration) (n.d.). Export pricing strategy. www.trade.gov/pricing-strategy

ITA (2016). Canadian visitors to the U.S. by activity. https://travel.trade.gov/outreachpages/download_data_table/2015%20Data%20Table%20G0%20Activities.pdf

ITA (2019). Fast facts: United States travel and tourism industry. https://travel.trade.gov/outreachpages/download_data_table/Fast_Facts_2018.pdf

Mazza, M. (2014, October). Capturing the hearts of Brazil's luxury consumers. McKinsey & Company. www.mckinsey.com/business-functions/marketing-and-sales/our-insights/capturing-the-hearts-of-brazils-luxury-consumers

CASE STUDY 11.2
Chanel Handbag Pricing

Chanel is pursuing an aggressive strategy through price increases and purchase restrictions. Since the end of 2019, Chanel has raised the price of some of its classic handbags by almost two-thirds (Aloisi, 2022). Soon after, it allowed individual customers to purchase only one item per year, making its products more exclusive. This strategy appears to show that Chanel is aiming for the status of competing luxury brand Hermès (Rascouet and Neumann, 2021).

For Chanel's aggressive strategy, South Korean consumers' reactions stand out and a luxury boom called "open run" was coined, which means running into the Chanel store as soon as it opens after camping outside the night before (Yang and Aloisi, 2022). Open run gradually spread as consumers wanted to buy products ahead of Chanel's price increase. A part-time job was created for the lineup, and even a waiting agency was created. The open run of consumers voluntarily created free advertising, as consumers posted reviews of their open run experience on social media. Demand for Chanel handbags was gradually increasing in the resale market because there were no products left despite waiting 10 hours. On Kream, a high-end reselling platform in South Korea, Chanel's classic handbag traded at $14,000 at the peak time in January 2022, 20 percent higher than its regular price (Yang and Aloisi, 2022). Consumers can potentially earn 20 percent (about $2,200) by just reselling it after an open run effort over a night, so there was no reason not to do it.

Soon, however, Chanel's aggressive pricing strategy had provoked adverse reactions among Korean consumers. So many people wanting to reap the benefit of reselling after the open run caused an oversupply in the resale market; all premiums in the resale market have fallen since February 2022 (Byun, 2022). People were doubtful whether their open run efforts were worth enough and whether the value of Chanel products corresponded to their high price (Kim, 2022). As more people own Chanel bags, its exclusive value appears to decrease.

Scarcity is one of the most critical values of luxury brands; if many own a brand's product, the brand value decreases. Chanel's strategy of continuously raising its prices and limiting purchases seemed to have worked in Korea for a short period, but consumers' enthusiasm toward the brand gradually faded.

Discussion Questions
1. What is open run? Where did it come from?
2. Do you think Chanel's strategy of increasing prices and limiting purchases is successful? Why?
3. Chanel's pricing strategy applies to all global markets. How do consumers in your country react to Chanel's strategy? Is it different from that in Korea? Why do you think it is different? If the same, discuss the reasons.

References

Aloisi, S. (2022, March 4). Chanel increases prices again in Europe and Asia. Reuters. www.reuters.com/business/retail-consumer/chanel-increases-prices-again-europe-asia-2022-03-04

Byun, H. (2022, March 24). Has frenzy for Chanel died down? Shoppers say rarity factor has faded. *The Korea Herald*. www.koreaherald.com/view.php?ud=20220324000730

Kim, J. (2022, February 17). Chanel losing brand value in Korea. *The Korea Times*. https://m.koreatimes.co.kr/pages/article.asp?newsIdx=324073

Rascouet, A. and Neumann, J. (2021, December 21). Chanel is aiming for Hermès status with handbag price hikes. Bloomberg. www.bloomberg.com/news/articles/2021-12-21/chanel-is-aiming-for-hermes-status-with-handbag-price-hikes

Yang, H. and Aloisi, S. (2022, March 18). Handbags at dawn: Chanel duels South Korean resellers in luxury boom. Reuters. www.reuters.com/business/retail-consumer/handbags-dawn-chanel-duels-south-korean-resellers-luxury-boom-2022-03-17

Summary

- Tariffs and taxes are placed on both imported and exported goods. Tariffs are government-imposed taxes, and import tariffs are assessed as a percentage of the landed cost of a product. The landed cost is the price after a product has landed in a host country and shipping and insurance costs have been added to the product cost. Duties are also placed on products, and they are levied on the consumer rather than the producer. Other taxes such as VAT or excise tariffs can be imposed on goods.

- Consumers sometimes travel to other countries or shop online to reap the benefits of lower taxes and more affordable goods, which is international outshopping.

- Some elements can escalate price, such as moving goods overseas, freight and insurance costs, and import tariffs. This results in price escalation, which adds up all costs resulting from exporting goods.

- Exchange rate fluctuations, inflation, and deflation also influence price escalation. They are outside a company's control and must be handled proactively.

- Some approaches to lower price escalation are: lowering the cost of goods sold, lowering tariffs, and lowering distribution costs.

- Four approaches to international pricing are: cost-plus pricing, flexible cost-plus pricing, penetration pricing, and skimming pricing.

- Company costs and goals impact pricing decisions as well. Price and volume increases can increase revenues, and cost of goods sold should be lowered to increase profit. Costs to make and sell should be lowered to increase profit. Companies should determine their goals to determine pricing, such as whether they are penetrating the market or working to secure their brand reputation. Some consumers associate quality with price, which should be taken into account.

- Market factors that impact pricing are: customer demand, competition, product life cycle stage, and economic conditions of the host market. Price should generate demand, not deter consumers from buying, so value must be justified.
- Parallel importation occurs when an unauthorized middleman transports products from lower-priced locations to countries where these products garner higher prices to make a profit. This process results in gray products that are present in the gray market. These products are not counterfeit; they are just moved around without the permission of the brand.
- With consumers being more sensitive to price and expecting transparency, brands need to be aware of competitors' prices, as consumers can easily look these up now.

Class Activities

1. Have you ever observed price differences in other countries for the same fashion brand? You can find this when you travel or search foreign e-commerce websites. Discuss your experience with your peers and its implications for consumers and fashion brands.
2. There are multiple ways you can buy a luxury item at a lower price than the price at their official boutiques or websites. Discuss the implications of the purchase for luxury brands.
3. Discuss the pros and cons of gray products for consumers and fashion brands.

Key Terms

- **Price quality association:** The common association consumers make between a product or brand's price and its respective quality. The higher the price, the better the quality.
- **Tariff:** Taxes the government imposes on goods when they cross national borders.
- **Duties:** Indirect taxes placed on the consumer of imported goods.
- **Landed cost:** Product price after it has arrived in a host country calculated by adding shipping and/or insurance cost to the product cost.
- **Value-added tax (VAT):** Tax added to a product at every point where value is added to it in the supply chain.
- **Cross-border shopping (international outshopping):** Consumers visit other countries or shop online to enjoy lower prices than in their home country.
- **De minimis tax:** A tax imposed by an importing country for cross-border e-commerce activities; a value cap for goods in which orders under this cap are exempt from the tax.
- **Price escalation:** Added costs incurred from the export of products from country to country.
- **Free on Board (FOB):** Price quote in which responsibility and liability of the goods are transferred from seller to buyer as soon as goods reach the port of origin.
- **Cost, Insurance and Freight (CIF):** Price quote in which the seller is responsible for the goods and pays insurance and freight and assumes liability until the goods reach the buyer's chosen port of destination.
- **Cost-plus pricing:** A pricing strategy calculated adding all costs incurred when goods cross national borders. Total cost depends on destination, transportation method, tariffs, fees, handling charges, and documentation costs.

- **Flexible cost-plus pricing:** Variation of cost-plus pricing strategy that ensures competitive pricing in particular market environments by adjusting price based on competitor pricing and other factors.
- **Penetration pricing:** A pricing strategy deliberately offering products at low prices to stimulate market growth.
- **Skimming pricing:** Charging a premium price to maximize products until competition forces a lower price, opposite of penetration pricing.
- **Parallel importing:** When unauthorized middlemen import identical products and brands from countries with lower prices to countries where the price is higher.
- **Gray product:** Authentic products that are imported from another country, often using parallel importation, without the permission of the brands.

CHAPTER 12
Retail and Distribution for Global Markets

Learning Objectives
After studying this chapter, you will be able to:

- Discuss why distribution channel decisions in overseas markets need to be aligned with a brand's global strategy.
- Articulate why fashion companies may need to modify their distribution channels in other countries.
- Examine the roles of local distributors and criteria in choosing the right distributors.
- Analyze the factors that influence the choice of distribution channel used by a firm.
- Compare three ways to distribute goods online and the best ways to leverage each method.
- Understand the challenges of distribution in emerging markets.

Once products are developed and prices are set, the next important decision to make is where to sell in foreign markets. Distribution channels connect consumers to fashion companies through various places where products are available for purchase, including department stores or shopping malls, both online and offline.

In Chapter 8, we learned the various methods a fashion company employs to enter a foreign market, which includes export, licensing, franchising, joint venture, wholly owned, and so on. Extending these topics, the focus of this chapter is the discussion of how the company develops and manages its distribution channels. Fashion firms may stick to their initial entry mode such as export, but they need to develop their distribution channels to increase their visibility and growth in the market. For example, a fashion company starts selling in a store in the domestic market but adds more channels to grow and make their products widely available. Zara first entered China by opening its offline stores (wholly owned direct investment) in 2006 (Fong, 2006), but as it grew, it added more stores and channels, such as online and Tmall (Wang, 2014).

The distribution channel structures, systems, and operations all vary greatly across countries. A successful distribution system in a domestic market may be hard to reproduce abroad, because it may not attract target consumers, so the distribution channel may need to be modified. In foreign markets, fashion companies may also need to contract with local distributors who know the distribution system, consumers, and market (indirect involvement), or they can choose to distribute themselves without intermediaries (direct involvement). Working with intermediaries or not, decisions regarding distribution channels require long-term commitments due to the expense associated with terminating the relationships. Therefore, local distributors should be chosen carefully.

This chapter starts with a discussion of the importance of developing distribution channels that align with brands' global strategies and why the channel may need to be localized in a host country. It then continues by introducing the various international distribution channel alternatives and moves on to fashion firms' direct and indirect involvement in managing distribution channels, with the pros and cons of each. With the growth and immense potential of e-commerce and its associated channels and platforms, digital distribution is examined in detail. Three options and their related advantages and challenges are introduced: via own brand website, selling through e-tailers (Amazon.com), and setting up a brand store on an online marketplace (such as Zalando and Alibaba's Tmall). The discussion of localization examples in a brand's own e-commerce website will also be examined. This chapter finishes with the challenges of distribution in developing countries and potential solutions.

International Distribution Channel Decision

International distribution is a vital and indispensable part of the marketing mix that links a fashion firm with its customers in markets around the world. A distribution channel represents a chain of businesses or intermediaries through which goods or services pass until they reach the final buyer or end consumer. Examples of distribution channels include wholesalers, retailers, distributors, and the internet.

This section introduces the importance of the international distribution channel decision and the reasons for channel localization.

International Distribution Channel Decisions Aligning with Brands' Strategy

The distribution channel plays a crucial role, conveying the brand image through factors such as the number of channels, intermediary type, and location. First, the number of channels should be aligned with their branding strategies. For example, for a mass brand, the greater the number of channels, the better. One example is Coca-Cola's strategy; the more consumers see it through multiple channels, the greater the chances to buy it. So, the more places these mass brands are sold, the better. Luxury brands, however, should control the number of channels to convey a prestige image and limit their availability in order to remain exclusive. Luxury brands do not use kiosks as a channel unlike mass brands.

Second, the intermediary type should be aligned with target marketing. For a premium brand, it should be distributed through high-end department stores or standalone stores. For a brand targeting young consumers, online may be better than a department store. Topshop exited the US in 2019 after ten years of operation, closing all its offline stores. One reason was ascribed to its store operations in standalone malls or kiosks within department stores, places that have seen a decline in foot traffic especially among their target consumers (Parisi, 2019).

Third, the location of stores also communicates the brand image. If you see certain brand stores located on a country's major fashion streets, such as Madison Avenue in New York City or Ginza shopping district in Tokyo, you will naturally consider the brand as a global fashion brand or well-known brand. So, just by having a flagship store in a prominent location, fashion companies can strategically create their brand image. This is often a major reason for having such flagship stores even though the profits are not great (Moore et al., 2000). Conversely, if you see a brand at JCPenney (mid-range department store in the US), you will think of the brand as a mid-range brand. In essence, distribution channel decisions should be aligned with positioning and branding strategies. The same applies to foreign markets. However, it will be challenging to identify intermediary types and locations that match well with target marketing and branding strategies in a foreign country, so working with intermediaries in the foreign market may be necessary.

Why Channel Localization Is Needed

The international distribution channel decision involves complex issues that do not exist in domestic distribution because of varying channel environments. For example, certain channels may not be available in other countries, and dominant channels vary. Shopping malls, common shopping places in the US, differ in many small European countries. M-commerce is more prevalent than e-commerce in some emerging countries (Petrov, 2022). Prevalent social media also varies. In China, many leading social media companies such as Facebook, Instagram, and YouTube are banned, but equivalent social media play the same function. This requires an understanding of such social media and their functions as a distribution channel. Therefore, as with other Ps of the marketing mix, the place of distribution decision needs to be localized. One example of distribution channel localization can be found in the UK's Body Shop. When the retailer entered the US, it was forced to open stores in shopping malls. That was a modification because Body Shop stores in other countries were small, freestanding boutiques in downtown locations (Johansson, 2009).

International Distribution Channel Selection

Fashion companies can choose from various distribution channels in foreign countries. Figure 12.1 presents the international distribution channels that fashion companies employ across countries. The fashion company can sell directly to global consumers through its directly managed stores, concession stores within department stores, its own websites, and factory outlet stores. It can also distribute indirectly via intermediaries, such as local distributors, franchise partners, and sales representatives. To consumers, however, it is indistinguishable whether a standalone store is a franchised store or directly operated store. The options and its advantages and disadvantages are now discussed.

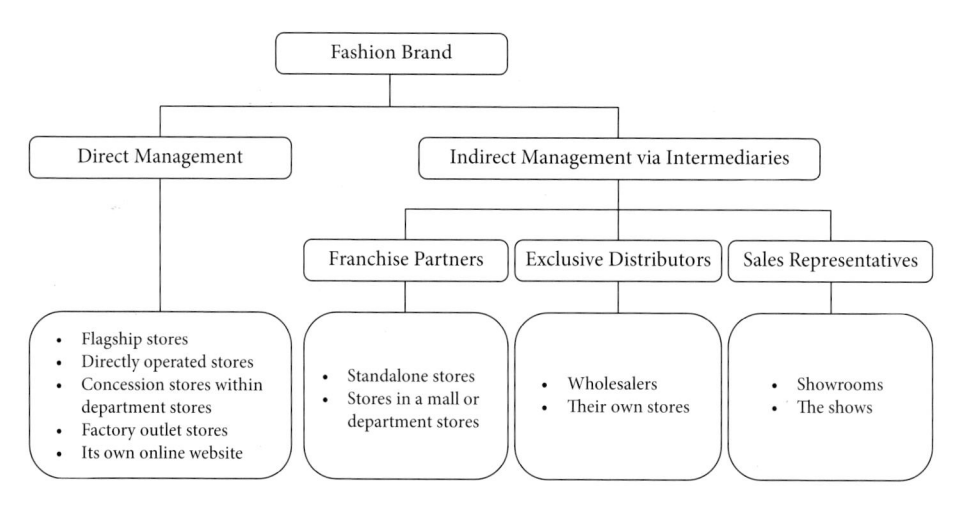

Figure 12.1 International distribution channels in the fashion industry.

Establishing Distribution Channels: Indirect Involvement

Distribution via Local Distributors

Distributing goods in other countries requires an understanding of consumers, markets, and distribution structures and systems. In the absence of such understanding, fashion brands may choose to work with local distributors who are provided with exclusive sales and distribution rights. These distributors take ownership of the merchandise and sell it via their distribution channels or wholesalers within a particular geographical location. Distributors are mostly large fashion or retail companies operating within a country. In India, for example, Genesis Colors Ltd., established in 1998, serves as an exclusive distribution partner for many global brands, including Paul Smith, Bottega Veneta, Jimmy Choo, Armani, Tumi, Michael Kors, Hugo Boss, Coach, and so on. The Chalhoub Group is the largest retail operator in the Middle East, active in the luxury, fashion, and beauty sectors. The group is a joint venture partner of Louis Vuitton, Dior Couture, Sephora, Fendi, Celine, Givenchy, Louboutin, and so on. It is also a franchise partner of Saks Fifth Avenue, Loewe, Carolina Herrera, Swarovski, Lacoste, Michael Kors, and so on. Table 12.1 presents major luxury distributors in selected countries.

There are many advantages of working with distributors. Fashion brands can capitalize on distributors' local market knowledge, including language, physical distribution, and communications. More importantly, since fashion brands utilize distributors' preexisting distribution channels, they can save time and capital they might otherwise have spent. Thus, it allows the brands' fast expansion into countries.

The major disadvantages of working with local distributors include losing control over their brand's strategy, which can hurt their brand image in the long run (Steenkamp, 2017). Korean brand On & On's initial partnership with a Chinese distributor in 1999 ended quickly because the partner copied On & On's design and sold under the partner's

Table 12.1 Major luxury distributors in selected countries

COUNTRY	LUXURY DISTRIBUTOR
China	DKSH Luxury & Lifestyle
India	Genesis Colors, Shreyans
Japan	Onward Kashiyama
Malaysia	Valiram Group
Hong Kong	Bluebell Group
Singapore	FJ Benjamin, Luxasia
United Arab Emirates	Chalhoub Group, Al Tayer Insignia, BinHendi Enterprises, Rivoli Group
Russia	Bosco di Ciliegi, Mercury

Source: Developed by the author based on Doran (2010).

brand name (Jin and Chung, 2016), which was detrimental to On & On when it tried to build brand awareness in the country. Fashion brands also lose the opportunity to learn about consumers in the host countries and therefore to tailor their product offerings based on evolving consumer needs. Companies basically cede the strategic marketing decisions to the distributors. Therefore, finding a qualified distributor who has ample experience in the fashion and retail business is critical for the success of fashion brands. These are some important points in finding the right partners (Arnold, 2000):

- *Select your distributors; don't let them select you*: A fashion company may choose to work with a distributor who approaches the company at a trade show or via other venues. The distributor may, however, already serve the company's competitors or have a different goal. The fashion company should proactively select local distributors that suit their needs through the list potentially obtained from the US Department of Commerce, the local chamber of commerce, or other related trade associations.
- *Look for distributors capable of developing markets, rather than those with a few good customer contacts*: Distributors with good customer contacts in the product category look promising for immediate return and revenues. However, for long-term goals, a better choice may be those distributors with a willingness to invest and accept an open relationship with the fashion company in marketing their products, even though the person may not have prior experience. Just having good customer contacts is not enough; instead, a distributor's capability or willingness in developing markets is more critical.
- *Maintain control over the marketing strategy*: Even though a local distributor should know the local market, it is not prudent to give them too much autonomy. From the start, fashion companies

should lead as to what products sell and how those products are positioned in the market.
- *Regard intermediaries as long-term partners, not as a temporary means of market entry*: Traditionally, a contract with local distributors addresses exclusive rights, which is good for the purpose of entry into the market but does not motivate them to undertake long-term business development. A more effective approach is to create an agreement that includes strong incentives for appropriate goals such as customer acquisition, so that distributors have an understanding of the fashion company's long-term perspective.

Distribution via Local Sales Representatives

Fashion companies may choose to establish a sales office or showroom and send managers and staff to a host country. They may hire a local sales representative if the size of the market and potential sales revenue is large enough for the investment. Similar to the functions of a manufacturer's representative in the US, overseas sales representatives promote a company's own products through diverse means, such as attending trade shows or visiting retailers and wholesalers in the host country. These representatives are normally compensated with a fixed salary plus commission. While such hires incur a resource commitment, they also give companies more control than working with local distributors. Employing a representative also allows companies to obtain a direct understanding of consumers in the host countries, providing opportunities to customize and improve product offerings accordingly. Figure 12.2 shows the examples of a showroom in Milan, Italy where sales representatives meet buyers with displayed products.

Establishing Distribution Channels: Direct Involvement

Fashion companies choose to establish their own distribution channels in foreign countries. Directly operated channels include

Figure 12.2 A building with many showrooms (left) and a showroom inside (right).
Source: Courtesy B. Ellie Jin.

flagship stores, directly managed stores, concession stores within department stores, brands' own websites, and factory outlet stores. In addition to these channels, more innovative store concepts are opened in major fashion cities. Nike Rise in Seoul, which opened in 2021, is a sort of flagship store but experiments with new concepts combining digital and physical experiences with localized digital services. Nike Rise is meant to be unique to a specific city that connects many local events and local runs (Nike Inc., 2021; Salpini, 2021). Another digital-led retail concept is Polo Ralph Lauren's new store in Beijing, developed by partnering with Tencent (a Chinese technology conglomerate holding company). It is the first of its kind featuring a Ralph's Coffee space, smart retail and digital technologies, virtual try-ons, an in-store treasure hunt that uses QR codes, and stations where shoppers can order customized products from their phones (Rozario, 2021; Wassel, 2021). Similar to flagship stores, these new concept stores require considerable capital investment but are effective in positioning brands as global and digital. By incorporating local components, the brands effectively approach consumers in the cities.

The advantages of brands having their own distribution channels are the control and freedom to create their own desired images for their positioning and branding strategies. One of the major disadvantages, however, is the cost of the investment. UK fashion retailer New Look entered China in 2014 directly without a local distributor. It required substantial investment to build its own distribution system, resulting in huge operational loss. New Look exited China in 2018 without recovering from the loss (Suen, 2019). Another downside lies in difficulties in navigating host countries where the cultural and retail environments differ hugely from the domestic market. In India, a market of immense potential, whose dynamism is matched only by its extreme complexity, Wrangler, Under Armour, and Lee initially entered the market without intermediaries but after a few years decided to work with local partners (Hall and Jay, 2021).

Factors Influencing a Firm's Choice of Distribution Channel

Distribution channels are the places to sell fashion brands' products, so it is desirable to cover a foreign country entirely. However, to build distribution channels across a country means resources and time for a fashion company. If working with a local distributor who already has these channels, these cost issues can be solved but control issues occur. That is, market development is mainly up to the distributor's capabilities, and less control is given to the fashion company. The loss of control in international distribution channels is greater than in domestic ones because the company has no one there to monitor the distributor's activities and performance. Moreover, goal differences between the distributor and the fashion firm can create conflict. For example, if the distributor focuses mainly on short-term profit when the fashion company pursues building up brand awareness slowly even though the sales are not great, the differing goal cannot be adequately reconciled. The ideal distribution channel would be one with optimum coverage and control at a minimum cost. So, decisions should be made based on market coverage, control, and cost.

One point to highlight is that companies can choose different distribution channels country by country. That is, while fashion brands may choose local distributors in some countries, they may choose to directly operate their own distribution channels in other countries. For example, luxury brands often leverage a network of exclusive distributors in Asia, Russia, and UAE where cultural and retail differences are great, while directly distributing via their own directly managed stores in home markets of Europe and the US.

Digital Distribution: Opportunities and Challenges in the Global Marketplace

With the increasing use of e-commerce, mobile platforms, and social media as distribution channels, fashion companies are expanding into global markets. Various methods can be used for digital distribution. Following Steenkamp (2017), they fall into three categories: selling through online marketplaces (Amazon.com), setting up a brand store on an online marketplace (Zalando and Alibaba's Tmall), and selling via a fashion brand's own website. These three ways are described with advantages and disadvantages.

Selling through Online Marketplaces

With the popularity of online shopping, an increasing number of large international e-tailers, such as Amazon.com, provide e-commerce marketplaces from which fashion firms distribute their merchandise to international consumers. For example, apparel companies in the US supply their goods to Amazon.com, who then sells and delivers to consumers in foreign markets via its distribution logistics. Similarly, small apparel firms in China sell their goods to international consumers via AliExpress.com, the Chinese version of Amazon.com. Unlike Amazon that sells to both domestic and international consumers, AliExpress was set up by Alibaba.com to sell mainly to international consumers. Alibaba.com has developed various e-commerce sites to target diverse consumer groups; for example, it established Tmall Global in 2014, which allows global fashion brands to sell to Chinese consumers without having a retail presence in China.

Table 12.2 summarizes the major online marketplaces in many different countries in which apparel firms sell their goods to domestic consumers as well as to international consumers. The popularity of these online marketplaces aligns with the trend of international consumers' shopping at other countries' websites without traveling to those countries (Ramkumar and Jin, 2019).

Among the three options, selling through online marketplaces might be the easiest way to reach consumers in other countries, in that fashion brands do not need to dispatch products or people to other countries as e-tailers handle order fulfillment such as delivery. They also do not need to develop their own websites. Another important advantage is the ease of attracting consumers, since e-tailers are known and have established their presence in home as well as international markets. In addition, fashion brands do not handle website design, management and security, which can be good for small firms with limited resources, but this also means less control. Fashion brands cannot feature their brand at its entirety, as presentations on the websites are mostly item-based, not brand-based. Consumers find the fashion brand by searching items as you do on Amazon.com.

Table 12.2 Major online marketplaces in selected countries

COUNTRY	ONLINE MARKETPLACE (YEAR ESTABLISHED)	OPERATING COUNTRIES (NUMBER OF COUNTRIES)
Argentina	Mercado Libre (1999)	Argentina, Bolivia, Brazil, Chile, Colombia, Costa Rica, Dominican Republic, Mexico, Spain, Ecuador, Guatemala, Honduras, Peru, Panama, Uruguay, Venezuela (16)
China	Alibaba (1999) Tmall (2008) AliExpress (2010)	China, Hong Kong, Taiwan, the US, the UK, Korea, Singapore, Italy, France, Germany, the Netherlands, Japan, Australia, New Zealand, India, Turkey, Pakistan, Canada (18)
Germany	Zalando (2008)	Germany, Austria, Switzerland, France, Belgium, the Netherlands, Italy, Spain, Poland, Sweden, Denmark, Finland, Norway, Slovenia, Ireland, Luxembourg, the Czech Republic, Slovakia, Croatia, the UK, Lithuania, Latvia, Estonia, Hungary, Romania (25)
India	Flipkart (2007) Myntra (2007)	India (1)
Japan	Rakuten (1997)	Japan, Taiwan, India, Singapore, China, Hong Kong, South Korea, the UK, the US, Spain, Luxembourg, Canada, Thailand, France (14)
Nigeria	Jumia (2012)	Nigeria, Egypt, South Africa, Ivory Coast, Kenya, Morocco, Tanzania, Algeria, Ghana, Cameroon, Tunisia, Uganda (12)
Singapore	Lazada (2012) Shopee (2015)	Singapore, Indonesia, Malaysia, the Philippines, Thailand, Vietnam (6) Singapore, Indonesia, Malaysia, Philippines, Thailand, Vietnam, Taiwan, Brazil, Chile, Colombia, Mexico, Poland (12)
South Korea	Coupang (2010)	South Korea (1)
US	Amazon (1994)	The US, Egypt, Brazil, Canada, Mexico, China, India, Japan, Saudi Arabia, Singapore, Turkey, UAE, France, Germany, Italy, the Netherlands, Poland, Spain, Sweden, the UK, Australia (21)
	eBay (1995)	The US, Australia, Austria, Belgium, Canada, France, Germany, Ireland, Italy, Hong Kong, Malaysia, the Netherlands, Philippines, Poland, Singapore, Spain, Switzerland, Taiwan, Thailand, the UK, Vietnam (21)

Gross margin is not great, as e-tailers typically command 30 percent of margin for fulfilling orders and handling websites. This option also does not allow fashion brands to interact with their customers directly, and important data that could be used for future product development purposes, such as consumers' search and purchase behavior, cannot be obtained. In sum, this option might be good for small firms that look for international opportunities but have fewer resources. It can also serve as a test before actually committing resources to international markets.

Digital Distribution via Fashion Brand's Own Brand Website

The next digital distribution option is selling via a fashion brand's own website. This typically involves allowing international consumers to order directly from the company's website. Companies then handle delivery to foreign consumers. American brand J.Crew ships directly to more than a hundred countries from the US upon receiving orders at its websites. Hong Kong, Japan, and Australia are among J.Crew's top five international e-commerce markets.

In addition to their own official website in the language of their home country (English in the case of J.Crew), many global fashion brands add various languages to reach international consumers. In the case of Nike, for example, when opening Nike.com, a viewer will be asked to choose their country. Once the viewer selects their country, a dropdown menu will appear listing a selection of different languages spoken in that country. The pages they are taken to not only are specialized for their language but use targeted marketing content as well (Praffulljain, 2016).

A brand's website for international consumers does not just mean translating the language to local languages. Website localization entails adapting websites to meet the linguistic, cultural, and commercial requirements of a target market. The following features need to be considered in web localization (Export.gov, 2018):

- *Language*: Some countries read from right to left or top to bottom. It should be more than a translation. Subtle nuances should also be considered. As mentioned in Chapter 10, correct clothing terms (pants in the US vs. trousers in the UK) should be used even in countries using the same language.
- *Cultural nuances*: In Chapter 4, we learned that contextual cues are more important in high-context cultures, while verbal expression works better in low-context cultures. Similarly, websites for consumers in high-context countries (Japan, Korea, and China) use more symbolic visuals, celebrity models, graphics, photographs, and illustrations than the ones designed for low-context nations (the US, the UK, and Germany) (An, 2007; Kim et al., 2009). Differences in color association and symbols should be also correctly reflected.
- *Payment preferences*: Credit cards are not widely used as payment in some countries. Cash on delivery (COD) is a common practice in many emerging markets in the Middle East, Africa, and India. COD allows buyers to pay cash when the order is delivered. WeChat and Alipay, similar to Apple Pay and PayPal

in the US, are largely used in China, and many diverse e-wallets, such as PayTM, Oxigen, Mobikwik, and PayUmoney, are used in India. Thus, websites should offer these payment options in the respective countries (Toppan, 2022).

- *Pricing and measurement*: If the prices are not in their currency, 33 percent of shoppers are likely to abandon their shopping carts (Benaiche, 2021). In addition, a proper unit system should be used in foreign websites. While the metric system is widely used, some countries use imperial units. Thus, appropriate modifications are needed to reflect the target country's currency and measurement system.

The advantages and disadvantages of distribution via a fashion brand's own website are the opposite to the selling through online marketplaces. Since fashion companies present and sell at their own websites, they can control the content and prices, featuring their desired brand images. Gross margin will also be higher since there are no middlemen between consumers and the firms (no need to pay 30 percent to the online marketplaces). Firms can utilize the consumer data available at their website, which can be used for future marketing plans and product development. However, if the brands are not well known, attracting consumers to their websites may be challenging, but this is not a problem for prestige brands and established brands.

One might think that this option is favored more by prestige and established brands, but an increasing number of new companies are opting for this option and are being successful. Good examples include the UK's Gymshark and China's Shein. Both were established in 2012 and sold directly to international consumers via their own websites without owning any physical stores. Gymshark and Shein now deliver worldwide to more than 131 and 150 countries, respectively. Both companies are very popular in the US. Forty percent of Gymshark's market share comes from the US (Bearne, 2018), and Shein outperforms H&M and Zara in the US (Chen, 2022; Kennedy, 2022; Lieber and Chen, 2022). However, Gymshark opened its first offline store in London in 2020.

Setting Up a Brand Store on an Online Marketplace

Fashion brands can choose to open a brand store on foreign online marketplaces that provide the brands with online platforms, such as Tmall and JD.com in China and Rakuten in Japan. That is, global fashion brands choose to have their website in a foreign online marketplace to reach consumers in that country. Tmall offers virtual storefronts to merchants who then sell directly to consumers in China and handle their own logistics (Morris, 2014). Tmall requires its merchants to have entities in China, thus merchants on Tmall tend to be larger Chinese brands and leading global brands such as Burberry, Zara, Ralph Lauren, Adidas, Calvin Klein, and so on. It lists more than 70,000 global and Chinese brands. This option is similar to having a brand store in a shopping mall where the brand can select the merchandise, set prices, and handle customer service. Like a shopping mall that does not own merchandise, Tmall provides a virtual space without owning merchandise.

The advantages and disadvantages of this option are broadly between the two options examined above. That is, by opening a brand store on a well-known online marketplace, it can create consumer traffic without much difficulty. Also, by having a brand store there, fashion brands have the freedom to directly market their goods to target consumers in foreign countries. Costs to put out their virtual storefront are also between the other two options. Tmall, for example, charges 5 percent or less (Steenkamp, 2017).

It is good that fashion companies have their independent virtual storefront at the online marketplace so they can control its content and order fulfillment, but they have to follow the format dictated by the marketplace and thus have little room to convey unique brand imagery. For this reason, Uniqlo shut its online store in JD.com in 2015. Since the fashion brands operate within the online marketplace system, consumer data on their website are shared with the marketplace. Having a virtual storefront at online marketplaces is growing as an attractive option for lesser known brands that desire to go global. Yet finding the right online marketplace is critical. The UK's Topshop initially entered China in 2014 by opening its website at Shangpin.com, an online luxury retailer in China but smaller than Tmall. Topshop's partnership with Shangpin.com was terminated early in 2018. Not having the right

Table 12.3 Comparison of three digital distribution options for global brands

	Own Brand Website (e.g., Nike.com)	Brand Store On Online Marketplace (e.g., Tmall.com, Zalando.com)	Selling Through E-Tailers (e.g., Amazon.com)
Control over marketing mixes	High	Intermediate	Limited
Control over brand image and website design	High	Intermediate. Can feature their brand image within the marketplace format	Limited
Gross margin	High	Medium	Low
Access to consumer data	High. Can analyze consumer data for future product development and marketing	Intermediate	Limited
Attracting consumers to the websites	Difficult for small businesses but easy for well-known brands	Intermediate	Easy, thanks to the popularity of e-tailers
Order fulfillment (e.g. delivery)	Complex. Needs to have its own order fulfillment system	Intermediate	Easy, as e-tailers will handle it

partner was seen as the reason for its failure in China (Bi, 2020; Suen, 2019).

Table 12.3 compares the three digital selling options. In many respects, establishing a brand store on an online marketplace falls between selling through a brand's own website and selling through online marketplaces. With the understanding of the three options, fashion companies can choose the right digital channel that fits their branding strategies, considering the digital and retail environments in foreign marketplaces. In other words, fashion companies can use different digital channels from country to country. For example, Japanese brand Uniqlo chose to have an online presence at Tmall in China but opened its own website in India (Hall and Jay, 2021).

Fashion brands can add more digital distribution channels to the existing ones as they grow in a foreign market. Zara opened an online flagship store on Tmall.com in 2014 in addition to its own website in China in 2012. Also, multiple digital channels can be added later to the offline distribution channel. Ralph Lauren has launched its online presence on many digital channels, including Tmall.com, JD.com, and WeChat, along with its standalone offline stores and its own websites in China (Wong, 2017). More information on WeChat is presented in Case Study 12.1. Fashion brands distribute their goods through multiple department stores and multiple e-commerce sites in their home country. Distribution in other countries is the same. Brands must choose the right distribution channels to suit their branding and strategic directions, given the retail and digital environments in foreign countries. They are also recommended to explore the new digital distribution channel of livestreaming to reach target consumers in foreign countries (see Box 12.1).

BOX 12.1

Livestreaming as a New Digital Distribution Channel

Streaming services of many kinds saw record growth during the Covid-19 pandemic, a trend that is continuing to grow. Livestream shopping is the instant purchase of a featured product during a livestream with audience participation through a chat function or reaction buttons on social media platforms. It is immersive and entertaining, allowing viewers to watch for long periods of time. For livestream shopping, typically a key opinion leader/consumer is engaged to host the show, showcase the product, and interact with the audience to drive sales. It opens cross-selling opportunities not only by showing the audience how to apply or use a particular product but also by suggesting how to coordinate with other products. This innovative format increases the appeal and distinctiveness of brands and attracts additional web traffic with time-limited tactics.

Livestream shopping is similar to home shopping networks like QVC in the US but with some key differences. While the majority of

US home shopping network viewers are aged 55 and over, livestream shopping is geared toward younger consumers. Additionally, in traditional home shopping, viewers make phone calls to order items, whereas livestream shopping is based on social media platforms, which allows viewers to respond and interact directly through comments, likes, and polls. For example, anyone watching a livestream shopping broadcast can ask a question about the products or ask the host to show them from different directions and angles. Moreover, home shopping is carried out in a broadcasting station studio, whereas livestream shopping is not limited to places, such as a host visiting a boutique shop in New York to broadcast inside the store.

China is at the frontier of livestreaming sales transactions utilizing social media platforms. It is already booming in China, as Chinese retail giants WeChat and Taobao pioneered a powerful new approach by connecting online livestream broadcasts to e-commerce platforms, allowing viewers to watch and shop at the same time. According to a survey, by 2020, two-thirds of Chinese consumers had experience of purchasing products via a livestream event (McKinsey Digital, 2021).

At the moment, livestream shopping is not as popular in the US as it is in China, but it is slowly gaining ground. Social media giants such as Facebook, Instagram, YouTube, and TikTok are making huge investments in order to take advantage of the new shopping features and functionalities. Livestream shopping is in its infancy, but it's worth noting that there's plenty of market potential. Several successful cases show its potential.

Tommy Hilfiger hosted a livestream show in China in summer 2020, which drew 14 million viewers and sold 1,300 hoodies in just two minutes (WARC, 2020). This encouraged the brand to later expand its livestreaming program into Europe and North America. Walmart held the first shoppable livestream fashion event with TikTok in December 2020. It received more than seven times the views it had anticipated and grew its TikTok followers by 25 percent. Walmart celebrated one year of livestreaming shopping shows on Twitter in November 2021 (White, 2021). Nordstrom, one of the biggest US department store retailers, also created its own new shopping channel called Livestream Shopping in 2021. According to its senior vice president: "Livestream Shopping enables us to stay closer to the customer with interactive and engaging experiences that allow for discovery, personalization and service at scale" (Nordstrom, 2021). During each Livestream Shopping event, customers can shop products available at Nordstrom.com and participate in a live chat.

In the post-pandemic situation and with growing functionality, livestream shopping is experiencing a surge in brands, consumers, and investor participation. Brands need to keep an eye on this new shopping channel to see how it works. At the very least, it has an entertainment component, while simplifying the consumer's purchase journey and improving their shopping experience.

References

McKinsey Digital (2021, July 21). It's showtime! How live commerce is transforming the shopping experience. McKinsey & Company. www.mckinsey.com/business-functions/

mckinsey-digital/our-insights/its-showtime-how-live-commerce-is-transforming-the-shopping-experience

Nordstrom (2021, March 18) Nordstrom introduces livestream shopping. https://press.nordstrom.com/news-releases/news-release-details/nordstrom-introduces-livestream-shopping

WARC (2020, October 13). US brands adopt e-commerce livestreaming to boost sales. www.warc.com/newsandopinion/news/us-brands-adopt-e-commerce-livestreaming-to-boost-sales/en-gb/44218

White, W. (2021, November 22). Walmart celebrates one year of livestreams with first shoppable livestream on Twitter. Walmart. https://corporate.walmart.com/newsroom/2021/11/22/walmart-celebrates-one-year-of-livestreams-with-first-shoppable-livestream-on-twitter

Challenges in Developing Countries: Payment and Logistics Challenges

Distribution in developing countries can be challenging as the distribution system and associated infrastructure are not equivalent to those of developed countries. In particular, paying with credit cards, which is commonplace in developed countries, is not widespread for two reasons. First, credit cards themselves are not widely available and, second, even if credit cards are available, consumers do not have confidence in using them for fear of fraud and a lack of legal protection if fraud occurs. A couple of solutions are used. As already noted, cash on delivery is a popular payment option in many developing countries. However, this method incurs high logistics costs for fashion companies because if consumers are not home multiple delivery attempts could be made for one order. Other solutions include the use of e-wallets such as Alipay or WeChat in China and PayTM in India. Mobile platforms, such as M-Pesa in Kenya, are also popular (Insider Intelligence, 2017).

The next challenge in developing countries is related to logistics. Some countries do not have house numbers, have invisible street signs or have complex address systems, so even the most up-to-date GPS cannot find them. Postal codes are not used in the UAE, for example, so there is a high chance of online orders being lost or returned during delivery. In some parts of the Middle East, it is estimated that up to 40 percent of packages are returned to senders because recipient locations cannot be found. E-commerce in Nigeria, the world's seventh most populous country, is now quickly growing, but 79 percent of the nation's homes and businesses still cannot receive door-to-door delivery (Jiang, 2017). To handle this issue, many e-commerce companies in India now use "kiranas" as physical pickup points beyond urban centers. Kiranas are small local independent mom and pop shops that sell groceries and a variety of other merchandise. Because of their personal knowledge of local clients, this delivery system works well. For example, Myntra, a major Indian fashion e-commerce company headquartered in Bengaluru, Karnataka, has partnered with over 15,000 small shops across India (Jay, 2020).

CASE STUDY 12.1
WeChat and Mobile Shopping in China

In China, online shopping largely means mobile shopping. China's smartphone ownership has reached 96 percent, surpassing the global average of 90 percent (Chou et al., 2019). More Chinese consumers shop weekly on mobile (45 percent) than via PC (35 percent) (Birtwhistle, 2017). Chinese consumers prefer to use social media for shopping significantly more than the global average (Accenture, 2017). About one-third of total online time is spent on social media, and between 2017 and 2019, the number of Chinese consumers making purchases directly from social media had almost quadrupled (Bu et al., 2019).

At the center of this trend is WeChat, the Chinese version of WhatsApp, the messaging app now owned by Facebook. Launched in 2011 by Tencent, one of China's top tech companies, WeChat is the most popular instant messaging app in China, with 1 billion monthly active users. Unlike WhatsApp, in addition to the messaging function, WeChat offers a wide range of features that allow users to carry out multiple activities, such as hailing a cab, paying bills, or booking a hotel. Because virtually everything is integrated into this one app, WeChat is referred to as "the super app." WeChat users can enjoy a multitude of different services without ever needing to leave and open a different app. This one-stop feature is possible because of the "mini-programs" or sub-apps that can be accessed only within WeChat (Rapp, 2018).

One of the main features that the mini-programs support is the WeChat store, a digital store linked to the company's official WeChat account. Among 2.3 million mini-programs, 18 percent are dedicated to e-commerce (Azoya Consulting, 2019). Within the store, customers can make a purchase through WeChat Pay, an integrated payment system that can be linked to Chinese debit or credit cards.

Apparel is among the most popular with the WeChat shoppers, with WeChat-initiated purchases accounting for about 30 percent of online spending in this category (Wang et al., 2016). For Chinese luxury consumers, over 60 percent of the product discovery and research done online comes from social media, and WeChat is the most utilized social platform for discovery and research. Cognizant of WeChat's role, quite a few global brands, particularly luxury brands such as Cartier, Burberry, Gucci, Louis Vuitton, and Longchamp have stores on WeChat (Ren, 2018). For example, Cartier sells around 60 products via WeChat. In 2017, on Valentine's Day, Cartier sold limited edition pink gold bracelets exclusively via WeChat, which sold out in a few days (Shannon, 2017). Gucci's mini-program store has full e-commerce functionality, including a live chat customer support mobile application (Azoya Consulting, 2019).

Without operating a full store, brands can still offer one-time sales or send promotional messages directly to customers (Kharpal, 2019). For example, in 2019, the Parisian fashion house Balenciaga hosted a flash sale of a single limited edition item—a pink monogram Logo Ville bag (Zheng, 2019). Chanel, on the other hand, uses WeChat primarily as a content marketing platform without e-commerce capabilities. On its account, Chanel shares information about products, brand history, makeup tips, and company news in the form of text-based content with pictures and videos (Chen, 2016).

For many businesses on WeChat, the mini-programs have paid off. According to a WeChat impact report by the China Academy of Information and Communications Technology (CAICT, 2018), 57 percent of registered businesses reported that the mini-programs contributed to over 10 percent of their new subscriptions, while 73 percent reported that the mini-programs boosted their sales. Given the sheer size of the user base and its integration into Chinese consumers' everyday life, WeChat, coupled with its user-friendly payment system, is undeniably a powerful sales and marketing tool for companies doing business in China.

Discussion Questions
1. What is the role of WeChat in China? What are the implications for global brands seeking to enter or already operating in China?
2. What are the advantage of using WeChat in China compared to other digital means?
3. What do you think are the benefits and challenges of operating a WeChat store for global brands?

References

Accenture (2017). Gen Z and millennials leaving older shoppers and many retailers in their digital dust. www.accenture.com/t20170503 t114448z__w__/us-en/_acnmedia/pdf-44/ accenture-retail-customer-research-executive-summary-2017.pdf

Azoya Consulting (2019). The WeChat mini-program playbook for e-commerce. www.azoyagroup.com/resources/view/the-wechat-mini-program-playbook-for-e-commerce

Bansal, S., Botta, A., Bruno, P., Denecker, O., Digiacomo, N. et al. (2019). *Global payments report 2019: Amid sustained growth, accelerating challenges demand bold actions.* Mckinsey & Company. www.mckinsey.com/~/media/mckinsey/industries/financial%20services/our%20insights/tracking%20the%20sources%20of%20robust%20payments%20growth%20mckinsey%20global%20payments%20map/global-payments-report-2019-amid-sustained-growth-vf.ashx

Birtwhistle, T. (2017). *Total retail report 2017: Ecommerce in China: the future is already here.* PWC. www.pwccn.com/en/retail-and-consumer/publications/total-retail-2017-china/total-retail-survey-2017-china-cut.pdf?

Bu, L., Wang, J., Wang, K.W. and Zipser, D. (2019). *China digital consumer trends 2019.* McKinsey. www.mckinsey.com/~/media/mckinsey/featured%20insights/china/china%20digital%20consumer%20trends%20in%202019/china-digital-consumer-trends-in-2019.ashx

CAICT (2018). *WeChat economic and social impact report 2017.* www.caict.ac.cn/kxyj/qwfb/ztbg/201805/P020180529380481819634.pdf

Chen, Y. (2016, June 1). How Burberry, Coach and Chanel win over WeChat users. Digiday. https://digiday.com/marketing/burberry-coach-chanel-win-wechat-users

Chou, W., Lam, Y. and Chung, R. (2019). *Chinese consumers at the forefront of digital technologies: 2018 Deloitte China*

Mobile Consumer Survey. www2.deloitte.com/content/dam/Deloitte/cn/Documents/technology-media-telecommunications/deloitte-cn-2018-mobile-consumer-survey-en-190121.pdf

Kharpal, A. (2019, February 3). Everything you need to know about WeChat – China's billion-user messaging app. CNBC. www.cnbc.com/2019/02/04/what-is-wechat-china-biggest-messaging-app.html

Rapp, J. (2018, June 23). How luxury brands use four social media apps in China to reach consumers who shop mostly online. *South China Morning Post*. www.scmp.com/lifestyle/fashion-beauty/article/2151762/how-luxury-brands-use-four-social-media-apps-china-reach

Ren, Y. (2018, November 19). Know your Chinese social media. *The New York Times*. www.nytimes.com/2018/11/19/fashion/china-social-media-weibo-wechat.html

Shannon, S. (2017, March 22). Cartier talks about cracking China with WeChat. *Financial Times*. www.ft.com/content/ea5402ae-e795-11e6-967b-c88452263daf

Wang, K.W., Lau, A. and Gong, F. (2016). How savvy, social shoppers are transforming Chinese e-commerce. McKinsey & Company. www.mckinsey.com/industries/retail/our-insights/how-savvy-social-shoppers-are-transforming-chinese-e-commerce

Zheng, R. (2019, January 17). Balenciaga blowout?: Paris brand tempts China market with WeChat flash sale. *Jing Daily*. https://jingdaily.com/balenciaga-china-flash-sale

Summary

- Distribution channels, such as department stores, shopping malls, or online retailers, are the next decision brands should make after developing products and prices. International distribution is important to connect global customers with fashion brands.
- The number of channels, the intermediary type, and the location of stores must align with the brand's target market and its image.
- Distribution decisions need to be localized to adapt to dominant channels and expectations of various market environments.
- Indirect involvement in distribution channels involves cooperation with local distributors who own the merchandise and use their own established channels and image in a specific geographic location to sell the merchandise for fashion brands. Indirect involvement allows brands the benefit of distributors' local knowledge of culture and consumers. One disadvantage is loss of control.
- Some key strategies for finding beneficial partners are: select distributors with purpose, look for distributors that can develop markets, maintain control over the marketing strategy, and regard intermediaries as long-term partners.
- Brands can hire local sales representatives or send managers and staff to a host country. Hiring local sales representatives can be expensive but gives brands more control and knowledge of local consumers than using local distributors.
- Direct involvement entails the establishment of a brand's own distribution channels, such as flagship stores, brand-owned websites, or factory outlet stores. Having brand-owned

channels benefits brands through control and freedom of positioning and strategies, but it is expensive and can lead to difficulty understanding cultural and retail environments.
- Factors that influence a firm's choice of distribution channel are cost and control. The best channel optimizes coverage and control while incurring the least cost to the brand. Brands can have different channel strategies for different countries.
- Online marketplaces allow brands to expand internationally with logistics handled by the marketplace. It is the easiest way to reach consumers as brands don't have to establish their own websites, and online marketplaces are already known. There is less control, but website operations, management, and security are handled by the online marketplace.
- Fashion brands' own websites let international consumers order products straight from a company. This requires more resources but gives brands more control than online marketplaces. Important considerations to localize a brand's website are language, cultural nuances, payment preferences, and pricing and measurement.
- Finally, brands can set up stores on online marketplaces, rather than just selling the products themselves in the online marketplace. This means that brands have their website on the online marketplace, like a store in a mall. Consumer traffic can be easily generated, brands can market directly to target consumers, and costs to set up the storefront are relatively low. However, there is little room to communicate brand image.
- Developing countries present challenges with payment and logistics issues. Payment and mailing systems are not always developed and can lead to consumers giving up on their attempt to purchase products.

Class Activities

1. Have you ever ordered fashion goods from e-commerce companies in other countries? How were your experiences? Were you able to navigate the websites easily and place your orders without difficulties? Share your challenges and compare them with your peers. What would you suggest for the companies?
2. Discuss the pros and cons of working with local distributors.
3. Recently, fashion companies that used their website as a major distribution tool in foreign countries have been successful. The UK's Gymshark and China's Shein are two examples. Explore similar examples and research their global strategies. Discuss if these strategies can be applied to small fashion companies in your country.

Key Terms

- **Distribution channel:** Chain of businesses or intermediaries through which the final buyer purchases goods or services. Distribution channels include wholesalers, retailers, distributors, and the internet.
- **Distribution localization:** Developing distribution channel strategies that best align with the foreign consumer market and culture.
- **Distributors:** Firms in international countries that gain exclusive sales and distribution rights

by a fashion brand. They take ownership of the product and sell it via their own distribution channels or wholesalers.

- **Showroom:** Presents a selection of products for buyers to shop from.
- **Local sales representative:** Individuals who promote a brand's product through various means. Selected from the population of the foreign country, they attend trade shows or visit retailers and wholesalers, and are compensated with salary plus commission.
- **Online marketplace:** E-commerce websites that sell a brand's products directly to consumers and handle shipping and logistics.
- **Virtual storefront:** A brand's website contained on a foreign online marketplace that consumers can purchase products from.
- **Website localization:** Adapting websites to meet the linguistic, cultural, and commercial requirements of a target market.
- **Cash on delivery (COD):** Allows buyers to pay cash when an order is delivered, common in many emerging markets.
- **E-wallets:** Online wallets that contain payment methods, such as Apple Pay or Alipay.
- **Livestream shopping:** The instant purchase of a featured product during a livestream event with audience participation through chats or reactions on social media platforms.
- **Direct involvement:** The establishment by fashion brands of their own distribution channels in foreign countries, such as flagship stores, directly managed stores, own websites, or factory outlet stores.
- **Indirect involvement:** Distributing goods in foreign countries without the establishment of own channels through local distributors or sales representatives.

CHAPTER 13
Communications and Advertising to Global Consumers

Learning Objectives

After studying this chapter, you will be able to:

- Articulate global advertising standardization and its pros and cons.
- Describe the barriers that deter advertising standardization.
- Illustrate the varying degrees of advertising adaptation from a simple change such as translating into local languages to new advertising campaign development.
- Discuss the pros and cons of global advertising adaptation.
- Demonstrate how effective advertising appeals and styles vary by cultures.
- Understand the challenges and regulations in international advertising across countries.

Once products are developed to meet target global consumers' needs, prices are set, and distribution channels are decided, global consumers must be informed of the offerings through communications. The last element of the marketing mix we will learn in this chapter is communication (promotion). Similar to domestic marketing, fashion companies need to take an integrated marketing communication approach, integrating all elements of the marketing communication mix—advertising, sales promotions, personal selling, public relations, and publicity—to achieve optimal synergies in global markets. With the differing economic, cultural, and legal environments, the same communication strategies may not work well in global markets. Global fashion companies, therefore, need to choose effective communication tools and the extent of standardization and adaptation in communication strategies. Effective communication tools differ by country. Personal selling may be effective in countries where comparison advertisement is legally banned such as Japan and low-wage countries enable the hiring of large local sales forces. But training sales associates in host countries may be challenging because service expectations and customer service level may vary country to country.

Among many communication tools, this chapter focuses on advertising, a major communication tool. First, this chapter will address international advertising standardization and localization issues and barriers to advertising standardization. One of the barriers of advertising standardization is cultural diversity among countries. Communication is a two-way process. Persons who receive messages need to interpret the messages created in a different cultural context. The differing cultural contexts can cause a greater chance of misunderstandings than in a domestic market. The chapter then turns to the cultural implications of international advertising. In general, studies suggest that advertising persuasion can be enhanced when it matches the cultural orientation of the society. The cultural frameworks we learned in Chapter 4 will be applied in discussing culturally effective messages. Third, the chapter explores the challenges in international advertising, in particular, highlighting advertising regulations and legal constraints across the world and their implications on fashion advertising.

Global Advertising: Standardization vs. Adaptation

Global fashion brand managers need to ask whether advertising messages and media strategy need to be changed from region to region or country to country. If changed, the extent of the changes should be decided. Advertising standardization means keeping the key elements of the advertising campaign the same across countries. This standardization approach saves time and resources, and with the same message, brand image consistency across the markets can be well maintained.

However, differences among countries make standardization a challenge. These are some of the barriers that deter advertising standardization:

- *Cultural differences among countries*: Advertising is created with the assumption that the sender's message will be interpreted by receivers as it is intended. If both sender and receiver share the same common experiences and history, there will be a high chance of interpreting the sender's intention and evaluating the content without misunderstanding. However, advertising created in one culture may not transfer well to other cultures as there are less shared experience and history. Also, values and purchase motivations differ by culture, thus using the same appeal and execution styles across cultures can be ineffective. For example, in high-context cultures, implicit and indirect messages are effective, while in low-context cultures, explicit and direct messages work better.
- *Legal constraints*: The same advertisement cannot be used in some countries owing to laws and regulations in host countries. For example, in countries where comparative advertising is banned, it must be modified. Hours of TV advertising are regulated in some European countries, and content is censored in many Muslim countries. Fashion companies must modify their advertisements to respect the host countries' laws and regulations.
- *Linguistic limitations*: Advertising messages, taglines, or slogans may need to be translated into the local language,

but capturing the same meaning is no easy task as the nuances may not be correctly transferred. Sometimes, the languages in host countries may not have proper words for translation. For this reason, visuals, rather than text that needs translation, have been used for standardizing print advertisements. Such highly standardized visual campaigns, however, are not always successful. For example, Benetton's 1989 advert showing a Black woman nursing a white baby was well received in Europe effectively showing the "United Colors of Benetton" slogan. The same ad was controversial in the US because the Black woman was interpreted as a nanny or in a subordinate role as a slave. As this case shows, even visuals are not uniformly understood across cultures (Callow and Schiffman, 2002).

- *Media limitations*: Preferred media as well as the extent of social media usage vary country to country. Social media use relative to population is higher in Eastern Asia (71 percent), North America (69 percent), and Northern Europe (67 percent) than Eastern Europe (49 percent), Southern Asia (27 percent), Western Africa (13 percent), and Eastern Africa (8 percent) (Kemp, 2020). Facebook is most common in the Philippines, Vietnam, Tunisia, Venezuela, and Kenya, while WhatsApp is most common in Mexico, Colombia, Jordan, South Africa, India, and Lebanon (Silver et al., 2019). Popular influencers and celebrities are also different. Thus assuming that the same social media platform is used across nations is impractical, and the particular platform, celebrities, and influencers should be carefully selected to fully utilize the power of social media.

To handle these barriers, fashion companies may need to change their advertising campaigns. Adaptation enhances not only the communication effectiveness but also revenues. One study discovered that brands that adequately adapted to local cultures generated higher revenue than their counterparts (Shi and Xu, 2020). As with other marketing elements, the extent of adaptation is broad on the standardization–adaptation continuum. It can vary from a simple change like translating into local languages to developing an entirely new advertising message. Developing an entirely different advertising campaign means higher costs and more time. It can also create consumer confusion as it conveys different messages within the same brand name framework. Most companies therefore decide to modify or revise to a certain degree; how much they modify their advertising is an important decision. Some typical advertising adaptation examples are presented:

- *Translating textual information into local languages*: Compared to other sectors, fashion brands can effectively communicate with visual images. Often, the ads of global fashion and jewelry brands that appear in fashion magazines (such as *Vogue*) are mainly in English with limited textual information other than brand or company name. In that case, seeing the English brand name and English slogans (Nike's Just Do It is a great example) is more effective because it naturally creates a global image and is thus perceived as cool (Hornikx et al., 2010). However, in the case of cosmetics, for which more textual information on the benefits is needed, translation into the local language is very much needed (Checchinato et al., 2014). As shown in Appendix 1, an advertisement for a Japanese Shiseido product is full of information about the product and the text information is directly translated into the local language.

- *Substituting models for local celebrities*: In the past, Caucasian models were almost exclusively portrayed across cultures in fashion magazine ads (Frith et al., 2005). This tendency, however, has moved somewhat to using Asian models for Asian markets. As an example, Puma's Run the Streets campaign in 2017 featured Canadian singer The Weeknd for the North American market but changed to Dean, a South Korean singer, for the Korean market (Puma, 2017) (see Appendix 2). More recently, with the increasing popularity of K-pop and K-drama, a growing number of Korean movie stars and singers serve as ambassadors for global luxury brands (see Box 13.1). Hoyeon Jung, who starred as a North Korean girl in the Netflix hit *Squid Game*, featured as the February 2022 cover star of *Vogue* (Kim, 2022; Sussman, 2022). This is a new shift seen in the fashion industry where once Caucasian models dominated in ads and Asian models served only for Asian markets.
- *Changing the verbal message slightly to reflect the cultural values of the countries entered*: Individualistic cultures use singular pronouns such as "I" while collectivistic cultures use plural pronouns "we" more (de Mooij, 2022) (see Chapter 4). L'Oréal successful "I am worth it" campaign was modified to "We are worth it" in Asia to address Asia's collectivist culture. L'Oréal also used a local actress in Asia for the campaign.
- *Adapting local media for communication*: In addition to substituting the main model in an ad for a local celebrity, fashion brands can choose popular local media for their ad campaign. Many luxury brands including Burberry and Montblanc launched an account in WeChat, a major social networking media in China, for communication purposes in China (Achim, 2021; Jones, 2014). Adopting local social media is critical in China, as many popular social media such as Facebook, YouTube, Instagram, Twitter, and Pinterest are banned in the country.
- *Developing a new advertising campaign to reflect the cultural values of the country entered*: The next degree of adaptation can be found when fashion brands create a new advertising campaign in a host country. As an example, Burberry featured three generations in its new Lunar New Year campaign in China starring Chinese actresses and brand ambassadors. The campaign celebrates family traditions and togetherness, a tradition of the Lunar New Year festive period (Jahshan, 2019) (see Further Reading).
- *Developing a new advertising campaign with local influencers*: The greater extent of localization can be observed when a new ad campaign with local influencers is featured in popular local media. Uniqlo developed a new advertising campaign to build its brand awareness in India. Soon after an entry into India in 2019 to build its brand awareness,

Uniqlo created the "Kurta Collection" with a local designer (product adaptation) and used local influencers and film stars like Kareena Kapoor Khan, who has over 7 million Instagram followers (Hall and Jay, 2021).

While local engagement strategies help companies build their brand images by connecting with local consumers, the highest level of localization in advertising may risk diluting brand image because consumers may not connect the advertising to their original brand images. Fashion brands, therefore, need to decide the extent of adaptation prudently.

BOX 13.1
Korean Girl Group Blackpink as Ambassadors for Luxury Brands

It was common that popular cultures in the West diffuse to the East, but now a noticeable shift is observed in a reverse flow from East to West. Award-winning movies and popular songs that charted on Billboard were used for the ones from the West like the US and Europe. This longstanding trend now appears to shift to the East (Hollingsworth, 2019; Tonby et al., 2019). In the center of the shift, South Korea's pop culture, from K-pop, K-drama, to K-beauty, leads the way. Korean songs have made the top of the Billboard starting with "Gangnam Style" in 2012, and movie stars and directors of Korean movies such as *Parasite* in 2020 and *Squid Game* in 2022 won prestigious awards such as Oscars and Golden Globes (Adams, 2022).

Leveraging the popularity of pop culture, fashion brands have featured those award-winning singers and movie stars in their marketing communication. Naturally, more Korean singers and movie stars are seen in fashion advertisements and serve as global brand ambassadors. One of them is Blackpink, a South Korean girl group consisting of four members: Jisoo, Jennie, Rosé, and Lisa. While many Korean girl groups have achieved success, until recently it was largely in the Asian market. Blackpink is the first girl group that made the top Billboard's Artist 100 and the first Korean girl group to enter and top Billboard's Emerging Artists chart. Each member of the group serves as an ambassador for luxury brands: Jisoo for Dior and Cartier, Jennie for Chanel, Rosé for Tiffany & Co. and Saint Laurent, and Lisa for Celine and Bulgari (Geddo, 2022). They have all appeared in a number of these brands' marketing communications, including magazine covers, runway shows such as Paris Fashion Week, and other events the brands host. All four girls are mega influencers with more than a million followers. However, Lisa is the most followed K-pop star on Instagram and Blackpink's most popular member: she has 82.6 million Instagram followers, indicating the power of the girls' Instagram messages.

A simple single message can create a huge reaction in consumers contributing to the luxury brands' communication effort. Blackpink is even more powerful because, according to a recent study, a great fit between product (luxury brands) and influencers (Blackpink), together with the high number of followers, results in a positive attitude toward adverts and products, as well as purchase intention (Janssen et al., 2022).

References

Adams, T. (2022, September 4). K-everything: The rise and rise of Korean culture. *The Guardian*. www.theguardian.com/world/2022/sep/04/korea-culture-k-pop-music-film-tv-hallyu-v-and-a

Geddo, B. (2022, August 1). The history behind Blackpink's many high fashion collabs. The Mary Sue. www.themarysue.com/blackpink-brand-ambassadors-all-brands-jennie-jisoo-rose-and-lisa-are-ambassadors-for

Hollingsworth, J. (2019, December 28). Why the past decade saw the rise and rise of East Asian pop culture. CNN. www.cnn.com/2019/12/28/entertainment/east-asia-pop-culture-rise-intl-hnk

Janssen, L., Schouten, A.P. and Croes, E.A. (2022). Influencer advertising on Instagram: Product-influencer fit and number of followers affect advertising outcomes and influencer evaluations via credibility and identification. *International Journal of Advertising*, 41(1): 101–27.

Tonby, O., Woetzel, J., Choi, W., Eloot, K., Dhawan, R. et al. (2019, September 18). The future of Asia: Asian flows and networks are defining the next phase of globalization. McKinsey & Company. www.mckinsey.com/featured-insights/asia-pacific/the-future-of-asia-asian-flows-and-networks-are-defining-the-next-phase-of-globalization

Cultural Implications of International Advertising

Communication is effective when the message sender (creator) and receiver (interpreter) share the same culture and share similar experiences and events in their lifetime. Even within a country, however, baby boomers and Gen Z have fewer shared events and experiences, so advertising campaigns targeting one generation may be ineffective for other generations. Imagine an advertising campaign featuring a popular American TV show; it cannot be understood by consumers in other countries who have not seen the show. Also, advertising appeals that include humor tend not to travel well because humor is different across countries. This section discusses effective advertising appeals and styles by cultures.

Differing Goals of Marketing Communications: Individualistic vs. Collectivistic Cultures

The major purpose of marketing communication differs across cultures. In general, an advertising campaign is effective and liked when it is congruent with the consumer's cultural values (Polegato and Bjerke, 2006). In individualistic cultures, appeals to individuality, personal benefits, and achievement are prevalent, while in collectivistic cultures, appeals to group benefits, harmony, and conformity (respect for collective values and beliefs) are emphasized (Cho et al., 1999; Kim and Markus, 1999). Naturally, a greater number of people are featured in ads in collectivistic cultures compared to those in individualistic cultures (de Mooij, 2022).

Similarly, in individualistic cultures, a brand's attributes and advantages are the focus in advertising (Polychroniou, 2019), whereas in collectivistic cultures, first the brand and company names (group) are emphasized and product attributes and benefits come later.

The major communication goal is also different; the goal in individualistic cultures is to persuade, while the goal in collectivistic cultures is to build relationships and trust between sellers and buyers. Specifically, in individualistic cultures, rational claims and information-driven hard sell approaches are commonly used to persuade, while collectivistic cultures focus on inducing positive feelings (emotional claims) and soft sell approaches to build the relationship and trust. Advertisements in Japan and Korea rely more on the emotional side of humans, utilizing symbolism, mood, and esthetics, and direct appeals such as comparisons with competitors are rarely used (Cho et al., 1999; Hong et al., 1987; Javalgi et al., 1995). These differences can be seen in Patagonia's Houdini jacket advertisement in two different cultures. In the US advertisement (individualistic culture), one man who wears the jacket shows the product in a plain background while he narrates the features and functions of the product (rational claims, information-driven). In contrast, the Korean advert of the same product features two men in a mountain climbing setting. The ad shows how light the product is in the story, not through detailed explanation in a voice narrative. Showing two men rather than one man is effective in group-oriented collectivistic cultures, while the background (mood) is used to persuade in a collectivistic culture (see Appendix 3 to compare the two ads).

The same pattern is found in website content. Individualistic cultures emphasize consumer–message and consumer–market interactivity, whereas collectivistic cultures emphasize consumer–consumer interactivity, consistent with the cultural values fostering interdependence and sociability (Cho and Cheon, 2005).

Effective Website Design: High- vs. Low-context Cultures

Website content and design can be effectively developed if those match their cultural orientations. The more the website design follows culturally familiar communication styles, the more trust can be established. As implicit and nonverbal communication is useful in high-context cultures (Japan, Saudi Arabia), more animation and visual layout, rather than texts, are effective in websites of high-context cultures. Consumers in high-context cultures can find hidden intentions and metaphors easily as they are used to contextual messages. By contrast, in low-context cultures, direct, informative, logical information, and a heavy text layout works well (de Mooij, 2022). Popular themes also match with cultural values in the society: a family or group theme appears frequently in China, hierarchy in India, clear gender roles in Japan, and so on (Singh, 2005).

Effective Advertising Appeals: Masculine vs. Feminine Cultures

Effective advertising appeals are consistent with cultural values in the society. Masculine cultures emphasize winning, competitiveness, mastery, bigness, success, achievement, and assertiveness, as we learned in Chapter 4. Advertising styles in masculine cultures are consistent with the cultural values. Therefore, "being first," "the one and only in the world," "be the best," and "a world without limits" types of hyperbole are often used. In Estée Lauder's campaign for its double wear foundation, the advertising copy, "Behind your beauty is confidence", was translated into local languages. However, in Korea, "it was Asia's number 1 foundation for the past eight years" was added in the local language (Korean) (Estée Lauder, 2021; Estée Lauder Korea market, 2022) to emphasize achievement and reputation (refer to Appendix 4 to compare the two ads). In contrast, reflecting a feminine culture's dominant values in caring for others and quality of life, advertising in feminine cultures uses understatement, such as "probably the best in the world" and showing off is viewed as negative (de Mooij, 2022).

Regulations and Challenges Related to Advertising across Countries

Advertising regulations differ by country. Some countries have a strict approach and others do not involve themselves in controlling advertising content and media usage. Global fashion brands should be cognizant of the regulations and restrictions imposed on advertising across the nations, so that they correctly tailor their ads to a particular country. Below, more specific regulations concerning advertising are illustrated.

Comparative Advertising Is Ineffective or Banned in Some Countries

Comparative advertising is directly comparing one brand's function and attributes over a competing brand, using the competing brand's name, pictures of packaging, and so on (FTC, 1979). It is legal in major markets such as the US but forbidden or heavily restricted in many countries. Comparative advertising is largely used in individualistic and weak to medium uncertainty avoidance cultures. It helps consumers choose the right product by providing contrasting information. Comparative advertising is ineffective or even banned in many collectivistic and feminine cultures because it is regarded as too aggressive and makes the other party lose face.

Communication Challenges in Arab Countries

Many Arab countries censor marketing and advertising materials although the extent varies widely among Arab countries. In general, in Arab countries, people are depicted less often, compared to ads in the US, and brevity is a virtue in ads. The use of comparative advertising claims is very limited. Particular attention is needed when featuring women in Arab countries. Women may only appear in those commercials that relate to the advertised product such as women's apparel. Still women must wear long dresses (Al-Olayan and Karande, 2000; Lugmani et al., 1989). In Dubai, a relatively liberal Arab country in the Middle East, H&M's ad featuring Gisele Bündchen was photoshopped to add a vest to cover her décolleté and armpits (Rawi, 2011). Arab countries vary greatly in their social attitudes and religiosity, but, in general, Muslim culture dictates that women dress modestly. Saudi Arabia interprets Islam more strictly than other Arab countries. Saudi Arabia censors, reviews, and edits marketing materials and blots out women's faces or body parts as needed. In Clarks ads in Saudi Arabia, a headscarf was added and knees were covered, but head and knees are not covered in the same ad in Kuwait (see Appendix 5 for a comparison). As these examples show, for a successful advertising adaptation, keen attention needs to be paid to understand varying cultures among Arab countries.

Regulating Advertising Hours and Content

Many European countries strictly control TV commercial time and content. For example, some European countries maintain that total advertising time may not exceed 12 minutes per hour (European Commission, 2016). Advertising or teleshopping cannot interrupt films, news, and children's programs more than once for each scheduled period of at least 30 minutes (European Commission, 2016). The control was traditionally applied to TV and video on-demand services (Netflix), but the scope has been recently extended to video-sharing platforms such as YouTube and Facebook (European Commission, 2018). The control and limits vary among EU countries. The limits on the amount of advertising are generally stricter in four EU members (France, Ireland, Italy, and the UK), and some other EU countries apply the 12-minute rule only to public service broadcasters (European Commission, 2016). Therefore, fashion companies should not assume that all EU countries have the same regulations and need to develop marketing communication programs with a proper understanding of such differences.

In Malaysia and Indonesia, foreign-made advertising is restricted to protect their local advertising industries. Also, 80 percent of ad production costs must be spent in Malaysia. Because of the regulations, Ray-Ban reshot its commercials with local talent. Moreover, Caucasians are not allowed to appear in TV commercials (Kotabe and Helsen, 2020), so adaptations are needed.

Regulating Unhealthy and Provocative Images in Advertising

Countries have their own measures to prevent unhealthy images from dissemination. For example, the UK's Advertising Standards Authority (ASA) reviews how ads can affect an audience. If judged to be unhealthy or socially irresponsible, an ad is advised to be banned. Given that the ideal body shape is often learned through repeated exposure to advertisements, fashion-conscious teenagers may put themselves under constant pressure to look like the ideal bodies seen on TV and in magazines. Recently, one Yves Saint Laurent's advert on *Elle UK* magazine was banned for being irresponsible, as the model was severely underweight with a visible ribcage, which may create unhealthy body images among viewers (ASA, 2022; BBC, 2015) (see Appendix 6 for the image). Another related example can be found in one of Miu Miu's advertisements. The ad featured a teenage girl sitting alone on a railroad track wiping her eye, suggesting she was crying. This ad was banned as it was deemed to be irresponsible and seemingly suggesting youth suicide (Sepre, 2011) (see Appendix 7 for the image).

France's advertising watchdog, the Autorité de Régulation Professionnelle de la Publicité, asked Yves Saint Laurent to cease distributing two ads, and modify the visuals, after consumers protested in front of the boutique and on social media postings. The models' poses and exposure were provocative and degrading to women. The ads breached the rules set by the advertising industry to maintain dignity and respect for the models featured in the ads (Reuters, 2017).

Regulating False Claims

Not all advertising claims are based on thorough testing and valid evidence. Restrictions against potentially false and misleading claims vary by country. Take Reebok's ad as an example. Reebok's TV and magazine ad campaigns for its EasyTone walking shoes and RunTone running shoes were banned. Reebok claimed that walking and running in the shoes could bring extra tone and strength to leg and buttock muscles, but both the US's Federal Trade Commission (FTC) and the UK's ASA viewed them as unsubstantiated claims (FTC, 2011; The Drum, 2010). As part of the settlement agreement for its deceptive advertisement, Reebok paid $25 million in the US (FTC, 2011).

Specifying Disclosure Requirements for Social Media Influencers

With the increasing impact of influencers on consumers, some countries are ahead in protecting consumers from potentially harmful influences. The UK's ASA, for example, specifies that influencers must make it clear that their post is an advertisement if they have been paid or have been gifted or loaned a product (Blair, 2018). India has a similar requirement. The Advertising Standards Council of India, a voluntary self-regulatory organization of the advertising industry, recently issued guidelines for influencer advertising. That is, advertisements published by social media influencers should add a disclosure label clearly stating that it as an advertisement when the influencer receives any benefits or incentives provided by the advertiser. In addition, when a virtual influencer is involved, consumers must be informed that they are not communicating with a real person (Khanna et al., 2021).

Regulating Digital Modifications

With the advancement of digital tools that can enhance visual images, images in advertising can be retouched, which may mislead consumers. Advertising regulations across Europe have recently targeted the beauty and fashion industries for misleading practices, which include digitally modifying images using a photo-editing tool (ASA, 2011; O'Neal, 2014). Self-regulatory bodies and legislation, especially in France and the UK, have been leading this charge, specifying unacceptable and acceptable practices. For instance, the

UK's ASA banned a Lancôme advertisement featuring Julia Roberts because it could mislead consumers about the benefits of cosmetics owing to excessive use of the photo-editing tool (Skarda, 2012) (see Appendix 8 for the image). Compared to Europe, the US is lenient in its imposition of similar regulations because of its strong commitment to free speech (McBride et al., 2019; O'Neil, 2014).

The global fashion industry is evolving; some regulations mentioned above (digital modification and disclosure requirements for influencers) may become universal but other regulations may become more diverse and vary country to country. Global fashion brands, therefore, need to keep up to date with changes in regulations when developing communication and advertising campaigns for the global market.

As communication touchpoints with consumers are ever increasing, more coordination across diverse communication channels and across markets will be required. In particular, social media is increasingly used as an effective communication tool, and its power has been proven with many successful small fashion brands (see Gymshark example in Case Study 13.1). Given the speed of information dissemination and its power on consumers, especially young consumers, the role of social media in communication will be greater in future. Communication, after all, is persuasion, whether it be verbal or visual. The fundamental cultural insights on the way people communicate will stay the same as culture is not something that changes over a short time period. Global fashion brands, therefore, need to be aware of changes in social media in order to maintain effective brand communication.

CASE STUDY 13.1

Gymshark's Impressive Rise: Social Media and Brand Community Strategies

Founded in 2012 by then 19-year-old Ben Francis, Gymshark is a fitness clothing brand based in the UK. In 2017, within six years of its launch, Gymshark's revenue was $50 million. In 2018, its sales had more than doubled, amounting to $128 million (Winkler, 2018). In the same year, Ben Francis was selected as one of Forbes' 30 Under 30 in the retail and ecommerce category (Cuccinello and Rachelle, 2018). Gymshark achieved its success without a single brick-and-mortar store. Gymshark sells its products exclusively via its online store but eventually opened its first offline store in London in 2020. Gymshark delivers worldwide to 131 countries. Orders are shipped from one of the three distribution centers in the UK, Belgium, and Canada. The US is Gymshark's biggest market, accounting for about 45 percent of its sales (Miller, 2022).

Gymshark's success can be attributed to its products, coupled with successful influencer marketing and a strong brand community. As of October 2022, Gymshark's main Instagram account has 5.8 million followers, including celebrity trainers and high-profile athletes with millions of followers on their own.

Gymshark was an answer to a gap in the polarized sportswear market where neither the low-end nor the high-end brands appealed to young gym-goers who wanted stylish and functional gym clothes that are affordable. Gymshark's leggings are known for being incredibly flattering, supportive, stretchy, and versatile, with a wide range of colors and flattering high-waisted fit. The clothes are affordable, with the price ranging between $25 and $60 for leggings. Bestselling shirts are priced as low as $25 (Leighton, 2018).

Gymshark enlisted fitness gurus and YouTube influencers, including high-profile body-builders like Lex Griffin and Chris Lavado, to promote its products. Gymshark now sponsors about 18 influencers with a combined following of over 20 million people (Hristova, 2020). Impressive returns on investment attest to how Gymshark successfully leverages the power of social media. For instance, Gymshark ran a "Blackout" campaign for Black Friday in 2017. About 40 percent of purchases made during the period came from Instagram posts that directed customers to Gymshark's online store, and the campaign on Instagram reached 16.4 million people (Facebook, n.d.).

Gymshark prioritizes building lasting relationships with its customers. The brand not only asks for feedback from its community but also actively incorporates them into the product design. The brand routinely conducts polls about favorite products and workouts on Twitter, and once heeded a comment from one customer by launching camo tops that became one of the most popular items (Barrie, 2020). In addition to creating and sharing workout videos on its YouTube channel for its customers to follow, Gymshark encourages active involvement from its community. Through the "Gymshark66 challenge," the brand encourages its fans to set a fitness goal and document their fitness journey by sharing a picture on the first day and another picture 66 days later to show their progress (Gilliland, 2019). Beyond virtually connecting via social media, Gymshark offers a chance to meet with its brand ambassadors in person. With the name "We Lift the City," the brand has been hosting multi-day conventions with fitness seminars by athletes, meet and greets with athletes, and exclusive merchandise. Gymshark demonstrates well how a startup brand can become a global brand within a short time period and how much social media and online and offline brand community contributes to the success, along with product and price strategies.

Discussion Questions
1. What do you think are Gymshark's success factors?
2. Why is it difficult for startup brands to open brick-and-mortar stores?
3. What are the limitations of having no physical stores for startup brands, and what can brands do to overcome the limitations?
4. Gymshark is an example of a direct-to-consumer (DTC) brand that achieved success in the global marketplace with effective social media strategies. Conduct your own research on DTC brands and identify other DTC brands that were successful in the global market. What have you found? Do you see some similarities among the brands in terms of their communication strategies?

References
Barrie, T. (2020, February 17). Gymshark founder Ben Francis's tips for success. GQ. www.gq-magazine.co.uk/lifestyle/article/gymshark-ben-francis-tips

Cuccinello, H.C. and Rachelle, B. (2018). 30 under 30: Retail & ecommerce. Forbes. www.forbes.

com/profile/ben-francis/?list=30under30-europe-retail-ecommerce#42d782842429

Facebook (n.d.). Gymshark: Shaping up for success. www.facebook.com/business/success/instagram/gymshark

Gilliland, N. (2019, February 27). Five marketing lessons from the success of Gymshark. Econsultancy. https://econsultancy.com/five-retail-lessons-sportswear-brand-gymshark

Hristova, K. (2020, August 28). How Gymshark disrupted the fitness industry. *CEO Today*. www.ceotodaymagazine.com/2020/08/how-gymshark-disrupted-the-fitness-industry

Leighton, M. (2018, November 6). Fitness apparel startup Gymshark was started by a 19-year-old and is now one of the fastest growing companies in the world – here's what the clothes are actually like. Business Insider. www.businessinsider.com/gymshark-workout-gear-clothes-leggings-review-2018-11

Miller, D-Y. (2022, May 23). Growing international sales boost Gymshark revenue and profits. Business of Fashion. www.businessoffashion.com/news/retailgrowing-international-sales-boost-gymshark-revenue-and-profits

Winkler, N. (2018). Holiday disaster to a $128M global brand: Behind Gymshark's multi-channel empire. Shopify. www.shopify.com/enterprise/gymshark-global-multi-channel

Summary

- Once products are developed to meet target global consumers' needs, prices are set, and distribution channels are decided, global consumers must be informed of the offerings through communications.
- Brands should decide between advertising standardization and adaptation when promoting their brand in multiple countries. Standardization is when key elements are kept the same in the campaign, and adaptation is when elements are changed to reflect cultural, linguistic, legal, and media differences among the countries.
- Brands adapt their advertising by translating textual information into local languages, changing the model with local celebrities, changing the verbal message to reflect the cultural values of the country entered, adapting a local media for communication, developing a new advertising campaign reflecting the cultural values of the country entered, or developing a new advertising campaign with local influencers.
- The degree of individualism vs. collectivism in cultures must be recognized for advertising. Individualistic cultures respond more to persuasion and the promotion of the brand's attributes and advantages. Collectivistic cultures respond more to brand names and building relationships and trust between the brand and the consumer.
- High-context and low-context cultures require different website designs. High-context cultures can understand nonverbal communication, such as animation and visuals, and metaphors more easily. Low-context cultures need direct, informative, and logical information.
- In masculine cultures, advertising reflecting winning, competitiveness, and achievement appeals to consumers. In feminine cultures, advertising reflecting caring for others and quality of life resonates more.
- Brands must be aware of regulations in countries in which they aim to advertise.

- Some countries ban comparative advertising, or it is ineffective based on certain cultures.
- In Arab countries, communication must be tailored to reflect their religiosity (or not, in the case of more liberal countries), and many Arab countries have restrictions on the use of women in advertising campaigns.
- Some countries restrict hours or number of advertisements within certain media programs.
- Many countries are implementing regulations on advertising that promotes poor body image and negative mental health struggles. Additionally, digital modification such as retouching is becoming more regulated.
- With an increase in social media marketing and influencer marketing, platforms are requiring the disclosure of an advertisement when products have been gifted or loaned to influencers or when influencers have been paid to promote them.

Class Activities

1. Compare a global fashion brand website in your country with one from a different culture. For example, if you are a student in the US (an individualistic culture), compare Polo Ralph Lauren's website in the US with the one in Italy (a collectivistic culture). Do you see any differences? Discuss the differences and similarities.

2. Choose a global fashion brand and visit the brand's Instagram in contrasting cultures (UK vs. Japan, US vs. Sweden). Are the postings similar or different? Discuss the similarities and differences according to the cultural dimensions.

Key Terms

- **Advertising standardization:** Keeping the key elements of the advertising campaign the same across countries.
- **Advertising adaptation:** Changing the key elements of the advertising campaign to reflect cultural, linguistic, legal, and media differences between different countries in which the advertising campaign is executed.
- **Comparative advertising:** Directly comparing one brand's function and attributes over its competing brands, with the competing brand name, picture of packages, and demonstration.

Further Reading: Burberry Ad in China

Jahshan, E. (2019, January 3). Burberry unveils first-ever Chinese New Year campaign. *Retail Gazette*. www.retailgazette.co.uk/blog/2019/01/burberry-unveils-first-ever-chinese-new-year-campaign

Appendix 1. Shiseido Advertisement on Instagram

Shiseido Hong Kong **Shiseido Global**

Shiseido Hong Kong [@shiseidohk]. (2022, August 17). 炎夏更需要無重底妝 最近天氣又熱又潮濕揀粉底當然希望可以令肌膚清爽冇負擔 [Video]. Instagram. www.instagram.com/p/ChW7DMBFksN/?utm_source=ig_web_copy_link

Shiseido Global [@shiseido]. (2022, July 20). Wherever summer takes you, SYNCHRO SKIN SELF-REFRESHING Foundation is always ready to go [Video]. Instagram. www.instagram.com/reel/CgPNHpDlNKn/?utm_source=ig_web_copy_link

Appendix 2. Puma's Run the Streets Campaign: US vs. Korea

US **Korea**

US: PUMA (2017, January 24). *The Weeknd Runs the Streets* [Video]. YouTube. https://youtu.be/S5_AdmhWiSA

Korea: PUMA (2017, September 3). [푸마] *PUMA X DEAN 거리를 지배하다, RUN THE STREETS* [Video]. YouTube. https://youtu.be/O5ZiP-9_P-M

Appendix 3. Patagonia Houdini Jacket Ad: Individualistic vs. Collectivistic Culture

US **Korea**

US: Patagonia. (2019, January 22). Patagonia® Men's Houdini® Jacket [Video]. YouTube. www.youtube.com/watch?v=Sq_gQ88LZvU

Korea: Patagonia Korea. (2021, March 12). 후디니 - 주머니 속으로 사라지는 초경량 바람막이 (Climbing ver./15s) [Video]. YouTube. www.youtube.com/watch?v=_sftrPnsYL0

Appendix 4. Estée Lauder's Advertisements: Masculine vs. Feminine Culture

US: Estée Lauder (2021, July 26). *Behind your beauty is confidence | Double Wear Foundation* [Video]. YouTube. https://youtu.be/zR2YkTMB0rQ

Korea: Estée Lauder Korea Market (2022, April 14). [에스티 로더] *"8년 연속 1위"* 아시아 *No.1* 파운데이션* #더블웨어 [Video]. YouTube. https://youtu.be/1rHuwUYswwQ

Appendix 5. Clarks' Advertisements: Saudi Arabia vs. Kuwait

deMilked (n.d.). 49 Examples of how the same products look in the West vs. Middle East. www.demilked.com/saudi-arabia-middle-east-product-censorship

Appendix 6. Yves Saint Laurent's Banned Ad in the UK

BBC (2015, June 3). "Unhealthily underweight model" Yves Saint Laurent advert banned. www.bbc.com/news/uk-32987228

Appendix 7. Miu Miu's Banned Advertisement in the UK

Sepre, G. (2011, November 28). Hailee Steinfeld's Miu Miu ad banned in Britain—but not for the reason you think. E News. www.eonline.com/news/277045/hailee-steinfeld-s-miu-miu-ad-banned-in-britain-but-not-for-the-reason-you-think

Appendix 8. Lancôme's Banned Advertisement in the UK

Skarda, E. (2012, February 3). Tough standards: 8 "misleading" ads banned by U.K. officials. *Time*. https://newsfeed.time.com/2012/02/06/tough-standards-8-misleading-ads-banned-by-u-k-standards-board/slide/julia-roberts-christy-turlington-for-loreal

References

Chapter 1

Amed, I. and Berg, C. (2020, April 8). The state of fashion 2020: Coronavirus update. *Business of Fashion*. www.businessoffashion.com/articles/intelligence/the-state-of-fashion-2020-coronavirus-update-bof-mckinsey-report-release-download

Campbell, L. (2016, May 7). Cushion foundation: What the hell they are and why they're big news. Huffington Post. www.huffingtonpost.com.au/2016/03/29/cushion-foundations_n_9535806.html

Duguid, K. (2017, May 8). Coach acquires Kate Spade, but overpays. *The New York Times*. www.nytimes.com/2017/05/08/business/dealbook/coach-acquires-kate-spade-but-overpays.html

Ell, K. (2018, December 31). Versace acquisition complete: Michael Kors Holdings changes name to Capri Holdings. WWD. https://wwd.com/business-news/mergers-acquisitions/michael-kors-acquisition-of-versace-1202942585

Enberg, J. (2019a, March 28). *Global digital ad spending 2019: Digital accounts for half of total media ad spending worldwide*. Emarketer. www.emarketer.com/content/global-digital-ad-spending-2019

Enberg, J. (2019b, March 28). *US digital ad spending 2019: Amazon gains on the duopoly, as digital ad spending exceeds 50% of market*. Emarketer. www.emarketer.com/content/us-digital-ad-spending-2019

Euromonitor International (2018, April). World market for apparel and footwear. www.euromonitor.com

Euromonitor International (2020). Market sizes. www.euromonitor.com

Euromonitor International (2022). *Market sizes: Apparel and footwear in all countries*. www-portal-euromonitor-com.prox.lib.ncsu.edu/portal/StatisticsEvolution/index

Gap Inc. (2022). Gap Inc.'s global footprint. https://gapinc-prod.azureedge.net/gapmedia/gapcorporatesite/media/images/investors/global-footprint-q2-22_8_9_22-002.pdf

George, G., Wiklund, J. and Zahra, S.A. (2005). Ownership and the internationalization of small firms. *Journal of Management*, 31(2): 210–33.

H&M Group (2021). *Annual and sustainability report 2021*. https://hmgroup.com/wp-content/uploads/2022/03/HM-Group-Annual-and-Sustainability-Report-2021.pdf

Inditex (2022). *Statement on non-financial information 2021*. https://static.inditex.com/annual_report_2021/en/documents/statement-of-non-financial-information-2021.pdf

Jin, B. (2004). Achieving an optimal global versus domestic sourcing balance under demand uncertainty. *International Journal of Operations and Production Management*, 24(12): 1292–1305.

Jin, B. (2006). Performance implications of information technology implementation in an apparel supply chain. *Supply Chain Management: An International Journal*, 11(4): 309–16.

Kalish, I. and Eng, V. (2020). *Global powers of retailing 2020*. Deloitte. www2.deloitte.com/global/en/pages/consumer-business/articles/global-powers-of-retailing.html

Kumar, N. and Steenkamp, J.-B. (2013). *Brand breakout: How emerging brands will go global*. Basingstoke: Palgrave Macmillan.

Levi Strauss & Co. (2022). Levi Strauss & Co. investor day 2022. https://s23.q4cdn.com/172692177/files/doc_presentations/2022/LSCo-Investor-Day_2022.pdf

Lieber, C. (2019, August 8). Live stream apps are changing the way people shop. Business of Fashion. www.businessoffashion.com/articles/professional/live-stream-apps-are-changing-the-way-people-shop

LVMH (2022). *2021 Financial documents.* https://r.lvmh-static.com/uploads/2022/01/financial-documents-december-31-2021.pdf

Nike (2022). *2021 Annual report and notice of annual meeting.* https://s1.q4cdn.com/806093406/files/doc_financials/2021/ar/386273(1)_20_Nike-Inc_Combo_WR.pdf

O'Connor, T. and Fernandez, C. (2020, November 9). Why Supreme sold to VF Corporation. Business of Fashion. www.businessoffashion.com/articles/professional/vf-corp-to-acquiresupreme

Schu, M., Morschett, D. and Swoboda, B. (2016). Internationalization speed of online retailers: A resource-based perspective on the influence factors. *Management International Review*, 56(5): 733–57.

Sherman, L. (2020, April 1). Next wave of luxury e-commerce. Business of Fashion. www.businessoffashion.com/case-studies/luxury/case-study-luxury-ecommerce-online-retail

Silver, L., Smith, A., Johnson, C., Jiang, J., Anderson, M. and Rainie, L. (2019, March 7). *Mobile connectivity in emerging economies.* Pew Research Center. www.pewresearch.org/internet/2019/03/07/use-of-smartphones-and-social-media-is-common-across-most-emerging-economies

Vogue Business (2020, March 5). China's live streaming boom. www.voguebusiness.com/consumers/live-streaming-china-shopping-kim-kardashian

WARC (2020, October 13). US brands adopt e-commerce livestreaming to boost sales. www.warc.com/newsandopinion/news/us-brands-adopt-e-commerce-livestreaming-to-boost-sales/en-gb/44218

White, W. (2021, November 22). Walmart celebrates one year of livestreams with first shoppable livestream on twitter. Walmart. https://corporate.walmart.com/newsroom/2021/11/22/walmart-celebrates-one-year-of-livestreams-with-first-shoppable-livestream-on-twitter

Chapter 2

Ahrendts, A. (2013). Burberry's CEO on turning an aging British icon into a global luxury brand. *Harvard Business Review*, 91(1/2): 39–42.

AMA (American Marketing Association) (n.d.). Definitions of marketing. www.ama.org/the-definition-of-marketing-what-is-marketing

Austen, I. (2015, April 21). Target's hasty exit from Canada leaves anger behind. *The New York Times.* www.nytimes.com/2015/04/22/realestate/commercial/targets-hasty-exit-from-canada-leaves-anger-behind.html

Booms, B.H. and Bitner, M.J. (1981). Marketing strategies and organization structures for services firms. In J.H. Donnelly and W.R. George (eds.) *Marketing of services*, pp. 47–51. Chicago, IL: American Marketing.

Booms, B.H. and Bitner, M.J. (1982). Marketing services by managing the environment. *The Cornell H.R.A. Quarterly*, 23: 35–9.

Chambers, S. (2016, April 7). Asos closes China business under weight of Alibaba competition. Bloomberg. www.bloomberg.com/news/articles/2016-04-07/asos-closes-china-business-under-weight-of-alibaba-competition

Faull, J. (2021, July 2). Gap: Where did it all go wrong for the iconic 90s brand? The Drum. www.thedrum.com/news/2021/07/02/gap-where-did-it-all-go-wrong-the-iconic-90s-brand

Green, D. (2018, January 26). Millennials' favorite place to shop online for clothing is launching a US invasion. Business Insider. www.businessinsider.com/asos-is-launching-a-us-invasion-2018-1?utm_source=copy-link

Hutchinson, K., Quinn, B., Alexander, N. and Doherty, A.M. (2009). Retail internationalization: Overcoming barriers to expansion. *International*

Jin, B. and Cedrola, E. (2017). Brands as core assets: Trends and challenges of branding in fashion business. In B. Jin and E. Cedrola (eds.) *Fashion branding and communication: Core strategies of European luxury and premium brands*, pp. 1–39. New York: Palgrave Macmillan.

Jin, B., Jung, S. and Jeong, S.W. (2018). Dimensional effects of Korean SMEs' entrepreneurial orientation on internationalization and performance: The mediating role of marketing capability. *International Entrepreneurship and Management Journal*, 14(1): 195–215.

Jing Daily (2020, August 12). Is Topshop's failure in China a fast fashion problem? https://jingdaily.com/is-topshops-failure-in-china-a-fast-fashion-problem

Johansson, J.K. (2009). *Global marketing: Foreign entry, local marketing and global management* (5th ed.). New York: McGraw-Hill/Irwin.

Lee, J.A. (1966). Cultural analysis in overseas operations. *Harvard Business Review*, 44(2): 106–14.

Lumpkin, G.T. and Dess, G.G. (1996). Clarifying the entrepreneurial orientation construct and linking it to performance. *Academy of Management Review*, 21(1): 135–172.

Parisi, D. (2019, May 30). There was almost a bit of arrogance: Why Topshop failed in the US. Digiday. https://digiday.com/retail/almost-bit-arrogance-topshop-failed-us

Parmar, H. (2018, December 6). Macy's ends Tmall store in second China strategy shift of 2018. Bloomberg. www.bloomberg.com/news/articles/2018-12-06/macy-s-ends-tmall-store-in-second-china-strategy-shift-of-2018

Picot-Coupey, K., Burt, S.L. and Cliquet, G. (2014). Retailers' expansion mode choice in foreign markets: Antecedents for expansion mode choice in the light of internationalization theories. *Journal of Retailing and Consumer Services*, 21(6): 976–91.

Restar, A. (2019, September 26). Forever 21 will pack bags and leave Japan by October. PublicWire. www.publicwire.com/forever-21-will-pack-bags-and-leave-japan-by-october

Salmon, W. and Tordjman, A. (1989). The internationalisation of retailing. *International Journal of Retailing*, 4(2): 3–16.

Shimp, T.A. and Sharma, S. (1987). Consumer ethnocentrism: Construction and validation of the CETSCALE. *Journal of Marketing Research*, 24(3): 280–9.

Steenkamp, J.-B. (2017). *Global brand strategy: World-wise marketing in the age of branding*. London: Palgrave Macmillan.

Sternquist, B. (1997). *International expansion by US retailers*. *International Journal of Retail and Distribution Management*, 25(8): 262–8.

Szymanski, D.M., Bharadwaj, S.G. and Varadarajan, P.R. (1993). Standardization versus adaptation of international marketing strategy: An empirical investigation. *Journal of Marketing*, 57(4): 1–17.

Timmins, B. (2021, July 1). Four reasons why gap is closing its shops in the UK. BBC News. www.bbc.co.uk/news/business-57677156

WWD (1994, September 23). VF in venture to make, sell Lee jeans in China. https://wwd.com/fashion-news/fashion-features/vf-in-venture-to-make-sell-lee-jeans-in-china–1167925

Chapter 3

Akamatsu, K. (1962). A historical pattern of economic growth in developing countries. *Journal of Developing Economies*, 1: 3–25.

Balabanis, G., Diamantopoulos, A., Mueller, R. and Melewar, T.C. (2001). The impact of nationalism, patriotism and internationalism on consumer ethnocentric tendencies. *Journal of International Business Studies*, 32(2): 157–75.

Bari, S. and Jin, B. (2021). Understanding apparel brand evolution patterns in Bangladesh: An industry life cycle perspective. *Journal of Fashion Marketing & Management*, 25(3): 548–66.

Batra, R., Ramaswamy, V., Alden, D.L., Steenkamp, J.-B. and Ramachander, S. (2000). Effects of brand local and nonlocal origin on consumer attitudes in developing countries. *Journal of Consumer Psychology*, 9(2): 83–95.

Cho, H.J., Jin, B. and Cho, H. (2010). An examination of regional differences in China by socio-cultural factors. *International Journal of Market Research*, 52(5): 611–31.

Cleveland, M., Laroche, M. and Papadopoulos, N. (2009). Cosmopolitanism, consumer ethnocentrism, and materialism: an eight country study of antecedents and outcomes. *Journal of International Marketing*, 17(1): 116–46.

Euromonitor International (2021). *Economies and Consumers Annual Data*. www.euromitor.com.

Gielens, K. and Dekimpe, M.G. (2007). The entry strategy of retail firms into transition economies. *Journal of Marketing*, 71(2): 196–212.

IMF (International Monetary Fund) (2022, April 19). World Economic Outlook Database. www.imf.org/en/Publications/WEO/weo-database/2022/April

Jin, B., Kendagal, P. and Jung, S. (2013). Evolution patterns of apparel brands in Asian countries: Propositions from an analysis of the apparel industry in Korea and India. *Clothing and Textiles Research Journal*, 31(1): 48–63.

Jin, B. and Moon, H.-C. (2006). The diamond approach to the competitiveness of Korea's apparel industry: Michael Porter and beyond. *Journal of Fashion Marketing and Management*, 10(2): 195–208.

Jin, B. and Son, J. (2013). Indian consumers: Are they the same across regions? *International Journal of Emerging Markets*, 8(1): 7–23.

Kang, J.H. and Jin, B. (2007). Determinants of the born global firm growth in apparel industry: Korean Case. *Journal of the Textile Institute*, 98(2): 137–45.

Katabe, M. and Helsen, K. (2020). *Global marketing management* (8th ed.). Hoboken, NJ: John Wiley & Sons.

Keller, C., Magnus, K.-H., Hedrich, S., Nava, P. and Tochtermann, T. (2014, September 1). *Succeeding in tomorrow's global fashion market*. McKinsey & Company. www.mckinsey.com/business-functions/marketing-and-sales/our-insights/succeeding-in-tomorrows-global-fashion-market

Kwan, C.H. (2002). The rise of China and Asia's flying-geese pattern of economic development: An empirical analysis based on US import statistics (Paper No. 52). Tokyo: Normura Research Institute.

Paris, M. (2022, March 4). Life after Ikea: A running list of retail closures in Russia. Bloomberg. www.bloomberg.com/news/articles/2022-03-04/ikea-lvmh-h-m-a-running-list-of-retail-closures-in-russia

Reinartz, W., Dellaert, B., Frafft, M., Kumar, V. and Varadarajan, R. (2011). Retailing innovations in a globalizing retail market environment. *Journal of Retailing*, 87(S1): 53–66.

Retail Insight Network (2022, February 25). Impact of Brexit on apparel: Retail trends. www.retail-insight-network.com/comment/impact-of-brexit-on-apparel-retail-trends

Ritchie, H. (2019, September 6). Which countries are most densely populated? Our World in Data. https://ourworldindata.org/most-densely-populated-countries

Samiee, S. (1993). Retailing and channel considerations in developing countries: A review and research propositions. *Journal of Business Research*, 27: 103–30.

Scott, A.J. (2006). The changing global geography of low-technology, labor-intensive industry: Clothing, footwear, and furniture. *World Development*, 34(9): 1517–36.

Sharma, P., Luk, S.T., Cardinali, S. and Ogasavara, M.H. (2018). Challenges and opportunities for marketers in the emerging markets. *Journal of Business Research*, 86(5): 210–16.

Sheth, J.N. (2011). Impact of emerging markets on marketing: Rethinking existing perspectives and practices. *Journal of Marketing*, 75(4): 166–82.

Singh, S.P. (2019). Impact of organized retail in changing perspective of unorganized retail sector in India. *Amity Journal of Commerce and Financial Review*, 2(2): 57–73.

Sternquist, B. and Goldsmith, E.B. (2018). *International retailing* (3rd ed.). New York: Fairchild Books.

Toyne, B., Arpan, J.S., Barnett, A.H., Ricks, D.A. and Shimp, T.A. (1984). *The global textile industry*. London: George Allen & Unwin.

US Census Bureau (2022, June 30). National population by characteristics: 2020–2021. Census.gov. www.census.gov/data/datasets/time-series/demo/popest/2020s-national-detail.html

Varshney, S. (2021, November 26). Indian unorganized retail: The largest consumer market.

Business World. https://bwdisrupt.businessworld.in/article/Indian-Unorganized-Retail-The-Largest-Consumer-Market/26-11-2021-412983/

Chapter 4

BBC (2019a, February 1). Year of the pig: Is it really a problem for Muslims? www.bbc.com/news/world-asia-47037757

BBC (2019b, June 19). What is India's caste system? www.bbc.com/news/world-asia-india-35650616

Cateora, P.R., Gilly, M.C. and Graham, J.L. (2013). *International marketing* (16th ed.). New York: McGraw Hill/Irwin.

Cho, H.J., Jin, B. and Cho, H. (2010). An examination of regional differences in China by socio-cultural factors. *International Journal of Market Research*, 52(5): 611–31.

De Mooij, M. and Hofstede, G. (2002). Convergence and divergence in consumer behavior: Implications for international retailing. *Journal of Retailing*, 79(1): 61–9.

Fam, K.S., Waller, D.S. and Erdogan, B.Z. (2004). The influence of religion on attitudes towards the advertising of controversial products. *European Journal of Marketing*, 38(5/6): 537–55.

Fan, Y. (2002). Questioning guanxi: Definition, classification and implications. International Business Review, 11(5): 543–61.

Goldstein, B.Z. and Tamura, K. (1975). *Japan and America: A comparative study in language and culture*. Rutland, VT: Charles E. Tuttle Company, Inc.

Graham, J.L. and Lam, N.M. (2003). The Chinese negotiation. *Harvard Business Review*, 81(10): 82–91.

Hall, E.T. (1976). *Beyond culture*. New York: Doubleday.

Hall, E.T. (1983). *The dance of life: The other dimension of time*. New York: Doubleday.

Hancocks, P. and Kwon, K.J. (2016, September 28). Three years jail for $50 gift? South Korea introduces strict anti-corruption law. www.cnn.com/2016/09/27/asia/korea-corruption-law-begins/index.html

Hofstede, G. (1980). Motivation, leadership, and organization: Do American theories apply abroad? *Organizational Dynamics*, 9(1): 42–63.

Hofstede, G. (1991). *Cultures and organizations: Software of the mind*. London: McGraw-Hill.

Hofstede, G. (2001). *Culture's consequences: Comparing values, behaviors, institutions and organization across nations* (2nd ed.). Thousand Oaks, CA: Sage Publications.

Hu, W. and Grove, C. (1999). *Encountering the Chinese: A guide for Americans* (2nd ed.). Yarmouth, ME: Intercultural Press.

Jin, B., Almousa, M. and Kim, N. (2018). Retailing amid regulation and religion: An analysis of the unique cultural challenges and opportunities facing market ventures in Saudi Arabia. *Journal of Cultural Marketing Strategy*, 3(1): 70–81.

Jin, B. and Kang, J.H. (2010). Face or subjective norm? Chinese college students' purchase behaviors toward foreign brand jeans. *Clothing & Textiles Research Journal*, 28(3): 218–33.

Jin, B. and Kang, J.H. (2011). Purchase intentions of Chinese consumers toward the U.S. apparel brand: A test of composite behavioral intention model. *Journal of Consumer Marketing*, 28(3): 187–99.

Jin, B. and Son, J. (2013). Indian consumers: Are they the same across regions? *International Journal of Emerging Markets*, 8(1): 7–23.

Jin, B. and Son, J. (2014). Face saving, materialism and desire for unique consumer products: Differences among three Asian countries. *Journal of the Textile Institute*, 105(3): 304–13.

Jin, B., Yu, H. and Kang, J.H. (2013). Challenges in Western-Chinese business relationships: The Chinese perspective. *Marketing Intelligence & Planning*, 31(2): 179–92.

Juliusson, H. (2015). Strategic fit in a new market: H&M's expansion to China. Master's thesis, Copenhagen business school. https://research.cbs.dk/en/studentProjects/48c7a926-c3df-4134-a6f6-7467392eda6f

Kumar, R. and Sethi, A.K. (2005). *Doing business in India*. New York: Palgrave Macmillan.

Lam, D., Lee, A. and Mizerski, R. (2009). The effects of cultural values in word-of-mouth communication. *Journal of International Marketing*, 17(3): 55–70.

Meyer, E. (2014). *The culture map: Breaking through the invisible boundaries of global business*. New York: Public Affairs.

Moshinky, B. (2015, August 6). This one chart shows how China's corruption crackdown put an end to extravagant parties. Business Insider. www.businessinsider.com/chinese-anti-corruption-campaign-nearly-destroyed-corporate-catering-2015-8

Nisbett, R.E. (2003). *The geography of thought: How Asians and Westerners think differently and why*. New York: The Free Press.

Pearce, J.A. and Robinson, R.B. (2000). Cultivating guanxi as a foreign investor strategy. *Business Horizons*, 43(1): 31–8.

Ranasinghe, D. (2014, June 19). Tough times for luxury retail in China. CNBC. www.cnbc.com/2014/06/19/tough-times-for-luxury-retail-in-china.html

Sari, D.K., Mizerski, D. and Liu, F. (2017). Boycotting foreign products: A study of Indonesian Muslim consumers. *Journal of Islamic Marketing*, 8(1): 16–34.

Shavitt, S. and Barnes, A.J. (2020). Culture and the consumer journey. *Journal of Retailing*, 96(1): 40–54.

Shneor, R., Munim, Z.H., Zhu, H. and Alon, I. (2021). Individualism, collectivism and reward crowdfunding contribution intention and behavior. *Electronic Commerce Research and Applications*, 47(3): 101045. DOI:10.1016/j.elerap.2021.101045

Squadrin, G. (2019, October 18). Difference between Saudi Arabia and UAE. Difference Between. www.differencebetween.net/miscellaneous/religion-miscellaneous/difference-between-saudi-arabia-and-uae

Thompson, M.F., Newman, A. and Liu, M. (2014). The moderating effect of individual level collectivist values on brand loyalty. *Journal of Business Research*, 67(11): 2437–46.

Triandis, H.C. (1995). *Individualism and collectivism*. London: Routledge.

Triandis, H.C. and Gelfland, M.J. (1998). Converging measurement of horizontal and vertical individualism and collectivism. *Journal of Personality and Social Psychology*, 74: 118–28.

Tzu, S. (2009). *The art of war*. Pax Librorum.

Zhang, X., Grigoriou, N. and Li, L. (2008). The myth of China as a single market: The influence of personal value differences on buying decisions. *International Journal of Market Research*, 50(3): 377–402.

Chapter 5

Amazon Web Services (n.d.). Amazon Web Services in China. www.amazonaws.cn/en/about-aws/china

Bray, C. (2013, April 22). Perfume, dresses and cash in Ralph Lauren bribe scheme: Ralph Lauren Corp. resolves U.S. government inquiries into customs payments. *The Wall Street Journal*. www.wsj.com/articles/SB10001424127887324235304578438704093187288

Chan, J. (2017). Raising the stakes in fighting fakes. Campaign Asia. www.campaignasia.com/article/raising-the-stakes-in-fighting-fakes/434153

Choe, S. (2016, September 29). Antigraft law stirs up wariness over South Koreans bearing gifts. *The New York Times*. www.nytimes.com/2016/09/30/world/asia/south-korea-bribery-law.html

Chopping, D. (2022, March 3). IKEA closes all 17 stores in Russia. *The Wall Street Journal*. www.wsj.com/livecoverage/russia-ukraine-latest-news-2022-03-03/card/ikea-closes-all-17-stores-in-russia-

Colurcio, M. and Melia, M. (2017). Harmont & Blaine: A successful dachshund to build the values and brand identity. In B. Jin and E. Cedrola (eds.) *Fashion Branding and Communication: Core Strategies of European Luxury Brands*, pp. 41–72. New York: Palgrave Macmillan.

Dastin, J., Cadell, C. and Wu, K. (2019, April 17). Amazon, facing entrenched rivals, says to shut China online store. Reuters. www.reuters.com/article/us-amazon-com-china/amazon-facing-entrenched-rivals-says-to-shut-china-online-store

Douglas, J. (2023, May 17). What is Saudization? www.linkedin.com/pulse/what-saudization-james-douglas-middle-east

Goodwin, S. (n.d.). *Development of retail industry in China* [PowerPoint slides]. SlidePlayer. https://slideplayer.com/slide/9277216

International Trade Administration (2022). Saudia Arabia – Country Commercial Guide. www.trade.gov/knowledge-product/saudi-arabia-market-challenges

Jakarta Post (2019). Indonesia to lower threshold for import taxes on e-commerce goods. www.thejakartapost.com/news/2019/12/24/government-to-lower-threshold-for-import-taxes-on-e-commerce-goods.html

Jay, P. (2020). How to plug into India's dynamic e-commerce market. The Business of Fashion. www.businessoffashion.com/articles/global-markets/india-e-commerce-opportunity-myntra-amazon-flipkart

Jin, B.E., Almousa, M.O. and Kim, N. (2018). Retailing amid regulation and religion: The unique cultural challenges and opportunities facing market ventures in Saudi Arabia. *Journal of Cultural Marketing Strategy*, 3(1): 70–81.

Jin, B.E. and Kim, G. (2021). Assessing Malaysia and Indonesia as emerging retail markets: An institution-based view. *International Journal of Retail & Distribution Management*, 50(60): 692–707.

Koppad, S.C. and Hundekar, S.G. (2014). An analysis of liberalization of the retail sector and beneficial stakeholders in India with special reference to FDI in retail. *Journal of Business and Economic Policy*, 1(2): 97–105.

Lattman, P. (2013, April 22). Ralph Lauren Corp. agrees to pay fine in bribery case. *The New York Times*. https://dealbook.nytimes.com/2013/04/22/ralph-lauren-pays-1-6-million-to-resolve-bribery-case

Mahajan, R., Bansal, A. and Bhattacharya, S. (2015, July). Fighting corruption in the Maritime Industry: What you need to do to navigate in transparent waters. Deloitte. www2.deloitte.com/content/dam/Deloitte/in/Documents/finance/in-fa-fighting-corruption-in-maritime-industry-noexp.pdf

Masharu, U. and Nasir, M.A. (2018). Policy of foreign direct investment liberalization in India: Implications for retail sector. *International Review of Economics*, 65(4): 465–87.

Mitnick, D. (2012, August 20). How Victoria's Secret learned about domain law. Digiday. https://digiday.com/marketing/how-victorias-secret-learned-about-domain-law

Molin, A. (2012, October 1). IKEA regrets cutting women from Saudi ad. *The Wall Street Journal*. https://online.wsj.com/article/SB10000872396390444592404578030274200387136.html

Moon, L. (2020, April 24). New Balance rightful owner of "N" logo, rules Chinese court. *South China Morning Post*. www.scmp.com/business/companies/article/3081315/new-balance-wins-copyright-case-against-chinese-firm-over-n-logo

Moshinky, B. (2015, August 6). This one chart shows how China's corruption crackdown put an end to extravagant parties. Business Insider. www.businessinsider.com/chinese-anti-corruption-campaign-nearly-destroyed-corporate-catering-2015-8

Müller, U. (2016). Corruption in Russia: IKEA's expansion to the East. *Emerald Emerging Marketing Case Studies*, 6(2): 1–25.

Nast, C. (2021, March 3). How China's resale market can win consumer trust. Vogue Business. www.voguebusiness.com/consumers/china-resale-market-consumer-trust

Ng, Y. (2022, January 18). Brands struggle to navigate China's new data privacy law. Business of Fashion. www.businessoffashion.com/briefings/china/brands-struggle-to-navigate-chinas-new-data-privacy-law

Nguyen-Chyung, A. and Faulk, E. (2014). *Amazon in emerging markets*. Harvard Business Publishing. https://hbsp.harvard.edu/product/W94C01-PDF-ENG

NRF (National Retail Federation) (n.d.). About retail jobs. https://nrf.com/insights/economy/about-retail-jobs

Ranasinghe, D. (2014, June 19). Tough times for luxury retail in China. CNBC. www.cnbc.com/2014/06/19/tough-times-for-luxury-retail-in-china.html

Rao, L. (2016). Amazon may face regulatory hurdles in India. Fortune. https://fortune.com/2016/04/08/amazon-regulatory-hurdles-india

Raszewski, E. (2017, March 30). Argentina's Macri faces rising complaints over import policies. Reuters. www.reuters.com/article/us-argentina-economy-trade-idUSKBN1712Y4

Salomón, J. (2019, November 27). Argentina customs "Mafia" earns millions from China imports. Insight Crime. www.insightcrime.org/news/brief/argentina-customs-mafia-dodges-millions-china-imports

SEC (Securities and Exchange Commission) (2013). SEC Announces non-prosecution agreement with Ralph Lauren Corporation involving FCPA misconduct. www.sec.gov/news/press-release/2013-2013-65htm

Song, X. and Cheng, W. (2012). Perception of corruption in 36 major Chinese cities: Based on survey of 1,642 experts. *Social Indicators Research*, 109(2): 211–21.

Sternquist, B. and Jin, B. (1998). South Korean retail industry: Government's role in retail liberalization. *International Journal of Retail & Distribution Management*, 26(9): 345–53.

Sulistiyono, A.G. (2016). Indonesian "Pierre Cardin" wins lawsuit against the French designer. *The Jakarta Post*. www.thejakartapost.com/news/2016/09/07/indonesian-pierre-cardin-wins-lawsuit-against-the-french-designer.html

The Fashion Law (2021, February 9). New Balance lands $3.85 million win in Chinese trademark case against copycat New Barlun. www.thefashionlaw.com/new-balance-lands-3-85-million-win-in-chinese-trademark-case-against-copycat-new-barlun/

Transparency International (2022). *Corruption perceptions index 2021*. www.transparency.org/en/cpi/2021

USPTO (United States Patent and Trademark Office) (2011). America Invents Act: Effective dates. www.uspto.gov/sites/default/files/aia_implementation/aia-effective-dates.pdf

Webber, J. (2012, January 11). Argentina tightens import controls. *Financial Times*. www.ft.com/content/92bb2e38-3c77-11e1-8d38-00144feabdc0

Weise, K. (2019, April 18). Amazon gives up on Chinese domestic shopping business. *The New York Times*. www.nytimes.com/2019/04/18/technology/amazon-china.html

WIPO (World Intellectual Property Organization) (n.d.). What is intellectual property? www.wipo.int/about-ip/en/index.html

Chapter 6

Andersen, O. (1997). Internationalization and market entry mode: A review of theories and conceptual frameworks. *Management International Review*, 37(2): 7–42.

Brook, B. (2017, October 2). US fast fashion brand Forever 21 looks set to exit Australia as Woolworths takes over flagship store. News.com.au. www.news.com.au/finance/business/retail/us-fast-fashion-brand-forever-21-looks-set-to-exit-australia-as-woolworths-takes-over-flagship-store/news-story

Childs, M. and Jin, B. (2014). Is Uppsala model valid to fashion retailers? An analysis from internationalisation patterns of fast fashion retailers. *Journal of Fashion Marketing and Management*, 18(1): 36–51.

Coviello, N.E. and Munro, H.J. (1997). Network relationships and the internationalisation process of small software firms. *International Business Review*, 6(4): 361–86.

Dunning, J. (1988). The theory of international production. *The International Trade Journal*, 3(1): 21–66.

Dunning, J. (2001). The eclectic (OLI) paradigm of international production: Past, present and future. *International Journal of the Economics of Business*, 8(2): 173–90.

Evans, J., Treadgold, A. and Mavondo, F.T. (2000). Psychic distance and the performance of international retailers: A suggested theoretical framework. *International Marketing Review*, 17(4/5): 373–91.

Gymshark (n.d.). About us. www.gymshark.com/pages/about-us

Howland, D. (2023, February 13). Bed Bath & Beyond Canada is going out of business. Retail Dive. www.retaildive.com/news/bed-bath-beyond-canada-going-out-of-business

Jannarone, J. (2011). Victoria's overseas Secret is behind closed doors. *The Wall Street Journal*. http://online.wsj.com/articles/SB10001424052970204485304576641430635247262

Jin, B., Chung, J.-E., Yang, H. and Jeong, S.W. (2018). Entry market choices and post-entry growth patterns among born globals in consumer goods sectors. *International Marketing Review*, 36(6): 958–80.

Johanson, J. and Mattsson, L.-G. (1988). Internationalisation in industrial systems. A network approach. In P.J. Buckley and P. Ghauri (eds.) *The internationalization of the firm: A reader*, pp. 303–21. Cambridge, MA: Academic Press.

Johanson, J. and Vahlne, J.-E. (1977). The internationalization process of the firm: A model of knowledge development and increasing foreign market commitments. *Journal of International Business Studies*, 8: 22–32.

Johanson, J. and Wiedersheim-Paul, F. (1975). The internationalization of the firm: Four Swedish cases. *Journal of Management Studies*, 12(3): 305–22.

Knight, G. and Cavusgil, S. (2004). Innovation, organization capabilities, and the born global firm. *Journal of International Business Studies*, 35(2): 124–41.

Lu, Y., Karpova, E.E. and Fiore, A.M. (2011). Factors influencing international fashion retailers' entry mode choice. *Journal of Fashion Marketing and Management: An International Journal*, 15(1): 58–75. https://doi.org/10.1108/13612021111112340

Madsen, T.K. and Servais, P. (1997). The internationalization of born globals: An evolutionary process? *International Business Review*, 6(6): 561–83.

Maheshwari, S. (2019, September 30). Forever 21 bankruptcy signals a shift in consumer tastes. *The New York Times*. www.nytimes.com/2019/09/29/business/forever-21-bankruptcy.html

Martin, K. (2023, March 3). Nordstrom leaving Canada, cutting 2,500 jobs. FOXBusiness. www.foxbusiness.com/markets/nordstrom-leaving-canada-cutting-2500-jobs

Nijssen, E., Reinders, M., Krystallis, A. and Tacken, G. (2019). Developing an internationalization strategy using diffusion modeling: The case of greater amberjack. *Fishes*, 4(1): 12. https://doi.org/10.3390/fishes4010012

O'Grady, S. and Lane, H. (1996). The psychic distance paradox. *Journal of International Business Studies*, 27(2): 309–33.

Olejnik, E. and Swoboda, B. (2012). SME's internationalisation patterns: Descriptives, dynamics and determinants. *International Marketing Review*, 29(5): 466–95.

Oviatt, B.M. and McDougall, P.P. (1994). Toward a theory of international new ventures. *Journal of International Business Studies*, 25: 45–64.

Pellegrini, L. (1991). The internationalization of retailing and 1992 Europe. *Journal of Marketing Channels*, 1(2): 3–27.

Picot-Coupey, K., Burt, S.L. and Cliquet, G. (2014). Retailers' expansion mode choice in foreign markets: Antecedents for expansion mode choice in the light of internationalization theories. *Journal of Retailing and Consumer Services*, 21(6): 976–91.

Punchard, H. (2023, February 14). Bed Bath & Beyond Canada's store closures are one of the largest recent retail failures: Analyst. BNN Bloomberg. www.bnnbloomberg.ca/bed-bath-beyond-canada-s-store-closures-are-one-of-the-largest-recent-retail-failures-analyst-1.1883729

Repko, M. (2023, March 2). Nordstrom earnings top expectations as retailer starts winding down Canada operations. CNBC. www.cnbc.com/2023/03/02/nordstrom-jwn-earnings-q4-2022.html

Rialp, A., Rialp, J. and Knight, G.A. (2005). The phenomenon of early internationalizing firms: What do we know after a decade (1993-2003)? *International Business Review*, 14(2): 147–66.

Rindfleisch, A. and Heide, J.B. (1997). Transaction cost analysis: Past, present, and future applications. *Journal of Marketing*, 61(4): 30–54.

Stremersch, S. and Tellis, G.J. (2004). Managing international growth of new products. *International Journal of Research in Marketing*, 21(4): 421–38.

Turner, A. (2018, April 9). Gymshark plans to go global as fitness brand breaks £100m sales. West Midlands. www.thebusinessdesk.com/westmidlands/news/2016416-staying-humble-while-going-global

Williamson, O.E. (1981). The economics of organization: The transaction cost approach. *American Journal of Sociology*, 87(3): 548–57.

Williamson, O.E. (1985). *The economic institutions of capitalization*. Cambridge: The Free Press.

Chapter 7

Andersen, O. and Buvik, A. (2002). Firms' internationalization and alternative approaches to the international customer/market selection. *International Business Review*, 11(3): 347–63.

Cebeci, D. (2020, February 18). Why Amazon failed in China: The one that got away. Transport Intelligence. www.ti-insight.com/briefs/why-amazon-failed-in-china-the-one-that-got-away

Childs, M. and Jin, B. (2014). Is Uppsala model valid to fashion retailers? An analysis from internationalisation patterns of fast fashion retailers. *Journal of Fashion Marketing and Management*, 18(1): 36–51.

Doherty, A.M. (2009). Market and partner selection processes in international retail franchising. *Journal of Business Research*, 62(5): 528–34.

Douglas, S.P. and Craig, C.S. (2011). The role of context in assessing international marketing opportunities. *International Marketing Review*, 28(2): 150–62.

Eshleman, J.R., Cashion, B.G. and Basirico, L.A. (1993). *Sociology: An introduction* (4th ed.). Northbrook, IL: Scott Foresman.

Fernandez, C. (December 14, 2017). L Catterton acquires majority stake in Ganni. Business of Fashion. www.businessoffashion.com/articles/finance/l-catterton-acquires-majority-stake-in-ganni

Fisher, L.A. (2019, March 19). This Brazilian brand is about to become every fashion girl's favorite. *Harper's Bazaar*. www.harpersbazaar.com/fashion/trends/a26840661/farm-rio-fashion

Gaston-Breton, C. and Martín, O. (2011). International market selection and segmentation: A two-stage model. *International Marketing Review*, 28(3): 267–90.

Gomes, R.M., Carneiro, J. and Dib, L.A. (2018). Branded retailer expansion on a continent-sized emerging market. *International Journal of Retail & Distribution Management*, 46(9): 820–34.

Han, C.M. and Won, S.B. (2017). Cross-country differences in consumer cosmopolitanism and ethnocentrism: A multilevel analysis with 21 countries. *Journal of Consumer Behaviour*, 17(1): e52–66.

Hannerz, U. (1990). Cosmopolitans and locals in world culture. *Theory, Culture and Society*, 7(2/3): 237–51.

He, J. and Wang, C.L. (2015). Cultural identity and consumer ethnocentrism impacts on preference and purchase of domestic versus import brands: An empirical study in China. *Journal of Business Research*, 86(6): 1225–33.

Hutchinson, K., Quinn, B., Alexander, N. and Doherty, A.M. (2009). Retailer internationalization: Overcoming barriers to expansion. *International Review of Retail, Distribution and Consumer Research*, 19(3): 251–72.

Jannarone, J. (2011, October 20). Victoria's overseas Secret is behind closed doors. *The Wall Street Journal*. http://online.wsj.com/articles/SB10001424052970204485304576641430635247262

Jin, B., Chung, J.E., Jeong, S.W. and Yang, H.S. (2015). 브랜드, 세계를 삼키다: 작지만 강한 한국 중소기업의 성공 DNA (*Brands rule the world: Unlocking the DNA of successful Korean SMEs in the global marketplace*). Idam Books.

Jin, B., Chung, J.-E., Yang, H. and Jeong, S.W. (2018). Entry market choices and post-entry growth patterns among born globals in consumer goods sectors. *International Marketing Review*, 36(6): 958–80.

Jin, B., Kendagal, P. and Jung, S. (2013). Evolution patterns of apparel brands in Asian countries: Propositions from an analysis of the apparel industry in Korea and India. *Clothing and Textiles Research Journal*, 31(1): 48–63.

Johanson, J. and Vahlne, J.-E. (1977). The internationalization process of the firm: A model of knowledge development and increasing foreign market commitments. *Journal of International Business Studies*, 8(1): 23–32.

Johanson, J. and Vahlne, J.E. (1990). The mechanism of internationalisation. *International Marketing Review*, 7(4): 11–24.

Kumar, V., Stam, A. and Joachimsthaler, E.A. (1994). An interactive multicriteria approach to identifying potential foreign markets. *Journal of International Marketing*, 2(1): 29–52.

Le, H. (2019, November 13). Foreign brands eager to enter booming fashion market. VnExpress International. https://e.vnexpress.net/news/business/industries/foreign-brands-eager-to-enter-booming-fashion-market-4009814.html

Lopez, C. and Fan, Y. (2009). Internationalisation of the Spanish fashion brand Zara. *Journal of Fashion Marketing and Management*, 13(2): 279–96.

Martín, O.M. and Papadopoulos, N. (2007). Internationalization and performance: Evidence from Spanish firms. *Journal of Euromarketing*, 16(1/2): 87–103.

Papadopoulos, N. and Denis, J. (1988). Inventory, taxonomy and assessment of methods for international market selection. *International Marketing Review*, 5(3): 38–51.

Portell, G., Mukherjee, D., Warschun, M., Pathak, S., Inoue, M. et al. (2021). *The 2021 Global Retail Development Index*. Kearney. www.kearney.com/global-retail-development-index/2021

Riefler, P. and Diamantopoulos, A. (2009). Consumer cosmopolitanism: Review and replication of the CYMYC scale. *Journal of Business Research*, 62(4): 407–19.

Riefler, P., Diamantopoulos, A. and Siguaw, J.A. (2011). Cosmopolitan consumers as a target group for segmentation. *Journal of International Business Studies*, 43(3): 285–305.

Sakarya, S., Eckman, M. and Hyllegard, K.H. (2007). Market selection for international expansion: Assessing opportunities in emerging markets. *International Marketing Review*, 24(2): 208–38.

Srivastava, A., Gupta, N. and Rana, N.P. (2021). Influence of consumer cosmopolitanism on purchase intention of foreign vs local brands: A developing country perspective. *International Journal of Emerging Markets*. DOI:10.1108/IJOEM-01-2021-0057

Strizhakova, Y., Coulter, R.A. and Price, L.L. (2011). Branding in a global marketplace: The mediating effects of quality and self-identity brand signals. *International Journal of Research in Marketing*, 28(4): 342–51.

Wong, Y.H. and Merrilees, B. (2007). Multiple roles for branding in international marketing. *International Marketing Review*, 24(4): 384–408.

Woo, H. and Jin, B. (2014). Asian apparel brands aiming for global: The cases of internationalization of Giordano and Uniqlo. *Fashion & Textiles*, 1(1): 1–14.

WTO (World Trade Organization) (2021). *World Trade Statistical Review 2021*. www.wto.org/english/res_e/statis_e/wts2021_e/wts2021_e.pdf

Chapter 8

Agarwal, S. and Ramaswami, S. (1992). Choice of foreign entry mode: Impact of ownership, location and internationalization factors. *Journal of International Business*, 23(1): 1–16.

Alexander, B., Nobbs, K. and Varley, R. (2018). The growing permanence of pop-up outlets within the international location strategies of fashion retailers. *International Journal of Retail & Distribution Management*, 46(5): 487–506.

Alexander, N. and Doherty, A.M. (2009). *International Retailing*. New York: Oxford University Press.

Alon, I. Madanoglu, M. and Shoham, A. (2017). Strategic agility explanations for managing franchising expansion during economic cycles. *Competitive Review*, 27(2): 113–31.

Atwal, G. and Bryson, D. (2017). *Luxury brands in China and India*. London: Palgrave Macmillan.

Baena, V. (2012). Master franchising as foreign entry mode: Evidences from the Spanish franchise system. *International Scholarly Research Notices*, 1–8. https://doi.org/10.5402/2012/293478

Bailay, R. (2017, May 24). Japanese retailers looking to enter Indian market dominated by European, US brands. *The Economic Times*. https://economictimes.indiatimes.com/industry/services/retail/japanese-retailers-looking-to-enter-indian-market-dominated-by-european-us-brands/articleshow/58814769.cms

Bailay, R. (2018, December 4). After online success, global brands are coming to a store near you. *The Economic Times*. https://economictimes.indiatimes.com/industry/services/retail/after-online-success-global-brands-are-coming-to-a-store-near-you/articleshow/66929833.cms

Bhushan, R. (2005, September 22). Planet Sports to enter India. The Times of India. https://timesofindia.indiatimes.com/business/india-business/planet-sports-to-enter-india/articleshow/1238645.cms

Bladd, J. (2010, January 25). Bloomingdale's Dubai set to open on Feb 1. Arabian Business. www.arabianbusiness.com/bloomingdale-s-dubai-set-open-on-feb-1-9335.html

Business Insider (2010, January 31). First international Bloomingdale's opens in Dubai. www.businessinsider.com/first-international-bloomingdales-opens-in-dubai-2010-1

Business Standard (2013, January 21). Road cleared for Gucci's India entry for single brand retail. www.business-standard.com/article/companies/road-cleared-for-gucci-s-india-entry-for-single-brand-retail-109120300145_1.html

Business Standard (2014, September 1). Nike to open fully-owned stores in India. www.business-standard.com/article/companies/nike-to-open-fully-owned-stores-in-india-114090101497_1.html

Butler, S. (2013, November 12). Online fashion retailer Asos launches Chinese website. *The Guardian.* www.theguardian.com/business/2013/nov/12/asos-launches-chinese-website

Cho, H.J. and Jin, B. (2012, November). An application of Uppsala model to internationalization of U.S. fashion companies: The cases of Tiffany & Co. and Polo Ralph Lauren in Japan. Paper presented at the annual conference of the International Textile and Apparel Association, Honolulu.

Clifford, S. and Alderman, L. (2011, June 15). American retailers try again in Europe. *The New York Times.* www.nytimes.com/2011/06/16/business/global/16retail.html

Computer Business Review (2006, October 31). Samsung to exit joint venture with Tesco. www.cbronline.com/news/samsung_to_exit_joint_venture_with_tesco

Diderich, J. (2016, December 22). Pierre Cardin won't get out of bed for less than a billion euros. Business of Fashion. www.businessoffashion.com/articles/news-analysis/pierre-cardin-wont-get-out-of-bed-for-less-than-a-billion-euros

Doland, A. (2014, May 08). Selling Americana to China: Abercrombie and Old Navy take on the mainland. AdAge. https://adage.com/article/global-news/abercrombie-navy-china/293076

Durand, A. (2019). *Marketing and globalization.* New York: Taylor & Francis.

ET Retail.com (2017, September 25). Skechers eyes up to 500 stores in India in 5 yrs https://retail.economictimes.indiatimes.com/news/apparel-fashion/footwear/skechers-eyes-up-to-500-stores-in-india-in-5-yrs/60821757

Fashion United (2013, April 15). Zalando explains its strategy for Italy. https://fashionunited.uk/v1/fashion/zalando-explains-its-strategy-for-italy/2013041512381

Fernie, J., Moore, C.M., Lawrie, A. and Hallsworth, A. (1997). The internationalisation of the high fashion brand: The case of central London. *Journal of Product & Brand Management,* 6(3): 151–62.

Filieri, R. (2015). From market-driving to market-driven: An analysis of Benetton's strategy change and its implications for long-term performance. *Marketing Intelligence and Planning,* 33(3): 238–57.

Financial Times (2016, April 7). Asos to pull out of China. www.ft.com/content/f931d8ee-98d9-3add-b2ca-03ce42fb45f0

FranCity (2015). Types of franchise arrangements. http://francity.com/about-franchising/types-of-franchise-arrangements

Gap Inc. (2010, June 23). Gap Inc. outlines comprehensive China market entry plans, starting with four gap brand stores and online shopping site in late 2010. www.gapinc.com/en-us/articles/2010/06/gap-inc-outlines-comprehensive-china-market-entry

Gauzente, C. and Dumoulin, R. (2010). Franchise as an efficient mode of entry in emerging markets: A discussion from the legitimacy point of view. In S. Singh (ed.) *Handbook of business practices and growth in emerging markets.* Singapore: World Scientific Publishing.

Hendriksz, V. (2017, July 7). Mulberry launches joint venture with Onward Global Fashion. Fashion United. https://fashionunited.uk/news/business/mulberry-launches-joint-venture-with-onward-global-fashion/2017070725102

Hitt, M.A., Ireland, R.D. and Hoskisson, R.E. (2019). *Strategic management: Competitiveness and globalization: Concepts and cases* (13th ed.). Mason, OH: South-Western College Publishing

Jin, B. and Chung, J.-E. (2016). Beaucre Merchandising Co., Ltd.: A successfully internationalizing Korean apparel company. In B. Jin and E. Cedrola (eds.) *Fashion brand internationalization: Opportunities and challenges,* pp. 115–38. New York: Palgrave Macmillan.

Kim, E. and Levy, A. (2019, January 29). Amazon plans to launch a new Middle East marketplace, two years after buying Souq for $580 million. CNBC. www.cnbc.com/2019/01/29/amazon-new-middle-east-marketplace-rivals-souq.html

King, K. (2017, May 21). Manhattan tallies vacant storefronts. *The Wall Street Journal.* www.wsj.com/articles/manhattan-tallies-vacant-storefronts-1495393079

Korukcuoglu, S. (2012, November 12). Fashion business and promotional strategies in the Middle East. Fashionbi. http://fashionbi.com/newspaper/fashion-business-and-promotional-strategies-in-the-middle-east

Kozinets, R.V., Sherrya, J.F., DeBerry-Spencea, B., Duhacheka, A., Nuttavuthisita, K. et al. (2002). Themed flagship brand stores in the new millennium: Theory, practice, prospects. *Journal of Retailing*, 78(1): 17–29.

Kumar, M. (2016, September 1). Puma moves out of joint venture, will now be on its own in India. Fashion United. https://fashionunited.in/news/business/puma-moves-out-of-joint-venture-will-now-be-on-its-own-in-india/2016090114098

Lee, K., Jarvis, J., Kundra, S., Mihoubi, B. and Grueneberg, S. (2012). Alternatives to master franchising: Area development agreements, area representatives and joint ventures. *International Journal of Franchising Law*, 10(4). www.macrothink.org/journal/index.php/jebi/article/view/10819

Long, G. (2005). China's policies on FDI: Review and evaluation. In H.M. Theodore, M.G. Edward and B. Magnus (eds.) *Does foreign direct investment promote development?*, pp. 315–36. Washington, DC: Institute for International Economics, Center for Global Development.

Lopez, C. and Fan, Y. (2009). Internationalisation of the Spanish fashion brand Zara. *Journal of Fashion Marketing and Management*, 13(2): 279–96.

Lu, Y., Karpova, E.E. and Fiore, A.M. (2011). Factors influencing international fashion retailers' entry mode choice. *Journal of Fashion Marketing and Management: An International Journal*, 15(1): 58–75.

Mitra, S. (2015, November 4). Adidas gets govt nod to open 100% foreign owned stores in India. Livemint. www.livemint.com/Companies/VpcqZXrhUXGIjKdEzFdInO/Adidas-gets-100-FDI-nod-to-open-own-stores-in-India.html

Moore, C.M., Doherty, A.M. and Doyle, S.A. (2010). Flagship stores as a market entry method: The perspective of luxury fashion retailing. *European Journal of Marketing*, 44(1/2): 139–61.

Moore, C.M., Fernie, J. and Burt, S. (2000). Brands without boundaries: The internationalization of the designer retailer's brand. *European Journal of Marketing*, 34(8): 919–37.

Ng, J. and Sanchanta, M. (2012, July 31). J.Crew brings its brand to China. *The Wall Street Journal*. www.wsj.com/articles/SB10000872396390444226904577560600321514134

Nguyen-Chyung, A. and Faulk, E. (2014). Amazon in emerging markets. Michigan Ross School of Business.

Okonkwo, U. (2007). *Luxury fashion branding: Trends, tactics, techniques*. New York: Palgrave Macmillan

Oxberry, E. (2009, November 20). Burberry signs new Indian partner. Drapers. www.drapersonline.com/news/burberry-signs-new-indian-partner

Pavarini, M. C. (2013, April 16). Zalando opens pop-up store in Milan. *Sportswear International*. www.sportswear-international.com/news/stories/Zalando-Opens-Pop-Up-Store-In-Milan-6649

Picot-Coupey, K., Burt, S.L. and Cliquet, G. (2014). Retailers' expansion mode choice in foreign markets: Antecedents for expansion mode choice in the light of internationalization theories. *Journal of Retailing and Consumer Services*, 21(6): 976–91.

Rai, N. (2007, November 30). DLF may buy Ferragamo franchise. Rediif India Abroad. www.rediff.com/money/2007/nov/30dlf.htm

Russell, J. (2018a, August 20). Walmart completes its $16 billion acquisition of Flipkart. Tech Crunch. https://techcrunch.com/2018/08/20/walmart-flipkart-deal-done

Russell, J. (2018b, December 11). Walmart partners with Rakuten to open its first e-commerce store in Japan. Tech Crunch. https://techcrunch.com/2018/12/10/walmart-ecommerce-japan

Shamnani, H. (2018, January 1). How Zara and H&M are reshaping the Indian branded apparel market? LinkedIn. www.linkedin.com/pulse/how-zara-hm-reshaping-indian-branded-apparel-market-hiren-shamnani

Sharma, A. and Sahu, P. (2012, January 11). India lifts some limits on foreign retailers. *The Wall Street Journal*. www.wsj.com/articles/SB10001424052970204257504577152342214405180

Tandon, S. (2018, May 9). Japan's biggest fashion chain is finally coming to India. Quartz India. https://

qz.com/india/1273211/uniqlo-is-finally-coming-to-india

The Corner (2012, September 14). Zara launches online shopping in China. http://thecorner.eu/companies/zara-launches-online-shopping-in-china/13961/

The Economic Times (2009, January 7). Puma, knowledge fire in retail JV. https://economictimes.indiatimes.com/industry/services/retail/puma-knowledge-fire-in-retail-jv/articleshow/3944764.cms?from=mdr

Tran, Q. (2015, May 22). Gap partners with Zalando for German re-entry. *WWD*. https://wwd.com/fashion-news/fashion-scoops/gap-at-zalando-for-german-re-entry-10134000

Vitorovich, L. (2008, May 15). Tesco to acquire Korea's homever from E-Land for $902.7 million. *The Wall Street Journal*. www.wsj.com/articles/SB121074934366591505?ns=prod/accounts-wsj

Walmart (n.d.). Our history. https://corporate.walmart.com/our-story/our-history

Well, J. (2018, May 2). L'Oréal acquires South Korea's Stylenanda. WWD. https://wwd.com/beauty-industry-news/products/loreal-acquires-south-koreas-stylenanda-1202663851

White, S. (2018, May 2). L'Oréal snaps up South Korean cosmetics firm Nanda. Reuters. www.reuters.com/article/us-loreal-stylenanda/loreal-snaps-up-south-korean-cosmetics-firm-nanda-idUSKBN1I32BO

Woo, H. and Jin, B. (2014). Asian apparel brands aiming for global: The cases of internationalization of Giordano and Uniqlo. *Fashion & Textiles*, 1(1): 1–14.

Chapter 9

Aichner, T., Forza, C. and Trentin, A. (2017). The country-of-origin lie: Impact of foreign branding on customers' willingness to buy and willingness to pay when the product's actual origin is disclosed. *International Review of Retail, Distribution and Consumer Research*, 27(1): 43–60.

Alden, D.L., Steenkamp, J.-B. and Batra, R. (1999). Brand positioning through advertising in Asia, North America, and Europe: The role of global consumer culture. *Journal of Marketing*, 63(1): 75–87.

Batra, R., Ramaswamy, V., Alden, D.L., Steenkamp, J.B. and Ramachander, S. (2000). Effects of brand local and non-local origin on consumer attitudes in developing countries. *Journal of Consumer Psychology*, 9(2): 83–95.

Chitrakorn, K. (2017, April 28). When the name game gets serious in China. Business of Fashion. www.businessoffashion.com/articles/china/chinese-brand-names-belle-li-ning-meipai/

Hanbury, M. (2018, August 16). TJ Maxx has a different name in Europe and Australia, and there's a simple reason why. Business Insider. www.businessinsider.com/tj-maxx-and-tk-maxx-are-same-company-2018-8

Inside Retail (2013, April 8). Mango tries again. https://insideretail.com.au/news/Mango-tries-again-201304

Jin, B., Almousa, M., Yang, H. and Kim, N. (2018). Differential effects of macro and micro country images by product category and by country among Saudi consumers. *Management Decision*, 56(8): 1663–81.

Johansson, J. (2009). *Global marketing: Foreign entry, local marketing, and global management* (5th ed.). New York: McGraw-Hill/Irwin.

Josiassen, A., Lukas, B A., Whitwell, G.J. and Assaf, A.G. (2013). The halo model of origin images: Conceptualisation and initial empirical test, *Journal of Consumer Behavior*, 12(4): 253–66.

Leclerc, F., Schmitt, B.H. and Dubé, L. (1994). Foreign branding and its effects on product perceptions and attitudes. *Journal of Marketing*, 31(2): 263–70.

Melnyk, V., Klein, K. and Völckner, F. (2012). The double-edged sword of foreign brand names for companies from emerging countries. *Journal of Marketing*, 76(6): 21–37.

Pappu, R., Quester, P.G. and Cooksey, R.W. (2007). Country image and consumer-based brand equity: Relationships and implications for international marketing. *Journal of International Business Studies*, 38(5): 726–45.

Steenkamp, J.-B. (2017). *Global brand strategy: World-wise marketing in the age of branding*. London: Palgrave Macmillan.

Steenkamp, J.-B., Batra, R. and Alden, D. (2003). How perceived brand globalness creates brand value. *Journal of International Business Studies*, 34(1): 53–65.

Vrontis, D. and Vronti, P. (2004). Levi Strauss: An international marketing investigation. *Journal of Fashion Marketing and Management*, 8(4): 389–98.

Wang, C. and Chen, Z. (2004). Consumer ethnocentrism and willingness to buy domestic products in a developing country setting: Testing moderating effects. *Journal of Consumer Marketing*, 21(6): 391–400.

Woo, H. (2016). Single brand with multiple country images: The effect of discrepancies between country images on brand credibility and prestige. Unpublished doctoral dissertation, University of North Carolina at Greensboro.

Chapter 10

Alkhalisi, Z. (2017, March 7). Nike has a new product for Muslim women: The "pro hijab". CNNMoney. https://money.cnn.com/2017/03/07/news/nike-pro-hijab

Arab America (2019, December 11). Colors of the Arab world: Meaning and symbolism. www.arabamerica.com/colors-of-the-arab-world-meaning-and-symbolism

Atwal, G. and Bryson, D. (2017). Learning from mistakes. In G. Atwal and D. Bryson, *Luxury brands in China and India*, pp. 207–31. London: Palgrave Macmillan.

Boyd, C. (2019, January 28). "Just don't do it!" Thousands of Muslims demand Nike withdraw "insulting" Air Max trainers "that have Allah written on the sole". Dailymail.com. www.dailymail.co.uk/news/article-6640481/Muslims-demand-Nike-withdraw-insulting-Air-Max-trainers-Allah-written-sole.html

Chen, C. (2018, December 3). How Victoria's Secret conquered China. The Business of Fashion. www.businessoffashion.com/articles/intelligence/as-victorias-secret-loses-relevance-in-the-us-china-may-offer-the-solution

Chen, C. (2022, June 10). How to take a brand from local to global. Business of Fashion. www.businessoffashion.com/articles/retail/farm-rio-global-expansion-contemporary-womenswear

Childs, M. and Jin, B. (2017). Nike: An innovation journey. In B. Jin and E. Cedrola (eds.) *Product innovation in the global fashion industry*, pp. 79–111. London: Palgrave Macmillan.

Chitrakorn, K. (2015, November 18). Can Halal cosmetics outgrow their niche? Business of Fashion. www.businessoffashion.com/articles/inside-beauty/can-halal-cosmetics-outgrow-their-niche

Dishman, L. (2012, March 23). The strategic retail genius behind Zara. Forbes. www.forbes.com/sites/lydiadishman/2012/03/23/the-strategic-retail-genius-behind-zara

Elwazer, S. (2011, November 28). UAE flag colours on Puma shoes anger nationals. CNN. www.cnn.com/blogarchive/insidethemiddleeast.blogs.cnn.com/2011/11/28/uae-flag-colours-on-puma-shoes-anger-nationals

Fitzgerald, B.F. (2022, July 15). Nike opens first-ever Nike style store in Seoul, Shanghai next. FashionNetwork.com. www.fashionnetwork.com/news/Nike-opens-first-ever-nike-style-store-in-seoul-shanghai-next,1424252.html

George, J. (2011, November 29). Puma apologies for shoes with UAE flag colours. Emirates 24/7. www.emirates247.com/news/emirates/puma-apologises-for-shoes-with-uae-flag-colours-2011-11-29-1.430783

Hall, C. and Jay, P. (2021). Case study: Unpacking Uniqlo's India strategy. Business of Fashion. www.businessoffashion.com/case-studies/global-markets/unpacking-uniqlos-india-strategy-download-the-case-study

Jin, B., Ramkumar, B. and Chou, W.H. (2018). Identifying sources and roles of networks in international expansion among small businesses in a less-technology-intensive industry. *International Journal of Entrepreneurship and Small Business*, 34(4): 421. https://doi.org/10.1504/ijesb.2018.093599

Jury, L. (1997, June 25). Nike to trash trainers that offended Islam. *Independent*. www.independent.co.uk/news/nike-to-trash-trainers-that-offended-islam-1257776.html

Kaye, L. (2018). H&M struggles repairing a battered reputation in South Africa. TriplePundit. www.triplepundit.com/story/2018/hm-struggles-repairing-battered-reputation-south-africa/13616

Lee, L. and Wang, L. (2014, July 21). J. Crew's XXXS size, Alibaba IPO, Asia woolmark prize. Business of Fashion. www.businessoffashion.com/articles/china/china-edit-j-crews-xxxs-size-alibaba-ipo-asia-woolmark-prize

McClelland, M. (2022, April 13). Your guide to the exclusive capsule collections designed for Ramadan 2022. *Grazia*. https://graziamagazine.com/me/articles/fashion-ramadan-capsule-collections

Palmer, N.S. (2018, February 3). The Muslim fashion market is not a monolith. Business of Fashion. www.businessoffashion.com/opinions/news-analysis/op-ed-the-muslim-fashion-market-is-not-a-monolith

Segran, E. (2016, October 27). How Tommy Hilfiger is reimagining this brand. Fast Company. www.fastcompany.com/3064125/how-tommy-hilfiger-is-reimagining-his-brand

Shoulberg, W. (2018, July 31). Why Ikea succeeds around the world while other retailers falter. Forbes. www.forbes.com/sites/warrenshoulberg/2018/07/30/put-another-stamp-on-the-ikea-passport

Sizeguide.net. (n.d.). Women's clothing sizes: International conversion charts and size charts. www.sizeguide.net/womens-clothing-sizes-international-conversion-chart.html

Solca, L. and Zhu, J. (2021, November 1). The biggest mistakes luxury brands make in China. Business of Fashion. www.businessoffashion.com/opinions/china/the-biggest-mistakes-luxury-brands-make-in-china

Tulshyan, R. (2011, October 12). Hermes is now selling saris in India, and it's a big deal. Forbes. www.forbes.com/sites/worldviews/2011/10/12/hermes-is-now-selling-saris-in-india-and-its-a-big-deal/?sh=308d6135f241

Waldmeir, P. (2010, August 18). Levi's launches new brand in China. *Financial Times*. www.ft.com/content/0a7a1c2e-aaaa-11df-80f9-00144feabdc0

Chapter 11

BBC (2021, July 1). Gap to close all 81 stores in UK and Ireland. BBC News. www.bbc.com/news/business-57670737.

Blake, D., McIlvaine, H., Hui-Miller, J.-A. and Pattabiraman, R. (2013, April 8). Mango tries again. Inside Retail. https://insideretail.com.au/news/mango-tries-again-201304

Bloomberg (2021, June 14). How Trump's trade war built Shein, China's first global fashion giant. www.bloomberg.com/news/articles/2021-06-14/online-fashion-giant-shein-emerged-from-china-thanks-to-donald-trump-s-trade-war

Ceballos, L.M., Jin, B. and Ortega, A.M. (2018). Colombian consumers' outshopping of apparel in the U.S. *International Review of Retail, Distribution and Consumer Research*, 8(2): 137–56.

Choi, B. (2010, March 22). Global fashion brands kneeled to Korean mom's request. Chosun Biz. https://biz.chosun.com/site/data/html_dir/2010/03/21/2010032100736.html

Coyle, J.J., Bardi, E.J. and Langley, C.J. (2003). *The management of business logistics: A supply chain perspective* (9th ed.). Mason, OH: South-Western/Thomson Learning.

Geoghegan, J. (2016, October 20). Analysis: Why US retailers can't crack the UK market. Drapers. www.drapersonline.com/news/analysis-why-us-retailers-cant-crack-the-uk-market

Gillespie, K. and Hennessey, D. (2016). *Global marketing* (4th ed.). New York: Routledge.

Huda, D., Rahaman, Md., Hasan, K. and Ziauddin, A. (2017). Study of the free port or free trade zone concept of Bangladesh. ResearchGate. www.researchgate.net/publication/330753546_Study_of_the_Free_Port_or_Free_Trade_Zone_Concept_of_Bangladesh

ICC (International Chamber of Commerce) (2012). De minimis: Definition. http://tfig.unece.org/contents/de-minimis.htm

Jin, B. and Chung, J.-E. (2016). Beaucre merchandising Co., Ltd.: A successfully internationalizing Korean apparel company. In B. Jin and E. Cedrola (eds.) *Fashion brand internationalization: Opportunities and challenges*, pp. 115–38. New York: Palgrave Macmillan.

Ju, J. and Chang, K.C. (2022, April 14). De minimis tax thresholds and cross-border e-commerce. GEODIS India. https://geodis.com/in/blog/customs/de-minimis-tax-thresholds-and-cross-border-e-commerce

McDowell, M. (2019, August 14). Europe is still a bargain for luxury shoppers. Vogue Business. www.voguebusiness.com/companies/global-luxury-price-discrepancies-louis-vuitton-gucci-balenciaga

Musco, F. (2017, January 25). Zara has a pricing and sizing problem. https://peacockplume.fr/fashion/zara-has-pricing-and-sizing-problem

Paton, E. (2021, August 24). Luxury's gray market is emerging from the shadows. *The New York Times*. www.nytimes.com/2021/08/24/fashion/fashion-luxury-gray-market.html

Redrup, Y. (2013, April 9). Spanish fashion giant Mango forms alliance with David Jones after initial struggle. SmartCompany. www.smartcompany.com.au/finance/economy/spanish-fashion-giant-forms-alliance-with-david-jones-after-initial-struggle

Shannon, S. (2018, August 16). Fashion's dirty secret: Millions in grey market sales. Business of Fashion. www.businessoffashion.com/articles/luxury/fashion-dirty-little-secret-grey-market-luxury-paralleling

Shannon, S. (2020, January 30). Brands beware: The digital grey market is growing. Business of Fashion. www.businessoffashion.com/…/brands-beware-the-digital-grey-market-is-growing

Son, J. and Jin, B. (2012, November). The price of Levi's jeans across countries: Why and how they are different? Paper presented at the annual conference of International Textile and Apparel Association, Honolulu.

USCIB (United States Council for International Business) (2016). Value added tax rates (VAT) by country. www.uscib.org/valueadded-taxes-vat-ud-1676

Chapter 12

An, D. (2007). Advertising visuals in global brands' local websites: A six-country comparison. *International Journal of Advertising*, 26(3): 303–32.

Arnold, D. (2000). Seven rules of international distribution. *Harvard Business Review*, 78(6): 131–7.

Bearne, S. (2018, October 1). The 26-year-old with a £100m sportswear brand. BBC. www.bbc.com/news/business-45246999

Benaiche, E. (2021, January 28). Prepare your ecommerce site for an international audience and secure new market shares. Goaland. www.goaland.com/blog/e-commerce/prepare-your-ecommerce-site-for-an-international-audience

Bi, R. (2020, August 12). Is Topshop's failure in China a fast fashion problem? *Jing Daily*. https://jingdaily.com/is-topshops-failure-in-china-a-fast-fashion-problem

Chen, C. (2022, March 9). How to compete with Shein. Business of Fashion. www.businessoffashion.com/articles/retail/how-to-compete-with-shein

Doran, S. (2010, December 23). 16 key luxury brand distributors. www.luxurysociety.com/en/articles/2010/12/16-key-luxury-brand-distributors

Export.gov (2018, March 14). 1. Steps to create a globalized website. https://legacy.export.gov/article?id=Steps-to-Create-a-Globalized-Website

Fong, M. (2006, February 20). Zara joins a fashion parade as China opens to retailers. *The Wall Street Journal*. www.wsj.com/articles/SB114038784361278113

Hall, C. and Jay, P. (2021). Case study: Unpacking Uniqlo's India strategy. Business of Fashion. www.businessoffashion.com/case-studies/global-markets/unpacking-uniqlos-india-strategy-download-the-case-study/

Insider Intelligence (2016, June 24). Cash on delivery remains the preferred method of payment in India. www.insider.com/cash-on-delivery-remains-the-preferred-method-of-payment-in-india-2016-6

Jay, P. (2020, July 30). How to plug into India's dynamic e-commerce market. Business of Fashion. www.businessoffashion.com/articles/professional/india-e-commerce-opportunity-myntra-amazon-flipkart

J.Crew. (n.d.). International. www.jcrew.com/help/international-orders

Jiang, E. (2017, August 14). In global e-commerce, the race to solve the "last mile". Business of Fashion. www.businessoffashion.com/articles/global-currents/in-e-commerce-the-race-to-solve-the-last-mile

Jin, B. and Chung, J.-E. (2016). Beaucre merchandising Co., Ltd.: A successfully internationalizing Korean apparel company. In B. Jin and E. Cedrola (eds.) *Fashion brand internationalization: Opportunities and challenges*, pp. 115–38. New York: Palgrave Macmillan.

Johansson, J.K. (2009). *Global marketing: Foreign entry, local marketing and global management* (5th ed.). New York: McGraw-Hill.

Kennedy, J. (2022, April 5). Why Shein might be worth $100 billion, in four charts. Business of Fashion. www.businessoffashion.com/articles/retail/why-shein-might-be-worth-100-billion-in-four-charts

Kim, H., Coyle, J.R. and Gould, S.J. (2009). Collectivist and individualist influences on website design in South Korea and the U.S.: A cross-cultural content analysis. *Journal of Computer-Mediated Communication*, 14(3): 581–601.

Lieber, C. and Chen, C. (2022, April 8). The $100 billion Shein phenomenon, explained. Business of Fashion. www.businessoffashion.com/briefings/retail/the-100-billion-shein-phenomenon-explained

Moore, C.M., Fernie, J. and Burt, S. (2000). Brands without boundaries: The internationalization of the designer retailer's brand. *European Journal of Marketing*, 34(8): 919–37.

Morris, S. (2014, June 11). Zara owner Inditex to join Tmall to reach more Chinese shoppers. https://uk.reuters.com/article/us-inditex-tmall/zara-owner-inditex-to-join-tmall-to-reach-more-chinese-shoppers-id

Nike Inc. (2021, August 10). First look at Nike Rise Seoul. Nike News. https://news.nike.com/news/nike-rise-seoul.

Parisi, D. (2019, May 30). "There was almost a bit of arrogance": Why Topshop failed in the US. https://digiday.com/retail/almost-bit-arrogance-topshop-failed-us

Petrov, C. (2022, August 19). 63+ wowing m-commerce statistics for 2022. Techjury. https://techjury.net/blog/mcommerce-statistics

Praffulljain. (2016, June 27). Global site structure (Nike.com): Part 2. Experience Labs. https://experiencelabs.wordpress.com/2016/06/27/global-site-structure-nike-com-part-2

Ramkumar, B. and Jin, B. (2019). Examining pre-purchase intention and post-purchase consequences of international online outshopping (IOO): The moderating effect of e-tailer's country image. *Journal of Retailing and Consumer Services*, 49: 186–97.

Rozario, K. (2021, August 3). Ralph Lauren soars as China leads Asian growth. *Jing Daily*. https://jingdaily.com/ralph-lauren-retail-beijing-q1-2022

Salpini, C. (2021, August 11). Nike doubles down on localization with Nike Rise Concept. Retail Dive. www.retaildive.com/news/nike-doubles-down-on-localization-with-nike-rise-concept/604819

Steenkamp, J-B. (2017). *Global brand strategy: Worldwise marketing in the age of branding.* London: Palgrave Macmillan.

Suen, Z. (2019, May 9). Why fast fashion brands are fleeing China. Business of Fashion. www.businessoffashion.com/articles/china/fast-fashion-in-china-go-hard-or-go-home

Toppan (2022, April 22). 9 key factors to consider when localising your website for international markets. Toppan Digital Language. https://toppandigital.com/translation-blog/9-key-factors-to-consider-when-localising-your-website-for-international-markets

Wang, Z. (2014, June 11). Zara to enter China's largest online platform. *China Daily*. www.chinadaily.com.cn/business/tech/2014-06/11/content_17580243.htm

Wassel, B. (2021, November 3). Ralph Lauren plans 90 new stores and additional localized websites in 2021. www.retailtouchpoints.com/topics/omnichannel-alignment/ralph-lauren-plans-90-new-stores-and-additional-localized-websites-in-2021

Wong, S.H. (2017, November 2). Ralph Lauren's retreat from discounting helps bolster profit. Bloomberg. www.bloomberg.com/news/articles/2017-11-02/ralph-lauren-s-retreat-from-discounting-helps-bolster-profit

Chapter 13

Achim, A.-L. (2021, March 17). These Western brands are winning China's local markets. *Jing Daily*. https://jingdaily.com/western-brands-winning-china-localization-gucci-burberry

Al-Olayan, F.S. and Karande, K. (2000). A content analysis of magazine advertisements from the United States and the Arab world. *Journal of Advertising*, 29(3): 69–82.

ASA (Advertising Standards Authority) (2011, April 4). Guidance on the use of pre and post-production techniques in ads for cosmetics. www.asa.org.uk/resource/cosmetic-production-techniques.html

ASA (2022, August 1). Social responsibility body image. www.asa.org.uk/advice-online/social-responsibility-body-image.html

BBC (2015, June 3). "Unhealthily underweight model" Yves Saint Laurent advert banned. www.bbc.com/news/uk-32987228

Blair, O. (2018, October 3). Influencers now have to follow these new rules when posting on Instagram. *Cosmopolitan*. www.cosmopolitan.com/uk/reports/a23577731/influencer-rules-instagram-asa

Callow, M. and Schiffman, L. (2002). Implicit meaning in visual print advertisements: A cross-cultural examination of the contextual communication effect. *International Journal of Advertising*, 21(2): 259–277.

Checchinato, F., Colapinto, C. and Giusto, A. (2014). Advertising in a luxury sector in China: Standardisation or adaptation? A comparison between China and Italy. In R. Taylor (ed.) *The globalization of Chinese business: Implications for multinational investors*, pp. 241–64. Oxford: Chandos Publishing.

Cho, B., Kwon, U., Gentry, J.W., Jun, S. and Kropp, F. (1999). Cultural values reflected in theme and execution: A comparative study of U.S. and Korean television commercials. *Journal of Advertising*, 28(4): 59–73.

Cho, C.H. and Cheon, H.J. (2005). Cross-cultural comparisons of interactivity on corporate websites. *Journal of Advertising*, 34(2): 99–115.

De Mooij, M. (2022). *Global marketing & advertising: Understanding cultural paradoxes* (6th ed.). London: Sage.

Estée Lauder (2021, July 26). *Behind your beauty is confidence | Double Wear Foundation* [Video]. YouTube. https://youtu.be/zR2YkTMB0rQ

Estée Lauder Korea Market (2022, April 14). [에스티 로더] "8년 연속 1위" 아시아 *No.1* 파운데이션* #더블웨어 [Video]. YouTube. https://youtu.be/1rHuwUYswwQ

European Commission (2016). Defining a framework for the monitoring of advertising rules under the Audiovisual Media Services Directive. https://ec.europa.eu/newsroom/dae/document.cfm?action=display&doc_id=15875

European Commission (2018, October 2). Digital single market: Updated audiovisual rules. https://ec.europa.eu/commission/presscorner/detail/en/MEMO_18_4093

Frith, K., Cheng, H. and Shaw, P. (2005). The construction of beauty: A cross-cultural analysis of women's magazine advertising. *Journal of Communication*, 55(1): 56–70.

FTC (Federal Trade Commission) (1979, August 13). Statement of policy regarding comparative advertising. www.ftc.gov/legal-library/browse/statement-policy-regarding-comparative-advertising

FTC (2011, September 28). Reebok to pay $25 million in customer refunds to settle FTC charges of deceptive advertising of EasyTone and RunTone shoes. www.ftc.gov/news-events/news/press-releases/2011/09/reebok-pay-25-million-customer-refunds-settle-ftc-charges-deceptive-advertising-easytone-runtone

Hall, C. and Jay, P. (2021). Case study: Unpacking Uniqlo's India strategy. Business of Fashion. www.businessoffashion.com/case-studies/global-markets/unpacking-uniqlos-india-strategy-download-the-case-study

Hong, J.W., Muderrisoglu, A. and Zinkhan, G.M. (1987). Cultural differences and advertising expression: A comparative content analysis of Japanese and U.S. magazine advertising. *Journal of Advertising*, 16(1): 55–62.

Hornikx, J., van Meurs, F. and de Boer, A. (2010). English of a local language in advertising? The appreciation of easy and difficult English slogans in the Netherlands. *Journal of Business Communication*, 47(2): 169–88.

Jahshan, E. (2019, January 3). Burberry unveils first-ever Chinese New Year campaign. *Retail Gazette*. www.retailgazette.co.uk/blog/2019/01/burberry-unveils-first-ever-chinese-new-year-campaign

Javalgi, R.G., Cutler, B.D. and Malhortra, N.K. (1995). Printing advertising at the component level: A cross-cultural comparison of the United States and Japan. *Journal of Business Research*, 34(2): 117–24.

Jones, S. (2014, October 17). Global digital marketing requires country-specific strategies. *Luxury Daily*. www.luxurydaily.com/global-digital-marketing-requires-country-specific-strategies

Kemp, S. (2020, January 30). Digital 2020: Global digital overview. Datareportal. https://datareportal.com/reports/digital-2020-global-digital-overview

Khanna, T., Jain, A. and Gokhale, G. (2021, July 12). Social media vs. reality (check): ASCI's new influencer guidelines. National Law Review. www.natlawreview.com/article/social-media-vs-reality-check-asci-s-new-influencer-guidelines

Kim, H.S. and Markus, H.R. (1999). Deviance or uniqueness, harmony or conformity? A cultural analysis. *Journal of Personality & Social Psychology*, 77(4): 785–800.

Kim, M. (2022, January 5). From *Squid Game* to supernova: Inside the whirlwind with Hoyeon Jung. *Vogue*. www.vogue.com/article/hoyeon-jung-squid-game-actress-cover-story-profile

Kotabe, M. and Helsen, K. (2020). *Global marketing management* (8th ed.). Hoboken, NJ: Wiley.

Lugmani, M., Yavas, U. and Quraeshi, Z. (1989). Advertising in Saudi Arabia: Content and regulation. *International Marketing Review*, 6(1): 59–72.

McBride, C., Costello, N., Ambwani, S., Wilhite, B. and Austin, S.B. (2019). Digital manipulation of images of models' appearance in advertising: Strategies for action through law and corporate social responsibility incentives to protect public health. *American Journal of Law & Medicine*, 45(1): 7–31.

O'Neil, A. (2014). A call for truth in the fashion pages: What the global trend in advertising regulation means for U.S. beauty and fashion advertisers. *Indiana Journal of Global Legal Studies*, 21(2): 619–41.

Polegato, R. and Bjerke, R. (2006). The link between cross-cultural value associations and liking: The case of Benetton and its advertising. *Journal of Advertising Research*, 46(3): 263–73.

Polychroniou, C.G. (2019). *Cultural influence on global marketing*. San Diego, CA: Congnella Publishing.

Rawi, M. (2011, May 16). Gisele censored! Supermodel photoshopped for H&M ads in Dubai. *Daily Mail*. www.dailymail.co.uk/femail/article-1369252/Supermodel-Gisele-censored-Middle-East-H-M.html

Reuters (2017, March 6). Saint Laurent told to modify ad campaign after uproar in France. www.reuters.com/article/us-fashion-saintlaurent-advertising-idUSKBN16D1YM

Sepre, G. (2011, November 28). Hailee Steinfeld's Miu Miu ad banned in Britain—but not for the reason you think. E News. www.eonline.com/news/277045/hailee-steinfeld-s-miu-miu-ad-banned-in-britain-but-not-for-the-reason-you-think

Shi, X.-S. and Xu, W.-J. (2020). Do Chinese brands culturally adapt their overseas websites?: Evidence from top Chinese brands' Sino-US websites. *Asian Journal of Communication*, 30(1): 58–78.

Silver, L., Smith, A., Johnson, C., Jiang, J., Anderson, M. et al. (2019, March 7). Mobile connectivity in emerging economies. Pew Research Center. www.pewresearch.org/internet/2019/03/07/use-of-smartphones-and-social-media-is-common-across-most-emerging-economies

Singh, N., Zhao, H. and Hu, X. (2005). Analyzing the cultural content of web sites: A cross-national comparison of China, India, Japan and US. *International Marketing Review*, 22(2): 129–46.

Skarda, E. (2012, February 3). Tough standards: 8 "misleading" ads banned by U.K. officials. *Time*. https://newsfeed.time.com/2012/02/06/tough-standards-8-misleading-ads-banned-by-u-k-standards-board/slide/julia-roberts-christy-turlington-for-loreal

Sussman, S. (2022, January 8). Images of the week: Hoyeon Jung is our February cover star. *Vogue*. www.vogue.com/slideshow/images-of-the-week-hoyeon-jung-is-our-february-cover-star

The Drum (2010, December 1). ASA bans misleading Reebok ad. www.thedrum.com/news/2010/12/01/asa-bans-misleading-reebok-ad

Index

Note: Page locators in **bold** refer to tables and page locators in *italic* refer to figures.

A

Acqua di Parma 151, 152
acquisitions **125**, 134, 141
   of global fashion brands by companies in Asia 13–15, **14**, 17–19
adaptation/localization 29–32, *31*, *32*, 39, 149
   discretionary adaptation 160, 170, 172
   distribution channels 193, 208, 209
   mandatory adaptation 160, 172
   products 163–9, 171, 172
   websites 200–1, 210
Adidas 6, 88, 137, *138*
advertising
   adaptation 213–15, 224
   adaptation vs. standardization 212–16, 223
   comparative 218, 224
   cultural implications of international 214–15, 216–18, 223, 225–6
   regulations and challenges related to 218–21, 223–4, 226
   spending on digital 9
   standardization 212, 224
Al Tayer Insignia 131
Alibaba 12, 198
AliExpress 198
Alipay 10, 200, 205
Amazon 86, 134, 198
Amazon Live 13
Amer Sports 18
animal symbols 63
Ansoff's product/market growth matrix 25–6, *26*, 38
Anta Sports Products Limited 17–19
Argentina 91, 92–3
Asos 137, 164, 185
associative counterfeits 88, 89, *89*, 95

B

Balenciaga 184, 185, 206
Bangladesh 48, 178
bans resulting from geopolitical tensions 87
Beaucre 8, 15–17
Bed Bath & Beyond 103
benefits of fashion brand internationalization 8
Benetton 148, 151, 213
big-box retailers 134, 136, 141
Blackpink 170, 215–16
Bloomingdale's 131
body image, unhealthy 219–20, 226
body mass index (BMI) 54, **54**
Body Shop 27, 193
born globals 27, 101–2, *102*, 110
Bottega Veneta 148, 151, 167
boycotts, consumer 61, 75–7, 163, 172
brand ambassadors 215–16
brand image 5, 8, 31, 41, 127, 215
   boycotts and damage to 61, 75–7, 163
   building global 8, 133
consistency 33, 35, 38, 129, 145, 150
   distribution and 193, 194, 201, 202
   home country image and 118, 119–20
   protecting 129, 135, 136
brand management for global markets 145–57
brand names, registering 88, 89, 147–9, 155, 157
Brazil 35, 174, 186
   brands in international markets 118, 119–20
Brexit 41
bribery 91, 92–3, 95
BRICS 45–6, 59
Burberry 167, 214, 224
   licensing agreements 35–6, 129, 139–40
bureaucracy and red tape 91
business networks 105, 114, 115–16, 122
buyer's market 52, **53**, 60

C

Canada 176, 185
   American retail failures in 33, 103, 106–8
care labels *166*
Cartier 206
cash on delivery (COD) 49, 60, 200, 205
celebrities, local 17, 169–70, 214, 215–16

247

censorship of marketing and advertising materials 86, 218–19, 226
challenges of global marketing 33–7
Chanel 148, 181, 184, 206–7
　handbag pricing 187–8
characteristics of the fashion business 4–5
China
　acquisition of global fashion brands by companies in 13, **14**, 17–19
　anti-corruption campaign 92
　boycott of Dolce & Gabbana 75–7, 82
　brand names in Chinese 148
　Burberry's new advertising campaign 214, 224
　color and symbols 63, 165
　companies exiting 33, 34, 36–7, 117, 132, 137, 164, 197
　cross-border shopping 185, 186
　cultural understanding in negotiations with US companies 73–4
　"daigou" 185
　foreign direct investment in 85, 132
　"guanxi" 75, 81
　high price of luxury goods 185
　Indian ban on Chinese apps 87
　intellectual property 88, 89, 90, *90*
　largest apparel and footwear market 21
　Levi's new brand in 168
　limited editions 31, 167
　livestream shopping 12–13, 204
　Macy's exit from 34, 36–7, 132
　mobile shopping 206–8
　On & On in 8, 15–17, 132, 181, 194–5
　phases of international brands' entry into 16
　regional diversity within 50, 55–6
　restrictions on foreign e-commerce companies 86
　retail formats *51*
　retail market liberalization 84, **85**
　second-hand clothing market 77–8
　social media 32, 193, 206–8, 214
Clarks 219, 226
classification and characteristics of countries, economic 44–6, *45*
closet size 54
clothing terms, localizing 164–5, **167**
collectivism **70**, 74, 75
collectivism vs. individualism 66–7, **67**, 80
　marketing communications 214, 216–17, 223, 225
colors
　cultural meanings 63
　localizing 165–7
commercial risk 34
communication 211–26
company costs 179–80, 188
company goals 180, 188
comparative advertising 218, 224
competition
　assessment of level of 112–13, **113**
　pricing and 181
competitive advantage 27–9, 38, 39, 161
　first-mover advantage 7–8, 15–17, 20, 104, 179
compound annual growth rates (CAGR) 6, 9
concessions **125**, 133, 141
consumer acceptance of global brands 117, 121
consumer culture positioning (CCP) 150–2, 156, 157
consumer demand
　for branded goods 116–17, 121
　pricing and 181
　uncertainty 4
consumer privacy 87
contractual entry mode 124, 127–30, 141
coordination of marketing activities 32–3, 35–6, 39
copyright 83, 88, 95
Corruption Perceptions Index (CPI) 91, 95
cosmopolitanism 117, 122
Cost, Insurance and Freight (CIF) 176–7, 189
cost of goods sold, lowering 178
cost-plus pricing 179, 189
costs, company 179–80, 188
counterfeiting 87–8, 89, 95
country image 152–3, *153*, 156, 157
country of brand (COB) 153, 157
country of company (COM) 153, 157
country of manufacturing (COM) 153, 157
country of origin (COO) effect 152, 156, 157
country risks 34
cross-border
　e-commerce 175–6, 185
　shopping 175, 185–6, 189
cross-cultural risk 33–4
cultural change, economic development and 75
cultural differences
　a barrier to advertising standardization 212
　within a culture 74
　modification of products to address 160
　in negotiations 73–4
cultural dimensions
　Hall's 34–5, 64–6, **65–6**
　Hofstede's 66–71, **70–1**, 80
　implications for international advertising 216–18, 223, 225–6
cultural elements related to apparel industry 62–4, *63*

248　Index

cultural environment 61–82
    implications for global fashion marketing 73–5
cultural frameworks 72–3, **73**
cultural proximity 104
cultural symbols 63–4, 165
    avoiding bad associations with 163, 171
culturally appropriate products, developing 162–3
culture, definition 62, 80
currency 201
    exchange rate fluctuations 177–8, 185
    risks 34
customer demand *see* consumer demand

D

D2C (direct-to-consumer) startups 11–12, 179
"daigou" 185
Danish brands, Muslim boycott of 75–6
data protection regulations 87
de minimis tax 175–6, 189
decision to enter a foreign market 26–9, 54
    selection of new markets 111–22
deflation 178
dENiZEN 149, 168
developing countries
    apparel industry development patterns 46–7, 48, 59–60
    consumer acceptance of branded goods 121
    consumer demand for branded goods 116–17
    distribution challenges 205, 209
    grouping of 44–6, **45**
    lowering of barriers to entry in 15
    m-commerce popularity 10, *11*
    market opportunities 51
    payment systems 10–11, 205
    see also emerging markets; least developed markets, retailing in; newly industrialized economies (NIEs)
development patterns, apparel industry 46–8, **47**, 59–60
digital distribution 198–205, **202**
digital modification of images, regulation of 220–1
Dior 8, 167, 184
direct export 126, 141
direct franchise 129, *130*
direct involvement 196–7, 208–9, 210
disclosure requirements 220
discretionary adaptation/modification 160, 170, 172
disposable income 182
distribution channels 191–210
distribution costs, lowering 178–9
distribution localization 193, 208, 209
distributors 194–6, **195**, 197–8, 208, 209–10
Dolce & Gabbana 31, 168
    Chinese boycott of 76–7, 82
Dr. Jart + 101, 118
Dubai 74, 131, 219
Dunning's eclectic paradigm 102–4, 109, 110
duties 41, 174, 175, 176, 188, 189

E

e-commerce 9
    competitive pricing 185
    cross-border 175–6, 185
    D2C model 179
    gray products 184
    livestream shopping connecting to platforms 204
    reentering markets with 138
    restrictions on foreign companies 85, 86
    a testing ground in potential markets 136–7
    see also online marketplaces
e-payment systems 10–11, **12**
e-wallets 201, 205, 210

Ease of Doing Business Index 91
economic conditions and pricing decisions 181–3
economic development and cultural change 75
economic development levels 44–52, 116
    characteristics and challenges of retail markets by 48–52, *50*, *51*, **53**
    country classification 44–6, **45**
    modification addressing 161–2
economic environment 43–60
    implications for global fashion marketing 52–4
economic status, changing 52–3
economies of replication 8, 20
economies of scale 4, 8, 20
emerging markets 45–6, 59
    characteristics and challenges in retailing 49–52, *50*, *51*, **53**
    finding a balance between mature and 53–4
    modifications addressing 162
enablers of fashion brand internationalization 8
entry mode decisions 123–41
    factors related to 135–6, 140
    implications for companies 136–8, 140
    market entry choices 124–35, 140
    multiple modes at same time 138
    reentering markets 137–8
entry to foreign markets
    entry decisions 26–9, 54
    selection of new markets 111–22
environmental influences on price escalation 177–8
Ermenegildo Zegna 127, 128, 135
Estée Lauder 127, 128, 160, 218, 226
ethnocentrism 35, 39, 117, 122
Everlane 28, 52
ex ante costs 105

ex poste costs 105
exchange rate fluctuations 177–8, 185
exporting 123, 124, *124*, 125–7, **125**, 141
    cost escalations 176–7, **177**
    direct 126, 141
    indirect 126, 141

F

face-saving 67, 81
false claims, regulation of 220
Farfetch 14
Farm Rio 118, 161
Fawaz Al Hokair Group 130
femininity vs. masculinity 69–70, **71**, 80
    effective advertising appeals 218, 223, 226
firm factors affecting market entry decisions 117–20, 121, 122
first-mover advantage 7–8, 20, 104, 179
    Beaucre 15–17
first to file (registration) vs. prior use ownership of intellectual property rights 90–1, 95
flags, national 162, 172
flagship stores **125**, 133, 141, 193, 197
flexible cost-plus pricing 179, 190
flying geese model 46–8, 59–60
foreign branding 153–4, 156, 157
foreign consumer culture positioning 151, 156, 157
Foreign Corrupt Practices Act (FCPA) 1977 91, 92, 95
foreign direct investment (FDI) 85, 123, 132
    in China 85, **85**, 132
    in India 57, 85, **85**, 132, 137
    OLI model effective in explaining 103–4
foreign market evaluation process 112–13, 122
Forever 21 33, 102, 161

4Ps of marketing (marketing mix) 24, 38
    global strategy options 150, 155–6
    standardization and adaptation 29–32, 31, *32*
franchising *124*, **125**, 129–30, 141
    advantages and disadvantages **131**
    direct franchise 129, *130*
    master franchise 129, 130, *131*
Free on Board (FOB) 176, 177, 189
free trade zones 178
fun brands 146, 147

G

Ganni 113
Gap Inc. 3–4, 7, 29, 138, 164, 181
Gentle Monster 169–70
gift-giving culture 64, 92, 167
Giordano 133
global brand strategic management process 147–50, 155, 157
global brands 5–6, 145, 155, 157
    acquisitions by Asian companies 13–15, **14**, 17–19
    consumer acceptance of 117, 121
    drivers of profitability *180*
    vs. local brands 146
    types 146–7
global consumer culture positioning 151, 156, 157
global integration 33, 36, 39
Global Retail Development Index (GRDI) 112, 115, 122
global STP strategy 145, 149–50, *150*, 155
global vs. multinational retailers 30
glocalization 32, 39
government regulations in retail sector 84–7, 94, 95
    at both state and federal level 87, 94

graphics resembling important symbols or words 163
gray products 184, 190
gross domestic product (GDP) per capita 44, 59
gross national income (GNI) per capita 44, 59
gross profit 180
growth matrix, Ansoff's product/market 25–6, *26*, 38
"guanxi" 75, 81
Gucci 31, 131, 135, 184, 206
Gymshark 41, 101, 201, 221–3

H

H&M 6, 63, 118, 163, 172, 219
halal certification 160
Hall's cultural dimensions 34–5, 64–6, **65–6**
Harmont & Blaine 25, 90
Havaianas 118, 119–20
Hermès 167, 181, 187
high-context culture 80
    vs. low-context culture 64–5, **65**, 200, 217, 223
Hofstede's cultural dimensions 66–71, **70–1**, 80
home country image 122
    brand image and 118, 119–20
home shopping networks 203–4
hospitality industry, expansion into 24–5
host country factors affecting market entry decisions 116–17, 121, 122

I

IKEA 86, 91, 149, 151, 162
imitations 88, 89, *89*, 90, 95
import taxes 86–7, 174–6, *175*, 188, 189
in-group favoritism 66–7, 80
India
    ban on Chinese apps 87
    developing product lines for 168
    distribution channels 197, 205

foreign direct investment 57, 85, **85**, 132, 137
high power distance culture 68
import taxes 86
joint ventures 132, *132*, 135–6
kiranas 205
limited editions 167–8
new advertising campaign 214–15
prospects for apparel market 56–8
regional differences within 50–1
resource commitment increase after 2012 137, *138*
restrictions on foreign e-commerce companies 85, 86
retail market liberalization 85, **85**
retailing characteristics and challenges 50–1, *50*, *51*
testing market through online sales 136
wholly owned subsidiaries 132, 135, 137
indirect export 126, 141
indirect involvement 194–6, 208, 210
individualism **70**, 74, 75
individualism vs. collectivism 66–7, **67**, 80
marketing communications 214, 216–17, 223, 225
Indonesia 87, 90, 113, **113**, 161, 219
inflation 178
influencers 214–15, 222
disclosure requirements 220
information-oriented vs. relationship-oriented cultures 72, 73, **73**, 81
Instagram 9–10, 32, 76, 215, 221, 222
intellectual property 87–91, 95
international distribution channel selection 193–8, *194*
international new ventures (born globals) 27, 101–2, *102*, 110

international outshopping (cross-border shopping) 175, 185–6, 189
internationalization advantages 104, 110
internationalization process model 99–102, *100*, 108–9, 110, 118, 135
vs. born global's expansion pattern 101–2, *102*
internationalization scope 9, 20
trends affecting 8–15
internationalization speed 9, 20
trends affecting 8–15
internationalization theories 99–110
investment entry mode 124, 130–5
Italy 118, 136, 137, 151, 152, 153, 196

J
Japan
advertisements 217
Burberry in 129, 139–40
cultural dimensions 68, 69, 72, 75, 79
Ralph Lauren in 137, *137*
JCPenney 28, 148, 149, 193
J.Crew 133, 164, 200
joint ventures (JV) *124*, **125**, 131–2, *132*, 135–6, 141

K
Kuwait 106, 114, 136, 168, 219, 226

L
labor costs 178
Lancôme 221, 226
landed cost 174, **177**, 189
least developed markets, retailing in 48–9, **53**
mistaken assumptions 53
Lee 36, 149, *150*
legal and regulatory environment 7, 83–95
Levi Strauss & Co, 5, 27, 28
dENiZEN 149, 168

pricing by country 182–3
licensing *124*, **125**, 139–40, 141
agreements 35, 127–9, *127*
limited editions 31, 167–8
linguistic limitations of standardized advertising 212–13
livestream shopping 12–13, 203–5, 210
local brands 146, 157
vs. global brands 146
local consumer culture positioning 151, 156, 157
local distributors 194–6, 197–8, 208, 209–10
local sales representatives 196, 208, 210
localization/adaptation 29–32, *31*, *32*, 39, 149
discretionary adaptation 160, 170, 172
distribution channels 193, 208, 209
mandatory adaptation 160, 172
product 163–9, 171, 172
websites 200–1, 210
location of stores 193
locational advantages 104, 110
L'Occitane en Provence 151
logistics challenges in developing countries 205
long- vs. short-term orientation 70, **71**, 80–1
L'Oréal 134, 214
Louis Vuitton 184, 185
low-context culture 80
vs. high-context culture 64–5, **65**, 200, 217, 223

M
m-commerce (mobile commerce) 10, *11*, 49, 205, 206–8
macro country image 152
Macy's 34, 36–7, 131, 132
Malaysia 167, 219
Mango 148, 181
manufacturing costs 178
market entry choices 124–35, 140

Index 251

market entry decisions
    firm factors affecting 117–19, 121, 122
    host country factors affecting 116–17, 121, 122
market factors affecting pricing 180–2, 189
marketing
    challenges of global 33–6
    coordination of activities 32–3, 35–6, 39
    definition of global fashion 24–6
    strategy 23–39
    three step strategy 26–9
marketing mix (4Ps) 24, 38
    global strategy options 150, 155–6
    standardization and adaptation 29–32, *31*, *32*
markets, size of apparel 3, 13, 21, 22
Marks & Spencer 164
masculinity vs. femininity 69–70, **71**, 80
    effective advertising appeals 218, 223, 226
mass brands 146, 147, 192
master franchise 129, 130, *131*
mature markets
    characteristics and challenges in retailing 52, **53**
    modification of products and services 161–2
measurement, units of 201
micro country image 152–3
Miu Miu 220, 226
modification of products and services for global markets 159–63, 170–1
monitoring costs 105
monochronic time (M-time) culture 80
    vs. polychronic time culture 34–5, 65, **66**
Montblanc 167, 214
motivators of fashion brand internationalization 7–8
Muji 132, *132*

Mulberry 124
multinational vs. global retailers 30
Muslim countries
    communication challenges 218–19, 224, 226
    gender separation 62
    product modifications 160, 161
    religion 62, *63*, 74, 161
Muslims
    boycott of Danish brands 75–6
    boycott of Nike 163, 172
    developing product lines for 168

N

nature of global fashion business 3–22
negotiations, understanding culture in 73–4
network model 105–6, 109, 110
New Balance, associative counterfeiting of 89, *90*
new brands for certain markets 168–9
New Look 197
newly industrialized economies (NIEs) 44–5, 46, 59
Nike 137, 148, *150*, 167, 168, 200
    offending graphics 163, 172
    shopping experience 161, 197
Nike Rise 197
Nike Style 161
non-systematic approach (descriptive model) to selecting new markets 113–14, 115–16, 121, 122
    vs. systematic approaches **114**
nonphysical culture 62, 80
Nordic countries 68, 69
Nordstrom 25, 103, 204
number symbols 63

O

On & On 8, 15–17, 132, 181, 194–5
online marketplaces 209, 210
    selling through 198–200, **199**, *202*

setting up brand stores on 201–3, **202**, 209
open run 187
operating profit 180
opportunism 105, 110, 114
organic growth 134, 141
orientation, short- vs. long-term 70, **71**, 80–1
original brand manufacturing (OBM) 48, 60
original design manufacturing (ODM) 48, 60
original equipment manufacturing (OEM) 48, 60
ownership advantages 104, 110
ownership-location-internationalization (OLI) model 102–4, 109, 110

P

parallel importing 184–5, 189, 190
Patagonia 217, 225
patent 88
patterns of development, apparel industry 46–8, **47**, 60
payment systems 10–11, **12**, 205
Paypal 10
penetration pricing 179, 190
personal and social networks 105, 114, 122
photo-editing of images, regulation of 220–1
physical culture 62, 80
Pierre Cardin 90, 128–9, *128*
piracy 88
polychronic time culture (P-time) 80
    vs. monochronic time culture 35, 65, **66**
pop-up stores 137, 140
positioning strategies 149, *150*, 154–5
    aligning distribution channel decisions with 193
    consumer culture positioning strategy 150–2, 156, 157
power distance, high vs. low 68–9, **69**, **71**, 80

252 Index

pre-owned clothing market 12, 64, 77–8
premium brands 147
prestige brands 147
price escalation 176–9, 188, 189
    approaches to lessening 178–9
price quality association 173, 189
pricing for global markets 173–90
Primark 148
prior use vs. registration, ownership of intellectual property rights 90–1, 95
privacy, consumer 87
product development for global markets 159–72
product evaluation 5, 28, 118, 152, 153
product life cycle (PLC) 4, 27, 39, 179, 181
product lines for certain markets 168
product localization 163–9, 171, 172
provocative images, regulation of 219–20
psychic distance 100, 101, 110
    paradox 100, 103, 106–8, 110
Puma *138*, 162, 172, 214, 225

R

racism 76, 82, 162–3
Ralph Lauren 137, *137*, 197, 203
    bribery in Argentina 91, 92–3
The RealReal 12, 89, 161
red tape and bureaucracy 91
Reebok 220
reentering markets 137–8
registration (first to file) vs. prior use ownership of intellectual property rights 90–1, 95
registration of brand names 88, 89, 147–9, 155, 157
regulations and challenges related to advertising 218–21, 223–4
regulations in retail sector, government 84–7, 94, 95
    at both state and federal level 87, 94
regulatory and legal environment 7, 83–95
REI (Recreational Equipment Inc.) 161–2
relationship-based cultures 81
    vs. task-based cultures 72
relationship-oriented vs. information-oriented cultures 72, 73, **73**, 81
Reliance Brands 132, *132*, 136
religion 62, *63*, 74, 161
rentals 9, 11, 52
Replay 132, 138
retail liberalization 84–5, **84**, 95
revenues, retail 5–6, **6**
risks of entering foreign markets 33–4

S

sales representatives, local 196, 208, 210
Salvatore Ferragamo 167
Samsung Tesco 131
Sanyo Shokai Ltd. 139
Saudi Arabia 62, 74, 86, 130, 219, 226
"Saudization" 86
season, modification addressing 161
second-hand clothing market 12, 64, 77–8
selection of new markets 111–22
self-reference criterion (SRC) 34–5, 39
seller's market **53**, 60
7Ps of service marketing 24–5
sexual images 160
Shang Xia 151
Shein 179, 201
Shiseido 160, 214, 225
shopping experiences 161–2, 197
ShopShops 12–13
short- vs. long-term orientation 70, **71**, 80–1
showrooms 196, *196*, 210
size, clothing 54, 164, *166*
    conversion chart **165**
size of apparel markets 3, 13, 21, 22
Skechers 135
skimming pricing 179, 190
social and personal networks 75, 105, 106, 114, 122
social media
    in China 32, 193, 206–8, 214
    as a distribution channel 193
    dominance of 9–10
    influencers 214–15, 220, 222
    livestream shopping on platforms 203–4
    role in communication 9, 221–3
    usage differences between countries 213
    using local 32, 193, 214
South Korea
    advertisements 217, 218, 225, 226
    ambassadors for luxury brands 215–16
    apparel industry development 46, **47**, 48
    celebrities 17, 169–70, 214, 215–16
    Chanel handbag pricing 181, 187–8
    consumer demand for branded goods 116–17
    Gentle Monster 169–70
    Improper Solicitation and Graft Act 92
    On & On in 8, 15–17, 132, 181, 194–5
    popular culture 215–16
    Puma's campaign in 214, 225
    retail market liberalization 84–5, **85**
    Samsung Tesco joint venture 131
sprinkler vs. waterfall strategy 102, 110
stage model 99–102, *100*, 108–9, 110, 118, 135

Index   253

vs. born global's expansion
	pattern 101–2, *102*
standardization 29–32, *31*, *32*, 39,
	150, 155, 159
	vs. adaptation in advertising
		212–16, 223
status of fashion brand
	internationalization 5–7
Stitch Fix 9, 11, 28, 52, 161
stock-keeping units (SKUs) 4, 20
STP strategy, global 145, 149–50,
	150, 155
strategic global brand
	management process
	147–50, 155, 157
superstitions, cultural 64, 78
SWOT analysis 27–9, *29*, 39
symbols, cultural 63–4, 165
	avoiding bad associations with
		163, 171
systematic approach (normative
	model) to selecting new
	markets 112–13, 121, 122
	vs. non-systematic approaches
		114

T

Taobao Live 12
Target 33, 106–8
targeting strategies 149, *150*
	aligning distribution channel
		decisions with 192–3
tariffs 174–6, 188, 189
	lowering 178
task-based cultures 81
	vs. relationship-based cultures
		72
taxes, import 86–7, 174–6, *175*,
	188, 189
tech packs 3, 20
terms, localizing clothing 164–5,
	167
Tiffany & Co 137, *137*
time, cultural attitudes to 65, **66**, 80

T.J. Maxx 148
Tmall Global 36, 37, 198, 201–2,
	203
Tommy Hilfiger 168, 179, 204
	positioning across countries
		154–5
Toms 27, 28
top global retailers 6–7, **6**, 21
Topshop 33, 164, 192–3, 202–3
Toyne's six stage industry
	development 46, **47**, 60
trade secrets, copying of 5
trade shows 126, **126**
trademarks 88
transaction cost analysis (TCA)
	framework 104–5, 109, 110
transaction cost economics (TCE)
	105
transaction costs 105, 110
translation of text into local
	languages 212–13, 213–14
trends affecting scope and speed
	of internationalization 8–15
trust building 72

U

uncertainty avoidance, weak vs.
	strong 67–8, **71**, 80
unhealthy images, regulation of
	219–20, 226
Uniqlo 118, 135, 202, 203
	flagship stores 133
	in India 135, 168, 214–15
United Arab Emirates (UAE) 74,
	131, 162, 172, 205
United States (US)
	cultural understanding in
		negotiations with Chinese
		companies 73–4
	de minimis tax thresholds
		176
	Foreign Corrupt Practices
		Act (FCPA) of 1977 91,
		92, 95

Macy's exit from China 34,
	36–7, 132
ownership of intellectual
	property rights 90
retail expansion failures in
	Canada 33, 103, 106–8
unorganized retailing 49, *50*, 60
Uppsala/U model 99–102, *100*,
	108–9, 110, 118, 135
	vs. born global's expansion
		pattern 101–2, *102*

V

value-added tax (VAT) 174, 189
value brands 146, 147
Victoria's Secret 83, 106, 160
Vietnam **113**, 117, 128
virtual storefronts 201, 202, 210

W

Walmart 85, 132, 134, 204
waterfall vs. sprinkler strategy 102,
	110
websites
	brands' own 200–1, **202**, 209
	design 217
	localization 200–1, 210
WeChat 203, 206–8, 214
wholesale trade 126, **126**
wholly owned subsidiaries **125**,
	126, 134–5, 141
Wrangler 149

X

xenocentrism 117, 122

Y

Yves Saint Laurent 219–20, 226

Z

Zara 14, 118, 132, 161
	in China 133, 191, 203
	in Middle East 130, 135
	pricing 182, 184